Student Handbook

American Government

Institutions and Policies

NINTH EDITION

James Q. Wilson and John J. DiIulio, Jr.

P. S. Ruckman, Jr.

Rock Valley College

Houghton Mifflin Company BOSTON NEW YORK

Sponsoring Editor: *Katherine Meisenheimer*
Development Editor: *Julie Hassel*
Editorial Assistant: *Sabrina Abhyankar*
Production/Design Assistant: *Bethany Schlegel*
Manufacturing Manager: *Jane Spelman*
Marketing Manager: *Nicola Poser*
Marketing Assistant: *Laura McGinn*

Printed in the U.S.A.

ISBN: 0-618-29984-X

3456789-MA-07 06 05 04

Contents

TO THE STUDENT V

PART ONE: THE AMERICAN SYSTEM 1

    CHAPTER 1 - THE STUDY OF AMERICAN GOVERNMENT 1

    CHAPTER 2 - THE CONSTITUTION 14

    CHAPTER 3 - FEDERALISM 33

    CHAPTER 4 - AMERICAN POLITICAL CULTURE 51

    PART 1 - CLASSIC STATEMENT: FEDERALIST NO. 39 67

PART TWO: OPINIONS, INTERESTS, AND ORGANIZATIONS 71

    CHAPTER 5 - PUBLIC OPINION 71

    CHAPTER 6 - POLITICAL PARTICIPATION 88

    CHAPTER 7 - POLITICAL PARTIES 103

    CHAPTER 8 - ELECTIONS AND CAMPAIGNS 122

    CHAPTER 9 - INTEREST GROUPS 142

    CHAPTER 10 - THE MEDIA 157

    PART 2 - CLASSIC STATEMENT: "THE OMNIPOTENCE OF THE MAJORITY IN THE UNITED STATES AND ITS EFFECTS," FROM *DEMOCRACY IN AMERICA*, BY ALEXIS DE TOCQUEVILLE 174

PART THREE: INSTITUTIONS OF GOVERNMENT 178

    CHAPTER 11 - CONGRESS 178

    CHAPTER 12 - THE PRESIDENCY 201

    CHAPTER 13 - THE BUREAUCRACY 218

    CHAPTER 14 - THE JUDICIARY 234

    PART 3 - CLASSIC STATEMENT: "BUREAUCRACY," FROM MAX WEBER: *ESSAYS IN SOCIOLOGY* 253

PART FOUR: THE POLITICS OF PUBLIC POLICY 257

    CHAPTER 15 - THE POLICY-MAKING PROCESS 257

    CHAPTER 16 - ECONOMIC POLICY 272

    CHAPTER 17 - SOCIAL WELFARE 287

    CHAPTER 18 - CIVIL LIBERTIES 301

    CHAPTER 19 - CIVIL RIGHTS 317

    CHAPTER 20 - FOREIGN AND MILITARY POLICY 333

    CHAPTER 21 - ENVIRONMENTAL POLICY 354

    PART 4 - CLASSIC STATEMENT: *WEST VIRGINIA BOARD OF EDUCATION V. BARNETTE* (1943) 371

PART FIVE: THE NATURE OF AMERICAN DEMOCRACY 373

CHAPTER 22 - WHO GOVERNS? TO WHAT ENDS? 373

PART 5 - CLASSIC STATEMENT: "WHY DEMOCRATIC NATIONS SHOW A MORE ARDENT AND ENDURING LOVE OF EQUALITY THAN OF LIBERTY, AND HOW THAT LEADS THEM TO CONCENTRATE POLITICAL POWER," FROM *DEMOCRACY IN AMERICA*, BY ALEXIS DE TOCQUEVILLE 382

PRACTICE EXAMINATIONS 386

To the Student

This *Student Handbook* is a self-study accompaniment to *American Government,* Eighth Edition, by James Q. Wilson and John J. Dilulio, Jr. It serves two purposes. First, it supplements, but does not replace the text. By using the *Student Handbook* and the text together, you will reap maximum benefits from the course and enhance your general knowledge of the structure and operation of U.S. government. Second, this *Student Handbook* will assist you in practicing and preparing for your exams and will improve your test-taking skills. These two purposes are inseparable. Good studying habits—hard work, practice, and review—are critical to learning and understanding any subject matter, and a thorough understanding is the best preparation for exams

This introduction begins with an overview of what you should expect to learn from a college-level course on U.S. American government. Following is detailed advice on how to get the most from this *Student Handbook* as well as suggestions for obtaining additional supplementary information from the Internet.

THE STUDY OF U.S. GOVERNMENT

In colleges and universities, U.S. government is usually taught as part of an academic discipline known as *political science.* Political science differs from typical high school courses in two important respects. High school government courses customarily emphasize history. Furthermore, high school courses generally seek to promote citizenship by encouraging you to vote.

While this approach and goal is important, college-level political science develops a broader, more theoretical perspective on government. Political science is often about contemporary government rather than history. It compares the U.S. political system with other systems and does not necessarily assume that our system or Constitution is superior to others. It focuses mainly on how government really works. It provides, for instance, answers to and explanations for the following questions: Why do senior citizens have more political influence than college students? Why do members of Congress spend more time talking with constituents and lobbyists, attending committee meetings/hearings, and participating in fact-finding missions than they do debating legislation? How and why have presidential candidates and the media contributed to more candidate-centered campaigns that focus less on issues and party labels? Do the federal courts merely apply to law or do they make policy and are sensitive to public opinion? Why do interest groups sometimes seem to reflect the views of the top leadership of their organization rather than the views of the rank and file membership on policy issues?

Political science occasionally frustrates students seeking one correct or perfect solution to real-world problems. Political science theories often provide conflicting or even equally valid perspectives on issues. A case in point deals with the issue of *symbolic speech*: according to one constitutional theory, flag and draft card burning and painting exhibits that some people find offensive and indecent are forms of free "expression" protected by the First Amendment. Yet, according to another constitutional theory, only "speech" and "press" are protected by the First Amendment, while the First Amendment does not extend to flag and draft card burning and painting exhibits. Another case involves search and seizures: according to one constitutional perspective, evidence obtained by police without a search warrant based on probable cause is a violation of the Fourth Amendment protection against illegal searches and seizures, and hence, inadmissible in court ("exclusionary rule"). Nonetheless, according to another constitutional perspective, evidence seized by police with the aid of a search warrant they believe to be valid is still admissible in court ("good-faith exception") if it later turns out that the warrant was defective (e.g., the judge used the wrong form).

Political science sometimes forces students to grapple with uncertainties. Students wrestle with debatable assumptions about human nature and with competing explanations for why humans behave as they do. For instance, they discover inherent contradictions between cherished ideals such as liberty and democracy. Moreover, they investigate basic value conflicts between interest groups, each with a good argument to support the assertion that its cause is just.

This is not meant to suggest that political science is an abstract or subjective field of study. To the contrary, political science requires precise conceptualizations and rigorous, objective analysis. It at times even involves the utilization of mathematical logic and quantitative data. Some have dismissed the importance of what political scientists do as nothing more than "precision guesswork." Yet, there is some truth to this claim because political science does attempt to explain government logically, and like any other science that tries to understand human beings, it is hardly exact. The complexities of humans create many challenges in political science. They also make it a fascinating subject, and one well worth your time and effort to study.

HOW TO USE THIS STUDENT HANDBOOK

You should use this *Student Handbook* to do exactly what the title says—to guide you through the text material. This guide will highlight what is important in each chapter (the study objectives located under the rubric "Chapter Focus"). In addition, the guide will assist you in reviewing each chapter to make sure that you have covered and understood the pertinent facts, principles, and processes presented (Study Outline, Key Terms Match, Did You Know That…?, and Data Check). This guide also includes a Practice for Exams section that consists of true/false, multiple choice, and essay questions. You should not treat these questions merely as a practice exam. Use each set of questions as a way of furthering your understanding of what Professors Wilson and Dilulio have written and your instructor has presented in class. As you answer each question, review the text material, as well as your own notes (from both the text and your class). Understanding the subject will help you to do well on exams. Preparing for exams will, in turn, help you to understand the subject.

Chapter Focus

Before beginning each chapter of *American Government*, read through the study objectives in the Chapter Focus section. You can utilize these objectives to organize your thoughts and understand the textbook material. Keep the framework of each objective in mind as you read through the chapter, using each component of each objective as a heading for summarizing, in your own words, the important facts, concepts, ideas, and explanations presented. By the time you have completed each chapter, you should be able to write out a clear and accurate statement fulfilling each objective. You should always remember to think about how current U.S. government and politics conform, or do not conform, to the expectations of the Framers of the U.S. Constitution.

Chapter Outline

The Chapter Outline presents a section-by-section overview of the chapter. You should check the outline both before and after reading each text chapter. It should serve to reinforce in your mind the major chapter topics and clarify the relationships among them. But, you should not use the outline as a replacement for reading the text. You need to understand the material on its own terms. This can be done only by reading each chapter and not by simply relying on the chapter outline.

Key Terms Match

This section reviews the terms considered central to an understanding of the chapter's material. Test yourself on each of these terms, court cases, and political figures. If a term, make sure that you can give more than just a simple definition. When pertinent, give an example, cite an appropriate court case, and place the term in a broader theoretical context (answer the question: "so what?"). If a court case, be able to discuss the specifics of the case, the reasons why the decision was made, and its political significance or implications (again, "so what?"). If a political figure, discuss who that person is and how he/she has contributed to U.S. government and politics.

Did You Know That…?

This section presents several statements that, on closer examination, prove mythical. Your task is to explain *why* each statement is incorrect. Completing this section will help you focus on important distinctions made in the chapter

Data Check

The *Data Check* exercises emphasize points made in the various graphs, maps, and tables appearing in the text chapter. Too often, students neglect these helpful aids to comprehension. Completing this section will help you get the most out of the text's valuable visual resources.

True/False Questions

Mark the response you think is correct (true or false). Make sure that you understand, for each statement that you think is false, why it is false (space is provided after each true/false item to explain your choice). You can also use the space to indicate why you think a statement is true. Check your responses with the ones provided in the Answer Key.

Multiple-Choice Questions

A multiple-choice question will generally not have just one obvious answer. Each choice listed may have some term or idea that is related to the question, but *only one will correctly complete the statement introduced or answer the question asked*. Only one choice is correct.

Use the multiple-choice items to help you to review and understand the textbook material. Make sure that you understand why your choice correctly completes each statement or answers each question and why the other choices do not. Refer to the text to review the appropriate material addressed in each multiple-choice item. Check your answers with the ones provided in the Answer Key.

Essay Questions

Each chapter is accompanied by a series of essay questions. Most of these questions refer to specific details or an analysis provided in a particular section of a chapter. Others require you to tie together information from throughout a chapter, or, on occasion, ask you to connect themes and information from different chapters.

It is not unusual for college students (particularly, first-year students) to have great difficulty in answering essay questions. You may encounter questions that can be answered correctly in different ways from different perspectives. The best answers, however, are usually the most complete. Others may not be correct at all, either because they contain factual errors or, more commonly, because they do not address the question asked. To assist you with crafting successful answers to essay questions, the following simple guidelines are provided:

1. Read each question carefully. Focus. Reread. Figure out what the question really asks and answer accordingly. Do not simply read the question superficially and then start to write the first thing that comes to mind. Never write an answer based on "what you think the professor wants." If you approach the question in this manner, there is a high probability that you don't understand the question.

2. Organize. Outline each essay before you start to write. Use the outline to divide your essay into paragraphs, with each paragraph addressing a different part of the question. Begin each paragraph with a topic sentence or thesis statement, and use subsequent sentences in the paragraph to present supporting factual evidence, examples, finer points of logic, and conclusions. Organization saves time. Moreover, it improves both the strength of your reasoning and recollection of information.

3. Attack questions directly, and stay focused. Do not waste time restating questions. Use the first sentence of each essay either to introduce your major arguments(s) or to explain a term that reasonably requires explanation at the beginning of the essay. Then, develop your logic more fully, and discuss specific facts and examples. You should remember that summary is simply not enough. You should evaluate material and organize ideas into coherent, cogent arguments. If relevant, acknowledge opposing points of view without diluting strength of argument. Try not to repeat yourself. Stick to what the question asks. Do not get sidetracked onto peripheral arguments and constantly review your essay for contradictions.

4. Make sure to devote enough space and time to each part of the question. In short, be sure that your essay is balanced, while covering all aspects of the question.

5. Define key concepts clearly and accurately. Essay questions usually demand logical application of concepts to relevant facts, and good essays almost inevitably result from clear and accurate concept definitions. Conversely, vague, inaccurate, or even erroneous concept definitions almost always lead to confused and incomplete essays.

6. Always be as specific as possible. Try to find words that express exactly what you mean.

7. Explain fully. Never assume that certain points are obvious or that the grader of your essay can read your mind. If you want the grader to know what you mean, then say it! Develop *cause-and-effect* relationships as explicitly as possible. Support conclusions with well-reasoned arguments and evidence. If you claim that something is true, explain why you believe it to be true. Also, try to explain why possible alternatives to the correct answer can be logically refuted. Use examples to illustrate and clarify key points.

Answer Key

Answers to all chapter exercises (except for essay questions) appear at the end of the *Student Handbook*.

Classic Statements

In addition to these chapter components, the *Student Handbook* includes five *"Classic Statements"* derived from the literature of American government and corresponding to one or more chapters of the text. These selections shaped political thought at the time they appeared and remain influential today. As you read each essay, consider (1) what the author is saying, (2) in what ways the author's central themes are relevant to American government and politics today, and (3) how the reading is related to the textbook coverage. Questions following each reading will help you focus on these three issues.

Following the last *Handbook* chapter you will find two practice exams. The first covers Chapters 1 to 14. The second one covers Chapters 15 to 22 and includes some review questions from the first part of the text. Avail yourself of this opportunity to see how well you have integrated a large amount of material. And at the same time get some practice for your class exams.

In conclusion, it should be remembered that a student handbook is useful only if it supplements your diligent study of the text itself. As mentioned earlier, it cannot replace the text, nor can it guarantee success on examinations. Used with the text, however, this *Student Handbook* should noticeably boost your course performance and, hopefully, heighten your appreciation of American government.

PART ONE: The American System

CHAPTER 1

The Study of American Government

REVIEWING THE CHAPTER

CHAPTER FOCUS

The purpose of this chapter is to give you a preview of the major questions to be asked throughout the textbook, as well as to introduce some key terms in the basic vocabulary of American politics. After reading and reviewing the material in this chapter, you should be able to do each of the following:

1. List the two basic questions to be asked about American (or any other) government, and show that they are distinct questions.

2. Explain what is meant by *power* in general human terms and by *political power* in particular, relating the latter to authority, legitimacy, and democracy in the context of American government.

3. Distinguish among the three concepts of democracy mentioned in the chapter, explaining in which of these senses the textbook refers to American government as *democratic*.

4. Differentiate between majoritarian politics and elitist politics, explaining the four major theories of the latter.

5. Explain how political change makes political scientists cautious in stating how politics works or what values dominate it.

STUDY OUTLINE

I. What is political power?
   A. Two great questions about politics
      1. Who governs: the people who govern affect us
      2. To which ends: in which ways government affects our lives
      3. And then how the government makes decisions on a variety of issues
   B. Power
      1. Definition: the ability of one person to cause another person to act in accordance with the first person's intentions
      2. Text's concern: power as it is used to affect who will hold government office and how government will behave
      3. Authority: the right to use power; not all who exercise political power have it
      4. Legitimacy: what makes a law or constitution a source of right
      5. Struggles over what makes authority legitimate
      6. Necessity to be in some sense democratic in the United States today
II. What is democracy?

A. Aristotelian "rule of the many" (participatory democracy)
1. Fifth-century B.C. Greek city-state
2. New England town meeting
3. Community control in self-governing neighborhood
4. Citizen participation in formulating programs
B. Acquisition of power by leaders via competitive elections (representative democracy)
1. Sometimes disapprovingly referred to as the *elitist theory*
2. Justifications of representative democracy
a) Direct democracy is impractical.
b) The people make unwise decisions based on fleeting emotions.
III. Direct versus representative democracy
A. Text uses the term *democracy* to refer to *representative democracy.*
1. The Constitution does not contain the word *democracy* but the phrase "republican form of government."
2. Representative democracy requires leadership competition if the system is to work.
a) Individuals and parties must be able to run for office.
b) Communication must be free.
c) Voters perceive that a meaningful choice exists.
3. Many elective national offices
4. Most money for elections comes from special interests
B. Virtues of direct democracy should be reclaimed through
1. Community control
2. Citizen participation
C. Framers: "will of people" not synonymous with the "common interest" or the "public good"
1. They strongly favored representative over direct democracy.
2. Direct democracy minimized chances of abuse of power by tyrannical popular majority or self-serving office holders.
IV. How is power distributed in a democracy?
A. Majoritarian politics
1. Leaders constrained to follow wishes of the people very closely
2. Applies when issues are simple, clear, and feasible
B. Elitism
1. Rule by identifiable group of persons who possess a disproportionate share of political power
2. Four theories of Elite Influence
a) Marxism: government merely a reflection of underlying economic forces
b) C. Wright Mills: power elite composed of corporate leaders, generals, and politicians
c) Max Weber: bureaucracies based on expertise, specialized competence
d) Pluralist view: no single elite has a monopoly on power; hence must bargain and compromise
C. Cynical view that politics is self-seeking
1. Good policies may result from bad motives
2. Self-interest is an incomplete guide to actions (Alexis de Tocqueville on America)
a) September 11 and self interest
b) AFL-CIO and civil rights
3. Some act against long odds and without the certainty of benefit
V. Political change
A. Necessary to refer frequently to history because no single theory is adequate
1. Government today influenced by yesterday
2. Government today still evolving and responds to changing beliefs

B.   Politics about the public interest, not just who gets what
VI. Finding out who governs
    A.   We often give partial or contingent answers.
    B.   Preferences vary, and so does politics.
    C.   Politics cannot be equated with laws on the books.
    D.   Sweeping claims are to be avoided.
    E.   Judgments about institutions and interests should be tempered by how they behave on different issues.
    F.   The policy process can be an excellent barometer of change in who governs.

KEY TERMS MATCH

Match the following terms and descriptions:

1.   The ability of one person to cause another person to act in accordance with the first person's intentions

2.   Power when used to determine who will hold government office and how government will behave

3.   The right to exercise political power

4.   The widely-shared perception that something or someone should be obeyed

5.   Conferring political power on those selected by the voters in competitive elections

6.   An identifiable group of people with a disproportionate share of political power

7.   A relatively small political unit within which classical democracy was practiced

8.   A political system in which the choices of the political leaders are closely constrained by the preferences of the people

9.   A philosopher who defined *democracy* as the "rule of the many"

10. A theory that government is merely a reflection of underlying economic forces

11. A sociologist who presented the idea of a mostly nongovernmental power elite

12. A sociologist who emphasized the phenomenon of bureaucracy in explaining political developments

13. A political system in which local citizens are empowered to govern themselves directly

14. A political system in which those affected by a governmental program must be permitted

a.   Aristotle
b.   authority
c.   bureaucracy
d.   bureaucratic theory
e.   citizen participation
f.   city-state
g.   community control
h.   democracy
i.   direct or participatory democracy
j.   elite (political)
k.   elitist theory
l.   legitimacy
m.   majoritarian politics
n.   Marxist theory
o.   Mills
p.   pluralist theory
q.   political power
r.   power
s.   representative democracy
t.   Schumpeter
u.   Weber

to participate in the program's formulation

15. A theory that no one interest group consistently holds political power

16. Structures of authority organized around expertise and specialization

17. An economist who defined *democracy* as the competitive struggle by political leaders for the people's vote

18. A theory that appointed civil servants make the key governing decisions

19. A term used to describe three different political systems in which the people are said to rule, directly or indirectly

20. A political system in which all or most citizens participate directly by either holding office or making policy

21. A theory that a few top leaders make the key decisions without reference to popular desires

DID YOU THINK THAT . . . ?

Below are listed a number of misconceptions. You should be able to refute each statement in the space provided, referring to information or argumentation contained in this chapter. Sample answers appear at the end of this chapter.

1. "The legitimacy of the American system rests solely on democratic values and practices."

_____

_____

2. "The meaning of the word *democracy* is generally agreed on in the world today."

_____

_____

3. "Only government officials influence policy making."

_____

_____

_____

4. "The Framers viewed the 'will of the people' as being synonymous with the 'common interest' or the 'public good.'"

_____

_____

_____

PRACTICING FOR EXAMS

TRUE/FALSE QUESTIONS

Read each statement carefully. Mark true statements *T.* If any part of the statement is false, mark it *F,* and write in the space provided a concise explanation of why the statement is false.

1. T F The two most important questions about politics concern who governs and for what purposes.

_____

2. T F Federal income taxes were higher in 1935 than they are today.

_____

3. T F Most people holding political power in the United States today are middle-class, middle-aged, white Protestant males.

_____

4. T F It is easy to discern political power at work.

_____

5. T F Much of American political history has been a struggle over what constitutes legitimate authority.

_____

6. T F Everyone in the ancient Greek city-state was eligible to participate in government.

_____

7. T F Some writers of the Constitution opposed democracy on the grounds that the people would be unable to make wise decisions.

_____

8. T F *Democracy* as used in this book refers to the rule of the many.

_____

9. T F The Framers hoped to create a representative democracy that would act swiftly and accommodate sweeping changes in policy.

_____

10. T F Majoritarian politics influences relatively few issues in this country.

_____

11.   T   F   Marxist theory sees society as divided into two classes: capitalists and workers.

_____

12.   T   F   C. Wright Mills included corporate, governmental, and labor officials in his power elite.

_____

13.   T   F   Weber included appointed officials—the bureaucracy—in his group of power elites.

_____

14.   T   F   Pluralists deny the existence of elites.

_____

15.   T   F   A policy can be good or bad independent of the motives of the person who decided it.

_____

16.   T   F   The self-interest of individuals is an incomplete guide to their actions.

_____

17.   T   F   AFL-CIO leaders in the 1960s opposed the civil rights movement for fear of racial confrontations in the unions.

_____

18.   T   F   In the 1920s it was widely assumed that the federal government would play a small role in citizens' lives.

_____

19.   T   F   Who wields power—that is, who made a difference in the outcome and for what reason—is harder to discover than who did what.

_____

20.   T   F   Political change is not always accompanied by changes in public laws.

_____

MULTIPLE CHOICE QUESTIONS

Circle the letter of the response that best answers the question or completes the statement.

1.   Most national political officeholders are middle-class, middle-aged, white Protestant males. Knowing this, we

   a.   still cannot explain many important policies.
   b.   have identified the power elite.
   c.   can answer the question, "To what ends?"
   d.   can predict little of importance to politics.
   e.   can predict most of the policies that come out of Washington.

2.   Which of the following statements about authority is correct?

   a.   It is defined as the right to use power.
   b.   It resides in government, not in the private sector.
   c.   It typically results from the naked use of force.

      d.   It is the opposite of legitimacy.

      e.   All of the above.

3.   Aristotle's notion of democracy is also referred to as:

      a.   New York Democracy.

      b.   direct democracy.

      c.   commoner democracy

      d.   participatory democracy

      e.   B and D.

4.   In Aristotle's view, democracy would consist of

      a.   the effective representation of the interests of the whole population.

      b.   political representation by all individuals in a society, regardless of race, age, or gender.

      c.   participation by all or most citizens in either holding office or making policy.

      d.   an elite group of policy makers elected by the will of the people.

      e.   a nocturnal council that made decisions without regard to public opinion.

5.   The theory of representative democracy holds that

      a.   individuals acquire power through competition for the people's vote.

      b.   it is unreasonable to expect people to choose among competing leadership groups.

      c.   government officials should represent the true interests of their clients.

      d.   the middle class has gained greater representation at the expense of the poor and minorities.

      e.   public elections on every issue directly affect the lives of voters.

6.   If you fear that people often decide big issues on the basis of fleeting passions and in response to demagogues, you are likely to agree with

      a.   recall elections.

      b.   the New England town meeting.

      c.   the referendum.

      d.   participatory democracy.

      e.   many of the Framers of the Constitution.

7.   The text suggests representative democracy is justified by all of the following concerns *except* that

      a.   the people have limited information and expertise.

      b.   direct democracy is impractical.

      c.   the people may decide large issues on the basis of fleeting passions.

      d.   the people cannot choose among competing leadership groups.

      e.   the people may respond to popular demagogues

8.   In the Marxist view government is a reflection of underlying _____ forces.

      a.   social

      b.   political

      c.   ideological

      d.   economic

      e.   teleological

9.   Marx concluded "modern" societies generally feature a clash of power between

      a.   farmers and industrialists

      b.   capitalists and workers

      c.   slave owners and the landed aristocracy

      d.   monarchists and anarchists

    e.   intellectuals and spiritualists

10. C. Wright Mills, an American sociologist, is best known for his work dealing with

    a.   the tyranny of the majority.
    b.   pork barrel legislation.
    c.   the nocturnal council.
    d.   neo-Marxist policy.
    e.   the power elite.

11. Which of the following statements is *not* consistent with Mills' position?

    a.   Corporate leaders are the primary, dominate nongovernmental influence in policy making,
    b.   Top military officials play an important role in the formulation of governmental policy.
    c.   The most important policies are made by a loose coalition of three groups.
    d.   A handful of key political leaders play an important role in the formulation of governmental policy.
    e.   Nongovernmental elites play an important role in the formulation of governmental policy.

12. Max Weber felt that the dominant social and political fact of modern times was

    a.   that "the Establishment" was dominated by Wall Street lawyers.
    b.   that all institutions have fallen under the control of large bureaucracies.
    c.   that capitalism is essential to modern-day forms of government.
    d.   the conflict between the government and the press.
    e.   a dialectical process made communism inevitable.

13. Weber concluded that the dominance of government agencies by those who operated them daily would enhance

    a.   democracy
    b.   capitalism
    c.   rational decision making
    d.   representation
    e.   responsiveness

14. The view that money, expertise, prestige, and so forth are widely scattered throughout our society in the hands of a variety of groups is known as the

    a.   pluralist view of American society.
    b.   economic theory of democracy.
    c.   elitist view of American society.
    d.   dispersed power theory of American politics.
    e.   monetary displacement theory of American politics.

15. One reason the text makes frequent reference to American history is that

    a.   what government does today is affected by what it did yesterday.
    b.   American political institutions have existed largely without change since the eighteenth century.
    c.   today's policies are largely the same as those that existed two hundred years ago.
    d.   the policies and institutions of yesterday differ enormously from those of today.
    e.   history is particularly useful for understanding domestic (but not international) politics.

16. Ronald Reagan's policy initiatives on social and economic problems sought to

    a.   return citizens' assumptions to what they had been during World War II.
    b.   make the government more efficient and capable of addressing social problems.

    c.   broaden government's social net for the truly needy.
    d.   move the United States into the front rank of nations involved in forward social planning.
    e.   return citizens' assumptions to what they had been before the 1930s.

17.   American foreign policy, according to the text, tends to alternate between

    a.   cold wars and hot wars.
    b.   idealism and realism.
    c.   bipolarism and multilateralism.
    d.   interventions and isolationism.
    e.   realism and existentialism.

18.   The kinds of answers that political scientists usually give to the fundamental political questions tend to be

    a.   highly abstract and speculative.
    b.   clear, concrete, and consistent.
    c.   partial, contingent, and controversial.
    d.   qualified to the point of unintelligibility.
    e.   empirical and void of theory.

19.   In the late 1970s many employees of the Civil Aeronautics Board worked hard to have their agency

    a.   expanded.
    b.   deregulated.
    c.   funded.
    d.   reformed.
    e.   abolished.

20.   The fact that people have been willing to die over competing definitions of political issues suggests that

    a.   ways of thinking about political issues can be of fundamental importance.
    b.   politics concerns who gets what, when, where, and how.
    c.   delusions are central to the political process.
    d.   human nature is fundamentally inconsistent.
    e.   political issues are rarely ever really understood.

21.   Power deals with relationships that are typically

    a.   coercive.
    b.   based on natural law.
    c.   competitive.
    d.   difficult to quantify.
    e.   exceptional, but transparent.

22.   According to the text, before making judgments about institutions and interests, we must first observe them

    a.   from a disinterested vantage point.
    b.   as manifestations of underlying economic relationships.
    c.   firsthand.
    d.   on a variety of different issues.
    e.   through the lenses of bureaucrats.

23.   The logical place to begin the study of how power is distributed in U.S. politics is

    a.   the Constitutional Convention.
    b.   your local town hall or courthouse.
    c.   the day-to-day lives of Americans.
    d.   the pages of this morning's newspaper.
    e.   the Civil War.

ESSAY QUESTIONS

Practice writing extended answers to the following questions. These test your ability to integrate and express the ideas that you have been studying in this chapter.

1.   What may be meant by the word democracy? What sort of democracy is the government of the United States supposed to be?

2.   What is the difference between power in general and political power? Give examples of both.

3.   Discuss the Framers' view of the "will of the people," and why they favored representative government.

4.   What are the various answers that have been given to the question, "Who governs?" How do we go about determining which is correct?

ANSWERS TO KEY TERMS MATCH QUESTIONS

1. r
2. q
3. b
4. l
5. s
6. j
7. f
8. m
9. a
10. n
11. o
12. u
13. g
14. e
15. p
16. c
17. t
18. d
19. h
20. i
21. k

ANSWERS TO "DID YOU THINK THAT . . . ?" QUESTIONS

1. Important nondemocratic values include government's limitation by a written constitution, minority rights against majority preference, and checks and balances of power—sometimes including checks on elected officials by nonelected judges.

2. Virtually all nations claim to be democratic, including those without genuinely competitive elections, those with hereditary monarchs, and the United States, where most of the people most of the time don't bother to vote.

3. Other sources of influence include public opinion, the mass media, researchers, and demonstrators.

4. They believed that government should mediate, not mirror, popular views, and that elected officials should represent, not register, majority sentiments.

ANSWERS TO TRUE/FALSE QUESTIONS

1. T

2. F. The average rate was about 4 percent in 1935. Today it is 21 precent.

3. T

4. F. More often power is exercised in subtle ways that may not be evident to participants.

5. T

6. F. Slaves, women, minors, and non-property owners were excluded.

7. T

8. F. It is used to mean "representative government."

9. F. To the contrary, there was great concern among the Framers about a government that could do great good quickly. That meant it could also do great harm quickly.

10. T

11. T

12. F. Mills focused on corporate leaders, top military officers and a handful of key political figures.

13. T

14. F. They simply argue power is distributed among several elites.

15. T

16. T

17. F. The AFL-CIO were among the most influential forces lobbying Congress for the passage of certain civil rights bills.

18. T

19. T

20. T

ANSWERS TO MULTIPLE CHOICE QUESTIONS

1. a
2. a
3. e
4. c
5. a
6. e
7. d
8. d
9. b
10. e
11. a
12. b

13. c
14. a
15. a
16. e
17. d
18. c
19. e
20. a
21. d
22. d
23. a

CHAPTER 2

The Constitution

REVIEWING THE CHAPTER

CHAPTER FOCUS

The purpose of this chapter is to introduce you to the historical context within which the U.S. Constitution was written and in particular to the colonists' quest for liberties they felt had been denied them under British rule. After reading and reviewing the material in this chapter, you should be able to do each of the following:

1. Compare the American and French Revolutions of the same era with respect to the ideals that motivated them.

2. Explain the notion of higher law by which the colonists felt they were entitled to certain natural rights. List these rights.

3. Discuss the Declaration of Independence as a lawyer's brief prepared for court argument of a case.

4. Compare what the colonists believed was a legitimate basis for government with what monarchies—such as that in Great Britain at the time—believed was a legitimate basis for government.

5. List and discuss the shortcomings of government under the Articles of Confederation.

6. Discuss the backgrounds of the writers of the Constitution, and explain why these men tended to be rather mistrustful of the notion of democracy.

7. Compare and contrast the Virginia and New Jersey plans, and show how they led to the Great Compromise.

8. Explain why the separation of powers and federalism became key parts of the Constitution. Hint: The Framers' intention was not to make the system more democratic, nor was it to make it more efficient.

9. Show how James Madison's notions of human nature played an important role in the framing of the Constitution.

10. Explain why the Constitution did not include a bill of rights. Then explain why one was added.

11. Explain why the Founders failed to address the question of slavery in a definitive way.

12. Discuss whether "women were left out of the Constitution."

13. Summarize Charles Beard's analysis of the economic motivations of the Framers and the counteranalyses of those who disagree with Beard.

14. List and explain the two major types of constitutional reform advocated today, along with specific reform measures.

STUDY OUTLINE

I. The problem of liberty
  A. The colonial mind
    1. Belief that because British politicians were corrupt, the English constitution was inadequate
    2. Belief in higher law of natural rights
      a) Life
      b) Liberty
      c) Property (Jefferson notwithstanding)
    3. A war of ideology, not economics
    4. Specific complaints against George III for violating unalienable rights
  B. The "real" revolution
    1. The "real" revolution was the radical change in belief about what made authority legitimate and liberties secure.
    2. Government by consent, not by prerogative
    3. Direct grant of power: written constitution
    4. Human liberty before government
    5. Legislature superior to executive branch
  C. Weaknesses of the confederation
    1. Could not levy taxes or regulate commerce
    2. Sovereignty, independence retained by states
    3. One vote in Congress for each state
    4. Nine of thirteen votes in Congress required for any measure
    5. Delegates picked, paid for by legislatures
    6. Little money coined by Congress
    7. Army small; dependent on state militias
    8. Territorial disputes between states
    9. No national judicial system
    10. All thirteen states' consent necessary for any amendments
II. The Constitutional Convention
  A. The lessons of experience
    1. State constitutions
      a) Pennsylvania: too strong, too democratic
      b) Massachusetts: too weak, less democratic
    2. Shays's Rebellion led to the fear the states were about to collapse.
  B. The Framers
    1. Who came: men of practical affairs
    2. Who did not come
    3. Intent to write an entirely new constitution
    4. Lockean influence
    5. Doubts that popular consent could guarantee liberty
    6. Results: "a delicate problem"; need strong government for order but one that would not threaten liberty
      a) Democracy of that day not the solution
      b) Aristocracy not a solution either
      c) Government with constitutional limits no guarantee against tyranny
III. The challenge
  A. The Virginia Plan
    1. Design for a true national government
    2. Two houses in legislature

   3. Executive chosen by legislature
   4. Council of revision with veto power
   5. Two key features of the plan
       a) National legislature with supreme powers
       b) One house elected directly by the people
  B. The New Jersey Plan
   1. Sought to amend rather than replace the Articles
   2. Proposed one vote per state
   3. Protected small states' interests
  C. The compromise
   1. House of Representatives based on population
   2. Senate of two members per state
   3. Reconciled interests of big and small states
   4. Committee of Detail
IV. The Constitution and democracy
  A. Founders did not intend to create pure democracy
   1. Physical impossibility in a vast country
   2. Mistrust of popular passions
   3. Intent instead to create a republic with a system of representation
  B. Popular rule only one element of the new government
   1. State legislators to elect senators
   2. Electors to choose president
   3. Two kinds of majorities: voters and states
   4. Judicial review another limitation
   5. Amendment process
  C. Key principles
   1. Separation of powers
   2. Federalism
  D. Government and human nature
   1. Aristotelian view: government should improve human nature by cultivating virtue
   2. Madisonian view: cultivation of virtue would require a government too strong, too dangerous; self-interest should be freely pursued
   3. Federalism enables one level of government to act as a check on the other
  E. The Constitution and liberty
  F. Whether constitutional government was to respect personal liberties is a difficult question; ratification by conventions in at least nine states a democratic feature but a technically illegal one
  G. The Antifederalist view
   1. Liberty could be secure only in small republics.
       a) In big republics national government would be distant from people.
       b) Strong national government would use its powers to annihilate state functions.
   2. There should be many more restrictions on government.
   3. Madison's response: personal liberty safest in large ("extended") republics
       a) Coalitions likely more moderate there
       b) Government *should* be somewhat distant to be insulated from passions
   4. Reasons for the absence of a bill of rights
       a) Several guarantees in Constitution
           (1) Habeas corpus
           (2) No bill of attainder
           (3) No ex post facto law
           (4) Trial by jury

(5)   Privileges and immunities

(6)   No religious tests

(7)   Obligation of contracts

     b)   Most states had bills of rights.

     c)   Intent to limit federal government to specific powers

  H.   Need for a bill of rights

     1.   Ratification impossible without one

     2.   Promise by key leaders to obtain one

     3.   Bitter ratification narrowly successful

V.   The Constitution and slavery

  A.   Slavery virtually unmentioned

  B.   Apparent hypocrisy of Declaration signers

  C.   Necessity of compromise: otherwise no ratification

     1.   Sixty percent of slaves counted for representation.

     2.   No slavery legislation possible before 1808

     3.   Escaped slaves to be returned to masters

  D.   Legacy: Civil War, continuing problems

VI.   The motives of the Framers

  A.   Acted out of a mixture of motives; economic interests played modest role

  B.   Economic interests of framers varied widely

     1.   Economic interests of Framers varied widely

     2.   Beard: those who owned governmental debt supported Constitution

     3.   However, no clear division along class lines found

     4.   Recent research: state considerations outweighed personal considerations; exception: slaveholders

  C.   Economic interests and ratification

     1.   Played larger role in state ratifying conventions

     2.   In favor: merchants, urbanites, owners of western land, holders of government IOUs, non-slave owners

     3.   Opposed: farmers, people who held no IOUs, slaveowners

     4.   But remarkably democratic process because most could vote for delegates

     5.   Federalists versus Antifederalists on ideas of liberty

  D.   The Constitution and equality

     1.   Critics: government today is too weak

       a)   Bows to special interests

       b)   Fosters economic inequality

       c)   Liberty and equality are therefore in conflict

     2.   Framers more concerned with political inequality; weak government reduces political privilege

VII. Constitutional reform—modern views

  A.   Reducing the separation of powers to enhance national leadership

     1.   Urgent problems remain unresolved

     2.   President should be more powerful, accountable, to produce better policies

     3.   Government agencies exposed to undue interference

     4.   Proposals

       a)   Choose cabinet members from Congress

       b)   Allow president to dissolve Congress

       c)   Empower Congress to require special presidential election

       d)   Require presidential/congressional terms

       e)   Establish single six-year term for president

       f)   Lengthen terms in House to four years

     5.   Contrary arguments: results uncertain, worse
  B.   Making the system less democratic
     1.   Government does too much, not too little
     2.   Attention to individual wants over general preferences
     3.   Proposals
         a)   Limit amount of taxes collectible
         b)   Require a balanced budget
         c)   Grant president a true line-item veto
         d)   Narrow authority of federal courts
     4.   Contrary arguments: unworkable or open to evasion
  C.   Who is right?
     1.   Decide nothing now
     2.   Crucial questions
         a)   How well has it worked in history?
         b)   How well has it worked in comparison with other constitutions?

KEY TERMS MATCH

Set 1

Match the following terms and descriptions:

1.   A set of principles, either written or unwritten, that makes up the fundamental law of the state

2.   Rights of all human beings that are ordained by God, discoverable in nature and history, and essential to human progress

3.   A document written in 1776 declaring the colonists' intention to throw off British rule

4.   The government charter of the states from 1776 until the Constitution of 1787

5.   A meeting of delegates in Philadelphia in 1787 charged with drawing up amendments to the Articles of Confederation

6.   A governing document considered to be highly democratic yet with a tendency toward tyranny as the result of concentrating all powers in one set of hands

7.   A state constitution with clear separation of powers but considered to have produced too weak a government

8.   An armed attempt by Revolutionary War veterans to avoid losing their property by preventing the courts in western Massachusetts from meeting

9.   A British philosopher whose ideas on civil

a.   Articles of Confederation

b.   Charles A. Beard

c.   Constitution

d.   Constitutional Convention

e.   Declaration of Independence

f.   federalism

g.   Federalist papers

h.   Great Compromise

i.   John Locke

j.   James Madison

k.   Massachusetts Constitution

l.   natural rights

m.   New Jersey Plan

n.   Pennsylvania Constitution

o.   separation of powers

p.   Shays's Rebellion

q.   Virginia Plan

government greatly influenced the Founders

10. A series of political tracts that explained many of the ideas of the Founders

11. A constitutional proposal that the smaller states' representatives feared would give permanent supremacy to the larger states

12. A constitutional proposal that would have given each state one vote in a new congress

13. A constitutional proposal that made membership in one house of Congress proportional to each state's population and membership in the other equal for all states

14. A constitutional principle separating the personnel of the legislative, executive, and judicial branches of government

15. A constitutional principle reserving separate powers to the national and state levels of government

16. A principal architect of the Constitution who felt that a government powerful enough to encourage virtue in its citizens was too powerful

17. A historian who argued that the Founders were largely motivated by the economic advantage of their class in writing the Constitution

Set 2

Match the following terms and descriptions:

1. A meeting of delegates in 1878 to revise the Articles of Confederation

2. The power of the legislative, executive, and judicial branches of government to block some acts by the other two branches

3. A form of democracy in which leaders and representatives are selected by means of popular competitive elections

4. An alliance between different interest groups or parties to achieve some political goal

5. Rights thought to be based on nature and providence rather than on the preferences of

a. amendment (constitutional)

b. Antifederalists

c. bill of attainder

d. Bill of Rights

e. checks and balances

f. coalition

g. confederation

h. Constitutional Convention

i. ex post facto law

people

6. Change in, or addition to, a constitution

7. A group of people sharing a common interest who seek to influence public policy for their collective benefit

8. The power of the courts to declare acts of the legislature and of the executive unconstitutional and therefore null and void

9. The first ten amendments to the U.S. Constitution

10. A series of eighty-five essays published in New York newspapers to convince New Yorkers to adopt the newly proposed Constitution

11. Supporters of a stronger central government who advocated ratification of the Constitution and then founded a political party

12. The power of an executive to veto some provisions in an appropriations bill while approving others

13. Those who opposed giving as much power to the national government as the Constitution did, favoring instead stronger states' rights

14. A law that would declare a person guilty of a crime without a trial

15. A law that would declare an act criminal after the act was committed

16. A philosophy holding that accommodating individual self-interest provided a more practical solution to the problem of government than aiming to cultivate virtue

17. An agreement among sovereign states that delegates certain powers to a national government

18. A court order requiring police officials to produce an individual held in custody and show sufficient cause for that person's detention

j. faction

k. Federalist papers

l. Federalists

m. judicial review

n. line-item veto

o. Madisonian view of

p. human nature

q. republic

r. unalienable rights

s. writ of habeas corpus

DID YOU THINK THAT . . . ?

Below are listed a number of misconceptions. You should be able to refute each statement in the space provided, referring to information or argumentation contained in this chapter. Sample answers appear at the end of this chapter.

1. "The American Revolution simply pitted the wellborn and landowners against the have-nots."

    _____

    _____

    _____

2. "The Declaration of Independence consisted primarily of a statement of abstract principles of political philosophy."

    _____

    _____

    _____

3. "The Constitution followed directly from the Revolutionary War."

    _____

    _____

    _____

4. "The Constitutional Convention was a legal assembly sanctioned by the thirteen original states."

    _____

    _____

    _____

5. "The process by which the Constitution was ratified was a legal one."

    _____

    _____

    _____

6. "The Constitution contained guarantees of those rights that citizens of the thirteen states already enjoyed at the time."

    _____

    _____

    _____

7. "The Constitution had nothing at all to say about slavery."

    _____

    _____

    _____

DATA CHECK

North America in 1787

1. How clear was it in 1787 that the destiny of most of North America was to become English speaking and dominated by the United States?

_____

_____

Ratification of the Federal Constitution by State Conventions, 1787–1790

2. What, if any, connection do you see between the pattern of support for or opposition to the ratification of the federal Constitution between 1787 and 1790 and the later pattern of support for or opposition to the federal government during the Civil War? (Of the states shown on the map, Virginia, North Carolina, South Carolina, and Georgia subsequently seceded from the Union.)

_____

_____

PRACTICING FOR EXAMS

TRUE/FALSE QUESTIONS

Read each statement carefully. Mark true statements *T.* If any part of the statement is false, mark it *F,* and write in the space provided a concise explanation of why the statement is false.

1. T F   The American and French Revolutions of the late 1700s were both fought for the ideals of liberty, fraternity, and equality.

_____

2. T F   The British constitution was not a single written document.

_____

3. T F   Revolutionary colonists rejected the notion that the king of England had a natural prerogative to be their legitimate ruler.

_____

4. T F   Commonly listed among the natural rights to which colonists felt entitled were life, liberty, and the pursuit of happiness.

_____

5. T F   The Declaration of Independence contained more paragraphs naming specific complaints against the king than paragraphs announcing the goals of the Revolution.

_____

6. T F   Revolutionary colonists largely held that the legislative branch of government should have a greater share of governmental power than the executive.

_____

7. T F   Under the Articles of Confederation the national government levied relatively modest taxes on the people.

_____

8. T F   There was no national judicial system under the Articles of Confederation.

_____

9. T F   The Articles required nine votes for the passage of any measure.

_____

10. T F   John Hancock was elected president in 1785 but never showed up to take the job.

_____

11. T F   Shays's Rebellion seemed to indicate the inability of state governments alone to cope with serious popular uprisings.

_____

12. T F   The Constitutional Convention lasted about one month.

_____

13. T F   The Pennsylvania state constitution was the most radically democratic.

_____

14. T F   Most of the Framers of the Constitution were experienced in government and were in their fifties or sixties.

_____

15. T F   The U.S. Constitution is the world's oldest written national constitution still in operation.

_____

16. T F   The Virginia Plan appeared to favor the larger states, whereas the New Jersey Plan was more acceptable to the smaller ones.

_____

17. T F   The Founders wanted to create the most efficient government possible.

_____

18. T F   James Madison, like Aristotle, thought that government had an obligation to cultivate virtue among those who were governed.

_____

19. T F   The Constitution did not contain a bill of rights originally, in part because the Founders did not believe that the national government would be able to infringe on those rights usually protected in such bills.

_____

20. T F   The evidence suggests the personal economic circumstances of the Framers influenced their decision-making more than the interests of the states they were supposed to represent.

_____

MULTIPLE CHOICE QUESTIONS

Circle the letter of the response that best answers the question or completes the statement.

1. The colonists believed that most politicians tended to be

    a. aristocratic.
    b. idealistic.
    c. benevolent.
    d. corrupt.
    e. incompetent.

2. At the time of the American Revolution, most citizens were

    a. self-employed.
    b. indentured servants.
    c. highly literate.
    d. propertyless.
    e. concerned with economic rather than political issues.

3. The colonists fought to protect liberties which they believed were

    a. discoverable in nature and history.
    b. based on a "higher law."
    c. essential to human progress.
    d. ordained by God.
    e. All of the above.

4. When he wrote the Declaration of Independence, Thomas Jefferson replaced _____ with "the pursuit of happiness."

    a. life
    b. property
    c. justice
    d. liberty
    e. equality

5. The essential complaints itemized in the Declaration are remarkable because

    a. each had been primary features in other revolutions.
    b. they were never actually mentioned to the King.
    c. most of the colonists were unable to understand them.
    d. none spoke of social or economic conditions in the colonies.
    e. Jefferson got most of the material from Washington and Adams.

6. The colonists new vision of government insisted that

    a. the executive branch be superior to the legislative branch.
    b. the judicial branch be superior to the legislative branch.
    c. the branches of government be unified.
    d. each branch of government be equal.
    e. the legislative branch be superior to the executive branch.

7. The Articles of Confederation attempted to create a

    a. firm league of friendship among the states.
    b. a centralized government.
    c. strong state commitment to the national government.

    d.   weak state governments

    e.   None of the above.

8.   All of the following were true of the government under the Articles *except*

    a.   Each state had one vote in Congress.

    b.   The national government could not regulate commerce.

    c.   The national government could not levy taxes.

    d.   There was no national judicial branch.

    e.   Amendments required the support of nine of thirteen states.

9.   The original purpose of the Constitutional Convention was to

    a.   draw up a bill of rights.

    b.   discuss trade regulation.

    c.   levy taxes.

    d.   build an army.

    e.   revise the Articles of Confederation.

10.   French political pundits and Thomas Paine praised the state constitution of Pennsylvania because it was radically

    a.   centralized.

    b.   democratic.

    c.   legalistic.

    d.   monarchical.

    e.   elitist.

11.   Shays's Rebellion stirred the fears of some that state governments were

    a.   becoming too powerful.

    b.   about to collapse.

    c.   controlled by British interests.

    d.   opposed to liberty.

    e.   seeking independence.

12.   Thomas Jefferson responded to the news of the Rebellion by noting

    a.   it was the logical result of the American Revolution.

    b.   no such problems were likely to occur again.

    c.   a little rebellion now and then is a good thing.

    d.   confederations are always plagued by such disturbances.

    e.   dissenters should be arrested and jailed as soon as possible.

13.   The philosophy of John Locke strongly supported the idea that

    a.   government ought to be limited.

    b.   property rights should be subordinated to human rights.

    c.   the state of nature was without flaw.

    d.   reason is an inadequate guide in establishing a political order.

    e.   equality of goods and income is necessary to political order.

14.   The majority of the delegates to the Constitutional Convention were

    a.   veterans of the Continental Army.

    b.   lawyers.

    c.   middle-aged.

    d.   doctors.

e.   intellectuals.

15. The delegates to the Constitutional Convention shared a commitment to

    a.   democracy.
    b.   equality.
    c.   fraternity.
    d.   liberty.
    e.   competition.

16. Supporters of a strong national government favored the

    a.   Virginia Plan.
    b.   New Jersey Plan.
    c.   Georgia Plan.
    d.   Rhode Island Plan.
    e.   Pennsylvania Plan.

17. The presiding officer at the Constitutional Convention was

    a.   James Madison.
    b.   Benjamin Franklin.
    c.   Patrick Henry.
    d.   George Washington.
    e.   Thomas Jefferson.

18. The Great Compromise

    a.   required Supreme Court justices to be confirmed by the Senate.
    b.   based House representation on population and Senate population on equality.
    c.   solved the conflict between those who wanted a powerful House and those who did not.
    d.   provided that the president be selected by the electoral college.
    e.   dealt with, without mentioning by name, "slavery."

19. The Great Compromise was supported by the votes of delegates from _____ states.

    a.   13
    b.   12
    c.   10
    d.   5
    e.   2

20. The Constitution called for Senators to be

    a.   elected by the people.
    b.   selected by members of the House.
    c.   selected by the previous administration.
    d.   chosen by the electoral college.
    e.   selected by the state legislatures.

21. The American version of representative democracy was based on two major principles:

    a.   self-interest and institutionalism.
    b.   separation of powers and federalism.
    c.   commerce and competition.
    d.   liberty and equality.
    e.   unification and centralism.

22. The *Federalist* papers were written

   a. at the suggestion of Benjamin Franklin.
   b. to explain democracy to European governments.
   c. to help win ratification of the Constitution in New York.
   d. principally by Madison and Jefferson.
   e. principally by John Jay.

23. The Antifederalists are best described as

   a. nationalists.
   b. radicals.
   c. neo-institutionalists.
   d. Framers.
   e. states' righters.

24. Which of the following liberties was included in the Constitution *before* the Bill of Rights was added?

   a. habeas corpus
   b. freedom of speech
   c. right to petition the government for redress of grievances
   d. right to bear arms
   e. protection from double jeopardy

25. In the Constitution slavery was

   a. not specifically mentioned.
   b. recognized as a necessary institution.
   c. outlawed after twenty years.
   d. denounced as inhuman.
   e. expressly permitted in the South.

26. The Framers believed that equality was

   a. protected by limited government.
   b. inconsistent with liberty.
   c. more than could be expected in a large republic.
   d. guaranteed by political privilege.
   e. a meaningless abstraction.

27. The U.S. Supreme Court was first established

   a. before the War for Independence.
   b. during the War for Independence.
   c. in 1787.
   d. after the Bill of Rights was added to the Constitution.
   e. In 1798.

28. Which of the following statements most accurately characterizes the support given to the Constitution by different Framers?

   a. Most Framers acted out of a mixture of motives, with economic interests playing only a modest role.
   b. The strongest supporters of the Constitution were veterans of the Revolutionary War.
   c. Those Framers who held government debt and who did not own slaves tended to oppose the Constitution.

d. Most Framers were more concerned about establishing a central government that was too weak than one that was too strong.

e. The Framers tended to divide along class lines in the support they gave to the Constitution.

29. Those who favor reforming the Constitution by lessening the separation of powers between the branches often draw their inspiration from the model of

a. Germany.
b. the Articles of Confederation.
c. Great Britain.
d. France.
e. the United Nations.

30. Sophisticated statistical analysis of the voting behavior of the Framers of the Constitution suggests

a. they generally pursued the interests of wealthy land owners and businessmen.
b. they generally acted in a manner to protect the interests of the poor.
c. they consciously ignored the interests of the commercial classes.
d. they generally represented the interests of their respective states.
e. they consciously ignored the interests of the slave-owners.

31. Women are specifically mentioned in the original Constitution

a. in the "privileges and immunities" clause [Art. IV].
b. under qualifications for office [Art. I].
c. in language regarding treason [Art. III].
d. in Article I, Section 8, Clause 3.
e. nowhere.

32. No women voted in state elections in the United States until

a. 1838, in Kentucky school board elections.
b. 1869, in territorial elections in Wyoming.
c. the ratification of the Fifteenth Amendment in 1875.
d. The Great Panic of 1872.
e. the ratification of the Twentieth Amendment in 1920.

ESSAY QUESTIONS

Practice writing extended answers to the following questions. These test your ability to integrate and express the ideas that you have been studying in this chapter.

33. Discuss the "colonial mind's" approach to political issues, and demonstrate how this kind of thinking was bound to come into conflict with continued British rule in America.

34. Show how historical experience with problems created by the Articles of Confederation led to the creation of a stronger form of government under the Constitution.

35. Review Madison's argument that liberty could be protected better in an "extended republic" than in a series of small democracies. State whether you find his argument persuasive and why.

36. Do you agree or disagree with those proponents of constitutional reforms who argue that this country suffers from an excess of democracy? Defend your answer.

ANSWERS TO KEY TERMS MATCH QUESTIONS

Set 1

1. c
2. l
3. e
4. a
5. d
6. n
7. k
8. p
9. i
10. g
11. q
12. m
13. h
14. o
15. f
16. j
17. b

Set 2

1. h
2. e
3. p
4. f
5. q
6. a
7. j
8. m
9. d
10. k
11. l
12. n
13. b

14. c

15. i

16. o

17. g

18. r

ANSWERS TO "DID YOU THINK THAT . . . ?" QUESTIONS

1. Political beliefs more than economic situations were the dividing line. Both the affluent and the indigent were found on either side of the struggle.

2. Although the Declaration is best remembered for its stirring preamble, the bulk of it consists of twenty-seven paragraphs of very specific complaints against the king.

3. An intervening period of eleven years under the Articles of Confederation saw considerable experimentation with the form of government.

4. Strictly speaking, the Convention, never approved by Rhode Island, decided to exceed its legal mandate of drafting *amendments* to the Articles and cloaked all of this by proceeding in secrecy.

5. Under the ruling Articles of Confederation, ratification of any changes had to be by unanimous consent of all thirteen states, not just the nine states called for in the Constitution.

6. No bill of rights was contained in the original Constitution; one had to be added after ratification.

7. The Constitution acknowledged slavery by allowing the slave trade to continue for twenty years, by providing for the return of fugitive slaves to their masters, and by counting a slave as three-fifths of a person for purposes of apportionment.

ANSWERS TO DATA CHECK QUESTIONS

1. Not at all clear.

2. Their connection is not strong, although North Carolina initially opposed the Constitution and the states which "strongly" favored the Constitution are in the Northeast.

ANSWERS TO TRUE/FALSE QUESTIONS

1. F. Equality was not a goal of the American Revolution.

2. T

3. T

4. F. Jefferson inserted the phrase "pursuit of happiness." Most colonists spoke of a natural right to property.

5. T

6. T

7. F. Under the Articles the national government could not levy taxes.

8. T

9. T

10. T

11. T

12. F. The Convention lasted four months.

13. T

14. F. They were, for the most part, young, but experienced.

15. T

16. T

17. F. The most important goal was to create a government with specific, limited powers.

18. F. The deliberate cultivation of virtue would require a government too strong and thus too dangerous to liberty.

19. T

20. F. The economic position of the states from which they came had a greater effect on their votes than did their own monetary condition.

ANSWERS TO MULTIPLE CHOICE QUESTIONS

1. d

2. a

3. e

4. b

5. d

6. e

7. a

8. e

9. e

10. b

11. b

12. c

13. a

14. b

15. d

16. a

17. d

18. b

19. d

20. e

21. b

22. c

23. e
24. a
25. a
26. a
27. c
28. a
29. c
30. d
31. e
32. a

CHAPTER 3

Federalism

REVIEWING THE CHAPTER

CHAPTER FOCUS

The central purpose of the chapter is to introduce you to some of the complexities of government in the United States caused by the adoption of a federal system, that is, one in which both the national and state governments have powers independent of one another. You should also note how the nature and the effects of U.S. federalism have changed throughout U.S. history and continue to change to this day. After reading and reviewing the material in this chapter, you should be able to do each of the following:

1. Explain the difference between federal and centralized systems of government, and give examples of each.

2. Show how competing political interests at the Constitutional Convention led to the adoption of a federal system, but one that was not clearly defined.

3. Outline the ways in which the courts interpreted national and state powers and why the doctrine of dual federalism is still alive.

4. State why federal grants-in-aid to the states have been politically popular, and cite what have proved to be the pitfalls of such grants.

5. Distinguish between categorical grants and block grants or general revenue sharing.

6. Explain why, despite repeated attempts to reverse the trend, categorical grants have continued to grow more rapidly than block grants.

7. Distinguish between mandates and conditions of aid with respect to federal grant programs to states and localities.

8. Define *devolution* and its roots.

9. Discuss whether or to what extent federal grants to the states have succeeded in creating uniform national policies comparable to those of centralized governments.

STUDY OUTLINE

I. Governmental structure
    A. Federalism: good or bad?
        1. Definition: political system with local governmental units, in addition to national one, that can make final decisions
        2. Examples of federal governments: Canada, India, and Germany
        3. Examples of unitary governments: France, Great Britain, and Italy
        4. Special protection of subnational governments in federal system is the result of:
            a) Constitution of country
            b) Habits, preferences, and dispositions of citizens

      c)   Distribution of political power in society

    5.   National government largely does not govern individuals directly but gets states to do so in keeping with national policy

    6.   Negative views: block progress and protect powerful local interests

        a)   Laski: states "poisonous and parasitic"

        b)   Riker: perpetuation of racism

    7.   Positive view: Elazar: strength, flexibility, and liberty

    8.   Federalism makes good and bad effects possible

        a)   Different political groups with different political purposes come to power in different places

        b)   *Federalist* No. 10: small political units dominated by single political faction

  B.   Increased political activity

    1.   Most obvious effect of federalism: facilitates mobilization of political activity

    2.   Federalism lowers the cost of political organization at the local level.

II.   The Founding

  A.   A bold, new plan to protect personal liberty

    1.   Founders believed that neither national nor state government would have authority over the other because power derives from the people, who shift their support.

    2.   New plan had no historical precedent.

    3.   Tenth Amendment was added as an afterthought, to define the power of states

  B.   Elastic language in Article I: necessary and proper

    1.   Precise definitions of powers politically impossible because of competing interests, such as commerce

    2.   Hence vague language—"necessary and proper"

    3.   Hamilton's view: national supremacy because Constitution supreme law

    4.   Jefferson's view: states' rights with people ultimate sovereign

III.   The debate on the meaning of federalism

  A.   The Supreme Court speaks

    1.   Hamiltonian position espoused by Marshall

    2.   *McCulloch v. Maryland* settled two questions.

        a)   Could Congress charter a national bank? (yes, because "necessary and proper")

        b)   Could states tax such a bank? (no, because national powers supreme)

    3.   Later battles

        a)   Federal government cannot tax state bank

        b)   Nullification doctrine led to Civil War: states void federal laws they deem in conflict with Constitution

  B.   Dual federalism

    1.   Both national and state governments supreme in their own spheres

    2.   Hence interstate versus intrastate commerce

        a)   Early product-based distinction difficult

        b)   "Original package" also unsatisfactory

  C.   State sovereignty

    1.   Mistake today to think that doctrine of dual federalism is entirely dead

    2.   Supreme Court limited congressional use of commerce clause, thus protecting state sovereignty under Tenth Amendment

    3.   Supreme Court has given new life to Eleventh Amendment

    4.   Not all recent Supreme Court decisions support greater state sovereignty.

    5.   New debate resurrects notion of state police powers

    6.   Many state constitutions open door to direct democracy through initiative, referendum, and recall.

    7.   Existence of states guaranteed while local governments exist at pleasure of states

IV.   Federal–state relations
   A.   Grants-in-aid
      1.   Grants show how political realities modify legal authority.
      2.   Began before the Constitution with "land grant colleges," various cash grants to states
      3.   Dramatically increased in scope in the twentieth century
      4.   Were attractive for various reasons
         a)   Federal budget surpluses (nineteenth century)
         b)   Federal income tax became a flexible tool
         c)   Federal control of money supply meant national government could print more money
         d)   "Free" money for state officials
      5.   Required broad congressional coalitions
   B.   Meeting national needs: 1960s shift in grants-in-aid
      1.   From what states demanded
      2.   To what federal officials found important as national needs
   C.   The intergovernmental lobby
      1.   Hundreds of state, local officials lobby in Washington
      2.   Purpose: to get more federal money with fewer strings
   D.   Categorical grants versus revenue sharing
      1.   Categorical grants for specific purposes; often require local matching funds
      2.   Block grants devoted to general purposes with few restrictions
      3.   Revenue sharing requires no matching funds and provides freedom in how to spend.
         a)   Distributed by statistical formula
         b)   Ended in 1986
      4.   Neither block grants nor revenue sharing achieved the goal of giving states more freedom in spending
      5.   Block grants grow more slowly than categorical grants.
         a)   Desire for federal control and distrust of state government
         b)   No single interest group has a vital stake in multipurpose block grants, revenue sharing
         c)   Categorical grants are matters of life or death for various agencies.
   E.   Rivalry among the states
      1.   Increased competition a result of increased dependency
      2.   Snowbelt (Frostbelt) versus Sunbelt states
         a)   Difficulty telling *where* funds spent
         b)   Difficulty connecting funds to growth rates
         c)   Focus on formulas and their impact
      3.   Census takes on monumental importance
V.   Federal aid and federal control
   A.   Introduction
      4.   Fear of "Washington control" and jeopardy of Tenth Amendment
      5.   Failed attempts at reversal in trends (block grants and revenue sharing)
      6.   Traditional and newer forms of federal controls on state governmental actions
         a)   Conditions of aid tell a state government what it must do to obtain grant money
         b)   Mandates tell state governments what to do, in some instances even when they do not receive grant money
   B.   Mandates
      1.   Most concern civil rights and environmental protection
      2.   Administrative and financial problems often result
      3.   Growth in mandates, 1981 to 1991
      4.   Features of mandates

        a)   Regulatory statutes and amendments of previous legislation
        b)   New areas of federal involvement
        c)   Considerable variation in clarity, administration, and costs
    5.   Additional costs imposed on the states through:
        a)   Federal tax and regulatory schemes
        b)   Federal laws exposing states to financial liability
    7.   Federal courts have fueled the growth of mandates
        a)   Interpretations of the Tenth Amendment have eased flow of mandates
        b)   Court orders and prisons, school desegregation, busing, hiring practices, police brutality

  C.   Conditions of aid
    1.   Received by states voluntarily, in theory
        a)   Financial dependence blurs the theory
        b)   Civil rights generally the focus of most important conditions in the 1960's, a proliferation has continued since the 1970's
        c)   Conditions range from specific to general
    2.   Divergent views of states and federal government on costs, benefits
    3.   Reagan's attempt to consolidate categorical grants; Congress's cooperation in name only
    4.   States respond by experimenting with new ways of delivering services (e.g., child care, welfare, education)

VI. A devolution revolution?
  A.   Renewed effort to shift important functions to states by Republican-controlled Congress in 1994
    1.   Key issue: welfare (i.e., the AFDC program)
    2.   Clinton vetoes two bills, then signed the third, to give management to states
  B.   These and other turn-back efforts were referred to as devolution.
    1.   Old idea, but led by Congress
    2.   Clinton agreed with need to scale back size and activities of federal government.
  C.   Block grants for entitlements
    1.   Most block grants are for operating and capital purposes (contra entitlement programs).
    2.   Republican efforts to make AFDC and Medicaid into block grant programs
    3.   Partial success and possible effects
        a)   AFDC and a number of related programs are now block grants
        b)   Possible triggering of second-order devolution
        c)   Possible triggering of third-order devolution
        d)   Dramatic decrease in welfare rolls increase in unspent dollars
        e)   Surpluses and Medicaid costs, shortfalls in state revenues and funding surges
  D.   What's driving devolution?
    1.   Beliefs of devolution proponents
    2.   Realities of budget deficit
    3.   Citizen views
  E.   Congress and federalism: nation far from wholly centralized
    1.   Members of Congress still *local* representatives
    2.   Members of Congress represent different constituencies from the same localities.
    3.   Link to local political groups eroded
    4.   Differences of opinion over which level of government works best

KEY TERMS MATCH

Match the following terms and descriptions

1. Governmental concerns considered to be primarily the responsibility of the central government

2. Government concerns considered to be primarily the responsibility of the state governments

3. Supreme or ultimate political authority

4. A system in which sovereignty is wholly in the hands of the national government

5. A system in which the state governments are sovereign and the national government may do only what the states permit

6. A system in which sovereignty is shared between the national and the state governments

7. The Founders' term for a federation

8. The clause that stipulates that powers not delegated to the United States are reserved to the states or to the people

9. A Supreme Court decision embodying the principle of implied powers of the national government

10. The phrase used by the Supreme Court to create the category of implied powers of the national government

11. A doctrine espoused by Calhoun that states could hold certain national policies invalid within their boundaries

12. The doctrine that both state and national governments are supreme in their respective spheres

13. Federal funds provided to states and localities

14. State educational institutions built with the benefit of federally donated lands

15. A program proposed in the 1960s to give federal funds to a small number of large cities with acute problems

16. A federal grant for a specific purpose, often with accompanying conditions

a. AFDC
b. block grants
c. categorical grant
d. conditions of aid
e. confederation or confederal system
f. devolution
g. dual federalism
h. federal system
i. federal republic
j. grants-in-aid
k. initiative
l. Intergovernmental lobby
m. interstate commerce
n. intrastate commerce
o. land grant colleges
p. James Madison
q. McCulloch v. Maryland
r. mandates
s. Medicaid
t. Model Cities
u. national interests
v. necessary-and-proper clause
w. nullification
x. police powers
y. recall
z. referendum
aa. revenue sharing
bb. second-order devolution
cc. sovereignty
dd. states' rights
ee. Tenth Amendment
ff. third-order devolution

and/or requiring a local match

gg.   unitary system

17. A federal grant that could be used for a variety of purposes, usually with few accompanying restrictions

18. Business that is conducted entirely within one state

19. Federal rules that states must follow, whether they receive federal grants or not

20. Federal rules that states must follow if they choose to receive the federal grants with which the rules are associated

21. An interest group made up of mayors, governors, and other state and local officials who depend on federal funds

22. The Federalist author who said that both state and federal governments "are in fact but different agents and trustees of the people constituted with different powers"

23. Business that is conducted in more than one state

24. Program to distribute welfare benefits that was formerly federally funded then devolved to the states in 1996

25. Federally funded medical care for the poor

26. An effort to shift responsibility for a wide range of domestic programs from Washington to the states

27. Those state laws and regulations not otherwise unconstitutional, that promote health, safety, and morals

28. A procedure whereby voters can remove an elected official from office

29. A procedure that enables voters to reject a measure adopted by the legislature

30. A procedure that allows voters to place legislative measures (and sometimes constitutional amendments) directly on the ballot by getting a specified proportion of voter signatures on a petition

31. Refers to a flow of power and responsibility from the states to local governments

32. a federal grant that requires no matching

       funds and provides freedom in how to
       spend it

33.   Refers to the increased role of nonprofit
       organizations and private groups in policy
       implementation

DID YOU THINK THAT . . . ?

Below are listed a number of misconceptions. You should be able to refute each statement in the space provided, referring to information or argumentation contained in this chapter. Sample answers appear at the end of this chapter.

1.   "The Constitution clearly established the powers of the national and state governments."

     _____

     _____

     _____

2.   "Today, the doctrine of dual federalism is entirely dead."

     _____

     _____

     _____

3.   "The nature of federalism has remained consistent throughout U.S. history."

     _____

     _____

     _____

DATA CHECK

Figure 3.2: The Changing Purposes of Federal Grants to State and Local Governments

1.   For what purpose did the percentage of federal grant money increase most between 1960 and 2001?

     _____

     _____

2.   What were the two categories in which the percentage of federal grant money declined?

     _____

     _____

Figure 3.3: Federal Aid to State and Local Governments, 1983–2003

3.   How many times, over the years reported, did the total outlay of federal aid decline from the year of the previous report?

_____

4.   In what year did federal aid first account for at least 15 percent of all federal spending?

_____

5.   In what year did federal aid peak as a percentage of all federal outlays?

_____

PRACTICING FOR EXAMS

TRUE/FALSE QUESTIONS

Read each statement carefully. Mark true statements *T*. If any part of the statement is false, mark it *F*, and write in the space provided a concise explanation of why the statement is false.

1.   T   F   Today, an effort is being made to scale back the size and activity of the national government.

_____

2.   T   F   The United States, Canada, and France are examples of federal governments.

_____

3.   T   F   The constitution of the former Soviet Union created a federal system in theory.

_____

4.   T   F   William Riker and Daniel J. Elazar have remarkably divergent viewpoints on the value of American federalism.

_____

5.   T   F   Federalism was intended by the Founders to operate as a protection for personal liberty.

_____

6.   T   F   If the Federalist papers are a guide, the Founders envisioned a system where neither the national or state government would have would have supreme authority over the other.

_____

7.   T   F   The Tenth Amendment has rarely had much practical significance.

_____

8.   T   F   Alexander Hamilton thought the national government was the superior and leading force in political affairs.

_____

9.   T   F   James Madison argued for state supremacy at the Constitutional Convention.

_____

10. T   F   *McCulloch* v. *Maryland* grew out of the refusal of a federal official to deliver a warrant to a duly appointed justice of the peace.

_____

11. T   F   The doctrine of nullification held that a state could refuse to enforce within its boundaries a federal law that exceeded the national government's authority.

_____

12. T . F   Dual Federalism implied Congress had the power to regulate interstate commerce.

_____

13. T   F   The existence of states is guaranteed by the federal Constitution.

_____

14. T   F   The federal government sometimes finds that the political limitations on its exercise of power over the states are greater than the constitutional limitations.

_____

15. T   F   Federal grants-in-aid began even before the Constitution was adopted.

_____

16. T   F   Cash grants-in-aid began in the late 1940's.

_____

17. T   F   Initially, the most attractive feature of federal grants-in-aid was the fact that there were surpluses in the federal budget.

_____

18. T   F   Governors and mayors complained about categorical grants.

_____

19. T   F   Both the Reagan and Bush administrations opposed the growth of mandates.

_____

20. T   F   Most Americans favor devolution but routinely oppose cutting back on the benefits of specific programs.

_____

MULTIPLE CHOICE QUESTIONS

Circle the letter of the response that best answers the question or completes the statement.

1. Today's effort to scale back the size and activities of the national government and shift responsibilities back to the states has become known as

   a. devolution.
   b. anti-federalism.
   c. reverse-federalism.
   d. statism.
   e. repatriation.

2. According to the text, the most obvious effect of federalism has been to

    a.   perpetuate slavery.
    b.   protect the interests of the upper classes.
    c.   facilitate the mobilization of political activity.
    d.   reverse the democratic tendency in the states.
    e.   increase the scope of the president's power.

3. Alexander Hamilton's view of federalism

    a.   held the federal government and the state governments as equals.
    b.   held that state governments were superior to the federal government.
    c.   held that the federal government was superior to the state governments
    d.   held that the principle threat to the rights of the people would be the federal government.
    e.   held that the government was the product of an agreement among the states.

4. The national supremacy view of the newly formed federal government was powerfully defended
    by Chief Justice

    a.   John Marshall.
    b.   James McCulloch.
    c.   Roger Taney
    d.   John C. Calhoun.
    e.   James Madison.

5. The landmark case *McCulloch v. Maryland* determined

    a.   a state had the power to tax the federal government.
    b.   the federal government had the power to tax a state.
    c.   Congress did not have the power to set up a national bank.
    d.   the "necessary and proper clause" allowed for the creation of a bank.
    e.   the Constitution was established by the states.

6. Although the doctrine of nullification is commonly associated with John C. Calhoun, the notion is
    plainly evident in

    a.   the Declaration of Independence.
    b.   the Articles of Confederation.
    c.   the Federalist Papers.
    d.   the Bill of Rights.
    e.   the Virginia and Kentucky Resolutions.

7. After the Civil War the debate about the meaning of federalism focused on the _____ clause
    of the Constitution.

    a.   defense
    b.   tax
    c.   currency
    d.   full faith and credit
    e.   commerce

8. According to the text, federal anti-trust laws do not affect

    a.   artists.
    b.   morticians.
    c.   professional baseball players.
    d.   lawyers.
    e.   window washers.

9. In the 2000 case *United States v. Morrison*, the Supreme Court refused to connect or extend the scope of the commerce clause to

    a.   school restrictions on guns.
    b.   background checks for gun owners.
    c.   copyright law suits.
    d.   abortion laws.
    e.   violence against women.

10. The existence of these governments is guaranteed by the U.S. Constitution.

    a.   city
    b.   county
    c.   municipal
    d.   town
    e.   the states

11. The greatest growth in grant-in-aid programs began in the

    a.   1920s
    b.   1930s
    c.   1940s
    d.   1950s
    e.   1960s

12. At first, federal money seemed attractive to state officials because

    a.   there were budget surpluses.
    b.   the federal income tax was a flexible tool of public finance.
    c.   the production and distribution of currency was managed by the federal government.
    d.   it seemed to be "free."
    e.   All of the above.

13. The intergovernmental lobby aimed at

    a.   reducing the economic powers of state governors.
    b.   obtaining more federal money with fewer strings attached.
    c.   encouraging states to raise taxes.
    d.   increasing the number of categorical grants available to states.
    e.   removing barriers to state representation in the judicial system.

14. The requirement that a state or locality match federal money is most common with

    a.   categorical grants.
    b.   land grants.
    c.   share-pay loans.
    d.   block grants.
    e.   revenue sharing.

15. In the federal highway program, Washington pays about _____ percent of the construction costs.

    a.   90
    b.   75
    c.   60
    d.   50
    e.   25

16. The Law Enforcement Assistance Act is an example of a

    a. categorical grant.
    b. share-pay loan.
    c. land grant.
    d. nullification.
    e. block grant.

17. Which of the following is (are) not among the coalition that prefers categorical grants to block grants and revenue sharing?

    a. Congress
    b. the federal bureaucracy
    c. organized labor
    d. liberal interest groups
    e. state and local officials

18. Which of the following has (have) grown fastest in recent years?

    a. categorical grants
    b. block grants
    c. revenue sharing
    d. All have grown at about the same rates.
    e. None have actually grown.

19. With the advent of grants based on distributional formulas, the _____ has taken on monumental importance.

    a. balance of trade
    b. electoral college
    c. gross national product
    d. crime rate
    e. census

20. Most federal mandates concern

    a. sexual harassment.
    b. civil liberties and civil rights.
    c. civil rights and environmental protection.
    d. waste management.
    e. law enforcement.

21. Which mandate is identified by the text as "hard to interpret, difficult to administer?"

    a. 1992 Voting Rights Act Amendments
    b. 1990 Americans with Disabilities Act
    c. 1986 Handicapped Children's Protection Act
    d. 1988 Ocean Dumping Ban Act
    e. 1988 Lead Contamination Control Act

22. The conditions attached to grants are by far the most important federal restriction on state action because

    a. the Tenth Amendment amplifies their effect.
    b. they can change, depending upon the size of the state.
    c. they are not subject to review in the courts.
    d. state officials play a major role in their interpretation.
    e. the typical state depends for a quarter or more of its budget on federal grants.

23. It appears that Reagan-era federal aid cutbacks lead to

    a. the slashing of programs by state and local governments.
    b. state and local governments finding new ways to deliver old services.
    c. lower service levels than otherwise would have been the case.
    d. increased communication and cooperation between states and the Senate.
    e. lesser state flexibility in program design.

24. When the election of 1994 brought Republican majorities in the House and the Senate, the first key issue in the drive to shift important functions back to the states was

    a. the war on drugs.
    b. welfare.
    c. social security.
    d. law enforcement.
    e. gender discrimination.

25. All of the following were reasons driving devolution efforts in the 1990s except

    a. deep-seated mistrust of the federal government.
    b. concern about the federal budget deficit.
    c. lack of flexibility on the part of the federal government.
    d. Americans' being in favor of devolution.
    e. A and B.

ESSAY QUESTIONS

Practice writing extended answers to the following questions. These test your ability to integrate and express the ideas that you have been studying in this chapter.

26. How do the objectives of the Founders in writing the Constitution (see Chapter 2) relate to the institution of federalism in theory, that is, in the thinking and political values of the Founders?

27. Given the changes that have occurred in federalism in practice in the past two centuries, does federalism today still serve the purposes for which it was designed?

28. What might be some of the consequences if, on the two-hundredth anniversary of the Constitutional Convention, a new constitutional convention were held at which it was decided to dispense with the two-layer system of government and move to a unitary state? What might be some of the advantages and disadvantages?

APPLYING WHAT YOU'VE LEARNED

In the federal system, the state governments serve as a barrier to protect individuals from persecution by the central government. The system operates by dividing the authority of government between national and local levels. This arrangement makes oppression less likely, because no government has a monopoly on power. A critical issue in the operation of the Constitution, therefore, is establishing which powers are assigned to each tier of government.

The powers of the federal government are enumerated in Article I of the Constitution. But these powers have not proved sufficient. In *McCulloch v. Maryland*, the Supreme Court used the elastic clause to supplement the scope of national authority. The powers left to the states, in contrast, are nowhere mentioned in the Constitution. For this reason the Tenth Amendment was added, declaring that all powers not expressly given to the national government belong to the states. These powers are the police powers that enable the states to make regulations relevant to the health, morals, and safety of their citizens.

But this discussion is entirely too theoretical; the nature of federalism cannot be understood without examining practical problems. Several difficulties are encountered in the real world of federalism. First, under the Constitution it is often unclear whether a particular policy issue should be settled at the national or at the state level. Second, if a power has not been specifically awarded to Congress, how far can the elastic clause be stretched to justify an exercise of power by the federal government? And third, to what extent can the federal government use grants-in-aid to dictate the use of police powers by the states without violating the Tenth Amendment?

Take the issue of education in the United States. Much debate has arisen over the declining performance of American public school students in recent years. Countries such as Japan and Germany are threatening to overtake U.S. economic superiority. The United States cannot compete, critics allege, because young people entering the labor market are poorly educated. Is the federal government responsible for correcting the deficiencies of public schools, or does this responsibility belong to the states?

1. Consider the constitutional issues involved. Public education has traditionally been considered an area under state and local control. Answer the following questions:

    a. Could Congress assume control over public education in light of the national consequences?

    _____

    _____

    b. Does the elastic clause authorize an assertion of federal power? In responding to this question, remember the rules outlined in McCulloch concerning the exercise of a power not enumerated in the Constitution; that is, McCulloch applies only if an enumerated power "implies" federal authority. Check Article I of the Constitution and determine whether any enumerated power implies congressional power over education.

    _____

    _____

    _____

2. If the constitutional avenue fails to vindicate federal authority, consider the use of grants-in-aid to coerce states to obey congressional regulations on education. To be sure, Congress is already supplying substantial amounts of educational funds. Consider the data in the following table.

Percentage of Education Revenues			
Year	Federal	State	Local
1940	1.8	30.3	68.0
1950	2.9	39.8	57.3
1960	4.4	39.1	56.5
1970	8.0	39.1	52.1
1980	9.8	46.8	43.4
1990	6.3	46.9	46.7
1996	6.7	43.4	47.9

Source: Clarke Cochran et al., *American Public Policy: An Introduction*, 6th ed. (New York: St. Martin's Press, 1999), p. 311.

Note that the Reagan administration reversed the early trend toward increased federal involvement in funding public education. This reversal underscores a different philosophical approach in balancing national and state power. President Reagan advocated a diminished role for the federal government.

a.   Why did Reagan endorse this position despite the deteriorating condition of American schools? Review the material in the text to answer this question.

_____

_____

_____

b.   How would a critic of Reagan respond to these arguments?

_____

_____

_____

3.   Evaluate the options available to Congress for improving public education through grants-in-aid.

a.   Which type of grant should Congress favor to achieve its objectives, block or categorical?

_____

_____

_____

b.   How might a grant deal with the problem of high school dropouts? What conditions for aid should be attached to a grant focusing on preventing students from dropping out of school?

_____

_____

_____

c.   Why are states demanding increased federal assistance in financing education when federal conditions in granting aid would take away state control over programs?

_____

_____

_____

ANSWERS TO KEY TERMS MATCH QUESTIONS

1. u
2. dd
3. cc
4. gg
5. e
6. h
7. i
8. ee
9. q
10. v
11. w
12. g
13. j
14. o
15. t
16. c
17. b
18. n
19. r
20. d
21. l
22. p
23. m
24. a
25. s
26. f
27. x
28. y
29. z
30. k
31. bb
32. aa
33. ff

ANSWERS TO "DID YOU THINK THAT . . . ?" QUESTIONS

1. Vague language regarding federal powers in the Constitution was deliberate, owing to unresolved political struggles.

2. Some recent Supreme Court rulings pertaining to the Tenth and Eleventh Amendments have supported greater state sovereignty, and hence, have served to revive the doctrine of dual federalism.

3. From differing interpretations by Hamilton and Jefferson, through attempts at nullification leading to the Civil War, right down to contemporary struggles between state and national officials, federalism has always been a bone of contention and subject to change (see entire chapter).

ANSWERS TO DATA CHECK QUESTIONS

1. Health, by 44 percent.

2. Transportation and highways (by 32 percent) and income security (14 percent).

3. Two (1986-1987, 1995-1996).

4. 1997.

5. 2003.

ANSWERS TO TRUE/FALSE QUESTIONS

1. T

2. F. France has a unitary system.

3. T

4. T

5. T

6. T

7. T

8. T

9. F. Madison argued for national supremacy at the Convention, then changed his mind later.

10. F. The case grew out of Maryland's attempt to tax an entity of the federal government, a bank.

11. T

12. T

13. T

14. T

15. T

16. F. They were around in the early 1800s.

17. T

18. T

19. T

20. T

ANSWERS TO MULTIPLE CHOICE QUESTIONS

1. a
2. c
3. c
4. a
5. d
6. c
7. d
8. c
9. e
10. e
11. e
12. e
13. b
14. a
15. a
16. e
17. e
18. a
19. e
20. c
21. b
22. e
23. b
24. b
25. c

CHAPTER 4

American Political Culture

REVIEWING THE CHAPTER

CHAPTER FOCUS

This chapter departs rather sharply from the previous ones, which focused on the legal and historical aspects of American government, and concentrates instead on the somewhat less concrete notion of *political culture,* or the inherited set of beliefs, attitudes, and opinions people (in this case, Americans) have about how their government ought to operate. After reading and reviewing the material in this chapter, you should be able to do each of the following:

1. Define what scholars mean by *political culture,* and list some of the dominant aspects of political culture in the United States.

2. Discuss how U.S. citizens compare with those of other countries in their political attitudes.

3. List the contributions to U.S. political culture made by the Revolution, by the nation's religious heritages, and by the family. Explain the apparent absence of class consciousness in this country.

4. Explain why some observers are quite concerned about the growth of mistrust in government and why others regard this mistrust as normal and healthy.

5. Define internal and external feelings of *political efficacy,* and explain how the level of each of these has varied over the past generation.

6. Explain why a certain level of political tolerance is necessary in the conduct of democratic politics, and review the evidence that indicates just how much political tolerance exists in this country. Agree or disagree with the text's conclusion that no group is truly free of political intolerance.

STUDY OUTLINE

I. Introduction
   A. The American model of government both here and abroad
   B. Tocqueville on American democracy
      1. Abundant and fertile soil for democracy to grow
      2. No feudal aristocracy; minimal taxes; few legal restraints
      3. Westward movement; vast territory provided opportunities
      4. Nation of small, independent farmers
      5. "Moral and intellectual characteristics," today called political culture
II. Political Culture
   A. Defined as a distinctive and patterned way of thinking about how political and economic life ought to be carried out (e.g. stronger American belief in political than in economic equality)
   B. Elements of the American political system
      1. Liberty
      2. Democracy

           3.   Equality

           4.   Civic duty

   C.   Some questions about the U.S. political culture

           1.   How do we know people share these beliefs?

               Before polls, beliefs inferred from books, speeches, and so on

           2.   How do we explain behavior inconsistent with beliefs?

               Beliefs still important, source of change

           3.   Why so much political conflict in U.S. history?

               Conflict occurs even with beliefs in common

           4.   Most consistent evidence of political culture

               Use of terms Americanism, un-American

   D.   The economic system

           1.   Americans support free enterprise but see limits on marketplace freedom

           2.   Americans prefer equality of opportunity to equality of result; individualist view

           3.   Americans have a shared commitment to economic individualism/self-reliance (see 1924 and 1977 polls)

III.   Comparing citizens of the United States with those of other nations

   A.   Political system

           1.   Swedes: more deferential than participatory

               a)   Defer to government experts and specialists

               b)   Rarely challenge governmental decisions

               c)   Believe in what is best more than what people want

               d)   Value equality over liberty

               e)   Value harmony and observe obligations

           2.   Japanese

               a)   Value good relations with colleagues

               b)   Emphasize group decisions and social harmony

               c)   Respect authority

           3.   Americans

               a)   Tend to assert rights

               b)   Emphasize individualism, competition, equality, following rules, treating others fairly (compare with the Japanese)

           4.   Cultural differences affect political and economic systems

           5.   Danger of overgeneralizing: many diverse groups within a culture

           6.   Almond and Verba: U.S. and British citizens in cross-national study

               a)   Stronger sense of civic duty, civic competence

               b)   Institutional confidence

               c)   Sense of patriotism

   B.   Economic system

           1.   Swedes (contrasted with Americans): Verba and Orren

               a)   Equal pay and top limit on incomes

               b)   Less income inequality

           2.   Cultural differences make a difference in politics: private ownership in United States versus public ownership in European countries

   C.   The Civic Role of Religion

           1.   Americans are highly religious compared with Europeans

           2.   Recent trends in religiosity

           3.   Putnam's "bowling alone" thesis

   D.   Religion and Politics

           1.   Religious movements transformed American politics and fueled the break with England.

       2.   Both liberals and conservatives use the pulpit to promote political change.

       3.   Bush, Gore and public support for faith based approaches to social ills

IV.   The sources of political culture

    A.   Historical roots

       1.   Revolution essentially over liberty; preoccupied with asserting rights

       2.   Adversarial culture the result of distrust of authority and a belief that human nature is depraved

       3.   Federalist-Jeffersonian transition in 1800 legitimated the role of the opposition party; liberty and political change can coexist

    B.   Legal-sociological factors

       1.   Widespread participation permitted by Constitution

       2.   Absence of an established national religion

           a)   Religious diversity a source of cleavage

           b)   Absence of established religion has facilitated the absence of political orthodoxy

           c)   Puritan heritage (dominant one) stress on personal achievement

               (1)   Hard work

               (2)   Save money

               (3)   Obey secular law

               (4)   Do good

               (5)   Embrace "Protestant ethic"

           d)   Miniature political systems produced by churches' congregational organization

       3.   Family instills the ways we think about world and politics

           a)   Great freedom of children

           b)   Equality among family members

           c)   Rights accorded each person

           d)   Varied interests considered

       4.   Class consciousness absent

           a)   Most people consider themselves middle class

           b)   Message of Horatio Alger stories is still popular

    C.   The culture war

       1.   Two cultural classes in America battle over values

       2.   Culture war differs from political disputes in three ways:

           a)   Money is not at stake

           b)   Compromises are almost impossible

           c)   Conflict is more profound

       3.   Culture conflict animated by deep differences in people's beliefs about private and public morality

       4.   Culture war about what kind of country we ought to live in

       5.   Two camps:

           a)   Orthodox: morality, with rules from God, more important than self-expression

           b)   Progressive: personal freedom, with rules based on circumstances, more important than tradition

       6.   Orthodox associated with fundamentalist Protestants and progressives with mainline Protestants and those with no strong religious beliefs

       7.   Culture war occurring within religious denominations

       8.   Current culture war has special importance historically because of two changes:

           a)   More people consider themselves progressives than previously

           b)   Rise of technology makes culture war easier to wage

V.   Mistrust of government

    A.   What the polls say

1. Since the 1950s, a steady decline in percentage who say they trust the government in Washington
2. Increase in percentage who think public officials do not care about what we think
3. Important qualifications and considerations:
    a) Levels of trust rose briefly during the Reagan administration
    b) Distrust of officials is not the same as distrust for our system of government
    c) Americans remain more supportive of the country and its institutions than most Europeans
B. Possible causes of apparent decline in confidence
1. Vietnam
2. Watergate and Nixon's resignation
3. Clinton's sex scandals and impeachment
4. Levels of support may have been abnormally high in the 1950s
    a) Aftermath of victory in World War II and possession of Atomic bomb
    b) From Depression to currency that dominated international trade
    c) Low expectations of Washington and little reason to be upset / disappointed
5. 1960's and 1970's may have dramatically increased expectations of government
6. Decline in patriotism (temporarily affected by the attacks of September 11)
C. Necessary to view in context
1. Decline in confidence not spread to all institutions
2. Decline in confidence also varies from group to group
3. American's loss of support for leaders and particular policies does not mean loss of confidence in the political system or each other
VI. Political efficacy
A. Definition: citizen's capacity to understand and influence political events
B. Parts
1. Internal efficacy
    a) Ability to understand and influence events
    b) About the same as in 1950s
2. External efficacy
    a) Belief that system will respond to citizens
    b) Not shaped by particular events
    c) Declined steadily through the 1960s and 1970s
C. Comparison: still much higher than Europeans'
D. Conclusion
1. Some say Americans are more "alienated" from politics
2. But current research has not easily established a relationship between trust in government and confidence in leaders and vote turnout
3. Decline in trust and confidence may mean support for non-incumbents and third party candidates
VII. Political tolerance
A. Crucial to democratic politics
1. Citizens must be reasonably tolerant
2. But not necessarily perfectly tolerant
B. Levels of American political tolerance
1. Most Americans assent in abstract
2. But would deny rights in concrete cases
    a) Liberals intolerant of extreme right
    b) Conservatives intolerant of extreme left
3. Most are willing to allow expression to most
4. Americans have become more tolerant in recent decades

C.   Question: How do very unpopular groups survive?
    1.   Most people do not act on beliefs
    2.   Usually no consensus on whom to persecute
    3.   Courts are sufficiently insulated from public opinion to enforce protection
D.   Conclusions
    1.   Political liberty cannot be taken for granted
    2.   No group should pretend it is always tolerant
      a)   Conservatives once targeted professors
      b)   Later, professors targeted conservatives

KEY TERMS MATCH

Match the following terms and descriptions.

1.   A distinctive and patterned way of thinking about how political life ought to be carried out

2.   The condition of being relatively free of governmental restraints

3.   The inclination to believe that one's efforts and rewards in life are to be conducted and enjoyed by oneself, apart from larger social groupings

4.   The condition in which people, although not guaranteed equal rewards, expect to have comparable chances to compete for those rewards

5.   Conducted a famous cross-national study of political participation.

6.   The feeling that one ought to do one's share in community affairs, irrespective of concrete rewards

7.   A word used in naming a congressional committee to merge the concepts of acceptance of national values and goodness itself

8.   A political party that opposes the majority party but within the context of the legal rules of the game

9.   A set of values that includes working hard, saving one's money, and obeying the law

10.   A persistent word in our vocabulary that indicates Americans are bound by common values and hopes.

11.   Published studies which indicated fewer and fewer Americans were joining clubs and organizations to promote civic trust and

a.   Almond and Verba
b.   Americanism
c.   civic competence
d.   civic duty
e.   class consciousness
f.   Congregational
g.   Erik Erikson
h.   equal opportunity
i.   external efficacy
j.   Individualism
k.   internal efficacy
l.   liberty
m.   opposition party
n.   orthodox (social)
o.   political culture
p.   political efficacy, sense of
q.   political ideology
r.   political tolerance
s.   progressive (social)
t.   Roger D. Putnam
u.   un-American
v.   work ethic

cooperation.

12. A kind of church in which members control activities, whether erecting a building, hiring a preacher, or managing its finances

13. A citizen's capacity to understand and influence political events

14. The confidence in one's own ability to understand and take part in political affairs

15. The belief that the system will respond to what citizens do

16. The willingness to allow people with whom one disagrees to have the full protection of the laws when they express their opinions

17. The belief that one can affect government policies

18. The awareness of belonging to a particular socioeconomic group whose interests are different from those of others

19. People who believe that moral rules are derived from God, are unchanging, and are more important than individual choice

20. Psychologist who noted distinct traits of American and European families.

21. A relatively consistent set of views of the policies government ought to pursue

22. People who believe that moral rules are derived in part from an individual's beliefs and the circumstances of modern life

DID YOU THINK THAT . . . ?

Below are listed a number of misconceptions. You should be able to refute each statement in the space provided, referring to information or argumentation contained in this chapter. Sample answers appear at the end of this chapter.

1. "The political culture can be used to predict exactly how people will behave."

_____

_____

_____

2. "The people's trust in government has decreased solely as a result of Watergate."

    _____

    _____

    _____

3. "Unemployed American workers always exhibit strong class consciousness."

    _____

    _____

    _____

DATA CHECK

Table 4.2: Patriotism in America, France and Germany

1. Citizens in which nation are more likely to agree with the statement, "I am very patriotic?"

    _____

2. Where are citizens most likely to say they are "proud" to be citizens of their country?

    _____

3. Where are citizens least likely to say they are "proud" to be citizens of their country?

    _____

Figure 4.1: Trust in the Federal Government, 1958–2001

4. When did the percentage of people who said they trusted government "just about always" begin to decline?

    _____

5. When did the percentage of people who said they trusted government "most of the time" begin to decline?

    _____

6. When did the percentage of people who said they trusted government "some of the time" begin to increase dramatically?

    _____

Table 4.9: Public Confidence in Institutions, 1973–2001

7. Which two institutions suffered the greatest losses in popular confidence during the twenty-six years covered by the surveys? Between which of the years covered by the surveys did each of the greatest declines take place?

    _____

Figure 4.2: Changes in the Sense of Political Efficacy, 1952–2000

8.   From what year does the general increase in the sense of inefficacy seem to date?

_____

Figure 4.4: Views of Tolerance and Morality

9.   What is the greatest worry of Americans?

_____

10.   What is most important to Americans?

_____

Figure 4.5: Changes in Levels of Political Tolerance, 1930–1999

11.   Which categories of candidates have gone from less than 50 percent acceptability to more than 50 percent?

_____

12.   Which categories are still not acceptable to the majority?

_____

PRACTICING FOR EXAMS

TRUE/FALSE QUESTIONS

Read each statement carefully. Mark true statements *T*. If any part of the statement is false, mark it *F*, and write in the space provided a concise explanation of why the statement is false.

1.   T   F   Other nations have attempted the American model of government and experienced military takeovers.

_____

2.   T   F   Americans are preoccupied with their rights.

_____

3.   T   F   A majority of Americans believe people should have the right to vote even if they cannot read or write or vote intelligently.

_____

4.   T   F   When the Southern states seceded from the Union, they modeled their government on the U.S. Constitution and duplicated some of its language.

_____

5.   T   F   The best way to learn what is distinctive about American political culture is to compare it with that of other nations.

_____

6.   T   F   Swedes have much higher rates of political participation than Americans.

_____

7. T   F   Americans are more interested in reaching decisions through the application of rules than are the Japanese.

_____

8. T   F   In cross-national surveys conducted in the 1990's, Americans expressed greater confidence in public institutions than citizens in other democracies.

_____

9. T   F   There is less income inequality in Sweden than in the United States.

_____

10. T   F   Religious ideas fueled the break with England.

_____

11. T   F   Both liberals and conservatives have used religious pulpits to promote political change.

_____

12. T   F   Federalists were suspicious that Jefferson intended to sell the country out to Spain.

_____

13. T   F   Erikson's study of American and European children noted a larger measure of equality among American family members.

_____

14. T   F   The United States is the only large industrial democracy without a significant socialist party.

_____

15. T   F   The culture war is occurring not just between religious denominations but also within them.

_____

16. T   F   Increasingly, individuals describe themselves as religiously orthodox.

_____

17. T   F   Levels of public trust in the government in Washington increased briefly during the Reagan administration.

_____

18. T   F   The attack of September 11 further eroded American's trust in the government.

_____

19. T   F   In concrete cases, Americans are not very tolerant of groups they dislike.

_____

20. T   F   Most of us are ready to deny some group its rights, we simply cannot agree on which group it should be.

_____

MULTIPLE CHOICE QUESTIONS

Circle the letter of the response that best answers the question or completes the statement.

1.   Americans think it very important that everyone should be

    a.   economically equal.
    b.   politically equal.
    c.   both politically and economically equal.
    d.   neither politically nor economically equal.
    e.   politically equal if economically advanced.

2.   Which of the following is *not* among the important elements in the American view of the political system?

    a.   civic duty
    b.   individualism
    c.   equality of opportunity
    d.   democracy
    e.   equality of condition

3.   Scholars infer the existence of political culture by observing

    a.   the kinds of books Americans read.
    b.   the political choices Americans make.
    c.   the slogans Americans respond to.
    d.   the speeches Americans hear.
    e.   All of the above.

4.   The Civil War provides an illustration of

    a.   political behavior inconsistent with personal values.
    b.   a radical rejection by the Confederacy of the constitutional order.
    c.   how governments cannot last long without internal conflict.
    d.   the conflict between existing constitutional values and institutional values.
    e.   the persistence of shared beliefs about how a democratic regime ought to be organized.

5.   One important piece of evidence that Americans have believed themselves bound by common values and common hopes has been

    a.   that free elections could indeed be conducted.
    b.   their hostile attitudes toward free speech.
    c.   their use of the word *Americanism.*
    d.   the importance of the frontier in American history.
    e.   their tendency toward idealism.

6.   When a 1924 study in Muncie, Indiana, was repeated in 1977, it found that 1977 respondents

    a.   judged those who failed more harshly.
    b.   were more sympathetic with failure.
    c.   had about the same attitudes as 1924 respondents.
    d.   were more critical of those who had great wealth.
    e.   were much more desirous of material success.

7.   Compared with people in other democracies, Americans are particularly preoccupied with

    a.   elections.
    b.   the assertion of rights.

c.   social harmony.
d.   institutions.
e.   equality.

8. Compared with Americans, the Japanese are more likely to

a.   emphasize the virtues of individualism and competition in social relations.
b.   reach decisions through discussion rather than the application of rules.
c.   emphasize the virtue of treating others fairly but impersonally, with due regard for their rights.
d.   see conflict as a means of getting to know and understand the psyche of other people.
e.   rely on individual decision making rather than decisions made by groups.

9. The classic study of political culture by Gabriel Almond and Sidney Verba concluded Americans

a.   were generally much like the citizens in four other nations.
b.   exhibited little that could be described as "culture."
c.   had a stronger sense of civic duty than citizens in other nations.
d.   had a stronger sense of civic competence than citizens in other nations.
e.   had a stronger sense of civic duty and competence than citizens in other nations.

10. Almond and Verba found some degree of similarity between citizens of the United States and citizens of

a.   Germany.
b.   Great Britain.
c.   Italy.
d.   Mexico.
e.   Sweden.

11. A 1985 study by Sidney Verba and Gary Orren compared the views of trade union and political party leaders in the United States and

a.   Germany.
b.   Great Britain.
c.   Italy.
d.   Mexico.
e.   Sweden.

12. Which statement is incorrect?

a.   In the 1830s, Tocqueville was amazed at how religious Americans were.
b.   The average American is more likely to believe in God than the average European.
c.   Religious revival movements of the 1700s transformed political life in the colonies.
d.   Today, America is less religious than most European countries.
e.   Candidates for national office in most contemporary democracies rarely mention religion.

13. According to the text, the notion that religious organizations that deliver social services deserve to receive government funding

a.   was criticized by Al Gore during the 2000 presidential election.
b.   was criticized by George W. Bush during the 2000 presidential election.
c.   was favored, in 2000, by three quarters of Americans
d.   is more acceptable in other nations than it is in America.
e.   is not popular among African Americans who are Democrats.

14. The American preoccupation with assertion and maintenance of rights has imbued the daily conduct of U.S. politics with

    a.   irregular sensitivity.
    b.   a willingness to compromise at great costs.
    c.   a lack of concern about the larger issues of politics.
    d.   a kind of adversarial spirit.
    e.   confusion.

15. While there has been no established religion in the United States, there has certainly been a dominant religious tradition. That tradition can be best described as

    a.   Catholicism
    b.   Protestantism
    c.   Protestantism, especially Lutheranism
    d.   Protestantism, especially Puritanism
    e.   None of the above.

16. Which of the following statements about class-consciousness in America is true?

    a.   It has been relatively unimportant.
    b.   It powerfully affects attitudes.
    c.   It is particularly salient among the unemployed.
    d.   It implies an ideology of class struggle.
    e.   It steers the campaigns of most presidential candidates.

17. The culture war is basically a conflict over

    a.   economic issues.
    b.   foreign affairs.
    c.   international norms.
    d.   differing religious ideologies.
    e.   private and public morality.

18. America has always had cultural conflicts, but they have acquired special importance today as a result of

    a.   a growing number of traditionalists.
    b.   an increasing gap between the have's and the have-nots.
    c.   the decline of political parties.
    d.   a growing number of "progressives" and the rise of the news media.
    e.   conflict between Catholic, Protestant, and Jewish leaders.

19. The increase in cynicism toward our government has been specifically directed at

    a.   officials and policies.
    b.   the system of government itself.
    c.   the Constitution.
    d.   the Declaration of Independence.
    e.   capitalism in America.

20. When people feel that they have a say in what the government does, that public officials will pay attention to them, and that politics is understandable, they have a sense of political

    a.   trust.
    b.   tolerance.
    c.   efficacy.
    d.   legitimacy.

e.   reciprocity.

21. Which is a correct description of trends in the political efficacy of Americans from the mid-1960s to today?

a.   Internal efficacy has dramatically increased.
b.   External efficacy has dramatically increased.
c.   Internal efficacy and external efficacy have dramatically increased.
d.   Internal efficacy appears to be in decline while external efficacy has remained the same.
e.   Internal efficacy appears to be the same while external efficacy appears to be in decline.

22. A study of national opinion by Herbert McClosky and Alida Ball concluded

a.   Americans are generally more tolerant than their community leaders
b.   Americans do not support freedom of worship for extremist religious groups.
c.   Community leaders tend to be more tolerant than the average American.
d.   Americans have become increasingly intolerant.
e.   Americans opposed nonviolent protests on college campuses.

23. The McClosky and Ball study provided evidence that _____ were particularly tolerant of controversial political activities.

a.   ministers
b.   lawyers
c.   public administrators
d.   teachers
e.   the police

24. Judgments about political tolerance should be made with caution because

a.   Americans rarely have a clear idea of what is meant by the word "tolerance."
b.   there is actually very little reliable data on the topic.
c.   there is so very little intolerance in the world.
d.   no nation is completely tolerant of every kind of political activity.
e.   one person's intolerance is another person's civic "concern."

ESSAY QUESTIONS

Practice writing extended answers to the following questions. These test your ability to integrate and express the ideas that you have been studying in this chapter.

25. List some of the more interesting ways in which American civic culture differs from that in France, Italy, Sweden, or Japan.

26. Comment on the fact that the United States is perhaps the only sizable industrial country in the world that does not have a socialist party as a major competitor for power.

27. State and justify your own reaction to the author's contention that mistrust of government in the United States isn't really as severe as it is sometimes thought to be.

28. Explain what is meant by the different sorts of political efficacy and relate these to your own feelings as a citizen.

29. State whether you personally believe that all types of political groups should receive the full protection of American laws. If so, why? If not, to which groups would you deny which rights?

ANSWERS TO KEY TERMS MATCH QUESTIONS

1. o
2. l
3. j
4. h
5. a
6. d
7. u
8. m
9. v
10. b
11. t
12. f
13. p
14. k
15. i
16. r
17. c
18. e
19. n
20. g
21. q
22. s

ANSWERS TO "DID YOU THINK THAT . . . ?" QUESTIONS

1. The United States has a political culture that emphasizes civic obligations, but rates of voting are low and participation is lower than generally reported. Nevertheless, shifts in attitudes may forecast changes in behavior.

2. Various measures of distrust and cynicism show increases between 1958 and 1970, with subsequent and greater increases occurring between 1972 and 1976. These findings match a decrease in trust of nonpolitical institutions in the late 1960s. The problems of distrust and cynicism did not start or end with Watergate.

3. During the Depression of the 1930s, employed and unemployed workers often exhibited class consciousness. But such periods in American history are rare. Surveys taken in the 1970s showed the great majority of the unemployed did not identify with other unemployed or think their interests as a class were in opposition to those of management.

ANSWERS TO DATA CHECK QUESTIONS

1. America.
2. America.
3. Germany.
4. 1966.
5. 1964.
6. 1964.
7. Public schools, by 20 percent between 1973 and 2001; and Congress, by 16 percent between 1973 and 2001.
8. Early 1960s.
9. The country will become too tolerant of behaviors that are bad for society.
10. Defending standards of right and wrong.
11. Jews, women, blacks, homosexuals.
12. Atheists.

ANSWERS TO TRUE/FALSE QUESTIONS

1. T
2. T
3. T
4. T
5. T
6. F. Although almost all adult Swedes vote in national elections, few participate in politics in any other way.
7. T
8. T
9. T
10. T
11. T
12. F. The suspicion was that Jefferson intended to sell out the country to France.
13. T
14. T
15. T
16. F. In recent years, there has been a significant increase in the number of people who consider themselves to be progressive.
17. T
18. F. Trust in government increased significantly at first, then began a steady decline.

19. T
20. T

ANSWERS TO MULTIPLE CHOICE QUESTIONS

1. b
2. e
3. e
4. e
5. c
6. c
7. b
8. b
9. e
10. b
11. e
12. a
13. c
14. d
15. d
16. a
17. e
18. d
19. a
20. c
21. e
22. c
23. b
24. e

PART 1

Classic Statement: Federalist No. 39 [1]

INTRODUCTION

The article presented here was written by James Madison to address two questions: first, whether the form of government being proposed in the Constitution was strictly a republican one, and second, whether it was in addition a federal form of government that would preserve the nature of the union between the states that had existed until then.

You will note that his answer to the first question is strongly affirmative, whereas he responds to the second one in a rather more complex fashion.

TO THE PEOPLE OF THE STATE OF NEW YORK:

. . . The first question that offers itself is, whether the general form and aspect of the government be strictly republican. It is evident that no other form would be reconcilable with the genius of the people of America; with the fundamental principles of the revolution; or with that honorable determination which animates every votary of freedom. . . .

What, then, are the distinctive characters of the republican form? . . .

If we resort for a criterion to the different principles on which different forms of government are established, we may define a republic to be, or at least may bestow that name on, a government which derives all its powers directly or indirectly from the great body of the people, and is administered by persons holding their offices during pleasure, for a limited period, or during good behavior. It is *essential* to such a government that it be derived from the great body of the society, not from an inconsiderable proportion, or a favored class of it; otherwise a handful of tyrannical nobles, exercising their oppressions by a delegation of their powers, might aspire to the rank of republicans, and claim for their government the honorable title of republic. It is *sufficient* for such a government that the persons administering it be appointed, either directly or indirectly, by the people; and that they hold their appointments by either of the tenures just specified; otherwise every government that has been or can be well organized or well executed, would be degraded from the republican character. . . .

On comparing the Constitution planned by the convention with the standard here fixed, we perceive at once that it is, in the most rigid sense, conformable to it. The House of Representatives, like that of one branch at least of all the State legislatures, is elected immediately by the great body of the people. The Senate, like the present Congress, and the Senate of Maryland, derives its appointment indirectly from the people. The President is indirectly derived from the choice of the people, according to the example

---

[1] The Federalist, sometimes referred to as the Federalist papers, is a series of articles written by Alexander Hamilton, John Jay, and James Madison and addressed to the citizens of New York at the time that the Constitution was being considered for ratification. Because these articles were composed by some of the leading authors of the Constitution, they are widely regarded as an authoritative interpretation of the Constitution and one that spells out in much greater detail the intentions of the authors than is the case with the very brief Constitution itself. A collection of these articles from which the present one is excerpted can be found in the publication of the same name by the Modern Library (New York: Random House, 1941).

in most of the States. Even the judges with all other officers of the Union, will, as in the several States, be the choice, though a remote choice, of the people themselves. The duration of the appointments is equally conformable to the republican standard, and to the model of State constitutions. The House of Representatives is periodically elective, as in all the States; and for the period of two years. . . . The Senate is elective, for the period of six years. . . . The President is to continue in office for the period of four years. . . . In the other States the election is annual. In several of the States, however, no constitutional provision is made for the impeachment of the chief magistrate. . . . The President of the United States is impeachable at any time during his continuance in office. The tenure by which the judges are to hold their places, is, as it unquestionably ought to be, that of good behavior. The tenure of the ministerial offices generally, will be a subject of legal regulation, conformable to the reason of the case and the example of the State constitutions.

Could any further proof be required of the republican complexion of this system, the most decisive one might be found in its absolute prohibition of titles of nobility, both under the federal and the State governments; and in its express guaranty of the republican form to each of the latter.

"But it was not sufficient," say the adversaries of the proposed Constitutions, "for the convention to adhere to the republican form. They ought, with equal care, to have preserved the *federal* form, which regards the Union as a *Confederacy* of sovereign states; instead of which, they have framed a *national* government, which regards the Union as a *consolidation* of the States." And it is asked by which authority this bold and radical innovation was undertaken? The handle which has been made of this objection requires that it should be examined with some precision.

. . . It appears, on one hand, that the Constitution is to be founded on the assent and ratification of the people of America, given by deputies elected for the special purpose; but, on the other, that this assent and ratification is to be given by the people, not as individuals composing one entire nation, but as composing the distinct and independent States to which they respectively belong. It is to be the assent and ratification of the several States, derived from the supreme authority in each State,—the authority of the people themselves. The act, therefore, establishing the Constitution, will not be a *national,* but a *federal* act.

. . . It must result from the *unanimous* assent of the several States that are parties to it, differing no otherwise from their ordinary assent than in its being expressed, not by the legislative authority, but by that of the people themselves. . . . Each State, in ratifying the Constitution, is considered as a sovereign body, independent of all others, and only to be bound by its own voluntary act. In this relation, then, the new Constitution will, if established, be a *federal,* and not a *national* constitution.

The next relation is, to the sources from which the ordinary powers of government are to be derived. The House of Representatives will derive its powers from the people of America; and the people will be represented in the same proportion, and on the same principle, as they are in the legislature of a particular State. So far the government is *national,* not *federal.* The Senate, on the other hand, will derive its powers from the States, as political and coequal societies; and these will be represented on the principle of equality in the Senate, as they now are in the existing Congress. So far the government is *federal,* not *national.* The executive power will be derived from a very compound source. The immediate election of the President is to be made by the States in their political characters. The votes allotted to them are in a compound ratio, which considers them partly as distinct and coequal societies, partly as unequal members of the same society. The eventual election, again, is to be made by that branch of the legislature which consists of the national representatives; but in this particular act they are to be thrown into the form of individual delegations, from so many distinct and coequal bodies politic. From this aspect of the government, it appears to be of a mixed character, presenting at least as many *federal* as *national* features.

The difference between a federal and national government, as it relates to the *operation of the government,* is supposed to consist in this, that in the former the powers operate on the political bodies composing the Confederacy, in their political capacities; in the latter, on the individual citizens composing the nation, in their individual capacities. On trying the Constitution by this criterion, it falls under the *national,* not the *federal* character; though perhaps not so completely as has been understood. . . .

But if the government be national with regard to the *operation* of its powers, it changes its aspect again when we contemplate it in relation to the extent of its powers. The idea of a national government involves in it, not only an authority over the individual citizens, but an indefinite supremacy over all persons and things, so far as they are objects of lawful government. Among a people consolidated into one nation, this supremacy is completely vested in the national legislature. Among communities united for particular purposes, it is vested partly in the general and partly in the municipal legislatures. In the former case, all local authorities are subordinate to the supreme; and may be controlled, directed, or abolished by it at pleasure. In the latter, the local or municipal authorities form distinct and independent portions of the supremacy, no more subject, within their respective spheres, to the general authority, than the general authority is subject to them, within its own sphere. In this relation, then, the proposed government cannot be deemed a *national* one; since its jurisdiction extends to certain enumerated objects only, and leaves to the several States a residuary and inviolable sovereignty over all other objects. . . .

If we try the Constitution by its last relation to the authority by which amendments are to be made, we find it neither wholly *national* nor wholly *federal.* Were it wholly national, the supreme and ultimate authority would reside in the *majority* of the people of the Union; and this authority would be competent at all times, like that of a majority of every national society, to alter or abolish its established government. Were it wholly federal, on the other hand, the concurrence of each State in the Union would be essential to every alteration that would be binding on all. The mode provided by the plan of the convention is not founded on either of these principles. In requiring more than a majority, and particularly in computing the proportion by *States,* not by *citizens,* it departs from the *national* and advances towards the *federal* character; in rendering the concurrence of less than the whole number of States sufficient, it loses again the *federal* and partakes of the *national* character.

The proposed Constitution, therefore, is, in strictness, neither a national nor a federal Constitution, but a composition of both. In its foundation it is federal, not national; in the sources from which the ordinary powers of the government are drawn, it is partly federal and partly national; in the operation of these powers, it is national, not federal; in the extent of them, again, it is federal, not national; and, finally, in the authoritative mode of introducing amendments, it is neither wholly federal nor wholly national.

PUBLIUS

Questions for Understanding and Discussion

1. Why, according to Madison, is it altogether necessary that the new government be republican in nature?

2. What would be the difference, in his thinking, between a federal and a national government?

3. Using this distinction, how does Madison describe the following?

    a.   the proposed act of establishing a Constitution

    b.   the composition of Congress and the executive branch

    c.   the operation of governmental powers

    d.   the extent of those governmental powers

    e.   the process of amending the Constitution

4. He concludes that the proposed Constitution is neither federal nor national but a mixture. How do you think the Constitution might have been different if the authors had decided simply on each of the following?

   a. a national government

   b. a federal government

PART TWO:
Opinions, Interests, and Organizations
CHAPTER 5
Public Opinion

REVIEWING THE CHAPTER

CHAPTER FOCUS

The purpose of this chapter is to explore what we mean by *public opinion* and to ask what sorts of effects public opinion has on our supposedly democratic form of government. After reading and reviewing the material in this chapter, you should be able to do each of the following:

1. List the sources of our political attitudes, and indicate which are the most important sources. Assess the influence of various religious traditions on political attitudes.

2. Explain why there is no single cleavage between liberals and conservatives in this country and why there are crosscutting cleavages. Explain the significance of these facts. Assess the significance of race in explaining political attitudes.

3. Define *political ideology* and state why most Americans do not think ideologically. Summarize the liberal positions on the economy, civil rights, and political conduct. Describe the major policy packages in the Democratic party, and indicate which groups in the Democratic coalition can be identified with each package.

4. Identify which elite groups have become liberal, and compare their current attitudes with the past political preferences of these groups. Discuss the "new class" theory as an explanation for changes in attitudes. Analyze why these changes are causing strain in the political party system.

STUDY OUTLINE

I. Introduction
    A. Lincoln and the Gettysburg address ... "of the people, by the people, for the people."
        1. Yet the federal government's budget is not balanced
        2. Yet the people have opposed busing
        3. Yet the ERA was not ratified
        4. Yet most Americans opposed Clinton's impeachment
        5. Yet most Americans favor term limits for Congress
    B. Why government policy and public opinion may appear to be at odds
        1. Government not intended to do "what the people want"
            a) Framers of Constitution aimed for substantive goals
            b) Popular rule was only one of several means toward these goals.
            c) Large nations feature many "publics" with many "opinions."

(1) Framers hoped no single opinion would dominate
(2) Reasonable policies can command support of many factions
2. Limits on effectiveness of opinion polling; difficult to know public opinion
3. Government may give more weight to political elites who may think differently

II. What is Public Opinion?
  A. Influences and limitations
    1. Public ignorance: Monetary Control Bill ruse, poor name recognition of leaders
    2. Importance of wording of questions, affects answers
    3. Questions may focus one side of an issue at the expense of another (benefits / costs)
    4. Instability of public opinion
    5. Public has more important things to think about; need clear-cut political choices
    6. Specific attitudes less important than political culture

III. The origins of political attitudes
  A. The role of the family
    1. Child absorbs party identification of family but becomes more independent with age
    2. Much continuity between generations
    3. Declining ability to pass on identification
    4. Younger voters exhibit less partisanship; more likely to be independent
    5. Meaning of partisanship unclear in most families; less influence on policy preferences
    6. Few families pass on clear ideologies
  B. Religion
    1. Religious traditions affect families
      a) Catholic families somewhat more liberal
      b) Protestant families more conservative
      c) Jewish families decidedly more liberal
    2. Two theories on differences
      a) Social status of religious group
      b) Content of religion's tradition
  C. The gender gap
    1. A "problem" that has existed for a long time for both parties
      a) Men and women both identified with the Democratic Party at about the same levels in the 1950s
      b) By the 1990's men identified more with the Republican party while women continued to support the Democrats at earlier levels
    2. Possible explanations for the "gap"
      a) Attitudes about size of government, gun control, spending programs for the poor, and gay rights
      b) The conservative policy positions of men are increasingly matched by their party loyalty
      c) Presence of Democratic female candidates may also have an impact
  D. Schooling and information
    1. College education has liberalizing effect; longer in college, more liberal
    2. Effect extends beyond end of college
    3. Cause of this liberalization?
      a) Personal traits: temperament, family, intelligence
      b) Exposure to information on politics
      c) Liberalism of professors
    4. Effect growing as more go to college
    5. Increasing conservatism since 1960s?
      a) Yes (legalizing marijuana)
      b) No (school busing)

IV. Cleavages in public opinion
   A. Social class: less important in United States than in Europe
      1. More important in 1950s on unemployment, education, housing programs
      2. Less important in 1960s on poverty, health insurance, Vietnam, jobs
      3. Why the change?
         a) Education: occupation depends more on schooling
         b) Noneconomic issues now define liberal and conservative
   B. Race and ethnicity
      1. Social class becoming less clear-cut source of political cleavage
      2. Impact of race and ethnicity is less clear
         a) Some clear difference in opinion (party identification, O.J. Simpson, criminal justice system, affirmative action)
         b) Some similarities (quotas, getting tough on crime, abortion, etc.)
         c) Evidence that the gap in opinions is narrowing
         d) Further complication: gaps between the opinions of younger and older blacks
      3. Big opinion gap between black leaders and black people generally
         a) Still differences of opinions between blacks and whites on social issues; opinions similar on others
         b) Evidence that black-white differences are narrowing
      4. Few studies of the opinions of over 30 million Latinos
         a) California study of Latinos and Asian Americans
         b) Latinos identified themselves as Democrats / Asian Americans identified themselves as Republicans
         c) Latinos were somewhat more liberal than Anglo whites and Asian Americans, but less liberal than blacks
         d) Diversity within ethnic groups and limitations of such studies
   C. Region
      1. Southerners more conservative than northerners on military and civil rights issues but difference fading overall
      2. Southern lifestyle different
      3. Lessening attachment to Democratic party
V. Political ideology
   A. Consistent attitudes
      1. Ideology: patterned set of political beliefs about who ought to rule, their principles and policies
      2. Most citizens display little ideology; moderates dominate
      3. Yet most citizens may have strong political predispositions
      4. "Consistency" criterion somewhat arbitrary
      5. Some believe ideology increased in 1960s
      6. Others argue that poll questions were merely worded differently in 1960s
   B. What do *liberalism* and *conservatism* mean?
      1. Liberal and conservative labels have complex history
         a) Europe during French Revolution: conservative = church, state authority
         b) Roosevelt and New Deal: activism = liberalism
         c) Conservative reaction to activism (Goldwater): free market, states' rights, economic choice
         d) Today's imprecise and changing meanings
   C. Various categories
      1. Three useful categories emerge from studies
         a) Economic policy: liberals favor jobs for all, subsidized medical care and education, taxation of rich

    b) Civil rights: liberals prefer desegregation, equal opportunity, etc.

    c) Public and political conduct: liberals tolerant of demonstrations, favor legalization of marijuana, and so on

  D. Analyzing consistency: people can mix categories

    1. Pure liberals: liberal on both economic and personal conduct issues

    2. Pure conservatives: conservative on both economic and personal conduct issues

    3. Libertarians: conservative on economic issues, liberal on personal conduct issues

    4. Populists: liberal on economic issues, conservative on personal conduct issues

  E. Political elites

    1. Definition: those who have a disproportionate amount of some valued resource

    2. Elites, or activists, display greater ideological consistency

     a) More information than most people

     b) Peers reinforce consistency and greater difference of opinion than one finds among average voters

  F. Is there a "new class"?

    1. Definition: those who are advantaged by the power, resources, and growth of government (not business)

    2. Two explanations of well-off individuals who are liberals

     a) Their direct benefits from government

     b) Liberal ideology infusing postgraduate education

    3. Traditional middle class: four years of college, suburban, church affiliated, pro-business, conservative on social issues, Republican

    4. Liberal middle class: postgraduate education, urban, critical of business, liberal on social issues, Democratic

    5. Emergence of new class creates strain in Democratic party

VI. Political elites, public opinion, and public policy

  A. Elites influence public opinion in three ways

    1. Raise and form political issues

    2. State norms by which to settle issues, defining policy options

    3. Elite views shape mass views

  B. Limits to elite influence on the public

    1. Elites do not define problems

    2. Many elites exist; hence many elite opinions

KEY TERMS MATCH

Match the following terms and descriptions:

1. The political party for which one or one's family usually votes

2. People who say that they have been "born again" and who see certain moral questions as political issues

3. Differences in political views between men and women

4. Differences in political preferences based on more than one variable

5. A coherent and consistent set of beliefs about who ought to rule, what principles rulers should obey, and what policies they

a. conservative

b. crosscutting cleavages

c. Evangelical Christians

d. gender gap

e. liberal

f. libertarian

g. middle America

h. new class

i. norm

ought to pursue

6. People who have a disproportionate amount of political power

7. Middle-income people who usually live in suburbs, attend church, favor business, and have mostly conservative political views

8. Middle-income people who live in cities, skip church, and have mostly liberal political views

9. Young urban professionals

10. One who is liberal on both economic and personal conduct issues

11. One who is conservative on both economic and personal conduct issues

12. One who is conservative on economic issues, liberal on personal conduct issues

13. One who is liberal on economic issues, conservative on personal conduct issues

14. One who favors more limited and local government, less government regulation of markets, and more social conformity to traditional norms and values

15. One who favors more government regulation of business and support for social welfare but less regulation of private social conduct

16. Americans who have moved out of poverty but are not yet affluent and who cherish middle-class values

17. A standard of right or proper conduct that helps determine the range of acceptable social behavior and policy options

18. A survey of public opinion

19. A sample selected in such a way that any member of the population being surveyed has an equal chance of being interviewed

20. The moral teachings of religious institutions on religious, social, and economic issues

21. The difference between the results of two surveys or samples

22. A phrase used to describe people, whatever their economic status, who uphold traditional values, especially against the counterculture

j. party identification

k. political elites

l. political ideology

m. poll

n. populist

o. pure conservative

p. pure liberal

q. random sample

r. religious tradition

s. sampling error

t. silent majority

u. social status

v. traditional middle class

w. yuppies

of the 1960s

23.   A measure of one's social standing obtained
by combining such factors as education,
income, and occupation

DID YOU THINK THAT . . . ?

Below are listed a number of misconceptions. You should be able to refute each statement in the space
provided, referring to information or argumentation contained in this chapter. Sample answers appear at
the end of this chapter.

1.   "Differences of opinion in the United States are clearly related to differences in class."

_____

_____

_____

2.   "Most Americans take consistently liberal or conservative positions on issues."

_____

_____

_____

3.   "The leaders of African American organizations generally reflect the view of blacks nationwide."

_____

_____

_____

4.   "Affluent people are always politically conservative."

_____

_____

_____

DATA CHECK

Table 5.1: Religious Orientation of White Voters

1.   Which orientation (Secular, In-Between, Fundamentalist) is most strongly associated with
liberalism?

_____

2.   Which orientation is most strongly associated with the belief that we should spend more on
defense?

_____

3. Which orientation appears to be most supportive of allowing gays in the military?

   _____

4. Which orientation is least supportive of national health insurance?

   _____

5. In which orientations do a majority express the view that less money should be spent on welfare?

   _____

Table 5.2: The Gender Gap: Differences in Political Views of Women and Men

6. How would you describe the difference between the views of women and men on the topic of legalized abortion?

   _____

7. Which topic in the Table exhibits the greatest amount of difference between the views of women and men?

   _____

8. Where else are the views of women and men separated by at least 14 percentage point?

   _____

Table 5.3: The Changing College Student

9. Describe the trend in the percentage of college students who think the death penalty should be abolished.

   _____

10. Generalize about how college students feel about legalized abortion.

   _____

11. Describe the trend in the percentage of college students who think criminals have too many rights.

   _____

12. Generalize about how college students feel about military spending.

   _____

Figure 5.3 Ideological Self-Identification, 1976–1999

13. How do the largest percentage (or a plurality) of Americans typically describe themselves ideologically?

   _____

14. Which ideological label is typically claimed by the smallest percentage of respondents in surveys?

   _____

Table 5.6 How Liberals and Conservatives Differ

15. Who is more likely to oppose the death penalty for those convicted of murder?

_____

16. Who is more likely to believe homosexuals should be allowed to serve in the U.S. Armed Forces?

_____

17. Describe Liberal and Conservative support for the notion that women should have an equal role in running business, industry, and government.

_____

_____

18. Who is less supportive of the notion that it is the duty of government to guarantee a job and good standard of living for every person?

_____

PRACTICING FOR EXAMS

TRUE/FALSE QUESTIONS

Read each statement carefully. Mark true statements *T*. If any part of the statement is false, mark it *F*, and write in the space provided a concise explanation of why the statement is false.

1.   T   F   How a pollster words a question can dramatically affect the answer he or she gets.

_____

2.   T   F   The proportion of citizens who consider themselves Democrats or Republicans has steadily increased since the 1950s.

_____

3.   T   F   Younger voters have a weaker sense of partisanship than older ones.

_____

4.   T   F   The Christian Coalition is strongest in the South, Midwest, and West.

_____

5.   T   F   Since 1960, evangelical Christians have become more attached to Republican candidates.

_____

6.   T   F   Men have generally been more conservative than women on social issues such as gay rights, gun control, and spending programs for the poor.

_____

7.   T   F   Survey data suggest men and women have similar views on abortion.

_____

8. T F   College students today are clearly more conservative are clearly more conservative
             than they were ten or twenty years ago.

             _____

9. T F   In the United States public opinion is less divided by class than it is in Europe.

             _____

10. T F   Most national surveys consist of samples of four to five thousand respondents.

             _____

11. T F   Gallup and Harris use two different questions to measure how Americans feel about the
             president.

             _____

12. T F   The South has, on the whole, been less accommodating to business enterprises than
             other regions.

             _____

13. T F   People can have an ideology without describing themselves as liberals or
             conservatives.

             _____

14. T F   In the nineteenth century liberals favored personal and economic freedom.

             _____

15. T F   Conservatives are more likely to support decriminalization of marijuana.

             _____

16. T F   Liberals are more likely to want the government to reduce income inequality.

             _____

17. T F   Libertarians are conservative on economic issues and liberal on social ones.

             _____

18. T F   Populists are liberal on economic issues and conservatives on social ones.

             _____

19. T F   Delegates to presidential nominating conventions tend to be more ideological than the
             average voter.

             _____

20. T F   According to the text, elites do not define economic problems.

             _____

MULTIPLE CHOICE QUESTIONS

Circle the letter of the response that best answers the question or completes the statement.

1. The Framers of the Constitution understood that _____ would be the chief source of opinion on most matters.

    a. the general public
    b. elected representatives
    c. factions and interest groups
    d. political theorists and educators
    e. intellectuals

2. Which of the following goals is *not* listed in the Preamble to the Constitution?

    a. justice
    b. domestic tranquility
    c. the common defense
    d. equality
    e. the general welfare

3. Research indicates over half of children identify with the partisan preferences of at least one of their parents by they time they are

    a. in the first grade.
    b. in the fifth grade.
    c. juniors in high school.
    d. seniors in high school.
    e. high school graduates.

4. In adulthood, people whose party identification differs from their parents' usually call themselves

    a. radicals.
    b. independents.
    c. neo-institutionalists.
    d. conservatives.
    e. Democrats.

5. In recent years the influence of the family on party identification has

    a. decreased.
    b. increased.
    c. remained the same.
    d. disappeared.
    e. become too complex to study.

6. The correlation of children's attitudes with parental attitudes on issues involving civil liberties and racial questions

    a. is about the same as the correlation with their partisan identification.
    b. is stronger than the correlation with their partisan identification.
    c. is slightly lower than the correlation with their partisan identification.
    d. is much lower than the correlation with their partisan identification.
    e. has never been adequately examined.

7. The transfer of political beliefs from generation to generation does not appear in large national studies of political attitudes because

    a. most Americans are quite conservative.
    b. few Americans are either far left or far right of the political spectrum.
    c. polling techniques change radically from one generation to the next.
    d. most Americans are quite liberal.
    e. some generations participate in polls more than others.

8. Which religious group is most likely to have liberal political attitudes?

    a. Jews
    b. Protestants
    c. White Protestants
    d. Catholics
    e. There are no significant differences among these groups.

9. Political scientists reason that different religious groups' different political persuasions may have resulted from

    a. the content of their religious beliefs.
    b. their members' experiences as immigrants here.
    c. the perceptions of pollsters about religion
    d. both A and B.
    e. None of the above.

10. The increasing incidence of men "deserting" Democratic candidates for Republican ones involves attitudes about all of the following issues *except*

    a. spending programs aimed at the poor.
    b. the size of government.
    c. the economy.
    d. gun control.
    e. gay rights.

11. Attending college tends to make people more _____ than the general population.

    a. moderate
    b. conservative
    c. Democratic
    d. Republican
    e. liberal

12. Students attending more prestigious or selective colleges are more _____ than the general population.

    a. liberal
    b. conservative
    c. Democratic
    d. Republican
    e. moderate

13. Social scientists list all of the following among the reasons that higher education correlates with increased liberalism *except*

    a. the personal traits of those going to college.
    b. students' exposure to more information.
    c. the liberalism of many professors.

d.   the common beliefs held by teachers.

e.   B and C.

14.   An analysis of voting in one hundred of America's richest communities from 1980 to 1996 found

a.   voter turnout decreased slightly.

b.   voter turnout decreased significantly.

c.   the Independent share of the vote increased.

d.   the Republican share of the vote increased.

e.   the Democratic share of the vote increased.

15.   The opinions of whites and African Americans are quite similar on all of the following *except*

a.   the use of racial quotas.

b.   stronger affirmative action.

c.   the belief that too much is made of racial differences.

d.   abortion.

e.   getting tough on criminals.

16.   Latinos, the fastest growing ethnic group in the United States,

a.   tend to vote for Democratic candidates.

b.   tend to vote for Republican candidates.

c.   tend to vote for Independent candidates.

d.   generally vote the same, but in an unpredictable manner.

e.   are a diverse mix of groups, none of which has become predictably partisan.

17.   In a typical ideological self-identification survey, the largest group of Americans will

a.   classify themselves as liberal.

b.   classify themselves as conservative.

c.   classify themselves as moderate.

d.   refuse to classify themselves in any manner.

e.   None of the above.

18.   Those who favor increased taxation of the rich are usually described as

a.   Republicans.

b.   liberals.

c.   activists.

d.   conservatives.

e.   Taxicrats.

19.   If you favor universal medical insurance and a woman's right to choose abortion, according to the text you would be labeled a

a.   pure liberal.

b.   pure conservative.

c.   neo-conservative.

d.   libertarian.

e.   populist.

20.   If you favor reducing federal taxes and quarantining AIDS victims, you would be classified as

a.   pure liberal.

b.   neo-populist.

c.   pure conservative.

d.   libertarian.

e.   populist.

21. If you want the federal government to save small farmers from bankruptcy and allow prayer in public schools, according to the text you would be labeled a

   a.   pure liberal.
   b.   pure conservative.
   c.   neo-conservative.
   d.   libertarian.
   e.   populist.

22. If you want to cut back on federal spending and favor the decriminalization of marijuana, you would be labeled a

   a.   pure liberal.
   b.   pure conservative.
   c.   neo-populist
   d.   libertarian.
   e.   populist.

23. Which group displays the most consistency in political attitudes?

   a.   average citizens
   b.   political activists
   c.   females
   d.   blacks
   e.   manual workers

24. The characteristic that is *not* found in the new middle class is

   a.   a postgraduate education.
   b.   residence in or near big cities.
   c.   an attitude favorable to business interests.
   d.   A and B.
   e.   a liberal position on social issues.

25. Which of the following is an incorrect assessment of elite opinion?

   a.   Elites influence which issues will capture the public's attention.
   b.   Elites are unified in their interests and opinions.
   c.   Elites state the norms by which issues should be settled.
   d.   Elites raise and frame political issues.
   e.   Elites influence how issues are debated and decided.

ESSAY QUESTIONS

Practice writing extended answers to the following questions. These test your ability to integrate and express the ideas that you have been studying in this chapter.

26. Discuss the comparative roles played by the family, religion, gender, and education in forming Americans' political outlook. Of the four, which would you say have been gaining in importance recently, and why?

27. Explain what the words *liberal* and *conservative* mean in the United States today, compared with their earlier meanings. Discuss to what extent these terms are useful in characterizing the political attitudes of the average American.

28. Discuss the notion of gender gap and why it is more accurate to say that men rather than women have "deserted" Democratic candidates for Republican ones. Also, discuss some of the issues that divide men and women.

29. Compare and contrast the "new class" and the traditional middle class, or "old class," as to their makeup and their political beliefs and allegiances. What effect on American politics is growth of the "new class" likely to have?

ANSWERS TO KEY TERMS MATCH QUESTIONS

1. j
2. c
3. d
4. b
5. l
6. k
7. v
8. h
9. w
10. p
11. o
12. f
13. n
14. a
15. e
16. g
17. i
18. m
19. q
20. r
21. s
22. t
23. u

ANSWERS TO "DID YOU THINK THAT . . . ?" QUESTIONS

1. Poor blacks and poor whites disagree on racial issues; Protestants and Jews of similar status often disagree on social welfare policies; and a majority of poor whites vote Republican, whereas a majority of poor blacks vote Democratic. Combinations of factors, including race, religion, region, and party identification, as well as status and occupation, determine political opinions.

2. Most Americans do not display ideological thinking. They may take liberal positions on some issues and conservative positions on others. They may be inconsistent—by supporting government social welfare programs but at the same time applauding efforts to reduce government spending in general. There seem to be various combinations involving some liberal and some conservative positions, and each of these combinations attracts candidates and voters.

3. There is, in fact, a big opinion gap between the leaders of African American organizations and black people generally. One recent poll indicates that leaders were much more likely than the rank-in-file to favor abortions, school busing, and affirmative action.

4. Members of the "new class"—affluent, under-forty persons with technical, scientific, and professional occupations—are often more liberal than business elites. "New class" Democrats are likely to be more liberal than working-class Democrats.

ANSWERS TO DATA CHECK QUESTIONS

1. Secular.

2. Fundamentalist.

3. Secular.

4. Fundamentalist.

5. A majority of all three of the orientations believe we should spend less on welfare.

6. A majority of both females and males support legalized abortion and the difference between the groups appears to be quite minimal (57 percent to 60 percent).

7. Banning handguns (a 26 percent difference).

8. Sexual harassment and voting for Clinton in 1996.

9. 33 percent thought the death penalty should be abolished in the 1970s. By 1993, the percentage fell to 22.

10. Almost half (47 percent) supported legalization of marijuana in the 1970s. By 1993, the percentage fell to 28.

11. A majority felt criminals had too many rights in the 1970s and in 1993, though the percentages have increased from 52 to 68 percent.

12. Support for an increase in military spending fell from 39 to 23 percent.

13. Moderate.

14. Liberal.

15. Liberal.

16. Liberal.

17. Both Liberals and Conservatives exhibit high levels of support for these notions (96 and 81 percent respectively), though Liberals appear more supportive.

18. Conservatives are much less comfortable with this notion. Only 21 percent express agreement with it, while 55 percent of liberal respondents feel otherwise.

ANSWERS TO TRUE/FALSE QUESTIONS

1. T
2. F. The percentage has steadily decreased.
3. T
4. T
5. T
6. T
7. T
8. F. They are more conservative on some issues, but more liberal on others.
9. T
10. F. A typical sample is between one thousand and fifteen hundred.
11. T
12. F. The South has, on the whole been less accommodating to labor and more accommodating to the interests of business.
13. T
14. T
15. F. Liberals are more likely to favor this.
16. T
17. T
18. T
19. T
20. T

ANSWERS TO MULTIPLE CHOICE QUESTIONS

1. c
2. d
3. b
4. b
5. a
6. d
7. b
8. a
9. d
10. c
11. e

12. a
13. d
14. e
15. b
16. e
17. c
18. b
19. a
20. c
21. e
22. d
23. b
24. c
25. b

CHAPTER 6

Political Participation

REVIEWING THE CHAPTER

CHAPTER FOCUS

This chapter reviews the much-discussed lack of voter turnout and other forms of political participation in the United States, and concludes that individual Americans may not be at fault for their seeming nonparticipation but that other factors may be at work. After reading and reviewing the material in this chapter, you should be able to do each of the following:

1. Explain why the text believes that the description, the analysis, and the proposed remedy for low voter turnout rates in this country are off base.

2. Compare the way turnout statistics are tabulated for this country and for other countries, and explain the significance of these differences.

3. Describe how the control of elections has shifted from the states to the federal government, and explain what effects this shift has had on blacks, women, and youths.

4. State both sides of the debate over whether voter turnout has declined over the past century, and describe those factors that tend to hold down voter turnout in this country.

5. List and explain Nie and Verba's four categories of political participation.

6. Discuss those factors that appear to be associated with high or low political participation.

7. Compare participation rates in various forms of political activity here and in other countries.

STUDY OUTLINE

I. A closer look at nonvoting
    A. Alleged problem: low turnout compared with Europeans, but this compares registered voters with the eligible adult population
    B. Common explanation: voter apathy on election day, but the real problem is low registration rates
    C. Proposed solution: get-out-the-vote drives, but this will not help those who are not registered
    D. Apathy not the only cause of nonregistration
        1. Costs here versus no costs in European countries where registration is automatic
        2. Motor-voter law of 1993 (which took effect in 1995)
            a) Did not create a general boom in vote turnout
            b) Did increase registration among eligible voters
            c) Did not change the two party balance of registrants
            d) Did increase the number of independent registrants
            e) May actually add registrants who are less likely to vote
    E. Voting is not the only way of participating
II. The rise of the American electorate

A.   From state to federal control
    1.   Initially, states decided nearly everything
    2.   This led to wide variation in federal elections
    3.   Congress has since reduced state prerogatives
        a)   1842 law: House members elected by district
        b)   Suffrage to women
        c)   Suffrage to blacks
        d)   Suffrage to eighteen- to twenty-year-olds
        e)   Direct popular election of U.S. senators
    4.   Black voting rights
        a)   Fifteenth Amendment gutted by Supreme Court as not conferring a right to vote
        b)   Southern states then use evasive strategies
            (1)   Literacy test
            (2)   Poll tax
            (3)   White primaries
            (4)   Grandfather clauses
            (5)   Intimidation of black voters
        c)   Most of these strategies ruled out by Supreme Court
        d)   Major change with 1965 Voting Rights Act; black vote increases
    5.   Women's voting rights
        a)   Western states permit women to vote
        b)   Nineteenth Amendment ratified 1920
        c)   No dramatic changes in outcomes
    6.   Youth vote
        a)   Voting Rights Act of 1970
        b)   Twenty-sixth Amendment ratified 1971
        c)   Lower turnout; no particular party
    7.   National standards now govern most aspects
B.   Voting turnout
    1.   Debate over declining percentages: two theories
        a)   The percentages are real and the result of a decline in popular interest in elections and competitiveness of the two parties
            (1)   Parties originally worked hard to increase turnout among all voters
            (2)   The election of 1896 locked Democrats in the South and Republicans in the North
            (3)   Lopsided Republican victories caused citizens to lose interest
            (4)   Leadership in the major parties became conservative and resisted mass participation
        b)   The percentages represent an apparent decline induced, in part, by more honest ballot counts of today.
            (1)   Parties once printed ballots
            (2)   Ballots cast in public
            (3)   Parties controlled counting
        c)   Most scholars see several reasons for some real decline.
            (1)   Registration more difficult: longer residency, educational qualifications, and discrimination
            (2)   Continuing drop after 1960 cannot be explained
            (3)   Refinement of VAP data to VEP data also reveals a decline
        d)   Universal turnout probably would not alter election outcomes
III.   Who participates in politics?
  A.   Forms of participation

      1.   Voting the most common, but 8 to 10 percent misreport it

      2.   Verba and Nie's six types of participants

         a)   Inactives

         b)   Voting specialists

         c)   Campaigners

         d)   Communalists

         e)   Parochial participants

         f)   Complete activists

B.   Causes of participation

      1.   Schooling, or political information, more likely to vote

      2.   Church-goers vote more

      3.   Men and women vote same rate

      4.   Race

         a)   Black participation lower than that of whites overall

         b)   But controlling for SES, higher than whites

      5.   Level of trust in government?

         a)   Studies show no correlation

      6.   Difficulty of registering; as turnout declines, registration gets easier

      7.   Several small factors decrease turnout

         a)   More youths, blacks, and other minorities

         b)   Decreasing effectiveness of parties

         c)   Remaining impediments to registration

         d)   Voting compulsory in other nations

         e)   Ethnic minorities encounter language barriers, whereas blacks are involved in nonpolitical institutions

         f)   May feel that elections do not matter

      8.   Democrats and Republicans fight over solutions

         a)   No one really knows who would be helped

         b)   Nonvoters tend to be poor, black, and so on

         c)   But an increasing percentage of college graduates are also not voting

         d)   Hard to be sure that turnout efforts produce gains for either party: Jesse Jackson in 1984

C.   The meaning of participation rates

      1.   Americans vote less but participate more

         a)   Other forms of activity becoming more common

         b)   Some forms more common here than in other countries

      2.   Americans elect more officials than Europeans do and have more elections

      3.   U.S. turnout rates heavily skewed to higher status; meaning of this is unclear

KEY TERMS MATCH

Match the following terms and descriptions:

1.   The lack of interest among the citizenry in participating in elections

2.   Those citizens disqualified from voting (too young, in prison, and so forth)

3.   Those citizens registered to vote

4.   Requirement that voters be able to read; formerly used in the South to disenfranchise

a.   activist

b.   Australian ballot

c.   campaigners

d.   communalists

e.   complete activists

f.   eligible electorate

Chapter 6: Political Participation   **91**

blacks

5. Proof of tax payment, to be produced when voting; used to disenfranchise blacks

6. A southern expedient to keep blacks from participating in primary elections

7. Requirement that for an individual to automatically qualify to vote, his or her grandparent had to have voted (excluded former slaves and their descendants)

8. Legislation that made it illegal to exclude potential voters on the basis of race

9. Legislation that extended suffrage to women

10. Legislation that gave eighteen-year-olds the right to vote in federal elections

11. Legislation that gave eighteen-year-olds the right to vote in all U.S. elections

12. A document that is government printed, of uniform size, and cast in secret

13. Those who avoid all forms of political participation

14. Those who restrict their political participation to voting in elections

15. Those who both vote in elections and get involved in campaigns

16. Those who join organizations and participate in politics but not in partisan campaigns

17. Those who avoid elections and civic organizations but will contact officials regarding specific problems

18. Those who take part in all forms of political activity

19. An individual who actively promotes a political party, philosophy, or issue she or he cares personally about

20. A bill that requires states to allow voter registration by mail, when applying for a driver's license, and at some state offices that serve the disabled or poor

21. The citizens who are eligible to vote after reaching a minimum age requirement

g. Fifteenth Amendment

h. grandfather clauses

i. inactives

j. literacy tests

k. motor-voter bill

l. Nineteenth Amendment

m. parochial participants

n. poll tax

o. registered voters

p. Twenty-sixth Amendment

q. voter apathy

r. voting-age population

s. Voting Rights Act of 1970

t. voting specialists

u. white primaries

Copyright © Houghton Mifflin Company. All rights reserved.

DID YOU THINK THAT . . . ?

Below are listed a number of misconceptions. You should be able to refute each statement in the space provided, referring to information or argumentation contained in this chapter. Sample answers appear at the end of this chapter.

1. "The motor-voter bill has resulted in greater voter turnout."

   _____

   _____

   _____

2. "Because the United States holds more elections for more offices than most other nations, its party system is stronger than that of most other nations."

   _____

   _____

   _____

3. "Registered American voters vote less frequently than do their counterparts in Europe."

   _____

   _____

   _____

4. "The declining voter turnout rate is caused by the difficulties associated with registering to vote."

   _____

   _____

   _____

DATA CHECK

Figure 6.2: Voter Participation in Presidential Elections, 1860–2000

1. How does voter turnout in the twentieth century compare with that of the nineteenth?

   _____

2. Identify two time periods of considerable length that are characterized by a steady, general decrease in voter turnout.

   _____

Table 6:3 Two Methods of Calculating Turnout in Presidential Elections, 1948–2000

3. In how many years does the VAP reach 60 percent?

   _____

4. In how many years does the VEP reach 60 percent?

   _____

5. According to the VEP measure, what percentage of eligible voters participated in the 2000 presidential election?

_____

Table 6.4 : Voter Turnout in Presidential Elections by Age, Schooling, and Race 1964–1996.

6. Which age group is least likely to vote in a presidential election?

_____

7. Which group is least likely to vote according to their schooling, or level of education?

_____

8. Describe vote turnout among blacks and Hispanics.

_____

_____

Table 6.5: How Citizens Participate

9. Describe the trend in respondents claiming to vote regularly in presidential elections.

_____

10. Describe the trend in respondents claiming to always vote in local elections.

_____

11. How many of the twelve activities other than voting are characterized by an increase in activity from 1967 to 1987?

_____

12. Which three activities are associated with the highest levels of increased activity?

_____

_____

PRACTICING FOR EXAMS

TRUE/FALSE QUESTIONS

Read each statement carefully. Mark true statements *T*. If any part of the statement is false, mark it *F*, and write in the space provided a concise explanation of why the statement is false.

1. T F Low rates of voter registration may indicate people are reasonably well satisfied with how the country is being governed.

_____

2. T F At the time the Constitution was ratified, the only qualification for voters was that they were white and male.

_____

3.   T   F   The Supreme Court declared grandfather clauses unconstitutional.

_____

4.   T   F   The 1965 Civil Rights Act suspended the use of literary tests.

_____

5.   T   F   The Nineteenth Amendment nearly doubled the number of eligible voters in the United States.

_____

6.   T   F   When the Voting Rights Act of 1970 extended the right of eighteen-year-olds to vote in state elections, the Supreme Court declared the law unconstitutional.

_____

7.   T   F   Before 1961, residents of the District of Columbia could not vote in presidential elections.

_____

8.   T   F   Most scholars believe voter turnout did decrease somewhere around the 1890s.

_____

9.   T   F   The 1996 presidential election featured a relatively high turnout.

_____

10.   T   F   Over 40 percent of non-voters in the 1992 and 1996 elections had moved in the previous two years.

_____

11.   T   F   In a typical survey, 20 to 25 percent of Americans misrepresent their voting habits.

_____

12.   T   F   Political "activists" constitute about 11 percent of the population.

_____

13.   T   F   Parochial participants vote frequently but participate very little in the political process otherwise.

_____

14.   T   F   Men and women participate in politics at about the same rate.

_____

15.   T   F   The Supreme Court has prohibited residency requirements longer than thirty days in presidential elections.

_____

16.   T   F   Four states allow voters to register and vote all in the same day.

_____

17.   T   F   Democrats usually suspect higher turnout would work to their advantage.

_____

18. T   F   Nonvoters are more likely to be poor than voters.

_____

19. T   F   The kinds of people who vote here are different from the kinds of people who vote abroad.

_____

20. T   F   Blacks are more likely to be members of churches that stimulate political interests, activity, and mobilization than Latinos.

_____

MULTIPLE CHOICE QUESTIONS

Circle the letter of the response that best answers the question or completes the statement.

1. While 80 percent of the people vote in many European elections, about _____ of the people typically vote in American presidential elections.

    a. 20 percent
    b. 25 percent
    c. 40 percent
    d. 50 percent
    e. 70 percent

2. In this country about _____ of the voting age population is registered to vote.

    a. one-eighth
    b. one-quarter
    c. one-half
    d. two-thirds
    e. ninety-five percent

3. Which of the following statements about the motor-voter law is accurate?

    a. It has enabled about 50 million more people to vote.
    b. It requires states to allow people to register to vote when applying for driver's licenses.
    c. It took effect in 1993.
    d. It has changed the balance of registrants in favor of the Democrats.
    e. It allows illegal aliens and convicted felons to register to vote.

4. The most important changes in elections have included all of the following *except*

    a. extension of suffrage to women.
    b. extension of suffrages to African Americans.
    c. extension of suffrage to eighteen-year-olds
    d. direct popular election of Senators.
    e. direct popular elections of Representatives in the House.

5. Initially, following passage of the Nineteenth Amendment, women

    a. voted as often as men, but generally in the same manner.
    b. voted less often than men, but generally in the same manner.
    c. voted more often than men, but generally in the same manner.
    d. voted more often than men, but quite independently.
    e. voted as often as men, but quite independently.

6.   Which statement is incorrect?

   a.   The Twenty-fifth Amendment gave eighteen-year-olds the right to vote.
   b.   The 1972 elections were the first where eighteen- to twenty-year-olds were allowed to vote.
   c.   The turnout for eighteen- to twenty-year-olds is usually lower than that of the population as a whole.
   d.   Most young voters supported Richard Nixon.
   e.   Political participation rates for young people have actually been shown to be quite high.

7.   In the twentieth century voter turnout in U.S. presidential elections has generally varied between

   a.   30 and 40 percent.
   b.   40 and 50 percent.
   c.   50 and 60 percent.
   d.   60 and 70 percent.
   e.   70 and 80 percent.

8.   In the later part of the nineteenth century (1860–1896), voter turnout in U.S. presidential elections generally varied between

   a.   30 and 40 percent.
   b.   40 and 50 percent.
   c.   50 and 60 percent
   d.   60 and 70 percent.
   e.   70 and 80 percent.

9.   Until about 1890 ballots were printed by the

   a.   candidates.
   b.   House of Representatives.
   c.   state legislatures.
   d.   political parties.
   e.   local government.

10.   Adoption of the Australian ballot enabled United States citizens to vote

   a.   early and often.
   b.   more easily.
   c.   by absentee ballot.
   d.   without being informed.
   e.   in secret.

11.   After the 1890s voter-registration regulations became more burdensome because

   a.   they had longer residency requirements.
   b.   it became harder for African Americans to vote.
   c.   educational qualifications were added in some states.
   d.   voters were required to register far in advance of the election.
   e.   All of the above.

12.   VEP measures of turnout may have an advantage over VAP measures because

   a.   VEP measures attempt to remove ineligible voters from the data.
   b.   VEP measures are based on actual census data.
   c.   VEP measures include prisoners, but not felons or aliens.
   d.   VEP measures include felons, but not prisoners or aliens.
   e.   VEP measures are verified by each state legislature.

13. When one refocuses analyses of vote turnout in the last fourteen presidential elections to VEP measures, it is clear that

    a.   there never has been anything like a turnout problem in America.
    b.   the voter turnout problem disappeared in the most recent elections.
    c.   voters are participating more now than ever before.
    d.   vote turnout has generally declined in the most recent elections.
    e.   vote turnout has generally remained the same.

14. Studies of non-voters suggest that, had they voted in recent presidential elections,

    a.   the Democrats would have won more often.
    b.   the Republicans would have won more often.
    c.   the Democrats would have won more of the elections by "landslides."
    d.   the Republicans would have won more of the elections by "landslides."
    e.   there is reason to expect there would have actually been no impact on who won or lost.

15. In surveys, about what percentage of respondents claim to have voted in an election when they did not do so?

    a.   2 to 3 percent
    b.   8 to 10 percent
    c.   20 to 25 percent
    d.   30 to 35 percent
    e.   40 to 50 percent

16. Those who prefer to participate in politics by joining nonpartisan groups and dealing with various issues in them are referred to as

    a.   voting specialists.
    b.   campaigners.
    c.   communalists.
    d.   issue belligerents.
    e.   parochial participants.

17. Those who cast ballots in elections but engage in no other form of political participation are called

    a.   voting specialists.
    b.   campaigners.
    c.   issue belligerents.
    d.   communalists.
    e.   parochial participants.

18. Those who stay out of electoral contests and community organizations but will contact officials to deal with specific problems are called

    a.   voting specialists.
    b.   campaigners.
    c.   communalists.
    d.   parochial participants.
    e.   issue belligerents.

19. Studies show that feelings of mistrust toward government have _____ effect on voter turnout.

    a.   a stimulating
    b.   a depressing
    c.   an impressive
    d.   no
    e.   an unpredictable

20. In states that have instituted same-day voter registration, the effect on voter turnout has been

    a.   a major decline.
    b.   a slight decline.
    c.   a slight increase.
    d.   a major increase.
    e.   no effect at all.

21. Two careful studies of voter turnout in twenty-four democratic nations found that almost all of the difference in voter turnout could be explained by

    a.   the degree of party strength.
    b.   the presence or absence of automatic registration.
    c.   the presence or absence of compulsory voting laws.
    d.   All of the above.
    e.   None of the above.

22. The best evidence suggests Americans

    a.   are voting less, and participating in politics less.
    b.   are voting less, and participating in politics more.
    c.   are voting and participating in politics at about the same rate.
    d.   are voting more, and participating less in politics.
    e.   are voting more and participating more in politics.

23. Political demonstrations have been used by

    a.   antiwar activists.
    b.   farmers.
    c.   truckers.
    d.   civil rights activists
    e.   All of the above.

24. The number of elective offices in the United States, compared with European nations, is

    a.   much lower.
    b.   slightly lower.
    c.   about the same.
    d.   slightly higher.
    e.   much higher.

25. Compared with Europeans, American voters are offered the opportunity to vote

    a.   much less frequently.
    b.   slightly less frequently.
    c.   more frequently.
    d.   just as often.
    e.   much less frequently, but their vote counts more.

ESSAY QUESTIONS

Practice writing extended answers to the following questions. These test your ability to integrate and express the ideas that you have been studying in this chapter.

1. Discuss those aspects of elections that can be said to make American politics more democratic than the politics of most other countries, as well as those aspects of elections that can be said to make American politics less democratic.

2. What are the major factors that appear to hold down the level of voter turnout in the United States? What sort of program might you design if you wanted to overcome some of these problems and thus increase voter turnout?

3. Outline the history of the growth of the franchise in this country. Discuss where we are likely to go from here: broadening the franchise to include more groups of people, keeping it about the same, or constricting it.

4. Categorize yourself on Nie and Verba's six-way classification of political participants. Are you comfortable with the category in which you find yourself now? Why or why not?

5. What, if any, reforms of the voter registration system in this country would you advocate? What might be the consequences, intended and/or unintended, of such reforms?

ANSWERS TO KEY TERMS MATCH QUESTIONS

1. q
2. f
3. o
4. j
5. n
6. u
7. h
8. g
9. l
10. s
11. p
12. b
13. i
14. t
15. c
16. d
17. m
18. e
19. a
20. k
21. r

ANSWERS TO "DID YOU THINK THAT . . . ?" QUESTIONS

1. Turnout has not increased; however, voter registration has increased markedly.

2. Parties in the United States remain generally weaker than their European counterparts.

3. According to figures cited with the permission of the American Enterprise Institute, the turnout rates of *registered* Americans are comparable to rates of Europeans, who are registered by their governments.

4. Registration rules have grown easier, without any corresponding rise in voter turnout rates.

ANSWERS TO DATA CHECK QUESTIONS

1. About 20 percent lower in the twentieth century.

2. 1896 to 1920 / 1960 to 1988.

3. Four (1952, 1960, 1964, and 1968).

4. Six (1952, 1956, 1960, 1964, 1968, and 1992).

5. 55.6 percent.

6. 18 to 24.

7. Less than high school.

8. Turnout for blacks and Hispanics is lower than that of whites with Hispanics having the lowest rates for the three groups.

9. There was a decrease of 8 percent among such respondents.

10. There was a decrease of 12 percent among such respondents.

11. 10 of 12 activities featured increases in activity.

12. Contacting state or national officials: issue-based (11 percent), contacting local officials: issue-based (10 percent) and contributing money to a party or candidate (10 percent).

ANSWERS TO TRUE/FALSE QUESTIONS

1. T

2. F. Voters also had to be property owners or taxpayers.

3. T

4. T

5. T

6. T

7. T

8. T

9. F. It featured the lowest turnout of any election since 1924.

10. T

11. F. The figure is actually 8 to 10 percent.

12. T

13. F. Parochial participants do not vote, participate in campaigns, or join associations, but they are willing to contact public officials.

14. T

15. T

16. T

17. T

18. T

19. T

20. T

ANSWERS TO MULTIPLE CHOICE QUESTIONS

1. d
2. d
3. b
4. e
5. b
6. a
7. c
8. e
9. d
10. e
11. e
12. a
13. d
14. e
15. b
16. c
17. a
18. d
19. d
20. c
21. d
22. b
23. e
24. e
25. c

CHAPTER 7

Political Parties

REVIEWING THE CHAPTER

CHAPTER FOCUS

This chapter provides a fairly detailed exploration of one unique aspect of American politics: the two-party system that has evolved in the United States. After reading and reviewing the material in this chapter, you should be able to do each of the following:

1. Define the term *political party* and contrast the structures of the European and American parties, paying particular attention to the federal structure of the American system and the concept of party identification.

2. Trace the development of the party system through its four periods, and offer reasons that parties have been in decline since the New Deal period.

3. Describe the structure of a major party and distinguish powerful from powerless party organs.

4. Define *intraparty democracy* and state its effect on the last few Democratic nominating conventions in the last few contests. Evaluate the relative strengths of state party bosses in recent years, and discuss the increasing importance of primaries in relation to the boss system at conventions.

5. Describe the machine, discuss its functions, and trace its decline. Contrast its structure with that of ideological and reform parties.

6. Offer two explanations for the persistence of the two-party system. Explain why minor parties form, and discuss different kinds of parties. Analyze why they are so rarely successful.

7. Describe some of the issue differences between delegates at Democratic and Republican conventions, and indicate whether there are major differences between the parties. Compare these differences with those between members of the rank and file voters.

STUDY OUTLINE

I. Parties here and abroad
    A. Decentralization
        1. A party is a group that seeks to elect candidates to public office by supplying them with a label.
        2. Arenas
            a) A label in the minds of the voters
            b) Set of leaders in government
            c) Organization recruiting and campaigning
        3. American parties have become weaker in all three arenas
            a) As labels: more independents
            b) As organizations: much weaker since the 1960s

     c) As sets of leaders: the organization of Congress less under their control

  B. Reasons for differences from European parties

    1. Federal system decentralizes power

     a) Early on, most people with political jobs worked for state and local government.

     b) National parties were coalitions of local parties.

     c) As political power becomes more centralized, parties become weaker still

    2. Parties closely regulated by state and federal laws

    3. Candidates chosen through primaries, not by party leaders

    4. President elected separately from Congress

    5. Political culture

     a) Parties unimportant in life; Americans do not join or pay dues

     b) Parties separate from other aspects of life

II. The rise and decline of the political party

  A. The Founding (to the 1820s)

    1. Founders' dislike of factions

    2. Emergence of Republicans, Federalists: Jefferson versus Hamilton

     a) Loose caucuses of political notables

     b) Republicans' success and Federalists' demise

    3. No representation of clear economic interests

  B. The Jacksonians (to the Civil War)

    1. Political participation a mass phenomenon

     a) More voters to reach

     b) Party built from the bottom up

     c) Abandonment of presidential caucuses

     d) Beginning of national conventions to allow local control

  C. The Civil War and sectionalism

    1. Jacksonian system unable to survive slavery issue

    2. New Republicans become dominant because of

     a) Civil War and Republicans on Union side

     b) Bryan's alienation of northern Democrats in 1896

    3. In most states one party predominates

     a) Party professionals, or "stalwarts," one faction in GOP

     b) Mugwumps, Progressives, or "reformers" another faction

      (1) Balance of power at first

      (2) Diminished role later

  D. The era of reform

    1. Progressive push measures to curtail parties

     a) Primary elections

     b) Nonpartisan elections

     c) No party-business alliances

     d) Strict voter registration requirements

     e) Civil service reform

     f) Initiative and referendum elections

    2. Effects

     a) Reduction in worst forms of political corruption

     b) Weakening of all political parties

III. Party realignments

  A. Definition: sharp, lasting shift in the popular coalition supporting one or both parties

  B. Occurrences: change in issues

    1. 1800: Jeffersonians defeated Federalists

    2. 1828: Jacksonian Democrats came to power

   3. 1860: Whigs collapsed; Republicans won
   4. 1896: Republicans defeated Bryan
   5. 1932: FDR Democrats came to power
  C. Kinds of realignments
   1. Major party disappears and is replaced (1800, 1860)
   2. Voters shift from one party to another (1896, 1932)
  D. Clearest cases
   1. 1860: slavery
   2. 1896: economics
   3. 1932: depression
  E. 1980 not a realignment
   1. Expressed dissatisfaction with Carter
   2. Also left Congress Democratic
  F. 1972–1988: shift in presidential voting patterns in the South
   1. Fewer Democrats, more Republicans, more independents
   2. Independents vote Republican
   3. Now close to fifty-fifty Democratic, Republican
   4. Party dealignment, not realignment
  G. Party decline; evidence for it
   1. Fewer people identify with either party
   2. Increase in ticket splitting
IV. The national party structure today
  A. Parties similar on paper
   1. National convention ultimate power; nominates presidential candidate
   2. National committee composed of delegates from states
   3. Congressional campaign committees
   4. National chair manages daily work
  B. Party structure diverges in the late 1960s
   1. RNC moves to bureaucratic structure; a well-financed party devoted to electing its candidates
   2. Democrats move to factionalized structure to distribute power
   3. RNC uses computerized mailing lists to raise money
    a) Money used to run political consulting firm
    b) Democrats still manage to outspend GOP
    c) Public opinion polls used to find issues and to get voter response to issues and candidates
   4. RNC now tries to help state and local organizations
   5. Democrats remain a collection of feuding factions
  C. National conventions
   1. National committee sets time and place; issues call setting number of delegates for each state
   2. Formulas used to allocate delegates
    a) Democrats shift the formula away from the South to the North and West
    b) Republicans shift the formula away from the East to the South and Southwest
    c) Result: Democrats move left, Republicans right
   3. Democratic formula rewards large states and Republican-loyal states
   4. Democrats set new rules
    a) In the 1970s the rules changed to weaken party leaders and increase the influence of special interests.
    b) Hunt commission in 1981 reverses 1970s rules by increasing the influence of elected officials and by making convention more deliberative

     5.   Consequence of reforms: parties represent different set of upper-middle-class voters
        a)   Republicans represent traditional middle class
        b)   Democrats represent the "new class"
        c)   Democrats hurt because the traditional middle class closer in opinions to most citizens
     6.   To become more competitive, Democrats adopt rule changes
        a)   In 1988 the number of superdelegates increased and special interests decreased.
        b)   In 1992 three rules: winner-reward system, proportional representation, and states that violate rules are penalized
     7.   Conventions today only ratify choices made in primaries.

V.   State and local parties
   A.   The machine
      1.   Recruitment via tangible incentives
      2.   High degree of leadership control
      3.   Abuses
        a)   Gradually controlled by reforms
        b)   But machines continued
      4.   Both self-serving and public regarding
      5.   Winning above all else
   B.   Ideological parties
      1.   Principle above all else
      2.   Usually outside Democrats and Republicans
      3.   But some local reform clubs
      4.   Reform clubs replaced by social movements
   C.   Solidary groups
      1.   Most common form of party organization
      2.   Members motivated by solidary incentives
      3.   Advantage: neither corrupt nor inflexible
      4.   Disadvantage: not very hard working
   D.   Sponsored parties
      1.   Created or sustained by another organization
      2.   Example: Detroit Democrats controlled by UAW
      3.   Not very common
   E.   Personal following
      1.   Examples: Kennedys, Curley, Talmadges, Longs
      2.   Viability today affected by TV and radio
      3.   Advantage: vote for the person
      4.   Disadvantage: takes time to know the person

VI. The two-party system
   A.   Rarity among nations today
   B.   Evenly balanced nationally, not locally
   C.   Why such a permanent feature?
      1.   Electoral system: winner-take-all and plurality system
      2.   Opinions of voters: two broad coalitions

VII. Minor parties
   A.   Ideological parties: comprehensive, radical view; most enduring
      Examples: Socialist, Communist, Libertarian
   B.   One-issue parties: address one concern, avoid others
      Examples: Free Soil, Know-Nothing, Prohibition
   C.   Economic protest parties: regional, oppose depressions
      Examples: Greenback, Populist

    D.   Factional parties: from split in a major party

           Examples: Bull Moose, Henry Wallace, American Independent

    E.   Movements *not* producing parties; either slim chance of success or major parties accommodate

           Examples: civil rights, antiwar, labor

    F.   Factional parties have had greatest influence

VIII. Nominating a president

    A.   Two contrary forces: party's desire to win motivates it to seek an appealing candidate, but its desire to keep dissidents in party forces a compromise to more extreme views

    B.   Are the delegates representative of the voters?

        1.   Democratic delegates much more liberal

        2.   Republican delegates much more conservative

        3.   Explanation of this disparity not quota rules: quota groups have greater diversity of opinion than do the delegates

    C.   Who votes in primaries?

        1.   Primaries now more numerous and more decisive

           a)   Stevenson and Humphrey never entered a primary

           b)   By 1992: forty primaries and twenty caucuses

        2.   Little ideological difference between primary voters and rank-and-file party voters

        3.   Caucus: meeting of party followers at which delegates are picked

           a)   Only most-dedicated partisans attend

           b)   Often choose most ideological candidate: Jackson, Robertson in 1988

    D.   Who are the new delegates?

        1.   However chosen, today's delegates a new breed unlikely to resemble average citizen: issue-oriented activists

        2.   Advantages of new system

           a)   Increased chance for activists within party

           b)   Decreased probability of their bolting the party

        3.   Disadvantage: may nominate presidential candidates unacceptable to voters or rank and file

IX.   Parties versus voters

    A.   Democrats: win congressional elections but lose presidential contests

        1.   Candidates are out of step with average voters on social and tax issues

        2.   So are delegates, and there's a connection

    B.   Republicans had the same problem with Goldwater (1964)

    C.   Rank-and-file Democrats and Republicans differ on many political issues, but the differences are usually small

    D.   Delegates from two parties differ widely on these same issues

        1.   1996 conventions

           a)   Few conservatives at Democratic convention

           b)   Few liberals at Republican convention

        2.   Formula for winning president

           a)   Nominate candidates with views closer to the average citizen (e.g., 1996 election)

           b)   Fight campaign over issues agreed on by delegates and voters (e.g., 1992 election)

KEY TERMS MATCH

Match the following terms and descriptions.

1.   A group that seeks to elect candidates to   a.   caucus

public office by supplying them with a label

2. A name applied by some of the Founders to political parties, to connote their tendency toward divisiveness

3. The political party founded and led by Thomas Jefferson

4. The political party founded and led by Alexander Hamilton

5. The arrangement of political parties initiated by Andrew Jackson

6. A name for party professionals, as opposed to volunteers

7. A name for party volunteers who later come to form their own reform movement

8. An election in which candidates for office are not identified by party labels

9. A party that stresses national organization to raise money and give assistance to local candidates and party units

10. An election in which citizens directly approve or disapprove legislation proposed by the government

11. Features a sharp, lasting shift in the popular coalition supporting one or both parties

12. An election in which citizens can place on the legislative agenda proposals by nongovernment groups

13. Elected officials who serve as delegates to the national convention

14. An electoral system that gives the only office to the candidate with the largest vote total, rather than apportioning numerous offices by the percentage of the total vote

15. A party unit that recruits members with tangible rewards and that is tightly controlled by the leadership

16. A closed meeting of party leaders to select party candidates

17. Parties that value principle above all else

18. Parties organized around sociability, rather than tangible rewards or ideology

19. Party units established or maintained by

b. congressional campaign committee
c. critical (or realigning) period
d. Democratic-Republicans
e. factional parties
f. factions
g. Federalists
h. ideological parties
i. initiative
j. machine
k. Mugwumps
l. national (party) chair
m. national committee
n. national convention
o. nonpartisan election
p. office bloc ballot
q. organizational party
r. party column ballot
s. personal following
t. plurality system
u. political machine
v. political party
w. proportional representation
x. referendum
y. second-party system
z. solidary groups
aa. solidary incentives
bb. split ticket voting
cc. sponsored parties
dd. stalwarts
ee. superdelegates
ff. two-party system
gg. winner-take-all

outside groups

20. The practice of voting for one major party's candidate in state or local elections and the other's at the national level

21. An electoral system that distributes numerous seats to parties on the basis of their percentage of the popular vote

22. Parties formed by a split within one of the major parties

23. A ballot listing all candidates of a given party together under the name of that party

24. A committee in each party to help elect or reelect members

25. The person elected and paid to manage the day-to-day work of a national political party

26. Delegates from each state who manage party affairs between conventions

27. A meeting of elected party delegates every four years to nominate presidential and vice-presidential candidates and ratify a campaign platform

28. An electoral system with two dominant parties that compete in state and national elections

29. A ballot listing all candidates for a given office under the name of that office

30. An electoral system in which the winner is the person who gets the most votes but not necessarily a majority of votes

31. A party organization that recruits members by dispensing patronage

32. The social rewards that lead people to join political organizations

33. The political support provided to a candidate on the basis of personal popularity and networks

DID YOU THINK THAT . . . ?

Below are listed a number of misconceptions. You should be able to refute each statement in the space provided, referring to information or argumentation contained in this chapter. Sample answers appear at the end of this chapter.

1.   "National party organizations control state and local parties."

_____

_____

_____

2.   "Major parties generally adopt proposals first made by minor parties."

_____

_____

_____

3.   "The delegates to national party conventions have accurately reflected the sentiments of rank-and-file members since the intraparty reforms of convention rules in 1972."

_____

_____

_____

4.   "There is not a dime's worth of difference between the two major parties."

_____

_____

_____

DATA CHECK

Figure 7.1: Decline in Party Identification, 1952–2000

1.   Which of the major parties typically has a higher number of "strong" identifiers?

_____

2.   In which years has the percentage of "strong" or "weak" Democrats or Republicans risen above 30 percent?

_____

3.   In what decade do independent voters first represent at least 30 percent of respondents?

_____

Table 7.1: Who Are the Party Delegates?

4.   Which party's delegates seem to represent greater social and religious diversity?

_____

_____

Table 7.3: Party Voting in Presidential Elections

5.   In which elections did Democratic voters support Democratic candidates at a higher rate than Republican voters supported Republican candidates?

_____

6.   What can be concluded from how independents cast their vote in these five elections?

_____

_____

Table 7.4: The Public Rates the Two Parties

7.   On what issues do Americans think that Republicans do a better job?

_____

8.   On what issues do Americans think that Democrats do a better job?

_____

9.   On what issues do Americans rate Republicans and Democrats about the same?

_____

Table 7.6: Political Opinions of Delegates and Voters, 2000

For each issue the three sets of percentages indicate the proportion of convention delegates and voters who favor the issue. You can compare both differences between Democrats and Republicans and differences between delegates and voters.

10.   On what issues do Democratic and Republican *delegates* appear to differ most widely?

_____

11.   On what issues do *voters* and Democratic *delegates* appear to differ most widely?

_____

12.   On what issues do *voters* and Republican *delegates* appear to differ most widely?

_____

13.   What do these figures indicate?

_____

PRACTICING FOR EXAMS

TRUE/FALSE QUESTIONS

Read each statement carefully. Mark true statements *T*. If any part of the statement is false, mark it *F*, and write in the space provided a concise explanation of why the statement is false.

1.   T   F   Once in office, elected officials in Europe are expected to vote and act together with other members of their party.

_____

2.   T   F   Political parties have of late become more centralized.

_____

3.   T   F   Most Americans would resent partisanship becoming a conspicuous feature of other organizations to which they belong.

_____

4.   T   F   The Founders favored parties because they enhanced communication between the government and its citizens.

_____

5.   T   F   The first political party took for a name "Republicans."

_____

6.   T   F   The followers of Hamilton founded the first political party.

_____

7.   T   F   Popular support for the Federalist party was limited to sections of the country and particular classes of Americans.

_____

8.   T   F   The reforms of the Progressives had the effect of weakening political parties.

_____

9.   T   F   Economic issues triggered the alignments of 1896 and 1932.

_____

10. T   F   By law, the national parties can spend only $12 million each directly on their presidential candidates.

_____

11. T   F   The Hatch Act of 1939 made it illegal for federal civil service employees to work in partisan campaigns.

_____

12. T   F   Elections where party machines were active commonly featured high voter turnout.

_____

13. T   F   The ideological party values winning above all else.

_____

14. T   F   In 1992, Bill Clinton won 45 percent of the popular vote in Missouri, but all of the state's electoral votes.

_____

15. T   F   In the United States, a third party has never won the presidency.

_____

16. T   F   The laws of many states make it difficult, if not impossible, for third parties to get on the ballot.

_____

17. T   F   Before 1972, party leaders chose most party delegates.

_____

18. T   F   Only about half as many people vote in primaries as in general elections.

_____

19. T   F   Since 1968, the Democratic party has had no trouble winning congressional elections.

_____

20. T   F   Republican convention delegates appear to be more separated from the opinions of most citizens than Democratic convention delegates

_____

MULTIPLE CHOICE QUESTIONS

Circle the letter of the response that best answers the question or completes the statement.

1.   The oldest political parties in the world are currently found in

   a.   India.
   b.   the United States.
   c.   Great Britain.
   d.   Germany.
   e.   Switzerland.

2.   American political parties have become weaker as

   a.   labels in the minds of voters.
   b.   a set of political leaders who try to organize and control government.
   c.   organizations that recruit candidates.
   d.   All of the above.
   e.   None of the above.

3.   In Europe candidates for elective office are generally nominated by

   a.   local referenda.
   b.   aristocrats.
   c.   party leaders.
   d.   prime ministers.
   e.   national primaries.

4.   Decentralization of political authority in the United States is chiefly promoted by

   a.   the legal community.
   b.   federalism.
   c.   nationalism.
   d.   the church.
   e.   the mass media.

5.   Which of the following is *not* a reason for stronger political parties in Europe?

    a.   the greater age of European parties
    b.   the absence of primary elections
    c.   the ability of the legislature to choose the chief executive
    d.   the power of leaders to nominate candidates
    e.   a political culture more favorable to parties

6.   American political parties, unlike those of most other democratic nations, are closely regulated by

    a.   minorities.
    b.   the Constitution.
    c.   powerful machines.
    d.   the executive branch of government.
    e.   state and federal laws.

7.   Why should George Washington, among other Founders of our nation, have been so opposed to political parties?

    a.   because the Constitution made clear the dangers of partisanship in government
    b.   because political parties during the early years of the republic were both strong and centralized
    c.   because disputes over policies and elections were not easily separated from disputes over governmental legitimacy
    d.   because political parties during the early years of the Republic represented clear, homogeneous economic interests
    e.   because Washington was concerned that Hamilton would win the White House as a result of party mobilization.

8.   Thomas Jefferson considered his Republican party to be

    a.   secret monarchists.
    b.   a federalism broker.
    c.   antifederalist.
    d.   a temporary arrangement.
    e.   a permanent organization.

9.   Which description of the Jacksonian period of political parties is incorrect?

    a.   The North and the South became more divided.
    b.   The Democrats and the Whigs were fairly evenly balanced.
    c.   The number of eligible voters decreased.
    d.   The party convention system was invented.
    e.   It featured the first truly national system.

10.   In 1831 the _____ party held the first American party convention.

    a.   Anti-Masonic
    b.   Free Soil
    c.   Greenback
    d.   Whig
    e.   Know-Nothing

11.   The candidacy of William Jennings Bryan strengthened the Republican party because Bryan

    a.   was quite unpopular in the South.
    b.   alienated many voters in the populous northeastern states.

    c.   called for a strong national government.

    d.   alienated rural voters in the Midwest.

    e.   represented the narrow interests of industrialists.

12.   The Mugwumps were

    a.   a political branch of the American Legion.

    b.   a faction of the Republican party.

    c.   the forerunners of the Ku Klux Klan.

    d.   an activist Indian tribe.

    e.   Louisiana tobacco farmers who held land near the coast.

13.   All of the following were true of the so-called "progressives" *except*

    a.   They wanted more strict voter registration requirements.

    b.   They pressed for civil service reform.

    c.   They called for non-partisan elections at the city level.

    d.   They called for non-partisan elections in some cases at the state level.

    e.   The opposed the use of mass media in the conduct of political debate.

14.   Scholars recognize at least ____ periods of critical realignment in American politics.

    a.   two

    b.   five

    c.   fifteen

    d.   thirty

    e.   thirty-two

15.   Some observers have noted critical realignments take place roughly once every

    a.   four years.

    b.   eight years.

    c.   twelve years.

    d.   sixteen years.

    e.   thirty-two years.

16.   Even if one questions the validity of the concept of a critical election, it is quite clear that

    a.   Ronald Reagan's election in 1980 signaled a realignment.

    b.   Ronald Reagan's election in 1984 signaled a realignment.

    c.   The South is becoming more supportive of the Democratic Party.

    d.   The South is becoming more supportive of the Republican Party.

    e.   Parties are gaining in strength.

17.   As a result of changes made by the parties in the 1960s and 1970s, the Democrats have become more _____ and the Republicans Party has become more _____.

    a.   libertarian ... liberal

    b.   factionalized ... bureaucratized

    c.   unified ... people-oriented

    d.   traditional ... modern

    e.   organized ... popular

18.   The formulas for apportioning delegates to the national party conventions are such that the Democrats give extra delegates to _____ states and the Republicans give extra delegates to states that are _____.

    a.   small ... large

    b.   Midwestern ... heavily populated
    c.   large ... loyal
    d.   Southern ... heavily contested
    e.   conservative ... liberal

19. At the opposite extreme from the political machine is

    a.   the sponsored party.
    b.   a personal following.
    c.   the ideological party.
    d.   the party bundle.
    e.   the solidary group.

20. The chief disadvantage of a solidary association is that its members

    a.   are looking for patronage.
    b.   hold fanatical opinions.
    c.   see politics as mere sport.
    d.   dislike machines.
    e.   may not work hard.

21. Almost all elections in the United States are based on

    a.   the plurality system.
    b.   the majority system.
    c.   proportional representation.
    d.   retention and recall.
    e.   a combination of systems.

22. The two-party system has persisted in the United States for all of the following reasons *except* that

    a.   it is impossible to form broad coalitions.
    b.   the electoral system prevents minor parties from winning.
    c.   the Fourteenth Amendment limits access to the ballot.
    d.   religion is considered a matter of private choice.
    e.   A and B.

23. The Free Soil and Know-Nothing parties are examples of

    a.   factional parties.
    b.   backlash parties.
    c.   ideological parties.
    d.   economic protest parties.
    e.   one-issue parties.

24. Which type of minor party probably has the greatest influence on U.S. public policy?

    a.   factional
    b.   ideological
    c.   economic protest
    d.   backlash
    e.   one issue

25. Party activists are *not* likely to

    a.   take issues seriously.
    b.   resemble the average citizen.
    c.   vote with any degree of consistency.

    d.   work very hard.

    e.   support candidates with strong ideological appeal.

26.   The disadvantage to parties of the current system of presidential nomination is that it

    a.   affords little opportunity to minorities to voice their concerns.

    b.   decreases the chances of a faction's bolting the party.

    c.   decreases the chances of a realigning election.

    d.   increases the chances of nominating a candidate unappealing to the rank and file.

    e.   increases the chances of a faction's bolting the party.

27.   To obtain power within a political party, an individual must usually

    a.   move toward the center.

    b.   move away from the center.

    c.   remain above political conflict.

    d.   avoid publicity.

    e.   reflect the views of the average voter.

ANSWERS TO KEY TERMS MATCH QUESTIONS

1. v
2. f
3. d
4. g
5. y
6. dd
7. k
8. o
9. q
10. x
11. c
12. i
13. ee
14. gg
15. j
16. a
17. h
18. z
19. cc
20. bb
21. w
22. e
23. r
24. b
25. l
26. m
27. n
28. ff
29. p
30. t
31. u
32. aa
33. s

ANSWERS TO "DID YOU THINK THAT . . . ?" QUESTIONS

1. State and local parties control their own finances, membership, nominations for public office, and party platforms.

2. Ideological proposals of the left and right have generally not been adopted. Southern regional parties since the 1940s have not strongly influenced the Democratic party on most matters. Often a major party, as a result of public opinion, adopts something that a minor party had previously proposed, but the relationship is usually coincidental rather than causal.

3. Those who are likely to be chosen convention delegates—party activists—are more ideological or issue oriented than are the rank and file. Democratic delegates are more liberal and Republican delegates more conservative than party members. Paradoxically, the rule changes give activists more opportunity to make the party less representative of the sentiments of the rank and file.

4. On most issues, the differences between Democratic and Republican *voters* are not very large. Among party *delegates,* however, there are sharp differences on most issues, for reasons noted above. These differences often extend to party candidates as well.

ANSWERS TO DATA CHECK QUESTIONS

1. Democrats.
2. Never.
3. 1968.
4. Democrats.
5. 1992 and 1996.
6. Independent voters are more likely to vote Republican.
7. National Defense, foreign trade, crime, and campaign finance reform.
8. Poverty, environment, health care, and social security.
9. Economic prosperity and taxes.
10. Government should do more to solve national problems.
11. Government should do more to solve national problems.
12. Banning soft money.
13. That delegates take more extreme positions than voters.

ANSWERS TO TRUE/FALSE QUESTIONS

1. T
2. F. If anything, they have become weaker and more decentralized.
3. T
4. F. The Founders disliked parties and thought of them as "factions' motivated by ambition and self-interest.
5. T
6. F. The followers of Jefferson founded the first organized party.

7. T
8. T
9. T
10. T
11. T
12. T
13. T
14. T
15. F. The Republicans won in 1860.
16. T
17. T
18. T
19. T
20. F. This problem is more acute for the Democrats.

ANSWERS TO MULTIPLE CHOICE QUESTIONS

1. b
2. d
3. c
4. b
5. a
6. e
7. c
8. d
9. c
10. a
11. b
12. b
13. e
14. b
15. e
16. d
17. b
18. c
19. c

20. e
21. a
22. c
23. e
24. a
25. b
26. d
27. a

CHAPTER 8

Elections and Campaigns

REVIEWING THE CHAPTER

CHAPTER FOCUS

This chapter takes you on a cook's tour of some of the scholarly examinations, the common folklore, and the amazing intricacies of America's most enduring and exciting political institution, the election. Major topics include, but are not limited to, the debate over just how democratic they are (given a very low voter turnout), the new personalistic nature of campaigning in the latter part of the twentieth century, the role that money plays in determining outcomes, the role of special interest groups, so-called realigning elections, and the elements of successful coalition building by Democrats and Republicans. After reading and reviewing the material in this chapter, you should be able to do each of the following:

1. Explain why elections in the United States are both more democratic and less democratic than those of other countries.

2. Demonstrate the differences between the party-oriented campaigns of the nineteenth century and the candidate-oriented ones of today, explaining the major elements of a successful campaign for office today.

3. Discuss how important campaign funding is to election outcomes, what the major sources of such funding are under current law, and how successful reform legislation has been in purifying U.S. elections of improper monetary influences.

4. Discuss the partisan effects of campaigns, or why the party with the most registered voters does not always win the election.

5. Define the term *realigning election* and discuss the major examples of such elections in the past, as well as recent debates over whether realignment is again underway.

6. Describe what the Democrats and the Republicans, respectively, must do to put together a successful national coalition to achieve political power in any election.

7. Outline the major arguments on either side of the question of whether elections result in major changes in public policy in the United States.

STUDY OUTLINE

I. Presidential versus congressional campaigns
   A. Introduction
      1. Two phases: getting nominated and getting elected
      2. Getting nominated
         a) Getting a name on the ballot
         b) An individual effort (versus organizational effort in Europe)
         c) Parties play a minor role (compared with Europe)

       d)   Parties used to play a major role

B.   Major differences
1.   Presidential races are more competitive.
    a)   House races have lately been one-sided for Democrats.
    b)   Presidential winner rarely gets more than 55 percent of vote
    c)   Most House incumbents are reelected (more than 90 percent)
2.   Fewer people vote in congressional elections
    a)   Unless election coincides with presidential election
    b)   Gives greater importance to partisan voters (party regulars)
3.   Congressional incumbents can service their constituents.
    a)   Can take credit for governmental grants, programs, and so forth
    b)   President can't: power is not local
4.   Congressional candidates can duck responsibility.
    a)   "I didn't do it; the people in Washington did!"
    b)   President is stuck with blame
    c)   But local candidates can suffer when their leader's economic policies fail
5.   Benefit of presidential coattails has declined
    a)   Congressional elections have become largely independent
    b)   Reduces meaning (and importance) of party

C.   Running for president
1.   Getting mentioned
    a)   Using reporters, trips, speeches, and name recognition
    b)   Sponsoring legislation, governing large state
2.   Setting aside time to run
    a)   Reagan: six years
    b)   May have to resign from office first
3.   Money
    a)   Individuals can give $1,000, political action committees (PACs) $5,000
    b)   Candidates must raise $5,000 in twenty states to qualify for matching grants to pay for primary
4.   Organization
    a)   Need a large (paid) staff
    b)   Need volunteers
    c)   Need advisers on issues: position papers
5.   Strategy and themes
    a)   Incumbent versus challenger: defend or attack?
    b)   Setting the tone (positive or negative)
    c)   Developing a theme: trust, confidence, and so on
    d)   Judging the timing
    e)   Choosing a target voter: who's the audience?

D.   Getting elected to Congress
1.   Malapportionment and gerrymandering.
2.   Establishing the size of the House
3.   Winning the primary
    a)   Ballot procedures
    b)   Developing a personal following for the "party's" nomination
    c)   Incumbent advantage
4.   Sophomore surge
    a)   Using the perqs of office
    b)   Campaigning for / against Congress
5.   Impact of the way we elect individuals to Congress

        a)   Legislators closely tied to local concerns

        b)   Weak party leadership

II.   Primary versus general campaigns

    A.   Kinds of elections and primaries: general versus primary elections

    B.   Differences between primary and general campaigns

        1.   What works in a general election may not work in a primary

            a)   Different voters, workers, and media attention

            b)   Must mobilize activists with money and motivation to win nomination

            c)   Must play to the politics of activists

        2.   Iowa caucuses

            a)   Held in February of general election year

            b)   Candidates must do well

            c)   Winners tend to be "ideologically correct"

            d)   Most liberal Democrat, most conservative Republican

            e)   The caucus system: "musical chairs and fraternity pledge week"

        3.   The balancing act

            a)   Being conservative (or liberal) enough to get nominated

            b)   Move to center to get elected

            c)   True nationwide in states where activists are more polarized than average voter

            d)   The "clothespin vote": neither candidate is appealing

        4.   Even primary voters can be more extreme ideologically than the average voter
Example: McGovern in 1972

    C.   Two kinds of campaign issues

        1.   Position issues

        2.   Valence issues

    D.   Television, debates, and direct mail

        1.   Paid advertising (spots)

            a)   Has little (or a very subtle) effect on outcome: spots tend to cancel each other out

            b)   Most voters rely on many sources of information.

        2.   News broadcasts (visuals)

            a)   Cost little

            b)   May have greater credibility with voters

            c)   Rely on having TV camera crew around

            d)   May be less informative than spots

        3.   Debates

            a)   Usually an advantage only to the challenger

            b)   Reagan in 1980: reassured voters

            c)   Primary debates: the "dating game" in 1988

        4.   Risk of slips of the tongue on visuals and debates

            a)   Ford and Poland, Carter and lust, Reagan and trees

            b)   Forces candidates to rely on stock speeches

            c)   Sell yourself, not your ideas

        5.   Free television time to major presidential candidates in 1996

        6.   The computer

            a)   Makes direct mail campaigns possible

            b)   Allows candidates to address specific voters

            c)   Creates importance of mailing lists

        7.   The gap between running a campaign and running the government

            a)   Party leaders had to worry about reelection

            b)   Today's political consultants don't

III.   Money

A. How important is it?
  1. "Money is the mother's milk of politics."
  2. Presidential candidates spent $286 million in 1992; up from $177 million in 1988
  3. Are candidates being "sold" like soap? Answer is not so obvious
B. The sources of campaign money
  1. Presidential primaries: part private, part public money
     a) Federal matching funds
     b) Only match small donors: less than $250; $5,000 in twenty states
     c) Gives incentive to raise money from small donors
     d) Government also gives lump-sum grants to parties to cover conventions
  2. Presidential general elections: all public money
  3. Congressional elections: all private money
     a) From individuals, PACs, and parties
     b) Most from individual small donors ($100 to $200 a person)
     c) $1,000 maximum for individual donors
     d) Benefit performances by rock stars, etc.
     e) $5,000 limit from PACs
     f) But most PACs give only a few hundred dollars
     g) Tremendous PAC advantage to incumbents: backing the winner
     h) Challengers have to pay their own way; only one-sixth from PACs
C. Campaign finance rules
  1. Watergate
     a) Dubious and illegal money raising schemes
     b) Democrats and Republicans benefited from unenforceable laws.
     c) Nixon's resignation and a new campaign finance law
  2. Reform law
     a) Set limit on individual donations ($1,000 per election)
     b) Reaffirmed ban on corporate and union donations, but allowed them to raise money through PACs
     c) Set limit on PAC donations ($5,000 per election to individuals, $15,000 per year to a party)
     d) Federal tax money made available for primaries and general election campaigns.
  3. Impact of the law
     a) Increase in money spent on elections
     b) Increase in PAC spending
     c) Additional problems: independent expenditures and soft money
  4. Campaign finance reform
     a) Reforms can have unintended consequences
     b) Bipartisan Campaign Finance Reform Act of 2002
        (1) Ban on soft money
        (2) Increase on individual contributions (to $2,000 per candidate per election)
        (3) Restrictions on independent expenditures
D. Money and winning
  1. During peacetime, presidential elections usually decided by three things:
     a) Political party affiliation
     b) State of the economy
     c) Character of candidates
  2. Money makes a difference in congressional races
     a) Challenger must spend to gain recognition
     b) Jacobson: big-spending challengers do better
     c) Big-spending incumbents also do better

3. Party, incumbency, and issues also have a role
4. Advantages of incumbency
   a) Easier to raise money
   b) Can provide services for constituency
   c) Can use franked mailings
   d) Can get free publicity through legislation and such

IV. What decides elections?
   A. Party identification, but why don't Democrats always win?
      1. Democrats less wedded to their party
      2. GOP does better among independents
      3. Republicans have higher turnout
   B. Issues, especially the economy
      1. V. O. Key: most voters who switch parties do so in their own interests
         a) They know which issues affect them personally
         b) They care strongly about emotional issues (abortion, etc.)
      2. Prospective voting
         a) Know the issues and vote for the best candidate
         b) Most common among activists and special interest groups
         c) Few voters use prospective voting because it requires information.
      3. Retrospective voting
         a) Judge the incumbent's performance and vote accordingly
         b) Have things gotten better or worse, especially economically?
         c) Examples: presidential campaigns of 1980, 1984, 1988, and 1992
         d) Usually helps incumbent unless economy has gotten worse
         e) Most elections decided by retrospective votes
         f) Midterm election: voters turn against president's party
   C. The campaign
      1. Campaigns do make a difference
         a) Reawaken voters' partisan loyalties
         b) Let voters see how candidates handle pressure
         c) Let voters judge candidates' characters
      2. Campaigns tend to emphasize themes over details
         a) True throughout American history
         b) What has changed is the importance of primary elections and tone of campaigns
         c) Theme campaigns give more influence to single-issue groups
   D. Finding a winning coalition
      1. Ways of looking at various groups
         a) How *loyal,* or percentage voting for party
         b) How *important,* or number voting for party
      2. Democratic coalition
         a) Blacks most loyal
         b) Jews slipping somewhat
         c) Hispanics somewhat mixed
         d) Catholics, southerners, unionists departing the coalition lately
      3. Republican coalition
         a) Party of business and professional people
         b) Very loyal, defecting only in 1964
         c) Usually wins vote of poor because of retired, elderly voters
      4. Contribution to Democratic coalition
         a) Blacks loyal but small proportion
         b) Catholics, unionists, and southerners largest part but least dependable

V.   The Effect of Elections on Policy
   A.   Political scientists are interested broad trends in wining and losing
   B.   Cynics: public policy remains more or less the same no matter which official or party is in office
      1.   Comparison: Great Britain, with parliamentary system and strong parties, often sees marked changes, as in 1945
      2.   Reply: evidence indicates that many American elections do make great differences in policy
      3.   Why, then, the perception that elections do not matter? Because change alternates with consolidation; most elections are only retrospective judgments

KEY TERMS MATCH

Match the following terms and descriptions.

1.   A means of soliciting funds from millions of people

2.   A filmed episode showing a candidate doing something newsworthy

3.   Televised pictures showing nothing more than individuals speaking

4.   A voter describing herself or himself as neither a Democrat nor a Republican

5.   Can be given to the parties in limitless amounts so long as it is not used to back candidates by name

6.   The tendency for newly elected members of Congress to become strong in their districts very quickly

7.   A group legally able to solicit campaign contributions from individuals within an organization and, under certain restrictions, to funnel these to candidates for office

8.   An election intended to select a party's candidates for elective office

9.   An election used to fill an elective office

10. A primary election in which voters must first declare to which party they belong

11. A primary in which voters can vote for the candidates of either the Democratic or the Republican party

12. A primary in which voters can vote for the Democratic candidates, the Republican candidates, or some from each party

13. A primary in which, to be successful, the candidate must receive a majority of all

a.   blanket primary
b.   closed primary
c.   coattails
d.   direct mail
e.   general election
f.   gerrymandering
g.   incumbent
h.   Independent
i.   independent expenditures
j.   open primary
k.   malapportionment
l.   political action committee (PAC)
m.   position issue
n.   presidential primary
o.   primary election
p.   prospective voting
q.   retrospective voting
r.   runoff primary
s.   soft money
t.   sophomore surge
u.   spots
v.   talking heads
w.   valence issue
x.   visual

votes cast in that race

14. The tendency of lesser-known or weaker candidates to profit from the presence on the ticket of stronger candidate

15. The person currently in office

16. The result of having districts of very unequal size

17. Drawing a district in some bizarre or unusual manner in order to create an electoral advantage

18. An issue dividing the electorate on which rival parties adopt different policy positions to attract voters

19. A primary held to select delegates to the presidential nominating conventions of the major parties

20. Voting for a candidate because one favors his or her ideas for addressing issues after the election

21. Voting for the candidate or party in office because one likes or dislikes how things have gone in the recent past

22. Short television advertisements used to promote a candidate for government office

23. Ordinary advertising for or against candidates but not coordinated with or made at their direction

24. An issue on which voters distinguish rival parties by the degree to which they associate each party with conditions or goals that the electorate universally supports or opposes

DID YOU THINK THAT . . . ?

Below are listed a number of misconceptions. You should be able to refute each statement in the space provided, referring to information or argumentation contained in this chapter. Sample answers appear at the end of this chapter.

1. "Voters generally choose candidates on the basis of issues presented during campaigns."

   _____

   _____

   _____

2.   "Most money for presidential and congressional campaigns comes from large corporate donors, labor unions, and PACs."

_____

_____

_____

3.   "The choice of a vice-presidential candidate makes a big difference in who wins presidential elections."

_____

_____

_____

4.   "The Republican victory in the midterm congressional elections in 1994 was attributable to the 'angry white male,' and the 'soccer moms' for Clinton's victory in 1996."

_____

_____

_____

5.   "Independent candidates have little or no impact on the outcome of presidential elections because they rarely get a significant percentage of the vote and the people who support them do not typically vote otherwise."

_____

_____

_____

DATA CHECK

Table 8.2: Sources of Campaign Funds: All House and Senate Candidates in 1997–1998 by Incumbents, Challengers, and Open

1.   What percentage of funds raised by incumbents came from individuals?

_____

2.   What percentage of funds raised by challengers came from individuals?

_____

3.   Who received the largest percentage of their funds from PACs?

_____

4.   Who received the largest percentage of their funds from the political parties?

_____

Figure 8.2: Growth of PACs

5.   How does the recent growth of corporate PACs compare with that of PACs representing labor?

_____

Table 8.3: Percentage of Popular Vote by Groups in Presidential Election, 1960–2000

This table indicates how voters with each set of identifiers (Republicans, Democrats, Independents) claim to have voted in a series of presidential elections. For each year the total percentages for each party equal 100 percent, divided among the various candidates. Columns are read down to see how group support has changed from one election to the next. Columns are read across to see how a candidate won votes, whether he or she built a partisan or bipartisan coalition, and whether she or he won the independent vote. Remember again that these figures are based on how people *said* they voted, not on how they voted.

6.   In which elections did Republicans give the GOP candidate at least 90 percent of their vote?

_____

7.   In which elections did Democrats give the Democrat 90 percent or more of their vote?

_____

8.   What percentage of Republicans claimed to have voted for Ross Perot in 1992 and 1996?

_____

9.   What percentage of Democrats claimed to have voted for Ross Perot in 1992 and 1996?

_____

10.   Describe the vote of political Independents in the 2000 election.

_____

Table 8.5: Who Likes the Democrats?

Percentages refer to the proportion of the group stating that they voted for the Democratic presidential nominee in the indicated year.

11.   Describe the relationship between education and the tendency to vote for Democratic candidates.

_____

12.   Which group appears to consistently provide the highest level of support for Democratic candidates?

_____

13.   Which group appears to consistently provide the lowest level of support for Democratic candidates?

_____

14.   In what years has the difference between male and female support for Democratic candidates been greater than 5 percent?

_____

15. In what years has the difference between Protestants and members of the Jewish faith been greater than 10 percent?

_____

Figure 8.5: Partisan Division of the Presidential Vote in the Nation, 1856–1996

Each of the colored lines represents the percentage of the popular vote received by the major parties in presidential elections. Third parties receiving more than five percent of the popular vote are indicated by green dots.

16. The popular vote for Democratic candidates was higher than 60 percent in which election(s)?

_____

17. The popular vote for Republican candidates was higher than 60 percent in which election(s)?

_____

18. In which elections has popular support for either of the major parties fallen below 30 percent?

_____

19. Which third party has gained the highest percentage of the popular vote in a presidential election?

_____

PRACTICING FOR EXAMS

TRUE/FALSE QUESTIONS

Read each statement carefully. Mark true statements *T*. If any part of the statement is false, mark it *F*, and write in the space provided a concise explanation of why the statement is false.

1. T F   Presidential races are more competitive than races for the House of Representatives.

_____

2. T F   In Israel and the Netherlands, the names of candidates do not even appear on the ballot

_____

3. T F   Voter turnout is higher in years when there is no presidential contest.

_____

4. T F   Members of Congress can serve for an unlimited number of terms.

_____

5. T F   The Supreme Court decides how many seats a state will have in the House of Representatives.

_____

6. T F   The Supreme Court requires that a census is taken every ten years.

_____

7. T   F   It is quite unusual for an incumbent to lose a primary.

_____

8. T   F   Congressmen run for Congress by running against it.

_____

9. T   F   Television advertising probably has a greater impact on primaries.

_____

10. T   F   In 1980, Ronald Reagan slipped by suggesting trees cause pollution.

_____

11. T   F   In the 2000 campaign, fundraising on the internet frequently led to victory.

_____

12. T   F   Most of the money for congressional campaigns comes from big business and PACs.

_____

13. T   F   A PAC must have at least fifty members.

_____

14. T   F   The 1972 campaign finance laws led to a dramatic increase in PAC spending.

_____

15. T   F   Critics of 2002 campaign finance rules have challenged their constitutionality in the courts.

_____

16. T   F   In good economic times the party holding the White House normally does well.

_____

17. T   F   If the U.S. Supreme Court had allowed Al Gore's original request for hand counts of votes in Florida counties he would have won.

_____

18. T   F   If the U.S. Supreme Court had allowed the vote count ordered by the Florida Supreme Court to continue Al Gore would have won.

_____

19. T   F   The choice a presidential candidate makes for the vice-president slot is critical to winning or losing an election.

_____

20. T   F   In the general election one's position on abortion is not likely to be critical.

_____

21. T   F   Political activists are more likely to be prospective voters.

_____

22. T   F   Retrospective voters decide elections.

22. T   F   Retrospective voters decide elections.

_____

23. T   F   The Republicans are often described as the party of business and professional people.

_____

24. T   F   Studies by scholars confirm that elections are often a critical source of policy change.

_____

25. T   F   Elections in ordinary times are not "critical."

_____

MULTIPLE CHOICE QUESTIONS
Circle the letter of the response that best answers the question or completes the statement.

1.   All of the following statements about presidential and congressional races are true *except*

   a.   Presidential races are more competitive.
   b.   More people vote in presidential elections.
   c.   Congressional incumbents usually win.
   d.   Presidents can rarely take credit for improvements in a district.
   e.   Presidents can distance themselves from the "mess" in Washington.

2.   In the 1996 election Bill Clinton chose as a theme

   a.   trust.
   b.   compassionate conservatism.
   c.   competence.
   d.   stay the course.
   e.   we need change.

3.   In the 2000 election George W. Bush chose as a theme

   a.   trust.
   b.   compassionate conservatism.
   c.   competence.
   d.   stay the course.
   e.   we need change.

4.   According to the text, which of the following is a critical problem to solve in deciding who gets represented in the House?

   a.   Allocating seats in the House among the states.
   b.   Determining the shape of districts.
   c.   Determining the size of districts.
   d.   Establishing the total size of the House.
   e.   All of the above.

5.   In 1911, Congress fixed the size of the House at _____ members.

   a.   50
   b.   100
   c.   435
   d.   535

e.   537

6.   Which states posted the biggest gains in House representation after the 1990 census?

a.   Florida and California
b.   Illinois and Wisconsin
c.   Florida and Alabama
d.   New York and Pennsylvania
e.   Montana and Idaho

7.   The states did little about malapportionment and gerrymandering until ordered to do so by

a.   the president.
b.   Congress.
c.   the Supreme Court.
d.   political party leaders.
e.   the Justice Department.

8.   Which statement about the so-called "sophomore surge" is *correct*?

a.   It has been around since the 1940s.
b.   It usually means an 8 to 10 percent increase in votes.
c.   It benefits members of the Senate more than members of the House.
d.   It does not benefit members of the Senate at all.
e.   It is the result of an increase in trust of the federal government.

9.   In order to win the party nomination, candidates need to appear particularly

a.   liberal.
b.   conservative.
c.   void of anything that looks like an ideological disposition.
d.   liberal if Democrats, conservative if Republicans.
e.   conservative if Democrats, liberal if Republicans.

10.   Voters at the Iowa Democratic caucuses, compared with other Democrats from Iowa, tend to be

a.   void of anything that looks like an ideological disposition.
b.   more conservative.
c.   more liberal.
d.   younger.
e.   less educated.

11.   When a voter casts a "clothespin" vote, he or she picks the

a.   most comfortable, homelike candidate.
b.   candidate most likely to endure.
c.   most familiar candidate.
d.   candidate that appears most reliable in a time of crisis.
e.   least objectionable candidate.

12.   The campaign activity most on the increase now is

a.   large parades.
b.   radio and television appearances.
c.   whistle-stop train tours.
d.   rallies.
e.   appearances at malls and factories.

13.   In recent presidential elections the independent vote has usually favored

    a.   a third party.
    b.   the Republicans.
    c.   the Democrats.
    d.   no one party.
    e.   male candidates.

14.   An election that results in one party gaining long-term dominance over the others is called by
       scholars a _____ election.

    a.   nonaligning
    b.   dealigning
    c.   realigning
    d.   criticized
    e.   transparent

15.   A major difference between presidential and congressional campaigns is that

    a.   more people vote in congressional elections.
    b.   presidential races are generally less competitive.
    c.   presidential candidates can more credibly take credit for improvements in a district.
    d.   presidential incumbents can better provide services for their constituents.
    e.   congressional incumbents can more easily duck responsibility.

16.   Blacks and Jews have been the most loyal supporters of

    a.   the Democrats.
    b.   independent candidates.
    c.   minor parties.
    d.   non-ideological candidates.
    e.   the Republicans.

17.   Unlike funding for presidential campaigns, the money for congressional campaigns comes from

    a.   both private and public sources.
    b.   public sources only.
    c.   private sources only.
    d.   federal matching grants only.
    e.   state income taxes.

18.   To a political candidate the drawback of television visuals and debates is

    a.   their expense.
    b.   the risk of slipups.
    c.   the low audience response.
    d.   their lack of credibility.
    e.   the complications surrounding choice of backs-drops.

19.   Each of the two major U.S. political parties can best be described as a(n)

    a.   bureaucracy.
    b.   weak coalition of diverse elements.
    c.   group of strong-minded ideologues.
    d.   unchanging entity.
    e.   solidified unit, with little flexibility or incentive to innovate.

20. A congressional candidate raises millions of dollars, without regard to FEC limits, for a campaign to educate adolescents on the importance of voting. Has the candidate broken the law?

    a.   no, because the candidate does not have to accept federal financing
    b.   no, because this type of fund raising is considered a party activity
    c.   yes, because the money is not being spent on a particular campaign.
    d.   no, because the money was not spent on advertising on the candidate's behalf
    e.   yes, because FEC laws strictly prohibit this type of activity

21. As party organization has declined, _____ has become more important to the candidate.

    a.   voter registration
    b.   patronage
    c.   the federal bureaucracy
    d.   money
    e.   party identification

22. In 1972 and 1984 the effect that the campaigns had on the outcome of the presidential vote was

    a.   clear.
    b.   significant, but not as predicted.
    c.   significant and as predicted.
    d.   as predicted, but insignificant.
    e.   not discernible at all.

23. Campaign contributions by PACs generally favor

    a.   Republicans.
    b.   conservatives.
    c.   incumbents.
    d.   supporters of organized labor.
    e.   challengers

24. If presidential campaigns were decided simply by party identification, the

    a.   Democrats would always win.
    b.   Republicans would always win.
    c.   Democrats would win most of the time.
    d.   Republicans would win most of the time.
    e.   There is no intelligent way to know what the impact would be.

25. The 1974 campaign finance reform law prohibits cash contributions from any individual in excess of

    a. $10.
    b. $100.
    c. $1,000.
    d. $10,000.
    e.   There are no such limits for individuals.

26. Several factors have contributed to the emphasis on themes over details in recent elections. These include all of the following *except*

    a.   the rise in prospective voting.
    b.   the expectations of single-issue groups.
    c.   short radio and television ads.
    d.   computer-generated direct mail.
    e.   A, B and D.

27. When PACs make independent expenditures on behalf of a candidate, the legal limit on such expenditures is

    a. $1,000
    b. $3,000.
    c. $15,000.
    d. $20,000.
    e. whatever they want to spend.

28. Which of the following is a valence issue rather than a position issue?

    a. legal access to abortion
    b. nuclear disarmament
    c. civil rights legislation
    d. all of the above.
    e. wasted tax dollars

ESSAY QUESTIONS

Practice writing extended answers to the following questions. These test your ability to integrate and express the ideas that you have been studying in this chapter.

29. Explain how each of the major parties must put together a successful coalition to win national elections. Design a strategy for the Democrats or the Republicans to win the next presidential election.

30. Discuss several popular ideas for reforming campaign finance laws and the problems that each creates.

31. List the major regulations on campaign financing imposed by recent legislation and the effects that these regulations are likely to have on candidates, donors, parties, and American politics generally.

ANSWERS TO KEY TERMS MATCH QUESTIONS

1. d
2. x
3. v
4. h
5. s
6. t
7. l
8. o
9. e
10. b
11. j
12. a
13. r
14. c
15. g
16. k
17. f
18. m
19. n
20. p
21. q
22. u
23. i
24. w

ANSWERS TO "DID YOU THINK THAT . . . ?" QUESTIONS

1. As many as two-thirds of the electorate choose on the basis of party loyalty or personality themes rather than, or in addition to, issues. Many voters know how they intend to vote before the election campaign.

2. Presidential campaigns rely on a mixture of public and private sources of funds for their financing. In terms of private funding, however, both for presidential and congressional campaigns, most money comes from individual donors who, by law, are limited to donations of $250.

3. There has rarely been an election in which his/her identity made a difference.

4. Although the media confidently made these statements, credible national and state survey research findings do not support these analyses.

5. History teaches us that 80 percent of the vote will go to the candidates of the major parties, but the remaining vote can be critical. The difference between the top two choices has been less than 20 percent in each of the last seven elections and less than 10 percent in the last three. Evidence also suggest the presence of Ross Perot hurt Republicans in 1992 and 1996 and Ralph Nader's candidacy may have cost Al Gore Florida and the White House in 2000.

ANSWERS TO DATA CHECK QUESTIONS

1. 57.5 percent.

2. 51.9 percent.

3. Incumbents (37.6 percent).

4. Challengers (6.1 percent).

5. No comparison; labor PACs have hardly grown at all.

6. 1960, 1972, 1984, 1988, 2000.

7. None.

8. 1992 (17 percent); 1996 (6 percent).

9. 1992 (13 percent); 1996 (5 percent).

10. Independents claimed to have voted at a slightly higher rate (2 percent) for George W. Bush.

11. Higher levels of education (grad school) are associated with higher levels of support for Democratic candidates.

12. Probably non-whites, who have an average level of support of 78 percent across ten elections.

13. Probably those in business and professional occupations, who have an average level of support of only 39 percent in the seven elections for which data are available.

14. 1980, 1988, 1996, and 2000

15. 1972, 1988, 1992, and 1996

16. 1936 and 1964

17. 1920 and 1972

18. 1860 (Democrats), 1912 (Republicans) and 1924 (Democrats)

19. 1912, Bull Moose Party

ANSWERS TO TRUE/FALSE QUESTIONS

1. T

2. T

3. F. While turnout is around 50 percent in presidential election years, one can expect turnout to be around 36 percent during the mid term elections.

4. T

5. F. Congress decides how many seats are assigned in the House of Representatives.

6.   F. The census is required by the Constitution.

7.   T

8.   T

9.   T

10. T

11. F. McCain and Bradley were distinct for raising funds via the internet and both lost in the primaries.

12. F. Most of the money comes–and always has come–from individuals.

13. T

14. T

15. T

16. T

17. F. Bush would have still won by 335 votes.

18. F. Bush would have still won by 493 votes.

19. T

20. T

21. T

22. T

23. T

24. T

25. T

ANSWERS TO MULTIPLE CHOICE QUESTIONS

1.   e
2.   e
3.   b
4.   e
5.   c
6.   a
7.   c
8.   b
9.   d
10. c
11. e
12. b
13. b

14. c
15. e
16. a
17. c
18. b
19. b
20. d
21. d
22. e
23. c
24. a
25. c
26. d
27. e
28. e

CHAPTER 9

Interest Groups

REVIEWING THE CHAPTER

CHAPTER FOCUS

The purpose of this chapter is to survey the wide variety of interest groups or lobbies that operate in the United States and to assess the effect they have on the political system of the country. After reading and reviewing the material in this chapter, you should be able to do each of the following:

1. Explain why the characteristics of American society and government encourage a multiplicity of interest groups, and compare the American and British experiences in this regard.

2. Describe the historical conditions under which interest groups are likely to form, and specify the kinds of organizations Americans are most likely to join.

3. Describe relations between leaders and rank-and-file members of groups, including why the sentiments of members may not determine the actions of leaders.

4. Describe several methods that interest groups use to formulate and carry out their political objectives, especially the lobbying techniques used to gain public support. Explain why courts have become an important forum for public interest groups.

5. List the laws regulating conflict of interest, and describe the problems involved with "revolving door" government employment. Describe the provisions of the 1978 conflict-of-interest law. Explain the suggestions that have been made for stricter laws. Describe the balance between the First Amendment's freedom of expression and the need to prevent corruption in the political system.

STUDY OUTLINE

I. Explaining proliferation: why interest groups are common in the United States
   A. Many kinds of cleavage in the country
   B. Constitution makes for many access points
   C. Political parties are weak
II. The birth of interest groups
   A. Periods of rapid growth
      1. Since 1960, 70 percent have established an office in Washington, D.C.
      2. 1770s, independence groups
      3. 1830s and 1840s, religious, antislavery groups
      4. 1860s, craft unions
      5. 1880s and 1890s, business associations
      6. 1900s and 1910, most major lobbies of today
   B. Factors explaining the rise of interest groups
      1. Broad economic developments create new interests
         a) Farmers produce cash crops

> b)   Mass production industries begin
2.   Government policy itself
>> a)   Created veterans' groups—wars
>> b)   Encouraged formation of Farm Bureau
>> c)   Launched Chamber of Commerce
>> d)   Favored growth of unions
3.   Emergence of strong leaders, usually at certain times
4.   Expanding role of government

III.   Kinds of organizations
A.   Institutional interests
1.   Defined: individuals or organizations representing other organizations
2.   Types
>> a)   Businesses: example, General Motors
>> b)   Trade or governmental associations
3.   Concerns—bread-and-butter issues of concern to their clients
>> a)   Clearly defined, with homogeneous groups
>> b)   Diffuse, with diversified groups
4.   Other interests—governments, foundations, universities
B.   Membership interests
1.   Americans join some groups more frequently than people in other nations
>> a)   Social, business, and so on, same rate as elsewhere
>> b)   Unions, less likely to join
>> c)   Religious or civic groups, more likely to join
>> d)   Greater sense of efficacy and duty explains the tendency to join civic groups
2.   Most sympathizers do not join because
>> a)   Individuals not that significant
>> b)   Benefits flow to nonmembers too
C.   Incentives to join
1.   Solidary incentives—pleasure, companionship (League of Women Voters, AARP, NAACP, Rotary, etc.)
2.   Material incentives—money, things, services (farm organizations, retired persons, etc.)
3.   Purpose of the organization itself—public-interest organizations
>> a)   Ideological interest groups' appeal is controversial principles
>> b)   Engage in research and bring lawsuits
D.   Influence of the staff
1.   Staff has most influence if members joined for solidary or material benefits
2.   National Council of Churches and unions are examples

IV.   Interest groups and social movements
A.   Social movement is a widely shared demand for change
B.   Environmental movement
C.   Feminist movement: three kinds
1.   Solidary—LWV and others (widest support)
2.   Purposive—NOW, NARAL (strong position on divisive issues)
3.   Caucus—WEAL (material benefits)
D.   Union movement; left over after social movement dies

V.   Funds for interest groups
A.   Foundation grants
1.   Ford Foundation and public-interest groups
2.   Scaife foundations and conservative groups
B.   Federal grants and contracts
1.   National Alliance for Business and summer youth job programs

        2.   Jesse Jackson's PUSH
   C.   Direct mail
        1.   Unique to modern interest groups through use of computers
        2.   Common Cause a classic example
        3.   Techniques
            a)   Teaser
            b)   Emotional arousal
            c)   Celebrity endorsement
            d)   Personalization of letter

VI. Problem of bias
   A.   Reasons for belief in upper-class bias
        1.   More affluent more likely to join
        2.   Business or professional groups more numerous; better financed
   B.   Why these facts do not decide the issue
        1.   Describe inputs but not outputs
        2.   Business groups often divided among themselves
   C.   Important to ask what the bias is
        1.   Many conflicts are within upper middle class
        2.   Resource differentials are clues, not conclusions

VII. Activities of interest groups
   A.   Information
        1.   Single most important tactic
            a)   Nonpolitical sources insufficient
            b)   Provide detailed, current information
        2.   Most effective on narrow, technical issues
        3.   Officials also need cues; ratings systems
        4.   Dissemination of information and cues via fax
   B.   Public support: rise of new politics
        1.   Outsider strategy replacing insider strategy
        2.   New strategy leads to controversy that politicians dislike
        3.   Key targets: the undecided
        4.   Some groups attack their likely allies to embarrass them
        5.   Legislators sometimes buck public opinion, unless issue important
        6.   Some groups try for grassroots support
            a)   Saccharin issue
            b)   "Dirty Dozen" environmental polluters
        7.   Few large, well-funded interests are all-powerful (e.g., NRA)
   C.   Money and PACs
        1.   Money is least effective way to influence politicians
        2.   Campaign finance reform law of 1973 had two effects
            a)   Restricted amount interest groups can give to candidates
            b)   Made it legal for corporations and unions to create PACs
        3.   Rapid growth in PACs has not led to vote buying.
            a)   More money is available on all sides
            b)   Members of Congress take money but still decide how to vote
        4.   Almost any organization can create a PAC.
            a)   More than half of all PACs sponsored by corporations
            b)   Recent increase in ideological PACs; one-third liberal, two-thirds conservative
        5.   Ideological PACs raise more but spend less because of cost of raising money
        6.   In 2000 unions and business organizations gave most
        7.   Incumbents get most PAC money

        a)   Business PACs split money between Democrats and Republicans
        b)   Democrats get most PAC money
    8.   PAC contributions small
    9.   No evidence PAC money influences votes in Congress
        a)   Most members vote their ideology
        b)   When issue of little concern to voters, slight correlation but may be misleading
        c)   PAC money may influence in other ways, such as access
        d)   PAC money most likely to influence on client politics
  D.   The revolving door
    1.   Promise of future jobs to officials
    2.   Few conspicuous examples of abuse
  E.   Trouble
    1.   Disruption always part of American politics
    2.   Used by groups of varying ideologies
    3.   Better accepted since 1960s
    4.   History of proper persons using disruption: suffrage, civil rights, antiwar movements
    5.   Officials dread no-win situation
VIII. Regulating interest groups
  A.   Protection by First Amendment
  B.   1946 law accomplished little in requiring registration
  C.   1995 lobby act enacted by Congress
    1.   Broadens definition of a lobbyist
    2.   Lobbyists must report twice annually
    3.   Exempts grassroots organizations
    4.   No enforcement organization created
  D.   Significant restraints prior to 1995 still in effect
    1.   Tax code: threat of losing tax exempt status
    2.   Campaign finance laws

KEY TERMS MATCH

Match the following terms and descriptions. (*Note:* One of the descriptions should be matched with two terms.)

1.   Any group that seeks to influence public policy

2.   Individuals or groups representing other organizations

3.   Interest groups made up of those who join voluntarily

4.   The sense of pleasure, status, or companionship arising from group membership

5.   Money, things, or services obtainable from interest group membership

6.   The goals of an organization that, if attained, would benefit primarily nongroup members

7.   Organizations that attract members mostly by the appeal of their broad, controversial

a.   client politics

b.   cue (political)

c.   direct mail

d.   "Dirty Dozen"

e.   Federal Regulation of Lobbying Act of 1946

f.   grassroots support

g.   ideological interest groups

h.   incentive (political)

i.   insider strategy

j.   institutional interests

k.   interest groups

principles

8. Organizations that gather information on consumer topics (first organized by Ralph Nader)

9. The solicitation of funding through letter campaigns

10. The situation that arises when a government agency services as well as regulates a distinct group

11. Backing for a public policy that arises or is created in public opinion

12. A list, compiled by an environmental interest group, of those legislators who voted most frequently against its measures

13. Groups that can collect political donations and make campaign contributions to candidates for office

14. The practice of lobbying officials with such promises as employment after their government service

15. Its application restricted to lobbying efforts involving direct contacts with members of Congress

16. A signal to a member of Congress that identifies which values are at stake in a vote

17. A valued benefit obtained by joining a political organization

18. A person attempting to influence government decisions on behalf of an interest group

19. The sense of satisfaction derived from serving a cause from which one does not benefit personally

20. An assessment of a representative's voting record on issues important to an interest group

21. A widely shared demand for change in some aspect of the social or political order

22. Lobbyists working closely with a few key members of Congress, meeting them privately to exchange information and sometimes favors

l. lobbyist

m. material benefit incentives

n. membership interests

o. outsider strategy

p. PACs

q. PIRGs

r. public-interest lobby

s. purposive incentive

t. ratings

u. revolving-door influence

v. social movement

w. solidary incentives

23. Plan increasingly used by lobbyists with advent of modern technology and employing grassroots lobbying

DID YOU THINK THAT . . . ?

Below are listed a number of misconceptions. You should be able to refute each statement in the space provided, referring to information or argumentation contained in this chapter. Sample answers appear at the end of this chapter.

1. "All major interests are represented by national associations of interest groups."

_____

_____

2. "Interest groups automatically give expression to the sentiments of their membership."

_____

_____

3. "The unorganized are completely unrepresented in American politics."

_____

_____

4. "The most effective way for interest groups to advance their causes is to buy influence with money."

_____

_____

DATA CHECK

Table 9.1: Dates of Founding of Organizations Having Washington Offices

1. Using as a standard the formation of a Washington office, what type of interest group has grown the fastest since 1970?

_____

2. What type of interest group has grown the least since 1970?

_____

Table 9.5: How the PACs Spent Their Money in 2000

3.   Of the categories of PAC sponsors listed in the bottom section of the table, which ones provided more support to candidates for the House than to candidates for the Senate in 2000?

_____

4.   Which category of PAC sponsors provided vastly more support to Democratic candidates than to Republican ones in the 2000 election?

_____

5.   What conclusion can be drawn after comparing the PAC contributions received by incumbents and those received by challengers from all categories of PAC sponsors?

_____

PRACTICING FOR EXAMS

TRUE/FALSE QUESTIONS

Read each statement carefully. Mark true statements *T*. If any part of the statement is false, mark it *F*, and write in the space provided a concise explanation of why the statement is false.

1.   T   F   James Madison considered the causes of "faction" to be sown in "human nature."

_____

2.   T   F   The American system features more interest groups than that of Great Britain because there are more points of access and opportunities to influence policy.

_____

3.   T   F   In Austria, France and Italy, many interest groups are closely linked with political parties.

_____

4.   T   F   The League of Women Voters represents an organization based on solidary incentives.

_____

5.   T   F   The protestant-oriented National Council of the Churches of Christ has frequently taken liberal positions on political questions.

_____

6.   T   F   Membership in unions composed of government workers is decreasing.

_____

7.   T   F   Business-oriented interest groups are rarely divided among themselves.

_____

8.   T   F   When an issue is broad and highly visible, the influence of the lobbyist is reduced.

_____

9.   T   F   Interest groups produce "ratings" in order to generate support for, or opposition to, legislators.

_____

10. T   F   Republican activist William Kristol is given credit for creative use of billboards in an effort to defeat President Clinton's education programs.

_____

11. T   F   Most legislators deal with the interest groups that agree with them.

_____

12. T   F   Members of interest groups tend to work primarily with legislators with whom they agree.

_____

13. T   F   By the 1990s the National Rifle Association had a negative image even among most gun owners.

_____

14. T   F   The text suggests money is probably one of the least effective ways for interest groups to advance their causes.

_____

15. T   F   Some members of Congress tell PACs what to do rather than take orders from them.

_____

16. T   F   Members of Congress are not allowed to set up their own PACs.

_____

17. T   F   Almost 80 percent of all PACs are sponsored by corporations.

_____

18. T   F   In recent years, there has been little interest in the creation of ideological PACs.

_____

19. T   F   Ideological PACs tend to raise more money and to contribute more to candidates.

_____

20. T   F   Both parties are dependent upon PAC money.

_____

MULTIPLE CHOICE QUESTIONS

Circle the letter of the response that best answers the question or completes the statement.

1.   Where political parties are strong, interest groups are likely to be

   a.   equally strong.
   b.   independent.
   c.   weak.
   d.   more numerous.
   e.   non-ideological.

2.   The great era of organization building in America occurred during the years

   a.   1830–1840.

b. 1900–1920.
c. 1883–1896.
d. 1970-1980.
e. 1940-1960

3. Large labor unions had no reason to exist until the era of

a. mass production.
b. "ill feeling."
c. "good will"
d. anti-federalism.
e. consumerism.

4. Professional societies of doctors and lawyers first gained in importance because

a. their numbers increased more than those of other profession.
b. more and more legislators came from those professions.
c. the Supreme Court made several decisions favorable toward their interests.
d. state governments gave them authority to decide qualifications for their professions.
e. the Tenth Amendment was ignored by most state governments.

5. The great majority of "public interest" lobbies were established

a. after 1960.
b. after 1970.
c. after 1980.
d. after 1990.
e. after 1995.

6. It is often said that Americans are a nation of

a. linkers.
b. combinationists.
c. relaters.
d. joiners.
e. aggregationists.

7. Workers are *least* likely to belong to labor unions in

a. Sweden.
b. Germany.
c. Italy.
d. Great Britain.
e. the United States.

8. Solidary incentives involve

a. employment opportunities in government agencies.
b. the appeal of a stated goal.
c. a sense of pleasure, status or companionship.
d. money, or things and services readily valued in monetary terms.
e. assurances that partisanship will play no part in an organization's decision making.

9. Purposive incentives involve

a. employment opportunities in government agencies
b. the appeal of a stated goal
c. a sense of pleasure, status or companionship.

d.   money, or things and services readily valued in monetary terms.

e.   assurances that partisanship will play no part in an organization's decision making.

10.   Ralph Nader rose to national prominence on the issue of

    a.   school busing.

    b.   abortion.

    c.   auto safety.

    d.   nuclear power.

    e.   discrimination

11.   Interest groups with large staffs are likely to take political positions in accordance with

    a.   rank-and-file opinion.

    b.   editorial commentary in the media.

    c.   the view of the general public.

    d.   staff beliefs.

    e.   government policy.

12.   All of the following are examples of liberal public-interest law firms *except* the

    a.   American Civil Liberties Union.

    b.   Asian American Legal Defense Fund.

    c.   NAACP Legal Defense and Education Fund.

    d.   Criminal Justice Legal Defense Fund.

    e.   Women's Legal Defense Fund.

13.   The Center for Defense Information, the Children's Defense Fund, and the Economic Policy Institute are examples of

    a.   liberal public-interest law firms.

    b.   non-ideological public-interest think tanks.

    c.   conservative public-interest law firms.

    d.   liberal think tanks.

    e.   conservative think tanks.

14.   The National Organization for Women and the National Abortion Rights Action League are examples of organizations that feature

    a.   solidary incentives.

    b.   purposive incentives.

    c.   material incentives.

    d.   non-partisan incentives.

    e.   All of the above.

15.   Most public-interest groups pursue

    a.   conservative policies.

    b.   moderate policies.

    c.   liberal policies.

    d.   non-partisan policies.

    e.   bi-partisan policies.

16.   About _____ percent of the interest groups represented in Washington, D.C. are public-interest groups.

    a.   4

    b.   12

c.   15
d.   20
e.   40

17. Although farmers today have difficulty getting Congress to pass bills in their favor, they are still able to

a.   block bills that they don't like.
b.   appeal to public sentiment.
c.   win court cases.
d.   manipulate prices by withholding their produce.
e.   affect collective bargaining agreements and discourage strikes.

18. Probably the best measure of an interest group's ability to influence legislators and bureaucrats is

a.   the size of the membership.
b.   the dollar amount of its contributions.
c.   the occupational sketch of its members.
d.   its organizational skill.
e.   its contacts.

19. A conservative legislator will feel comfortable about a position that is favored by

a.   the American Medical Association.
b.   the NAACP.
c.   the American Civil Liberties Union.
d.   the Farmers' Union.
e.   a Naderite organization.

20. The "Dirty Dozen" refers to members of Congress who appear to be

a.   corrupt.
b.   anti-environment.
c.   beleaguered.
d.   free-thinking.
e.   parlor "pinks."

21. The passage of the campaign finance reform law in 1973 led to the rapid growth in

a.   political parties.
b.   interest groups.
c.   PACs.
d.   voter registration.
e.   revenue sharing.

22. The revolving door between government and business raises the possibility of

a.   poor communications.
b.   revenue sharing.
c.   conflicts of interest.
d.   duplication.
e.   ticket splitting.

23. Former executive branch employees may *not* represent anyone on any matter before their former agency for a period of _____ after leaving it.

a.   six months
b.   eight months.

c.   one year
d.   two years
e.   five years

24.   A protest march is an example of the political resource called

a.   subversion.
b.   making trouble.
c.   illegal activity.
d.   pop-arbitration.
e.   power politics.

25.   The most significant legal constraints on interest groups currently come from

a.   the 1946 Federal Regulation of Lobbying Act.
b.   the tax code.
c.   antitrust legislation.
d.   state labor leaders.
e.   the Supreme Court.
f.   the free-rider problem.

ESSAY QUESTIONS

Practice writing extended answers to the following questions. These test your ability to integrate and express the ideas that you have been studying in this chapter.

1.   List and comment on the various reasons commonly given for the unusually large variety of interest groups found in the United States.

2.   List and analyze the various periods of American history that have witnessed rapid growth in interest groups. Discuss whether any of the requisite conditions are present today.

3.   Explain the difference between organizational and membership-type interest groups, and discuss how you might expect their conduct in the political system to vary.

4.   Do you believe that the system of interest groups active in American politics today has an upper-class bias? Defend your answer, and discuss whether the system as you see it is a desirable or an undesirable one.

5.   Discuss 1946 and 1995 congressional efforts to regulate lobbying.

ANSWERS TO KEY TERMS MATCH QUESTIONS

1. k
2. j
3. n
4. w
5. m
6. r
7. p
8. q
9. c
10. a
11. f
12. d
13. g
14. u
15. e
16. b
17. h
18. l
19. s
20. t
21. v
22. i
23. o

ANSWERS TO "DID YOU THINK THAT . . . ?" QUESTIONS

1. At times major segments of society, such as blacks, farmers, the poor, and migrant workers, have been unrepresented. Movements arise in response to economic conditions, and, through much of American history, there has been a struggle to organize those without effective representation. Frequently, large numbers of constituents do not belong to the unions, civil rights organizations, or religious organizations that claim to speak in their name.

2. Leaders at times act according to their own perceptions, especially on civil rights issues and foreign policy matters. To create coalitions they may join with other groups and espouse their causes. Groups may also take positions because of sponsors or donors of funds.

3. Sponsored groups may act as surrogates. Other groups may join with sponsored groups in coalitions—a situation that occurred in the early stages of the civil rights movement. There are

executive branch agencies and members of Congress who also may take up the banner for a politically unorganized group.

4. Money is probably one of the *least* effective ways for an interest group to advance its cause; passage of the campaign reform law in 1973 saw to that. More effective are activities that supply credible information to legislators and bureaucrats. Other important activities include the public support campaign, such as mail and telegram campaigns.

ANSWERS TO DATA CHECK QUESTIONS

1. Public interest organizations.

2. Corporations

3. All of them.

4. Labor organizations.

5. Incumbents tend to attract far more PAC contributions than do challengers.

ANSWERS TO TRUE/FALSE QUESTIONS

1. T

2. T

3. T

4. T

5. T

6. F. They are becoming the most important part of the union movement, almost the only part that is growing in size.

7. F. On the contrary, they are often divided among themselves.

8. T

9. T

10. F. Kritsol's efforts were aimed against Clinton's health care plan.

11. T

12. T

13. T

14. T

15. T

16. F. Some members do create their own PACs.

17. F. It would be more accurate to say over half are sponsored by corporations.

18. F. The rise in ideological PACs has been the most remarkable development in interest group activity in recent years.

19. F. Instead, they tend to raise more money and contribute less to candidates.

20. T

ANSWERS TO MULTIPLE CHOICE QUESTIONS

1. c
2. b
3. a
4. d
5. a
6. d
7. e
8. c
9. b
10. c
11. d
12. d
13. c
14. b
15. c
16. a
17. a
18. d
19. a
20. b
21. b
22. c
23. c
24. b
25. b

CHAPTER 10

The Media

REVIEWING THE CHAPTER

CHAPTER FOCUS

In this chapter you examine the historical evolution and current status of relations between the government and the news media—how the media affect government and politics and how government seeks to affect the media.

After reading and reviewing the material in this chapter, you should be able to do each of the following:

1. Describe the evolution of journalism in American political history, and describe the differences between the party press and the mass media of today.

2. Demonstrate how the characteristics of the electronic media have affected the actions of public officials and candidates for national office.

3. Describe the effect of the pattern of ownership and control of the media on the dissemination of news, and show how wire services and television networks have affected national news coverage. Discuss the influence of the national press.

4. Describe the rules that govern the media, and contrast the regulation of electronic and print media. Describe the effect of libel laws on freedom of the press and of government rules on broadcasters.

5. Assess the effect of the media on politics, and discuss why it is difficult to find evidence that can be used to make a meaningful and accurate assessment. Explain why the executive branch probably benefits at the expense of Congress.

6. Describe the adversarial press and how reporters use their sources. Describe how an administration can develop tactics to use against the adversarial press.

STUDY OUTLINE

I. Journalism in American political history
   A. The party press
      1. Parties created and subsidized various newspapers
      2. Circulation was small, newspapers expensive, advertisers few
      3. Newspapers circulated among political and commercial elites
   B. The popular press
      1. Changes in society and technology made the press self-supporting and able to reach mass readership.
         a) High-speed press
         b) Telegraph
         c) Associated Press, 1848; objective reporting
         d) Urbanization allowed large numbers to support paper
         e) Government Printing Office; end of subsidies in 1860

2. Influence of publishers, editors created partisan bias
    a) "Yellow journalism" to attract readers
    b) Hearst foments war against Spain
3. Emergence of a common national culture

C. Magazines of opinion
1. Middle class favors new, progressive periodicals
    a) *Nation, Atlantic, Harper's* in 1850s and 1860s on behalf of certain issues
    b) *McClure's, Scribner's, Cosmopolitan* later on
2. Individual writers gain national followings through investigative reporting
3. Number of competing newspapers declines, as does sensationalism
4. Today the number of national magazines focusing on politics accounts for a small and declining fraction of magazines.

D. Electronic journalism
1. Radio arrives in the 1920s, television in the 1940s
2. Politicians could address voters directly but people could easily ignore them
3. But fewer politicians could be covered
    a) President routinely covered
    b) Others must use bold tactics
4. Recent rise in the talk show as a political forum has increased politicians' access to electronic media
    a) Big Three networks have made it harder for candidates by shortening sound bites
    b) But politicians have more sources: cable, early morning news, news magazine shows
    c) These new sources feature lengthy interviews
5. No research on consequences of two changes:
    a) Recent access of politicians to electronic media
    b) "Narrowcasting," which targets segmented audiences
6. Politicians continue to seek visuals even after they are elected

E. The Internet
1. Ultimate free market in political news
2. Voters and political activists talk to one another

II. The structure of the media
A. Degree of competition
1. Newspapers
    a) Number of daily newspapers has declined significantly
    b) Number of cities with multiple papers *has* declined
        (1) 60 percent of cities had competing newspapers in 1900
        (2) Only 4 percent in 1972
    c) Newspaper circulation has fallen since 1967
    d) Most people now get most of their news from television
2. Radio and television
    a) Intensely competitive, becoming more so
    b) Composed mostly of locally owned and managed enterprises, unlike Europe
    c) Orientation to local market
    d) Limitations by FCC; widespread ownership created

B. The national media
1. Existence somewhat offsets local orientation
2. Consists of
    a) Wire services
    b) National magazines
    c) Television networks

       d)   Newspapers with national readerships
  3. Significance
     a) Washington officials follow it closely
     b) Reporters and editors different from the local press
       (1) Better paid
       (2) From more prestigious universities
       (3) More liberal outlook
       (4) Do investigative or interpretive stories
  4. Roles played
     a) Gatekeeper: what is news, for how long
       (1) Auto safety
       (2) Water pollution
       (3) Prescription drugs
       (4) Crime rates
     b) Scorekeeper: who is winning, losing
       (1) Attention to Iowa, New Hampshire
       (2) Gary Hart in 1984 and John McCain in 2000
     c) Watchdog: investigate personalities and expose scandals
       (1) Hart's name, birth date, in 1984; Donna Rice in 1987
       (2) Watergate (Woodward and Bernstein)

III. Rules governing the media
  A. Newspapers versus electronic media
    1. Newspapers almost entirely free from government regulation; prosecutions only after the fact and limited: libel, obscenity, incitement
    2. Radio and television licensed, regulated
  B. Confidentiality of sources
    1. Reporters want right to keep sources confidential
    2. Most states and federal government disagree
    3. Supreme Court allows government to compel reporters to divulge information in court if it bears on a crime
    4. Myron Farber jailed for contempt
    5. Police search of newspaper office upheld
  C. Regulating broadcasting
    1. FCC licensing
     a) Seven years for radio
     b) Five years for television
     c) Stations must serve "community needs"
     d) Public service, other aspects can be regulated
    2. Recent movement to deregulate
     a) License renewal by postcard
     b) No hearing unless opposed
     c) Relaxation of rule enforcement
    3. Radio broadcasting deregulated the most
     a) Telecommunications Act of 1996 permits one company to own as many as eight stations in large markets (five in smaller ones)
     b) Results:
       (1) Few large companies now own most of the big-market radio stations
       (2) Greater variety of opinion on radio
    4. Other radio and television regulations
     a) Equal time rule
     b) Right-of-reply rule

        c)   Political editorializing rule
    5.   Fairness doctrine was abolished in 1987
  D.   Campaigning
    1.   Equal time rule applies
        a)   Equal access for all candidates
        b)   Rates no higher than least expensive commercial rate
        c)   Debates formerly had to include all candidates
           (1)   Reagan-Carter debate sponsored by LWV as a "news event"
           (2)   Now stations and networks can sponsor
    2.   Efficiency in reaching voters
        a)   Works well when market and district overlap
        b)   Fails when they are not aligned
        c)   More Senate than House candidates buy TV time
IV. The effects of the media on politics
  A.   Studies on media influence on elections
    1.   Generally inconclusive, because of citizens'
        a)   Selective attention
        b)   Mental tune-out
    2.   Products can be sold more easily than candidates
    3.   Newspaper endorsements of candidates
        a)   Often of Republicans locally, whereas of Democrats nationally
        b)   But worth 5 percent of vote to endorsed Democrats
  B.   Major effect is on how politics is conducted, not how people vote
    1.   Conventions scheduled to accommodate television coverage
    2.   Candidates win party nomination via media exposure, for example, Estes Kefauver
    3.   Issues established by media attention
        a)   Environment
        b)   Consumer issues
    4.   Issues that are important to citizens similar to those in media
        a)   TV influences political agenda
        b)   But people less likely to take media cues on matters that affect them personally
    5.   Newspaper readers see bigger candidate differences than do TV viewers
    6.   TV news affects popularity of presidents; commentaries have short-term effect
V. Government and the news
  A.   Prominence of the president
    1.   Theodore Roosevelt: systematic cultivation of the press
    2.   Franklin Roosevelt: press secretary a major instrument for cultivating press
    3.   Press secretary today: large staff, many functions
    4.   White House press corps is the focus of press secretary
    5.   Unparalleled personalization of government
  B.   Coverage of Congress
    1.   Never equal to that of president; members resentful
    2.   House quite restrictive
        a)   No cameras on the floor until 1978
        b)   Sometimes refused to permit coverage of committees
        c)   Gavel-to-gavel coverage of proceedings since 1979
    3.   Senate more open
        a)   Hearings since Kefauver; TV coverage of sessions in 1986
        b)   Incubator for presidential contenders through committee hearings
VI. Interpreting political news
  A.   Are news stories slanted?

1. Most people believe media, especially television, from which they get most news
    a) But the percentage that thinks the media is biased is increasing
    b) Press itself thinks it is unbiased
2. Liberal bias of national media elite
3. Various factors influence how stories are written
    a) Deadlines
    b) Audience attraction
    c) Fairness, truth imposed by professional norms
    d) Reporters' and editors' beliefs
4. Types of stories
    a) Routine stories: public events regularly covered
        (1) Reported similarly by all media; opinions of journalists have least effect
        (2) Can be misreported: Tet offensive
    b) Selected stories: public but not routinely covered
        (1) Selection involves perception of what is important
        (2) Liberal and conservative papers do different stories
        (3) Increasing in number; reflect views of press more than experts or public
    c) Insider stories: not usually made public; motive problem
5. Studies on effects of journalistic opinions
    a) Nuclear power: antinuclear slant
    b) School busing: probusing
    c) Media spin almost inevitable
6. Insider stories raise questions of informant's motives
    a) From official background briefings of the past
    b) To critical inside stories of post-Watergate era
B. Why do we have so many news leaks?
    1. Constitution: separation of powers
        a) Power is decentralized
        b) Branches of government compete
        c) Not illegal to print most secrets
    2. Adversarial nature of the press since Watergate
        a) Press and politicians distrust each other
        b) Media are eager to embarrass officials
        c) Competition for awards
        d) Spurred by Irangate: arms for hostages
    3. Cynicism created era of attack journalism
        a) Most people do not like this kind of news
        b) Cynicism of media mirrors public's increasing cynicism of media
        c) People believe media slant coverage
        d) Public support for idea of licensing journalists or fines to discourage biased reporting
    4. Public confidence in big business down and now media are big business
    5. Drive for market share forces media to use theme of corruption
    6. Increased use of negative advertising
C. Sensationalism in the media
    1. Prior to 1980, sexual escapades of political figures not reported
    2. Since 1980, sex and politics extensively covered
    3. Reasons for change
        a) Sensationalism gets attention in a market of intense competition.
        b) Sensational stories are often cheaper than expert analysis and/or investigation of stories about policy or substantive issues.

         c)   Journalists have become distrusting adversaries of government.

         d)   Journalists are much more likely to rely on unnamed sources today and, as a result, are more easily manipulated.

    4.   Impact of September 11

         a)   Public interest in national news

         b)   Greater confidence and trust in news organizations

  D.   Government constraints on journalists

    1.   Reporters must strike a balance between

         a)   Expression of views

         b)   Retaining sources

    2.   Abundance of congressional staffers makes it easier

    3.   Governmental tools to fight back

         a)   Numerous press officers

         b)   Press releases, canned news

         c)   Leaks and background stories to favorites

         d)   Bypass national press for local

         e)   Presidential rewards and punishments for reporters based on their stories

KEY TERMS MATCH

Match the following terms and descriptions:

1.   British legislation to punish officials who divulge private government business

2.   U.S. legislation guaranteeing citizens access to certain government documents

3.   An organization founded for the telegraphic dissemination of news in 1848

4.   Sensationalized news reporting

5.   Investigative reporters such as Lincoln Steffens

6.   Filmed stories for evening television news

7.   The government agency charged with regulating the electronic media

8.   Information from a government official who can be quoted by name

9.   Information from an official that cannot be printed

10.   Information from an official that can be printed but not attributed to the official by name

11.   Information from an official that can be printed but not attributed at all

12.   A court standard for finding the media guilty of libeling officials

13.   An official criterion for the renewal of

a.   Associated Press

b.   attack journalism

c.   canned news

d.   community needs

e.   equal time rule

f.   fairness doctrine

g.   FCC

h.   feature stories

i.   Freedom of Information Act

j.   insider stories

k.   loaded language

l.   market (television)

m.   muckrakers

n.   Official Secrets Act

o.   off the record

p.   on background

q.   on deep background

r.   on the record

s.   reckless disregard

t.   right-of-reply rule

broadcast licenses

14. A principle that formerly obligated broadcasters to present both sides of an issue

15. An obligation on broadcasters to give all candidates equal access to the media

16. An area easily reached by one television signal

17. The tendency of people to see what they like and ignore what they do not like

18. Reporters regularly assigned to cover the president

19. Public events regularly covered by reporters

20. Public events not regularly covered by reporters

21. Events that become public only if revealed to reporters

22. Press releases or other news items prepared for reporters

23. Journalism that seizes on information that might question the character or qualifications of a public official

24. Words that reflect a value judgment, used to persuade the listener without making an argument

25. An FCC rule permitting a person the right to respond if attacked on a broadcast other than in a regular news program

26. A brief statement no longer than a few seconds used on a radio or television broadcast

27. Information provided to the media by an anonymous source as a way of testing the reaction to a potential policy or appointment

28. Allows one company to own as many as eight radio stations in large markets (five in smaller ones) and as many as it wishes nationally

u. routine stories

v. selective attention

w. sound bite

x. Telecommunications Act of 1996

y. trial balloon

z. visuals

aa. White House Press Corps

bb. "yellow journalism"

DID YOU THINK THAT . . . ?

Below are listed a number of misconceptions. You should be able to refute each statement in the space provided, referring to information or argumentation contained in this chapter. Sample answers appear at the end of this chapter.

1. "Freedom of the press means that Congress cannot regulate the mass media."

    _____

    _____

    _____

2. "The media simply act as messengers that carry objective news."

    _____

    _____

    _____

3. "Media manipulation has had a major demonstrable effect on voting behavior in most elections."

    _____

    _____

    _____

4. "Negative advertising has no effect on elections."

    _____

    _____

    _____

DATA CHECK

Table 10.2: Journalist Opinion Versus Public Opinion

1. According to the Table, what percentage of journalists describe themselves as "liberal?"

    _____

2. How does the percentage of journalists that describe themselves as "conservative" compare to the public?

    _____

3. Which topics / issues feature the greatest degree of difference between the opinions of journalists and the opinions of the public?

    _____

    _____

    _____

Table 10.4: Self-Identified Ideology Among American Elites

4. What groups tend to be the most liberal?

    _____

5. What groups tend to be the most conservative?

    _____

Figure 10.3: Decline in Public Trust of the Media

6. What percentage of those polled stated that they had less confidence in the media than when they first started paying attention to news and current events?

   _____

7. What percentage felt the media have too much influence over what happens today?

   _____

8. What percentage believed the media abused the privileges that are enjoyed by the protections of the Bill of Rights?

   _____

PRACTICING FOR EXAMS

TRUE/FALSE QUESTIONS

Read each statement carefully. Mark true statements *T*. If any part of the statement is false, mark it *F*, and write in the space provided a concise explanation of why the statement is false.

1. T F   Public figures in England frequently sue newspapers for libel and collect.

   _____

2. T F   In the early years of the Republic, newspapers were relatively unbiased and placed a premium on reporting "just the facts."

   _____

3. T F   Randolph Hearst used his newspapers to agitate for war.

   _____

4. T F   In 1992, Ross Perot declared his willingness to run for the presidency on the television program "Meet the Press."

   _____

5. T F   The typical American newspaper has more local than national news in it.

   _____

6. T F   In general, your name and picture can be printed without your consent if they are part of a news story of some conceivable public interest.

   _____

7. T F   Licenses for radio stations must be renewed every seven years.

   _____

8. T F   Licenses for television stations must be renewed every five years.

   _____

9. T F   People are more likely to take cues from the media in matters that affect them personally.

   _____

10. T F In a study of the 1976 election, newspaper readers saw less of a difference between presidential candidates than did television viewers.

_____

11. T F Research indicates television "commentary" has little or no affect on the opinions of the public.

_____

12. T F Congress did not allow live coverage of committee hearings until the House considered the impeachment of Richard Nixon.

_____

13. T F Americans tell pollsters that they get most of their news from newspapers.

_____

14. T F Most Americans consider newspapers more reliable than television.

_____

15. T F In 1992, over 80 percent of media leaders in Washington voted for Bill Clinton.

_____

16. T F In other democratic countries there are far fewer leaks to members of the media because governments are more decentralized.

_____

17. T F Journalists are far less willing today to accept at face value the statements of elected officials.

_____

18. T F The texts suggests "negative" campaigns are on the increase because they work.

_____

19. T F Research indicates "negative" ads are associated with increased voter turnout.

_____

20. T F Newspapers knew that Franklin Roosevelt had a romantic affair in the 1930s but did not report it.

_____

MULTIPLE CHOICE QUESTIONS

Circle the letter of the response that best answers the question or completes the statement.

1. Politicians have become more heavily dependent on the media as

   a. the public has become better educated.
   b. the federal bureaucracy has enlarged itself.
   c. public affairs have become much more complex.
   d. the scope of government has expanded.
   e. political party organizations have declined.

2.   Compared with other Western democracies, the United States has

    a.   a more nationally oriented media.
    b.   a greater variety of extreme left- and right-wing views.
    c.   more government supervision of the content of media.
    d.   more private ownership of broadcast media.
    e.   greater concentration of control over the media in a few hands.

3.   Which of the following was a milestone in the development of a reasonably nonpartisan and unbiased press?

    a.   the establishment of the *Gazette of the United States* during the Washington administration
    b.   the establishment of the Associated Press in 1848
    c.   the creation of the *National Intelligence* by Jacksonian Democrats
    d.   the rise of magazines of opinion in the late 1800s
    e.   the rise of competition from radio in the 1920s

4.   Which of the following was *not* among the factors that made government subsidies of the press obsolete?

    a.   the establishment of the Government Printing Office
    b.   the rise of newspapers associated with particular political parties or factions
    c.   the development of the high-speed rotary press
    d.   urbanization
    e.   B and C.

5.   Which of the following was *not* among the achievements of the mass-based press, exemplified by Hearst and Pulitzer?

    a.   instituting responsible and unbiased journalism
    b.   beginning the creation of a national political culture
    c.   proving the feasibility of a press free of government subsidy or control
    d.   revealing public scandal
    e.   criticizing public policy

6.   Which of the following was *not* associated with the rise of national magazines around the turn of the century?

    a.   the middle class
    b.   muckraking
    c.   scandal mongering
    d.   high-impact photojournalism
    e.   nationally-known writers

7.   The invention of radio was a politically important media development because it

    a.   allowed public officials to reach the public in a less-filtered manner.
    b.   gave rise to the era of mass politics and a large electorate.
    c.   rendered image more important than substance in seeking political office.
    d.   more than doubled the number of persons who followed politics with interest.
    e.   reinforced the influence of political parties when it was first introduced.

8.   In 2000, the average sound bite of a presidential contender was _____ the average sound bite of such contenders in 1968.

    a.   considerably longer than
    b.   about the same length as
    c.   considerably shorter than

    d.   more controversial than

    e.   less complex

9.   By 1972, competing daily newspapers existed in _____ percent of American cities.

    a.   4

    b.   9

    c.   10

    d.   25

    e.   68

10.   All of the following are correct statements with respect to reporters and editors for the national press *except*

    a.   they are better paid than most other journalists.

    b.   they have often graduated from the most prestigious colleges and universities.

    c.   they generally hold more liberal political views.

    d.   they rarely have the opportunity to do investigative or interpretive stories about politics.

    e.   their work is given considerable attention by officials in Washington.

11.   One of Jimmy Carter's signal achievements in dealing with the press in the 1976 primary campaign was

    a.   keeping a low profile.

    b.   taking newsworthy positions on important issues.

    c.   defusing an initial bias against him among reporters.

    d.   refusing to buckle under the pressure of special interests.

    e.   getting himself mentioned with great frequency.

12.   Eugene McCarthy in the 1968 New Hampshire primary and George McGovern in the 1972 New Hampshire primary

    a.   were virtually ignored by the national press.

    b.   accused the press of a bias against them.

    c.   successfully managed to avoid issues.

    d.   were declared "winners" by the press, although they lost.

    e.   successfully managed to stress image.

13.   An irony concerning government regulation of the news media is that

    a.   American media are less regulated than foreign media despite the greater need for regulation here.

    b.   legislation designed to intimidate the media has in fact made them more hostile toward officials.

    c.   the least competitive part of the media is almost entirely unregulated, whereas the most competitive part is substantially regulated.

    d.   the most influential media, the broadcast media, show highly concentrated patterns of ownership by a few large corporations.

    e.   All of the above.

14.   Once something is published, a newspaper may be sued or prosecuted if the material

    a.   is libelous.

    b.   is obscene.

    c.   incites someone to commit an illegal act.

    d.   All of the above.

    e.   None of the above.

15. For a public official in the United States to win a libel suit against the press, he or she must prove that

    a. what was printed was untrue.
    b. the material was untrue and was printed maliciously.
    c. the material caused "emotional duress."
    d. his or her privacy was violated.
    e. the printing of the material in question has done "substantial harm" to the public interest.

16. Which regulation was abolished by the FCC in 1987 because it may have inhibited free discussion of issues ?

    a. The Equal Time Rule
    b. The Political Editorializing Rule
    c. The Right-of Reply Rule
    d. The No-Spin Rule
    e. The Fairness Doctrine

17. To date, there is _____ evidence that enables us to know the degree to which media influence the public's view of politics and policymaking.

    a. an extraordinary amount of
    b. a moderate amount of
    c. relatively little
    d. moderate, but highly convincing
    e. a great deal of highly convincing

18. Local newspapers have generally

    a. endorsed Republican candidates throughout this century.
    b. endorsed Democratic candidates throughout this century.
    c. endorsed Independent candidates throughout this century.
    d. have endorsed the candidates of the major parties equally.
    e. have generally refrained from making political endorsements.

19. The first politician to discover the powerful effect television coverage could have on a political career was

    a. Theodore Roosevelt.
    b. Franklin Roosevelt.
    c. Woodrow Wilson.
    d. Estes Kefauver.
    e. Richard Nixon.

20. If we compare the issues that citizens feel are important with the issues that newspapers and television newscasts feature, we find that

    a. they are much the same.
    b. they are vastly different.
    c. there is little about which to generalize one way or the other.
    d. the media are more likely to feature the concerns of political liberals.
    e. the media ignore the economic concerns of many citizens.

21. The first president to engage in the systematic cultivation of news reporters was

    a. Theodore Roosevelt.
    b. Franklin Roosevelt.
    c. Woodrow Wilson

    d.   John F. Kennedy.
    e.   Richard Nixon.

22. Which of the following presidents first made his press secretary a major instrument for dealing with the press?

    a.   Herbert Hoover
    b.   Franklin Roosevelt
    c.   Dwight Eisenhower
    d.   John F. Kennedy
    e.   Ronald Reagan

23. The president of the United States is unlike the chief executive of other nations with regard to the

    a.   hostility with which he is normally treated by the press.
    b.   use of the press secretary as an instrument for dealing with the press.
    c.   extreme difficulty that the press experiences in covering his activities.
    d.   close physical proximity between the press and the center of government.
    e.   manner in which he is required to conduct press conferences.

24. In an age in which the media are very important, who of the following is best positioned to run for president?

    a.   a House member
    b.   an innovative person with a business background.
    c.   a senator
    d.   a governor
    e.   a big-city mayor

25. In deciding which stories to include in the daily newspaper, editors

    a.   are rigidly constrained by the volume of hard news that must be included.
    b.   are rigidly constrained by the limited amount of material available to them.
    c.   are rigidly constrained by the limited about of time they have before publication.
    d.   are rigidly constrained by the need to include popular or catchy feature stories.
    e.   have considerable latitude to express their ideological biases in the selection of background or feature stories.

ESSAY QUESTIONS

Practice writing extended answers to the following questions. These test your ability to integrate and express the ideas that you have been studying in this chapter.

1. Compare and contrast the party press of the Federalist-Republican era with today's mass media, listing some major changes in technology and society that have brought about this evolution.

2. Discuss the major ways in which the focus on electronic media rather than print media has changed the conduct of American politics.

3. Compare government regulation of the print media with that of radio and TV, noting also recent trends in the latter.

4. Discuss the relationship between the economics of journalism and the rise of sensationalism in the media.

ANSWERS TO KEY TERMS MATCH QUESTIONS

1. n
2. i
3. a
4. bb
5. m
6. z
7. g
8. r
9. o
10. p
11. q
12. s
13. d
14. f
15. e
16. l
17. v
18. aa
19. u
20. h
21. j
22. c
23. b
24. k
25. t
26. w
27. y
28. x

ANSWERS TO "DID YOU THINK THAT . . . ?" QUESTIONS

1. Print media can be regulated as business (antitrust laws, postal regulations, labor-management laws). Courts can apply the laws of libel and obscenity. Electronic media are regulated because they use public airwaves and are considered a public trust.

2. Media owners are businesspeople who try to get audiences. They may choose to go after nonroutine news by sponsoring investigative units that will engage in exposés and muckraking.

Often editors will go on crusades to highlight an issue of particular concern in the hope of gaining additional readers or viewers. Reporters have their own political beliefs that may shape their perceptions of events, and columnists and editorial page writers are expected to promote their own values.

3. Surveys have not demonstrated a significant difference between those watching TV a great deal and those watching little during a campaign. Newspaper endorsements and editorials seem to have little effect. Advertisements provide more information than do news spots, and debates, which provide even more information, do seem to have had an influence on voters in 1960 and 1976. Perhaps the greatest effect of the media is on primary campaigns, especially benefiting those who are not well known.

4. Research shows that negative advertising not only changes voter preferences but also reduces voter turnout. Negative advertising may help a candidate win but only by turning people against elections.

ANSWERS TO DATA CHECK QUESTIONS

1. 55 percent.

2. 17 percent of journalists considered themselves conservative as opposed to 29 percent in the public.

3. Prayer in schools, favor hiring homosexuals, withdrawing investments from South Africa.

4. Television and labor.

5. Military and business.

6. 40 percent.

7. 59 percent.

8. 52 percent.

ANSWERS TO TRUE/FALSE QUESTIONS

1. T

2. F. In the early years of the Republic, politicians and parties created, sponsored, and controlled newspapers.

3. T

4. F. Perot declared his candidacy on CNN's *Larry King Live*.

5. T

6. T

7. T

8. T

9. F. They are less likely to take cues from the media on such matters.

10. F. Newspaper readers saw more of a difference between candidates.

11. F. It tends to have a large effect, although in the short run.

12. T

13. F. Most Americans tell pollsters they get their news from television.

14. F. They regard TV as more reliable than the printed press.
15. T
16. F. Power is instead centralized and prime ministers do not need to leak in order to get an upper hand with the legislature.
17. T
18. T
19. T
20. T

ANSWERS TO MULTIPLE CHOICE QUESTIONS

1. e
2. d
3. b
4. b
5. a
6. d
7. a
8. c
9. a
10. d
11. e
12. d
13. c
14. d
15. b
16. e
17. c
18. a
19. d
20. a
21. a
22. b
23. d
24. c
25. e

PART 2

Classic Statement: "The Omnipotence of the Majority in the United States and Its Effects," from *Democracy in America,* by Alexis de Tocqueville[1]

INTRODUCTION

Alexis de Tocqueville's classic book on American democracy is in many ways an admiring work: Tocqueville was particularly taken with the spirit of equality and energy he met from his first days in the United States in the 1830s. But he also discerned flaws and dangers in the world's newest democracy, and some of these were, in his view, very much bound up with the nation's strengths.

Nowhere is this more true than in his discussion of the will of the majority. Although the principle of majority rule is inseparable from the workings of a democratic system, majority rule can, if not challenged or limited, lead to tyranny and to the undoing of the democratic experiment. More than a century and a half later, see whether you find that any of Tocqueville's thoughts on this subject still ring true.

The absolute sovereignty of the will of the majority is the essence of democratic government, for in democracies there is nothing outside the majority capable of resisting it.

Most American constitutions have sought further artificially to increase this natural strength of the majority.

Of all political powers, the legislature is the one most ready to obey the wishes of the majority. The Americans wanted the members of the legislatures to be appointed *directly* by the people and for a *very short* term of office so that they should be obliged to submit only to the general views but also to the passing passions of their constituents.

In America several particular circumstances also tend to make the power of the majority not only predominant but irresistible.

The moral authority of the majority is partly based on the notion that there is more enlightenment and wisdom in a numerous assembly than in a single man, and the number of the legislators is more important than how they are chosen. It is the theory of equality applied to brains. This doctrine attacks the last asylum of human pride; for that reason the minority is reluctant in admitting it and takes a long time to get used to it.

---

[1] *Democracy in America* was published as a result of the French author's trip to America in 1831 to observe the workings of this New World democracy. His observations from the early days of Jacksonian democracy, published in two separate volumes, would be hailed as "the greatest book ever written on America." The excerpts presented here are taken from Volume I, Part II, Chapter 7, as presented in *Democracy in America* (New York: Harper and Row, 1966).

The idea that the majority has a right based on enlightenment to govern society was brought to the United States by its first inhabitants; and this idea, which would of itself be enough to create a free nation, has by now passed into mores and affects even the smallest habits of life.

The moral authority of the majority is also founded on the principle that the interest of the greatest number should be preferred to that of those who are fewer. Now, it is easy to understand that the respect professed for this right of the greatest number naturally grows or shrinks according to the state of the parties. When a nation is divided between several great irreconcilable interests, the privilege of the majority is often disregarded, for it would be too unpleasant to submit to it.

Hence the majority in the United States has immense actual power and a power of opinion which is almost as great. When once its mind is made up on any question, there are, so to say, no obstacles which can retard, much less halt, its progress and give it time to hear the wails of those it crushes as it passes.

The consequences of this state of affairs are fate-laden and dangerous for the future.

I have spoken before of the vices natural to democratic government, and every single one of them increases with the growing power of the majority.

To begin with the most obvious of all:

Legislative instability is an ill inherent in democratic government because it is the nature of democracies to bring new men to power. But this ill is greater or less according to the power and means of action accorded to the legislator.

In America the lawmaking authority has been given sovereign power. This authority can carry out anything it desires quickly and irresistibly, and its representatives change annually. That it is to say, just that combination has been chosen which most encourages democratic instability and allows the changing wishes of democracy to be applied to the most important matters.

Thus American laws have a shorter duration than those of any other country in the world today. Almost all American constitutions have been amended within the last thirty years, and so there is no American state which has not modified the basis of its laws within that period.

As for the laws themselves, it is enough to glance at the archives of the various states of the Union to realize that in America the legislator's activity never slows down. Not that American democracy is by nature more unstable than any other, but it has been given the means to carry the natural instability of its inclinations into the making of laws.

The omnipotence of the majority and the rapid as well as absolute manner in which its decisions are executed in the United States not only make the law unstable but have a like effect on the execution of the law and on public administrative activity.

My greatest complaint against democratic government as organized in the United States is not, as many Europeans make out, its weakness, but rather its irresistible strength. What I find most repulsive in America is not the extreme freedom reigning there but the shortage of guarantees against tyranny.

When a man or a party suffers an injustice in the United States, to whom can he turn? To public opinion? That is what forms the majority. To the legislative body? It represents the majority and obeys it blindly. To the executive power? It is appointed by the majority and serves as its passive instrument. To the police? They are nothing but the majority under arms. A jury? The jury is the majority vested with the right to pronounce judgment; even the judges in certain states are elected by the majority. So, however iniquitous or unreasonable the measure which hurts you, you must submit.

But suppose you were to have a legislative body so composed that it represented the majority without being necessarily the slave of its passions, an executive power having a strength of its own, and a judicial power independent of the other two authorities; then you would still have a democratic government, but there would be hardly any remaining risk of tyranny.

I am not asserting that at the present time in America there are frequent acts of tyranny. I do say that one can find no guarantee against it there and that the reasons for the government's gentleness must be sought in circumstances and in mores rather than in the laws.

It is when one comes to look into the use made of thought in the United States that one most clearly sees how far the power of the majority goes beyond all powers known to us in Europe.

Thought is an invisible power and one almost impossible to lay hands on, which makes sport of all tyrannies. In our day the most absolute sovereigns in Europe cannot prevent certain thoughts hostile to their power from silently circulating in their states and even in their own courts. It is not like that in America; while the majority is in doubt, one talks; but when it has irrevocably pronounced, everyone is silent, and friends and enemies alike seem to make for its bandwagon. The reason is simple: no monarch is so absolute that he can hold all the forces of society in his hands and overcome all resistance, as a majority invested with the right to make the laws and to execute them can do.

I know no country in which, speaking generally, there is less independence of mind and true freedom of discussion than in America.

There is no religious or political theory which one cannot preach freely in the constitutional states of Europe or which does not penetrate into the others, for there is no country in Europe so subject to a single power that he who wishes to speak the truth cannot find support enough to protect him against the consequences of his independence. If he is unlucky enough to live under an absolute government, he often has the people with him; if he lives in a free country, he may at need find shelter behind the royal authority. In democratic countries the aristocracy may support him, and in other lands the democracy. But in a democracy organized on the model of the United States there is only one authority, one source of strength and of success, and nothing outside it.

In America the majority has enclosed thought within a formidable fence. A writer is free inside that area, but woe to the man who goes beyond it. Not that he stands in fear of an *auto-da-fé*, but he must face all kinds of unpleasantness and everyday persecution. A career in politics is closed to him, for he has offended the only power that holds the keys. He is denied everything, including renown. Before he goes into print, he believes he has supporters; but he feels that he has them no more once he stands revealed to all, for those who condemn him express their views loudly, while those who think as he does, but without his courage, retreat into silence as if ashamed of having told the truth.

Formerly tyranny used the clumsy weapons of chains and hangmen; nowadays even despotism, though it seemed to have nothing more to learn, has been perfected by civilization. . . .

The influence of what I have been talking about is as yet only weakly felt in political society, but its ill effects on the national character are already apparent. I think that the rareness now of outstanding men on the political scene is due to the ever-increasing despotism of the American majority.

Governments ordinarily break down either through impotence or through tyranny. In the first case power slips from their grasp, whereas in the second it is taken from them.

Many people, seeing democratic states fall into anarchy, have supposed that government in such states was by nature weak and impotent. The truth is that once war has broken out between the parties, government influence over society ceases. But I do not think a lack of strength or resources is part of the nature of democratic authority; on the contrary, I believe that it is almost always the abuse of that strength and the ill use of those resources which bring it down. Anarchy is almost always a consequence either of the tyranny or of the inability of democracy, but not of its impotence.

One must not confuse stability with strength or a thing's size with its duration. In democratic republics the power directing society is not stable, for both its personnel and its aims change often. But wherever it is brought to bear, its strength is almost irresistible.

The government of the American republics seems to me as centralized and more energetic than the absolute monarchies of Europe. So I do not think that it will collapse from weakness.

If ever freedom is lost in America, that will be due to the omnipotence of the majority driving the minorities to desperation and forcing them to appeal to physical force. We may then see anarchy, but it will have come as the result of despotism.

Questions for Understanding and Discussion

1.   What did various American states and the federal Constitution do to make legislative bodies even more responsive to the wishes of the majority than the basic principle of democracy might demand?

2.   Why are Americans, more than members of more traditional societies, likely to recognize the rights of the majority?

3.   On what grounds does Tocqueville expect to find greater legislative instability in the United States than in other countries?

4.   Explain why the author, unlike others, is more fearful of the power of democratic regimes than of their weakness.

5.   How do you react to Tocqueville's assertion that there is more mind control in this country than in any other?

6.   What is his explanation for his observation that few truly outstanding individuals seek political office in this country?

7.   How, according to Tocqueville, might the "omnipotence" of the majority lead to anarchy?

8.   Of the various observations presented here by Tocqueville, which ones seem to you particularly relevant today? Why?

PART THREE
Institutions of Government

CHAPTER 11

Congress

REVIEWING THE CHAPTER

CHAPTER FOCUS

The central purpose of this chapter is to describe the Framers' understanding of the role of Congress and to describe the role and organization of Congress today. You should pay particular attention to the effects of organizational characteristics on the behavior of members of Congress and on the way that the House and the Senate perform their functions. After reading and reviewing the material in this chapter, you should be able to do each of the following:

1. Explain the differences between Congress and Parliament.

2. Delineate the role that the Framers expected Congress to play.

3. Pinpoint the significant eras in the evolution of Congress.

4. Describe the characteristics of members of Congress.

5. Discuss the relationship between ideology and civility in Congress in recent years.

6. Identify the factors that help to explain why a member of Congress votes as she or he does.

7. Outline the process for electing members of Congress.

8. Identify the functions of party affiliation in the organization of Congress.

9. Explain the effect of committee reform on the organization of Congress.

10. Describe the formal process by which a bill becomes a law.

11. Explain the ethical problems confronting Congress.

STUDY OUTLINE

I.   Congress: the "first branch"
     A.   This branch has considerable power
     B.   Many consider this branch to be the one most badly in need of repair
     C.   The puzzles, processes and actions of this branch say a great deal about America's representative democracy
II. Congress versus Parliament
     A.   Parliamentary candidates are selected by party
          1.   Members of Parliament select prime minister and other leaders

2. Party members vote together on most issues
3. Renomination depends on loyalty to party
4. Principal work is debating national issues
5. Very little power, very little pay

B. Congressional candidates run in a primary election, with little party control
1. Vote is for the man or woman, not the party
2. Result is a body of independent representatives
3. Members do not choose the president
4. Principal work is representation and action
5. Great deal of power, high pay; parties cannot discipline members

C. Congress a decentralized institution
1. Members more concerned with their views and views of their constituents
2. Members less concerned with organized parties and program proposals of president

D. Congress can be unpopular with voters

III. The evolution of Congress
A. Intent of the Framers
1. To oppose concentration of power in a single institution
2. To balance large and small states: bicameralism

B. Traditional criticism: Congress is too slow
1. Centralization needed for quick and decisive action
2. Decentralization needed if congressional constituency interests are to be dominant

C. Development of the House
1. Always powerful but varied in organization and leadership
   a) Powerful Speakers
   b) Powerful committee chairmen
   c) Powerful individual members
2. Ongoing dilemmas
   a) Increases in size have lead to the need for centralization and less individual influence
   b) Desire for individual influence has led to institutional weakness

D. Development of the Senate
1. Structural advantages over the House
   a) Small enough to be run without giving authority to small group of leaders
   b) Interests more carefully balanced
   c) No time limits on speakers or committee control of debate
   d) Senators not elected by voters until this century
      (1) Chosen by state legislators
      (2) Often leaders of local party organizations
2. Major changes
   a) Demand for direct popular election
      (1) Intense political maneuvering and the Millionaire's Club
      (2) Senate opposition and the threat of a constitutional convention
      (3) 17th Amendment approved in 1913
   b) Filibuster restricted by Rule 22 – though tradition of unlimited debate remains

IV. Who is in Congress?
A. The beliefs and interests of members of Congress can affect policy
B. Sex and race
1. House has become less male and less white
2. Senate has been slower to change, but several blacks and Hispanics hold powerful positions
C. Incumbency

1. Low turnover rates and safe districts common in Congress before 1980s
2. Incumbents increasingly viewed as professional politicians and out of touch with the people by the 1980s
3. Call for term limits; however, natural forces were doing what term limits were designed to do by the mid-1990s
4. Influx of new members should not distort incumbents' advantage

D. Party
   1. Democrats are beneficiaries of incumbency
   2. Gap between votes and seats: Republican vote higher than number of seats won
      a) One explanation: Democratic legislatures redraw district lines to favor Democratic candidates
      b) But research does not support; Republicans run best in high turnout districts, Democrats in low turnout ones
      c) Another explanation: incumbent advantage increasing
      d) But not the reason; Democrats field better candidates whose positions are closer to those of voters
   3. Advantages of incumbency for Democrats turn into disadvantages by the 1990s
   4. Republicans win control of Congress in 1994
   5. Republicans replace conservative Democrats in the South during the 1990s
   6. More party unity, especially in the House, since the 1990s

V. Do members represent their voters?
   A. Representational view
      1. Assumes that members vote to please their constituents
      2. Constituents must have a clear opinion of the issue
         a) Very strong correlation on civil rights and social welfare bills
         b) Very weak correlation on foreign policy
      3. May be conflict between legislator and constituency on certain measures: gun control, Panama Canal treaty, abortion
      4. Constituency influence more important in Senate votes
      5. Members in marginal districts as independent as those in safe districts
      6. Weakness of representational explanation: no clear opinion in the constituency
   B. Organizational view
      1. Assumes members of Congress vote to please colleagues
      2. Organizational cues
         a) Party
         b) Ideology
      3. Problem is that party and other organizations do not have a clear position on all issues
      4. On minor votes most members influenced by party members on sponsoring committees
   C. Attitudinal view
      1. Assumes that ideology affects a legislator's vote
      2. House members tend more than senators to have opinions similar to those of the public.
         a) 1970s: senators more liberal
         b) 1980s: senators more conservative
      3. Prior to 1990s, southern Democrats often aligned with Republicans to form a conservative coalition.
      4. Conservative coalition no longer as important since most southerners are Republicans
   D. Ideology and civility in Congress
      1. Members of Congress more sharply divided ideologically than they once were
      2. New members of Congress are more ideological

3. Members of Congress more polarized than voters
    a) Democrats more liberal/Republicans more conservative
    b) Voters closer to center of political spectrum
4. Members of Congress (especially the House) do not get along as well as they once did.
VI. The organization of Congress: parties and caucuses
   A. Party organization of the Senate
      1. President pro tempore presides; member with most seniority in majority party
      2. Leaders are the majority leader and the minority leader, elected by their respective party members
      3. Party whips keep leaders informed, round up votes, count noses
      4. Policy Committee schedules Senate business
      5. Committee assignments
         a) Democratic Steering Committee
         b) Republican Committee on Committees
         c) Emphasize ideological and regional balance
         d) Other factors: popularity, effectiveness on television, favors owed
   B. Party structure in the House
      1. Speaker of the House as leader of majority party; presides over House
         a) Decides whom to recognize to speak on the floor
         b) Rules of germaneness of motions
         c) Decides to which committee bills go
         d) Appoints members of special and select committees
         e) Has some patronage power
      2. Majority leader and minority leader
      3. Party whip organizations
      4. Democratic Steering and Policy Committee, chaired by Speaker
         a) Makes committee assignments
         b) Schedules legislation
      5. Republican Committee on Committees; makes committee assignments
      6. Republican Policy Committee; discusses policy
      7. Democratic and Republican congressional campaign committees
   C. The strength of party structure
      1. Loose measure is ability of leaders to determine party rules and organization
      2. Tested in 103d Congress: 110 new members
         a) Ran as outsiders
         b) Yet reelected entire leadership and committee chairs
      3. Senate different since transformed by changes in norms, not rules: now less party centered, less leader oriented, more hospitable to new members
   D. Party unity
      1. Recent trends
         a) Party unity voting higher between 1953 and 1965 and lower between 1966 and 1982
         b) Party unity voting increased since 1983 and was norm in the 1990s
         c) Party unity voting lower today than in the 1800s and early 1900s
         d) Party splits today may reflect sharp ideological differences between parties (or at least their respective leaders)
      2. Such strong differences in opinion are not so obvious among the public
         a) Impeachment vote did not reflect public opinion
         b) Congressional Democrats and Republicans also more sharply divided on abortion
      3. Why are congressional Democrats and Republicans so liberal and conservative?
         a) Most districts are drawn to protect partisan interests

          (1)   Few are truly competitive

          (2)   Primary elections count for more and ideological voters are more common in such a low turnout environment

      b)   Voters may be taking cues from the liberal and conservative votes of members of Congress

      c)   Committee chairs are typically chosen on the basis of seniority

          (1)   They are also usually from safe districts

          (2)   And hold views shaped by lifetime dedication to the cause of their party

   E.   Caucuses: rivals to parties in policy formulation

      1.   No longer supported by public funds

      2.   Six types

VII. The organization of Congress: committees

   A.   Legislative committees—most important organizational feature of Congress

      1.   Consider bills or legislative proposals

      2.   Maintain oversight of executive agencies

      3.   Conduct investigations

   B.   Types of committees

      1.   Select committees—groups appointed for a limited purpose and limited duration

      2.   Joint committees—those on which both representatives and senators serve

      3.   Conference committee—a joint committee appointed to resolve differences in the Senate and House versions of the same piece of legislation before final passage

      4.   Standing committees—most important type of committee

         a)   Majority party has majority of seats on the committees

         b)   Each member usually serves on two standing committees

         c)   Chairs are elected, but usually the most senior member of the committee is elected by the majority party

         d)   Subcommittee "bill of rights" of 1970s changed several traditions

           (1)   Opened more meetings to the public

           (2)   Allowed television coverage of meetings

           (3)   Effort to reduce number of committees in 1995–1996

   C.   Committee styles

      1.   Decentralization has increased individual member's influence

         a)   Less control by chairs

         b)   More amendments proposed and adopted

      2.   Ideological orientations of committees vary, depending on attitudes of members

      3.   Certain committees tend to attract particular types of legislators

         a)   Policy-oriented members

         b)   Constituency-oriented members

VIII. The organization of Congress: staffs and specialized offices

   A.   Tasks of staff members

      1.   Constituency service: major task of staff

      2.   Legislative functions: monitoring hearings, devising proposals, drafting reports, meeting with lobbyists

      3.   Staff members consider themselves advocates of their employers

   B.   Growth and influence of staff

      1.   Rapid growth: a large staff itself requires a large staff

      2.   Larger staff generates more legislative work

      3.   Members of Congress can no longer keep up with increased legislative work and so must rely on staff

      4.   Results in a more individualistic Congress

   C.   Staff agencies offer specialized information

       1.   Congressional Research Service (CRS)
       2.   General Accounting Office (GAO)
       3.   Office of Technology Assessment (OTA)
       4.   Congressional Budget Office (CBO)

IX.   How a bill becomes law
   A.   Bills travel through Congress at different speeds
       1.   Bills to spend money or to tax or regulate business move slowly
       2.   Bills with a clear, appealing idea move fast
            Examples: "Stop drugs," "End scandal"
   B.   Introducing a bill
       1.   Introduced by a member of Congress: hopper in House, recognized in Senate
       2.   Most legislation has been initiated in Congress
       3.   Presidentially-drafted legislation is shaped by Congress
       4.   Resolutions
            a)   Simple—passed by one house affecting that house
            b)   Concurrent—passed by both houses affecting both
            c)   Joint—passed by both houses, signed by president (except for constitutional amendments)
   C.   Study by committees
       1.   Bill is referred to a committee for consideration by either Speaker or presiding officer
       2.   Revenue bills must originate in the House
       3.   Most bills die in committee
       4.   Hearings are often conducted by several subcommittees: multiple referrals (replaced by sequential referral system in 1995)
       5.   Markup of bills—bills are revised by committees
       6.   Committee reports a bill out to the House or Senate
            a)   If bill is not reported out, the House can use the discharge petition
            b)   If bill is not reported out, the Senate can pass a discharge motion
       7.   House Rules Committee sets the rules for consideration
            a)   Closed rule: sets time limit on debate and restricts amendments
            b)   Open rule: permits amendments from the floor
            c)   Restrictive rule: permits only some amendments
            d)   Use of closed and restrictive rules growing
            e)   Rules can be bypassed by the House
            f)   No direct equivalent in Senate
   D.   Floor debate, House
       1.   Committee of the Whole—procedural device for expediting House consideration of bills but cannot pass bills
       2.   Committee sponsor of bill organizes the discussion
   E.   Floor debate, Senate
       1.   No rule limiting debate or germaneness
       2.   Entire committee hearing process can be bypassed by a senator
       3.   Cloture—sets time limit on debate—three-fifths of Senate must vote for a cloture petition
       4.   Both filibusters and cloture votes becoming more common
            a)   Easier now to stage filibuster
            b)   Roll calls are replacing long speeches
            c)   But can be curtailed by "double tracking"—disputed bill is shelved temporarily—making filibuster less costly
   F.   Methods of voting

1. To investigate voting behavior one must know how a legislator voted on amendments as well as on the bill itself.
2. Procedures for voting in the House
   a) Voice vote
   b) Division vote
   c) Teller vote
   d) Roll call vote
3. Senate voting is the same except no teller vote
4. Differences in Senate and House versions of a bill
   a) If minor, last house to act merely sends bill to the other house, which accepts the changes
   b) If major, a conference committee is appointed
      (1) Decisions are made by a majority of each delegation; Senate version favored
      (2) Conference reports back to each house for acceptance or rejection
5. Bill, in final form, goes to the president
   a) President may sign it
   b) If president vetoes it, it returns to the house of origin
      (1) Either house may override the president by a vote of two-thirds of those present
      (2) If both override, the bill becomes law without the president's signature

X. Reducing power and perks
   A. Many proposals made to "reform" and "improve" Congress
   B. Common perception it is overstaffed and self-indulgent
      1. Quick to regulate others, but not itself
      2. Quick to pass pork barrel legislation but slow to address controversial questions of national policy
      3. Use of franking privilege to subsidize personal campaigns
         a) Proposals to abolish it
         b) Proposals for restrictions on timing of mailings and a taxpayer "notice"
   C. Congressional Accountability Act of 1995
      1. For years Congress routinely exempted itself from many of the laws it passed
      2. Concern for enforcement (by Executive branch) and separation of powers
      3. 1995 Act
         a) Obliged Congress to obey eleven major laws
         b) Created the Office of Compliance
         c) Established an employee grievance procedure
   D. Trimming the pork
      1. Main cause of deficit is entitlement programs, not pork
      2. Some spending in districts represents needed projects
      3. Members supposed to advocate interests of district
      4. Price of citizen-oriented Congress is pork

XI. Ethics and Congress
   A. Separation of powers and corruption
      1. Fragmentation of power increases number of officials with opportunity to sell influence. Example: senatorial courtesy offers opportunity for office seeker to influence a senator
      2. Forms of influence
         a) Money
         b) Exchange of favors
   B. Problem of defining unethical conduct

1.   Violation of criminal law is obviously unethical
    a)   Since 1941, over one hundred charges of misconduct
    b)   Most led to convictions, resignations, or retirements
    c)   Ethics codes and related reforms enacted in 1978, 1989, and 1995 have placed members of Congress under tight rules
2.   Other issues are more difficult.
    a)   A substantial outside income from speaking and writing does not necessarily lead to vote corruption.
    b)   Personal friendships and alliances can have an undue influence on votes.
    c)   Bargaining among members of Congress may involve exchange of favors and votes.

XII.   Summary: The old and the new Congress
  A.   House has evolved through three stages
    1.   Mid-1940s to early 1960s
      a)   Powerful committee chairs, mostly from the South
      b)   Long apprenticeships for new members
      c)   Small congressional staffs
    2.   Early 1970s to early 1980s
      a)   Spurred by civil rights efforts of younger, mostly northern members
      b)   Growth in size of staffs
      c)   Committees became more democratic
      d)   More independence for members
      e)   Focus on reelection
      f)   More amendments and filibusters
    3.   Early 1980s to present
      a)   Strengthening and centralizing party leadership
      b)   Became apparent under Jim Wright
      c)   Return to more accommodating style under Tom Foley
    4.   Senate meanwhile has remained decentralized throughout this period
  B.   Reassertion of congressional power in 1970s
    1.   Reaction to Vietnam and Watergate
    2.   War Powers Act of 1973
    3.   Congressional Budget and Impoundment Act of 1974
    4.   Increased requirement for legislative veto
  C.   Congressional power never as weak as critics have alleged

KEY TERMS MATCH

Set 1

Match the following terms and descriptions:

1.   The system under which committee chairs are awarded to members who have the longest continuous service on the committee

2.   An assembly of party representatives that chooses a government and discusses major national issues

3.   An alliance of conservative Democrats with Republicans for voting purposes

    a.   bicameral legislature
    b.   closed rule
    c.   cloture rule
    d.   Committee on Committees
    e.   congressional caucus
    f.   conservative coalition

4. Indicated by votes in which a majority of voting Democrats oppose a majority of voting Republicans.

5. A rule issued by the Rules Committee that does not allow a bill to be amended on the House floor

6. A means by which senators can extend debate on a bill in order to prevent or delay its consideration

7. A Senate rule offering a means for stopping a filibuster

8. A rule issued by the Rules Committee that permits some amendments to a bill but not to others

9. Committee revisions of a bill

10. An association of members of Congress created to advocate a political ideology or a regional or economic interest

11. An individual who assists the party leader in staying abreast of the concerns and voting intentions of the party members

12. Assigns Republicans to standing committees in the Senate

13. The group that decides what business comes up for a vote and what the limitations on debate should be

14. A means by which the House can remove a bill stalled in committee

15. The process through which a bill is referred to several committees that simultaneously consider it in whole or in part

16. Assigns Democrats to standing committees in the Senate.

17. A meeting of the members of a political party to decide questions of policy

18. The extent to which members of a party vote together in the House or the Senate

19. A lawmaking body composed of two chambers or parts

20. Districts in which the winner got less than 55 percent of the vote

21. Unrelated amendments added to a bill

g. discharge petition
h. filibuster
i. House Rules Committee
j. marginal districts
k. markup
l. Millionaire's Club
m. multiple referral
n. Parliament
o. party caucus
p. party polarization
q. party vote
r. party whip
s. restrictive rule
t. riders
u. safe districts
v. seniority
w. sequential referral
x. Steering Committee

22. Districts in which the winner got more than 55 percent of the vote

23. The process through which a bill is referred to second committee after the first is finished acting

24. A traditional, pejorative name for the United States Senate.

Set 2

Match the following terms and descriptions:

1. The legislative leader elected by party members holding the majority of seats in the House or Senate

2. Congressional committees appointed for a limited time period and purpose

3. The ability of members of Congress to mail letters to their constituents free of charge

4. An association of members of Congress created to advocate a political ideology or a regional, ethnic, or economic interest

5. A congressional voting procedure that consists of members answering yea or nay to their names

6. The legislative leader elected by party members holding a minority of seats in the House or Senate

7. A committee on which both representatives and senators serve

8. A resolution used to settle housekeeping and procedural matters in either house but not having the force of law

9. A resolution used to settle housekeeping and procedural matters that affect both houses but not having the force of law

10. Legislation that deals with matters of general concern

11. An order from the Rules Committee in the House that permits a bill to be amended on the legislative floor

12. A method of voting used in both houses in

a. caucus (congressional)

b. Christmas tree bill

c. concurrent resolution

d. conference committees

e. division vote

f. double tracking

g. franking privilege

h. joint committee

i. joint resolution

j. majority leader

k. minority leader

l. open rule

m. pork barrel legislation

n. private bill

o. public bill

p. quorum call

q. roll call vote

r. select committees

s. simple resolution

t. standing committees

u. teller vote

v. voice vote

which members vote by shouting yea or nay

13. A congressional voting procedure in which members pass between two tellers, first the yeas and then the nays

14. A procedure to keep the Senate going during a filibuster; the disputed bill is shelved temporarily

15. A special type of joint committee appointed to resolve differences in the House and Senate versions of a piece of legislation

16. A bill that has many riders

17. A congressional voting procedure in which members stand and are counted

18. The permanent committees of each house with the power to report bills

19. Legislation that deals only with specific matters rather than with general legislative affairs

20. A resolution requiring approval of both houses and the signature of the president and having the same legal status as a law

21. Legislation that gives tangible benefits to constituents in the hope of winning their votes

22. A calling of the role in either house of Congress to determine whether the number of members in attendance meets the minimum number required to conduct official business

DID YOU THINK THAT . . . ?

Below are listed a number of misconceptions. You should be able to refute each statement in the space provided, referring to information or argumentation contained in this chapter. Sample answers appear at the end of this chapter.

1. "The Founders desired and expected the president and Congress to have equal authority."

_____

_____

_____

2.   "In Congress Democrats and Republicans are loyal to their respective parties and vote accordingly."

_____

_____

_____

3.   "Most members of Congress must be very sensitive to public opinion in their districts or they will soon find themselves out of a job."

_____

_____

_____

4.   "A good, strong code of ethics would largely eliminate the problems of corruption in Congress."

_____

_____

_____

DATA CHECK

Table 11.1: Blacks, Hispanics, and Women in Congress, 1971–2002

1.   Which chamber generally features a greater number of blacks, Hispanics, and women?

_____

2.   Which Congress featured the greatest number of blacks in the House of Representatives?

_____

3.   Which Congress featured the greatest number of women in the Senate?

_____

Table 11.2: Incumbents in Congress Reelected by 60 Percent or More

4.   What is the lowest number of House incumbents that have run for reelection in any given year from 1956–1998?

_____

5.   In which years have at least 75 percent of House incumbents running for reelection received at least 60 percent of the vote?

_____

6.   When is the last time less than 60 percent of House members running for reelection received at least 60 percent of the vote?

_____

Table 11.4: Party Polarization in Congress, 1953–2000

7.   How many times between 1953 and 1965 did a majority of all House votes pit a majority of voting Democrats against a majority of voting Republicans? How many times in the Senate?

_____

8.   How many times between 1966 and 1982 did a majority of all House votes pit a majority of voting Democrats against a majority of voting Republicans? How many times in the Senate?

_____

9.   How many times between 1983 and 2000 did a majority of all House votes pit a majority of voting Democrats against a majority of voting Republicans? How many times in the Senate?

_____

Figure 11.4: The Growth in Staff of Members and Committees in Congress, 1930–2000

10.   Describe trends in staff membership from 1930 to 1955.

_____

11.   Describe trends in staff membership from 1960 to 1980.

_____

12.   Describe trends in staff membership from 1980 to 2000.

_____

PRACTICING FOR EXAMS

TRUE/FALSE QUESTIONS

Read each statement carefully. Mark true statements *T*. If any part of the statement is false, mark it *F*, and write in the space provided a concise explanation of why the statement is false.

1.   T   F   Congress was designed by the Founders in ways that almost inevitably make it popular with voters.

_____

2.   T   F   By the end of the nineteenth century, the House was known as the "Millionaire's Club."

_____

3.   T   F   The Senate agreed to a constitutional amendment that changed the manner in which its members were elected.

_____

4.   T   F   Conservatives in the Senate used the filibuster for both lofty and self-serving purposes.

_____

5.   T   F   The tradition of unlimited debate remains strong in the Senate.

_____

6.   T   F   Senators are more likely to lose bids for reelection than members of the House.

_____

7.   T   F   In every election from 1968 to 1998, Republicans have gathered a higher percentage of the popular vote than they have the percentage of seats in the House of Representatives.

_____

8.   T   F   Democrats tend to do exceptionally well in low turnout districts.

_____

9.   T   F   Gary Jacobson's research indicates Democrats tend to field more experienced candidates in congressional races.

_____

10.   T   F   During the 1980s about forty members of Congress were charged with misconduct.

_____

11.   T   F   A member's final vote on a bill may conceal as much as it reveals.

_____

12.   T   F   Senators are often less in tune with public opinion than members of the House.

_____

13.   T   F   The Senate highlights the fact that the Republican party is more deeply divided than the Democratic party.

_____

14.   T   F   Today, members of the House are more likely to investigate and denounce each other.

_____

15.   T   F   The 2000 election created an evenly divided Senate.

_____

16.   T   F   Leadership carries more power in the Senate than in the House.

_____

17.   T   F   The votes of Republicans on the four impeachment articles against President Clinton did not even represent the views of their districts.

_____

18.   T   F   In a typical Congress about several hundred bills are introduced.

_____

19.   T   F   Pending legislation does not carry over from one Congress to the next.

_____

20.   T   F   Most bills that die in committee are often introduced only to get publicity for a member of Congress.

_____

21.   T   F   What the filibuster means in practice is that neither political party can control the Senate unless it has at least sixty votes.

_____

22.   T   F   Most bills require a conference of committees from each house.

_____

23.   T   F   Conferences tend to report bills that favor the Senate version.

_____

24.   T   F   In most instances, the conference report on a bill is accepted by the respective chambers.

_____

25.   T   F   The text suggests that the only way to get rid of congressional "pork" is to eliminate Congress altogether and replace it with a tightly controlled parliament.

_____

MULTIPLE CHOICE QUESTIONS

Circle the letter of the response that best answers the question or completes the statement.

1.   A person ordinarily becomes a candidate for representative or senator by

   a.   appealing to party leaders.
   b.   serving first in the state legislature.
   c.   serving in the state judiciary.
   d.   running in a primary election.
   e.   serving first in a government agency.

2.   Whereas the principal work of a parliament is debate, that of a congress is

   a.   representation.
   b.   oversight.
   c.   administration.
   d.   investigation.
   e.   discussion.

3.   Contemporary critics of Congress disagree with the Framers' vision of Congress in that the critics

   a.   believe that Congress should normally proceed slowly in its deliberations.
   b.   believe that Congress should rarely act without guidance from the executive branch.
   c.   view Congress as designed to check and balance strong leaders in the executive branch.
   d.   wish to end policy gridlock by making Congress capable of speedily adopting sweeping changes in national policies.
   e.   wish to make changes to prevent the American political system from resembling a parliamentary system.

4.   In the twentieth century the trend in congressional decision-making has been toward

   a.   centralization.
   b.   increasing the power of the Speaker.
   c.   increasing the power of party leaders.
   d.   increasing the power of the president.

e.   decentralization.

5.   Until 1913 senators were

a.   popularly elected.
b.   elected by state legislatures.
c.   appointed by state governors.
d.   selected by the state judiciaries.
e.   elected by the electoral college.

6.   Originally, filibusterers were sixteenth century

a.   auctioneers.
b.   lawyers.
c.   salesmen.
d.   cavalrymen.
e.   pirates.

7.   The typical representative or senator is

a.   white.
b.   male.
c.   protestant.
d.   a lawyer.
e.   All of the above.

8.   In 1994 Native American Ben Nighthorse Campbell

a.   was elected to the Senate.
b.   was elected to the House.
c.   used radio programs to argue persuasively in favor of term limits.
d.   was allowed to fill a congressional seat as the result of a resignation.
e.   ran for seats in the House and the Senate simultaneously.

9.   Political scientists define a "safe" district as one where the incumbent received ___ percent or more of the vote in the previous election.

a.   50
b.   55
c.   60
d.   65
e.   80

10. During the 1950s and 1960s, the Senate was dominated by

a.   northern senators.
b.   liberal senators.
c.   conservative Republicans.
d.   southern senators.
e.   freshman senators.

11. From the middle 1960s to the late 1970s, the Senate was dominated by

a.   northern senators.
b.   liberal senators.
c.   conservative Republicans.
d.   southern senators.
e.   freshman senators.

12. The real leadership in the Senate rests with the

    a. majority leader.
    b. president pro tempore.
    c. managers.
    d. vice president.
    e. Senate whip.

13. In the House the most important position is the

    a. majority leader.
    b. manager.
    c. Speaker.
    d. president pro tempore.
    e. floor leader.

14. In recent years, the Senate has become more hospitable to

    a. lawyers.
    b. ideologues.
    c. partisans.
    d. state legislators.
    e. freshmen.

15. Which statement best describes Democrats and Republicans in Congress since the early 1990s?

    a. They are both are more liberal.
    b. They are both more conservative.
    c. They are both more moderate.
    d. Republicans are more liberal and Democrats are more conservative.
    e. Democrats are more liberal and Republicans are more conservative.

16. An extreme example of party voting was the response to Clinton's 1993 budget plan in which every Republican in the

    a. House voted against it.
    b. Senate voted for it.
    c. House and Senate voted against it.
    d. House and Senate voted for it.
    e. House and Senate refused to vote on the matter at all.

17. The most important organizational feature of Congress is the

    a. party caucus.
    b. floor leader.
    c. committee structure.
    d. legislative leadership program.
    e. congressional campaign committee.

18. Each member of the House usually serves on ___ standing committees.

    a. 2
    b. 3
    c. 4
    d. 6
    e. 7

19. The text suggests that closed rules, proxy voting and strong committee chairmen

    a.   were desired by Democrats, but not the Republicans.
    b.   were a major campaign issue in 1976.
    c.   reduced the number of bills that were introduced in Congress.
    d.   made it easier to get things done.
    e.   enhanced the public reputation of Congress.

20. The Constitution requires that "all bills for raising revenue shall …

    a.   originate in the House of Representatives."
    b.   originate in the Senate."
    c.   originate in Conference Committee."
    d.   require a unanimous vote."
    e.   be exempt from the veto of the President."

21. In the House a stalled bill can be extracted from a committee and brought to the floor by means of

    a.   a discharge petition.
    b.   an extraction bill.
    c.   a committee rule.
    d.   cloture.
    e.   a unanimous consent vote.

22. In recent years the filibuster has occurred more frequently because

    a.   the Senate has increased in size.
    b.   Republicans have gained seats in the Senate.
    c.   Democrats have gained seats in the Senate.
    d.   participants are guaranteed media exposure.
    e.   it is easier to stage one.

23. For years Congress defended the manner in which it exempted itself from many of its own laws by reference to

    a.   federalism.
    b.   bicameralism.
    c.   the separation of powers.
    d.   legislative supremacy.
    e.   the committee structure.

24. According to the text most categories of pork spending have _____ in the last ten or fifteen years.

    a.   decreased
    b.   remained at approximately the same levels
    c.   increased
    d.   slightly increased
    e.   dramatically increased

25. A conference committee is a type of

    a.   standing committee.
    b.   joint committee.
    c.   select committee.
    d.   jurisdiction committee.
    e.   exclusive committee.

ESSAY QUESTIONS

Practice writing extended answers to the following questions. These test your ability to integrate and express the ideas that you have been studying in this chapter.

1. What role did the Founders expect Congress to play in national policy making? Do you think that Congress has generally played that role?

2. Analyze the factors that have led to the decline in party influence in Congress.

3. Identify and discuss the importance of several events since 1911 that have led to an increase in the decentralization of the operation of Congress.

4. Discuss three theories that purport to explain why members of Congress vote as they do.

5. Discuss some of the suggestions to reform the powers and perks of Congress.

ANSWERS TO KEY TERMS MATCH QUESTIONS

Set 1
1. v
2. n
3. f
4. p
5. b
6. h
7. c
8. s
9. k
10. e
11. r
12. d
13. i
14. g
15. m
16. x
17. o
18. q
19. a
20. j
21. t
22. u
23. w
24. l

Set 2
1. j
2. r
3. g
4. a
5. q
6. k

7. h

8. s

9. c

10. o

11. l

12. v

13. u

14. f

15. d

16. b

17. e

18. t

19. n

20. i

21. m

22. p

ANSWERS TO "DID YOU THINK THAT . . . ?" QUESTIONS

1. The Founders wanted Congress to be the dominant institution because of their fear of an executive dictatorship.

2. Party voting in the House is still relatively low because there is little party discipline and because members respond to important constituency interests that may not coincide with the policy of their party.

3. The proportion of House incumbents who have won reelection with at least 60 percent of the vote increased from about three-fifths in the 1950s and early 1960s to three-quarters in the 1970s and to almost nine-tenths in the later 1980s. Even as this trend began to change in 1990, most House districts remained safe. Thus, members of Congress have been relieved of the need to be unusually sensitive to district pressures.

4. The complexity of Congress and its reliance on exchanges of votes in developing a winning coalition in support of a bill leave many opportunities for senators and representatives to take advantage of their positions in unethical ways.

ANSWERS TO DATA CHECK QUESTIONS

1. The House.

2. 106th.

3. 107th.

4. 349.

5. 1970, 1972, 1986, 1988, 1990, 1998.

6.   1964.

7.   Six times in the House and two times in the Senate.

8.   Zero, for both the House and the Senate.

9.   Twelve times in the House, eight times in the Senate.

10.   While there were increases, they were slight or quite gradual.

11.   From 1960 to 1980 there was a continuous, sharp increase in the size of staff membership.

12.   From 1980 to 2000 the size of staff membership leveled off and, in some instances, decreased.

ANSWERS TO TRUE/FALSE QUESTIONS

1.   F. The opposite is true.

2.   F. The Senate was known by this title.

3.   T

4.   F. The filibuster has used by both conservatives and liberals.

5.   T

6.   T

7.   T

8.   T

9.   T

10.   T

11.   T

12.   T

13.   F. The Democratic party is in fact more divided that the Republican party.

14.   T

15.   T

16.   F. The opposite is true.

17.   T

18.   F. About 6,000 are introduced each Congress.

19.   T

20.   T

21.   T

22.   F. Very few bills require a conference committee.

23.   T

24.   T

25.   T

ANSWERS TO MULTIPLE CHOICE QUESTIONS

1. d
2. a
3. d
4. e
5. b
6. e
7. e
8. b
9. b
10. d
11. c
12. a
13. c
14. e
15. e
16. c
17. c
18. a
19. d
20. a
21. a
22. e
23. c
24. a
25. b

CHAPTER 12

The Presidency

REVIEWING THE CHAPTER

CHAPTER FOCUS

This chapter introduces you to the institution that has become the hub of American government during its two centuries of history: the presidency. The chapter demonstrates that this institution is unique or at least significantly different from other positions of government leadership. It also surveys the changes that have occurred in the office from the original, limited position intended by the Founders, through historical evolution, and down to the office of the president as we know it today. After reading and reviewing the material in this chapter, you should be able to do each of the following:

1. Explain the differences between the positions of president and prime minister.

2. Discuss the approach of the Founders toward executive power.

3. Sketch the evolution of the presidency from 1789 to the present.

4. List and describe the various offices that make up the office of the president.

5. Review discussions of presidential character and how these relate to the achievements in office of various presidents.

6. Enumerate and discuss the various facets—formal and informal—of presidential power.

STUDY OUTLINE

I. Presidents and prime ministers
   A. Characteristics of parliaments
      1. Parliamentary system twice as common
      2. Chief executive chosen by legislature
      3. Cabinet ministers chosen from among members of parliament
      4. Prime minister remains in power as long as his or her party or coalition maintains a majority in the legislature
   B. Differences
      1. Presidents are often outsiders; prime ministers are always insiders, chosen by party members in parliament
      2. Presidents choose their cabinet from outside Congress; prime ministers choose members of parliament
      3. Presidents have no guaranteed majority in the legislature; prime ministers always have a majority. The United States usually has a divided government.
      4. Presidents and the legislature often work at cross-purposes
         a) Even when one party controls both branches
         b) A consequence of separation of powers
         c) Only Roosevelt and Johnson had much luck with Congress
II. Divided Government

A. Divided versus unified government
  1. Fifteen of twenty-two congressional/presidential elections since 1952 produced divided government
  2. Americans dislike divided government because it can lead to gridlock.
B. Does gridlock matter?
  1. But divided government enacts as many important laws as a unified government
  2. Reason: Unified government is something of a myth in U.S.
C. Is policy gridlock bad?
  1. Unclear whether gridlock is always bad; it is a necessary consequence of representative democracy
  2. Representative democracy opposite direct democracy
III. The evolution of the presidency
A. Delegates feared both anarchy and monarchy
  1. Idea of a plural executive
  2. Idea of an executive checked by a council
B. Concerns of the Founders
  1. Fear of military power of president who could overpower states
  2. Fear of presidential corruption of Senate
  3. Fear of presidential bribery to ensure reelection
C. The electoral college
  1. Each state to choose own method for selecting electors
  2. Electors to meet in own capital to vote for president and vice president
  3. If no majority, House would decide
D. The president's term of office
  1. Precedent of George Washington and two terms
  2. Twenty-second Amendment in 1951 limits to two terms
  3. Problem of establishing the legitimacy of the office
  4. Provision for orderly transfer of power
E. The first presidents
  1. Prominent men helped provide legitimacy
  2. Minimal activism of early government contributed to lessening fear of the presidency
  3. Appointed people of stature in the community (rule of fitness)
  4. Relations with Congress were reserved; few vetoes, no advice
F. The Jacksonians
  1. Jackson sought to maximize powers of presidency
  2. Vigorous use of veto for policy reasons
  3. Challenged Congress
G. The reemergence of Congress
  1. With brief exceptions the next hundred years was a period of congressional ascendancy
  2. Intensely divided public opinion
  3. Only Lincoln expanded presidential power
    a) Asserted "implied powers" and power of commander in chief
    b) Justified by emergency conditions
  4. President mostly a negative force to Congress until the New Deal
  5. Since the 1930s power has been institutionalized in the presidency
  6. Popular conception of the president as the center of government contradicts reality; Congress often policy leader
IV. The powers of the president
A. Formal powers found in Article II
  1. Not a large number of explicit powers

          2.   Potential for power found in ambiguous clauses of the Constitution, such as power as commander in chief and duty to "take care that laws be faithfully executed"
    B.   Greatest source of power lies in politics and public opinion
          1.   Increase in broad statutory authority
          2.   Expectation of presidential leadership from the public

V.   The office of the president
    A.   The White House Office
          1.   Contains the president's closest assistants
          2.   Three types of organization
              a)   Circular
              b)   Pyramid
              c)   Ad hoc
          3.   Staff typically worked on the campaign: a few are experts
          4.   Relative influence of staff depends on how close one's office is to the president's
    B.   The Executive Office of the President
          1.   Composed of agencies that report directly to the president
          2.   Appointments must receive Senate confirmation
          3.   Office of Management and Budget most important
               a)   Assembles the budget
               b)   Develops reorganization plans
               c)   Reviews legislative proposals of agencies
    C.   The cabinet
          1.   Largely a fiction, not mentioned in Constitution
          2.   President appoints or controls more members of cabinet than does prime minister
          3.   Secretaries become preoccupied and defensive about their own departments
    D.   Independent agencies, commissions, and judgeships
          1.   President appoints members of agencies that have a quasi-independent status
          2.   Agency heads serve a fixed term and can be removed only "for cause"
          3.   Judges can be removed only by impeachment

VI.   Who gets appointed
    A.   President knows few appointees personally
    B.   Most appointees have had federal experience
          1.   "In-and-outers"; alternate federal and private sector jobs
          2.   No longer have political followings but picked for expertise
    C.   Need to consider important interest groups when making appointments
    D.   Rivalry between department heads and White House staff

VII.   Presidential character
    A.   Eisenhower: orderly
    B.   Kennedy: improviser
    C.   Johnson: dealmaker
    D.   Nixon: mistrustful
    E.   Ford: genial
    F.   Carter: outsider
    G.   Reagan: communicator
    H.   Bush: hands-on manager
    I.   Clinton: focus on details
    J.   Bush: a different kind of outsider

VIII.   The power to persuade
    A.   Formal opportunities for persuasion
    B.   The three audiences
          1.   Other politicians and leaders in Washington, D.C.; reputation very important

        2.   Party activists and officials inside Washington

        3.   The various publics

   C.   Popularity and influence

        1.   Presidents try to transform popularity into support in Congress

        2.   Little effect of presidential coattails

        3.   Members of Congress believe it is politically risky to challenge a popular president

        4.   Popularity is unpredictable and influenced by factors beyond the president's control.

   D.   The decline in popularity

        1.   Popularity highest immediately after an election

        2.   Declines by midterm after honeymoon period

IX.   The power to say no

   A.   Veto

        1.   Veto message

        2.   Pocket veto (only before end of Congress)

        3.   Congress rarely overrided vetoes in 1996

   B.   Executive privilege

        1.   Confidential communications between president and advisers

        2.   Justification

            a)   Separation of powers

            b)   Need for candid advice

        3.   *U.S. v. Nixon* (1973) rejects claim of absolute executive privilege

   C.   Impoundment of funds

        1.   Defined: presidential refusal to spend funds appropriated by Congress

        2.   Countered by Budget Reform Act of 1974

            a)   Requires president to notify Congress of funds he does not intend to spend

            b)   Congress must agree in forty-five days

X.   The president's program

   A.   Putting together a program

        1.   President can try to have a policy on everything (Carter)

        2.   President can concentrate on a small number of initiatives (Reagan)

        3.   Constraints

            a)   Public reaction may be adverse

            b)   Limited time and attention span

            c)   Unexpected crises

            d)   Programs can be changed only marginally

        4.   Need for president to be selective about what he wants

        5.   Heavy reliance on opinion polls

        6.   Impact of dramatic events and prolonged crises

   B.   Attempts to reorganize the executive branch

        1.   An item on presidential agendas since the administration of Herbert Hoover

        2.   Bush and the Department of Homeland Defense

            a)   White House Office of Homeland Security created in aftermath of terrorist attack of September 11

                (1)   Small staff

                (2)   Little budgetary authority

                (3)   No ability to enforce decisions

            b)   Bush's call for a reorganization

                (1)   Creation of third largest cabinet department encompassing twenty-two federal agencies

                (2)   170,000 employees and an annual budget of almost $40 million

            c)   Fate of proposal is pending, but it is neither the first of its kind nor the largest

        3.   Reasons for reorganizing
           a)   Large number of agencies
           b)   Easier to change policy through reorganization
        4.   Reorganization outside the White House staff must be by law

XI. Presidential transition

    A.   Few presidents serve two terms

    B.   The vice president
        1.   May succeed on death of president
           a)   Has happened eight times
           b)   John Tyler defined status of ascending vice president: president in title and in powers
        2.   Rarely are vice presidents elected president
           a)   Unless they first took over for a president who died
           b)   Only five instances otherwise: Adams, Jefferson, Van Buren, Nixon, and Bush
        3.   "A rather empty job"
           a)   Candidates still pursue it
           b)   Preside over Senate and vote in case of a tie
           c)   Leadership powers in Senate are weak

    C.   Problems of succession
        1.   What if the president falls ill?
           Examples: Garfield, Wilson

        2.   If vice president steps up, who becomes vice president?
           a)   Succession Act (1886): designated secretary of state as next in line
           b)   Amended in 1947 to designate Speaker of the House
        3.   Twenty-fifth Amendment resolved both issues
           a)   Allows vice president to serve as "acting president" if president is disabled; decided by president, by vice president and cabinet, or by two-thirds vote of Congress
           b)   Requires vice president who ascends to office on death or resignation of the president to name a vice president
               (1)   Must be confirmed by both houses
               (2)   Examples: Agnew and Nixon resignations

    D.   Impeachment
        1.   Judges most frequent targets of impeachment
        2.   Indictment by the House, conviction by the Senate

XII. How powerful is the president?

    A.   Both president and Congress are constrained

    B.   Reasons for constraints
        1.   Complexity of issues
        2.   Scrutiny of the media
        3.   Power of interest groups

KEY TERMS MATCH

Match the following terms and descriptions:

1. A constitutional procedure by which federal judges and civil officers can be removed from office before their terms expire

2. Legislation that specifies the conditions and order of succession to the presidency and vice presidency when the president leaves office before completion of his term

3. People who alternate between jobs in the federal government and employment in the private sector

4. Presidential staff who oversee the policy interests of the president

5. A statement sent to Congress by the president giving the reasons for vetoing a bill

6. The chief executive in a parliamentary system who is chosen by the legislature

7. The presidential assertion of the right to withhold certain information from Congress

8. The organization responsible for preparing the federal budget and for central clearance of legislative proposals from federal agencies

9. Agencies headed by appointees who serve for fixed terms and can be removed only "for cause"

10. A presidential refusal to spend money appropriated by Congress

11. Agencies that perform staff services for the president but are not part of the White House

12. View of presidential decision-making which stresses what the public wants

13. The power of some governors (and the president in a limited way between 1996 and 1998) to veto portions of a bill instead of having to veto the entire bill

14. A legal system by which states select electors who then vote for the president and vice president

15. A statement that defines the constitutional powers of the president

16. A method of organizing a president's staff in which several task forces, committees, and informal groups deal directly with the president

17. A president's council of advisers

a. ad hoc structure
b. Article II
c. cabinet
d. circular structure
e. delegate
f. direct democracy
g. divided government
h. electoral college
i. Executive Office of the President
j. Executive privilege
k. impeachment
l. impoundment of funds
m. "in-and-outers"
n. independent agencies
o. lame duck
p. legislative veto
q. line-item veto
r. Office of Management and Budget
s. perks
t. pocket veto
u. prime minister
v. pyramid structure
w. representative democracy
x. trustee
y. Twenty-fifth Amendment
z. unified government
aa. veto message
bb. White House Office

18. A method of organizing a president's staff in which several presidential assistants report directly to the president

19. View of presidential decision making which stresses what the public interest requires

20. A political system in which all or most citizens participate directly by either holding office or making policy

21. A government in which one party controls the White House and another party controls one or both houses of Congress

22. A politician who is still in office after having lost a reelection bid

23. The rejection of a presidential or administrative action by a vote of one or both houses of Congress without the consent of the president

24. The fringe benefits of holding an office

25. A form of veto in which the president fails to sign a bill passed by both houses within ten days and Congress has adjourned during that time

26. A method of organizing a president's staff in which most presidential assistants report through a hierarchy to the president's chief of staff

27. A political system in which leaders and representatives acquire political power by means of a competitive struggle for the people's vote

28. A government in which the same party controls the White House and both houses of Congress

DID YOU THINK THAT . . . ?

Below are listed a number of misconceptions. You should be able to refute each statement in the space provided, referring to information or argumentation contained in this chapter. Sample answers appear at the end of this chapter.

1. "The president has clear-cut authority over executive agencies and only needs to be urged to exercise it."

_____

_____

_____

2. "Because members of Congress generally win their seats on the strength of their individual efforts and not by riding the president's coattails, they do not pay special attention to the president on legislative matters."

_____

_____

3. "Presidents are constitutionally required to share all their information with Congress."

_____

_____

_____

4. "Presidential powers under the Constitution are complete."

_____

_____

_____

DATA CHECK

Table 12.3: Partisan Gains or Losses in Congress in Presidential Election Years

1. What hypothesis underlies the table?

_____

2. What does the 1956 election suggest about the popularity of Eisenhower (who won 57% of the popular vote) and the popularity of the Republican party as an institution?

_____

3. In which election was the greatest number of seats gained by the president's party in the House of Representatives?

_____

4. In which election was the greatest number of seats gained by the president's party in the Senate?

_____

5. In which election was the greatest number of seats lost by the president's party in the House of Representatives?

_____

Figure 12.2: Presidential Popularity

6. What question was asked of respondents in order to collect the data presented in this Figure?

_____

7. In which terms was it quite clear that the president was not as popular at the end of his term as he was at the very beginning?

_____

8. What do the terms that do not exhibit the trend identified in the previous question have in common?

_____

Table 12.4: Partisan Gains or Losses in Congress in Off-Year Elections

9. What does Table 12.4 tell us generally?

_____

10. In which election(s) did the party of the president lose more than fifty seats in the House?

_____

11. In which election(s) did the party of the president lose more than fifteen seats in the Senate?

_____

PRACTICING FOR EXAMS

TRUE/FALSE QUESTIONS

Read each statement carefully. Mark true statements *T*. If any part of the statement is false, mark it *F*, and write in the space provided a concise explanation of why the statement is false.

1. T   F   The general assumption of the Framers of the Constitution was that George Washington would be the first president.

_____

2. T   F   The Framers expected that the House of Representatives would frequently select the President.

_____

3. T   F   Congress decided no president's image would appear on currency until after his death.

_____

4. T   F   Andrew Jackson had been a member of both the House and the Senate.

_____

5. T   F   Abraham Lincoln praised Andrew Jackson's exceptional use of executive authority.

_____

6. T   F   Lincoln issued the Emancipation Proclamation without prior congressional approval.

_____

7. T   F   Peterson's study of legislative-executive relations from Eisenhower to Reagan indicates the president has generally taken the lead in setting the legislative agenda.

_____

8.   T   F   Presidents like to pretend the White House is not the large bureaucracy that it in fact
                has become.

_____

9.   T   F   President Carter employed the pyramid structure for organization of personal staff.

_____

10. T   F   There are ten major executive departments headed by cabinet officers.

_____

11. T   F   A president rarely knows more than a few of the people that he appoints.

_____

12. T   F   According to the text much of Eisenhower's bumbling, incoherent manner of speaking
                was a strategic "public disguise."

_____

13. T   F   Richard Nixon thrived on personal confrontation and face-to-face encounters with
                other politicians.

_____

14. T   F   President Roosevelt failed to "purge" members of Congress who opposed his program.

_____

15. T   F   The Constitution specifically requires the president to divulge private communications
                between himself and his principal advisors if a congressional investigation demands
                such information.

_____

16. T   F   The Constitution specifically requires the president to spend money that is appropriated
                by Congress.

_____

17. T   F   A sixty-hour workweek is typical for a president.

_____

18. T   F   Presidents routinely complain of what they feel is the limited scope of their power.

_____

19. T   F   In 1841, John Tyler became the first vice president to become president because of the
                death of his predecessor.

_____

20. T   F   The only official task of the vice president is to preside over the Senate and to vote in
                case of a tie.

_____

MULTIPLE CHOICE QUESTIONS

Circle the letter of the response that best answers the question or completes the statement.

1. In a parliamentary system the prime minister is chosen by the

    a. people.
    b. signatories.
    c. electors.
    d. legislature.
    e. monarch.

2. Which of the following statements is true of U.S. presidents but not of British prime ministers?

    a. Presidents and the legislature often work at cross-purposes.
    b. Presidents are selected by the legislature.
    c. Presidents have more strict control over members of their party.
    d. Presidents are most often government insiders.
    e. Presidents generally choose their cabinets from among members of Congress.

3. The text makes which of the following statements about the effect of divided government?

    a. Divided government produces worse gridlock than does a unified government.
    b. The end of gridlock is accomplished by a divided government.
    c. Important legislation is produced about as much with divided governments as with unified governments.
    d. Divided government slows the progress of necessary legislation and, in a time of crisis, almost ensures there will be no consensus.
    e. Divided government is a myth.

4. The text suggests that policy gridlock is a necessary consequence of

    a. representative democracy.
    b. big government.
    c. direct democracy.
    d. divided government.
    e. unified government.

5. Who called for something like an elective monarchy here in the United States?

    a. George Washington
    b. John Adams
    c. Thomas Jefferson
    d. John Jay
    e. Alexander Hamilton

6. The Framers first considered having _____ select the president.

    a. the Supreme Court
    b. Congress
    c. the state legislatures
    d. the various governors
    e. the large states

7. Which amendment formally limited presidents to two terms?

    a. 9th

    b.   10th
    c.   17th
    d.   22nd
    e.   26th

8.   Andrew Jackson's use of the veto power was conspicuous because

    a.   he rarely used it.
    b.   he used it more than all of the presidents before him combined.
    c.   all of his vetoes were overridden.
    d.   he would not use the power unless he thought legislation was unconstitutional.
    e.   he would not use the veto simply because of a policy disagreement

9.   The greatest source of presidential power is found in

    a.   the Constitution.
    b.   Congress.
    c.   public communication.
    d.   the bureaucracy.
    e.   politics and public opinion.

10.   The ability of a presidential assistant to influence the president is governed by the rule of

    a.   reason.
    b.   propinquity.
    c.   law.
    d.   the judiciary.
    e.   Congress.

11.   The Office of Management and Budget both assembles the president's budget and

    a.   manages the departments.
    b.   reviews departmental legislative proposals.
    c.   manages federal personnel.
    d.   organizes presidential cabinet meetings.
    e.   reviews the Senior Executive Service.

12.   Which modern president is almost the only one given credit for making his cabinet a truly deliberative body?

    a.   Harry Truman
    b.   Calvin Coolidge
    c.   John F. Kennedy
    d.   Dwight Eisenhower
    e.   Bill Clinton

13.   The main difference between a presidential agency and an independent agency is that heads of the former

    a.   cannot have their salaries reduced.
    b.   serve at the president's discretion.
    c.   can only be removed "for cause."
    d.   cannot sponsor legislation.
    e.   serve at Congress's pleasure.

14. In recent administrations there has been a tendency for presidents to place in their cabinet people known for their

    a. independent political power.
    b. personal wealth.
    c. creativity.
    d. loyalty to Congress.
    e. expertise.

15. Of the three audiences that the president confronts, the one most important for maintaining and exercising power is

    a. other politicians and leaders in Washington.
    b. the mass public throughout the nation.
    c. party activists.
    d. foreign leaders.
    e. officeholders outside Washington.

16. Once in office a president can expect to see his popularity

    a. increase over time.
    b. remain about the same.
    c. fluctuate in a manner that admits of no generalization.
    d. decline over time.
    e. be dependent on the actions of Congress.

17. Which of the following statements about George W. Bush's approval ratings is *incorrect*?

    a. His initial ratings were comparable to those of President Clinton's in 1993.
    b. His disapproval rating was the highest of any president since polling began.
    c. His approval rating for the first six months was fairly typical for modern presidents.
    d. His approval ratings after the September 11 attack were the highest ever recorded.
    e. None of the above.

18. Which of the following statements is true of a bill that is not signed or vetoed within ten days while Congress is still in session?

    a. It is considered to have received a pocket veto.
    b. It is returned to Congress.
    c. It must be given a veto message.
    d. It becomes a law until the next session of Congress.
    e. It becomes law automatically.

19. From George Washington to Bill Clinton, about ____ percent of over 2,500 presidential vetoes have been overridden.

    a. 4
    b. 15
    c. 20
    d. 25
    e. 30

20. The doctrine of executive privilege is based on separation of powers and on the

    a. constitutional requirements for secrecy.
    b. War Powers Act.
    c. president's need for confidential advice.
    d. White House *Sourcebook*.

e.   integrity of each branch of government.

21. The personal popularity of the president affects which of the following most directly?

   a.   how Congress treats presidential legislative proposals
   b.   how members of the president's party do in House elections
   c.   how members of the president's party do in Senate elections
   d.   the president's ability to conduct foreign affairs
   e.   B and D

22. A president suffers a stroke that leaves him or her partially paralyzed. The vice president, with the support of a majority of the cabinet, declares that the president is unable to discharge the duties of the office, but the president disagrees. What happens next?

   a.   Congress decides who is president.
   b.   Because the vice president has the support of a majority of the cabinet, the vice president assumes the presidency.
   c.   Because the president is still alive, he or she remains president.
   d.   Because the president and vice president disagree, a new election is held, allowing the people to decide who should be president.
   e.   The Supreme Court decides who is president.

23. Which of the following factors places the greatest constraint on a president's ability to plan a program?

   a.   the president's personal ideology
   b.   the limits of the president's time and attention
   c.   the need to campaign
   d.   the leaders in his own party.
   e.   the mass media

24. _____ was the last president *not* to use public opinion polls.

   a.   Woodrow Wilson
   b.   Herbert Hoover
   c.   John F. Kennedy.
   d.   Franklin Roosevelt
   e.   Harry Truman

25. Which of the following statements about efforts to reorganize the federal bureaucracy is true?

   a.   They may trigger bitter political battles.
   b.   They typically take place at the time of the election of a new president.
   c.   They have seldom been tried.
   d.   They require the support of the voters.
   e.   All of the above.

ESSAY QUESTIONS

Practice writing extended answers to the following questions. These test your ability to integrate and express the ideas that you have been studying in this chapter.

1. Your text asserts that the most important power of the presidency lies in politics and public opinion. Explain what this statement means.

2. Discuss the factors that lead to conflict in executive-legislative relations. Can they be neatly placed in constitutional and political categories?

3. If you were asked by the Founders to make recommendations on the presidency, what would you suggest, on the basis of two hundred years of experience?

ANSWERS TO KEY TERMS MATCH QUESTIONS

1. k
2. y
3. m
4. bb
5. aa
6. u
7. j
8. r
9. n
10. l
11. i
12. e
13. q
14. h
15. b
16. a
17. c
18. d
19. x
20. f
21. g
22. o
23. p
24. s
25. t
26. v
27. w
28. z

ANSWERS TO "DID YOU THINK THAT . . . ? QUESTIONS

1. The president only has direct authority over presidential agencies; he does not have such control over independent agencies.

2. Politicians tend to rise and fall together. Generally, they will not challenge a popular president of their own party.

3. Presidents have claimed an executive privilege to withhold certain information from Congress. The Supreme Court has said the president has only a qualified privilege to do so.

4. No; these powers are shared with Congress. For instance, the presidential veto may be overridden, presidential impoundment authority has been regulated, presidential executive privilege has been qualified, and presidential power to remove officials in independent agencies is restricted by Congress.

ANSWERS TO DATA CHECK QUESTIONS

1. There is a chance that individuals running for the House and the Senate who are of the same party as the individual who is elected presidency will win at a higher rate. That is, they will ride the president's coattails into office.

2. The relationship between the presidential candidate's popularity and the popularity of the party is not easy to detect.

3. 1932, Roosevelt, 90 seats.

4. 1980, Reagan, 12 seats.

5. 1992, Clinton, 9 seats.

6. "Do you approve of the way ___ is handling his job as president?"

7. Every administration except Eisenhower, Reagan, Clinton.

8. In each case, they are the first terms of two-term administrations.

9. The presidents party usually loses seats in the House and the Senate during the mid-term elections.

10. 1942, 1946, 1994.

11. None.

ANSWERS TO TRUE/FALSE QUESTIONS

1. T
2. T
3. T
4. T
5. F. Lincoln had been critical of Jackson's use of executive authority.
6. T
7. F. Congress, not the president, often took the lead in setting the legislative agenda.
8. T
9. F. Carter employed the circular structure.
10. F. There are fourteen major executive departments.
11. T
12. T
13. F. Nixon disliked personal confrontations and tended to shield himself behind an elaborate staff system.

14.   T

15.   F. The Constitution says nothing about this matter.

16.   F. Again, the Constitution is silent on this matter.

17.   F. According to the text, a ninety-hour workweek is "typical."

18.   T

19.   T

20.   T

ANSWERS TO MULTIPLE CHOICE QUESTIONS

1.   d
2.   a
3.   c
4.   d
5.   e
6.   b
7.   d
8.   b
9.   e
10.   b
11.   b
12.   d
13.   b
14.   e
15.   a
16.   d
17.   e
18.   e
19.   a
20.   c
21.   a
22.   a
23.   b
24.   b
25.   a

CHAPTER 13

The Bureaucracy

REVIEWING THE CHAPTER

CHAPTER FOCUS

This chapter introduces you to what is big about big government: the bureaucracy. Both the distinctiveness and the size of the federal government bureaucracy are reviewed, along with the various roles that have been assigned to it throughout its history. Significant aspects of the bureaucracy today include the extent and character of its authority, how members are recruited, and other factors that help explain the conduct of bureaucrats in office. Finally, the chapter looks at the ways in which Congress attempts to control the behavior of bureaucrats and at various "pathologies" of various large bureaucracies. After reading and reviewing the material in this chapter, you should be able to do each of the following:

1. Compare and contrast the American and British models of government bureaucracy.

2. Sketch the history of the growth of bureaucracy in this country and the different uses to which it has been put.

3. Show how bureaucracy continues to grow today, although the number of persons directly employed by government has not greatly increased lately.

4. Discuss the recruitment, retention, and personal characteristics of federal bureaucrats.

5. Show how the roles and missions of the agencies are affected by both internal and external factors.

6. Review congressional measures to control the bureaucracy, and evaluate their effectiveness.

7. List the "pathologies" that may affect bureaucracies, and discuss whether they are relevant to the federal government bureaucracy today.

8. Discuss why it is so difficult to reform the bureaucracy.

STUDY OUTLINE

I. Distinctiveness of the American bureaucracy
    A. Constitutional system and traditions
        1. Supervision shared
        2. A federalist structure shares functions
        3. Adversary culture leads to defense of rights and lawsuits
    B. Scope of bureaucracy
        1. Little public ownership of industry in the United States
        2. High degree of regulation in the United States of private industries
II. The growth of the bureaucracy
    A. The early controversies
        1. Senate consent to removal of officials is challenged by supporters of a strong president

        2.   President is given sole removal power but Congress funds and investigates

    B.   The appointment of officials

        1.   Officials affect how laws are interpreted, the tone of their administration, and their effectiveness

        2.   Use of patronage in the nineteenth and early twentieth centuries to reward supporters

        3.   Civil War a watershed in bureaucratic growth; showed the weakness of federal government

    C.   A service role

        1.   1861–1901: shift in role from regulation to service

        2.   Reflects desire for limited government, laissez-faire beliefs, and the Constitution's silence

    D.   A change in role

        1.   Depression and World War II lead to a role of government activism

        2.   Introduction of heavy income taxes supports a large bureaucracy

III.   The federal bureaucracy today

    A.   Direct and indirect growth

        1.   Modest increase in the number of government employees

        2.   Indirect increase through the use of private contractors much greater

    B.   Growth in discretionary authority

        1.   Delegation of undefined authority by Congress

        2.   Primary areas of delegation

            a)   Subsidies to groups

            b)   Grant-in-aid programs

            c)   Enforcement of regulations

    C.   Factors explaining behavior of officials

        1.   Recruitment and retention

            a)   The competitive service: most bureaucrats compete for jobs through OPM

                (1)   Appointment by merit based on a written exam

                (2)   Decreased to less than 54 percent of federal government work force

            b)   The excepted service: most are appointed by other agencies on the basis of qualifications approved by OPM

                (1)   Fastest growing sector of federal government employment

                (2)   Examples: Postal Service employees and FBI agents

                (3)   But president can also appoint employees: presidential appointments, Schedule C jobs, and NEA jobs

                (4)   Pendleton Act (1883): transferred basis of government jobs from patronage to merit

                (5)   Merit system protects president from pressure and protects patronage appointees from new presidents ("blanketing in")

            c)   The buddy system

                (1)   Name-request job: filled by a person whom an agency has already identified for middle- and upper-level jobs

                (2)   Job description may be tailored for person

                (3)   Circumvents usual search process

                (4)   But also encourages "issue networks" based on shared policy views

            d)   Firing a bureaucrat

                (1)   Most bureaucrats cannot be fired

                (2)   Exception: Senior Executive Service (SES)

                (3)   SES managers receive cash bonuses for good performance

                (4)   But very few SES members have been fired or even transferred

            e)   The agencies' point of view

    (1)   Agencies are dominated by lifetime bureaucrats who have worked for no other agency

    (2)   System assures continuity and expertise

    (3)   But also gives subordinates power over new bosses: can work behind boss's back through sabotage, delaying, and so on

2.   Personal attributes

    a)   Allegations of critics

        (1)   Higher civil servants are elitists

        (2)   Political appointees and career bureaucrats think about government and politics differently than public at large

    b)   Correlation between type of agency and attitudes of employees: activist versus traditional

    c)   Professional values of officials

3.   Do bureaucrats sabotage their political bosses?

    a)   If so, such sabotage hurts conservatives more than liberals; bureaucrats tend to be liberal

    b)   But loyalty to bosses runs strong—despite the power of bureaucrats to obstruct or complain

        (1)   Whistleblower Protection Act (1989) created Office of Special Counsel

        (2)   "Cooperation is the nature of a bureaucrat's job"

    c)   Most civil servants: highly structured roles make them relatively immune to personal attitudes

    d)   Professionals such as lawyers and economists in the FTC: loosely structured roles may be much influenced by personal attitudes, professional values help explain how power is used

4.   Culture and careers

    a)   Each agency has its own culture

    b)   Jobs with an agency can be career enhancing or not

    c)   Strong agency culture motivates employees but makes agencies resistant to change

5.   Constraints

    a)   Biggest difference between a government agency and a business: hiring, firing, pay, procedures, and so forth

    b)   General constraints

        (1)   Administrative Procedure Act (1946)

        (2)   Freedom of Information Act (1966)

        (3)   National Environmental Policy Act (1969)

        (4)   Privacy Act (1974)

        (5)   Open Meeting Law (1976)

        (6)   Assignment of single jobs to several agencies

    c)   Effects of constraints

        (1)   Government moves slowly

        (2)   Government acts inconsistently

        (3)   Easier to block than to take action

        (4)   Reluctant decision making by lower-ranking employees

        (5)   Red tape

6.   Why so many constraints?

    a)   Constraints come from us

    b)   They are an agency's response to our demands for openness, honesty, fairness, and so on

7.   Agency allies

        a)   Agencies often seek alliances with congressional committees or interest groups: "iron triangle"

        b)   Far less common today; politics has become too complicated

            (1)   More interest groups, more congressional subcommittees, and easier access for individuals

            (2)   Far more competing forces than ever given access by courts

        c)   "Issue networks": groups that regularly debate government policy on certain issues

            (1)   Contentious and partisan

            (2)   New president often recruits from networks

IV. Congressional oversight

    A.   Forms of congressional supervision

       1.   Approval necessary for creation

       2.   Statutes influence agency behavior (sometimes precisely)

       3.   Authorization of money, either permanent or fixed number of years

       4.   Appropriation of money allows spending

    B.   Congressional oversight and "homeland security"

       1.   Lieberman's call for Department of Homeland Defense after September 11 attack

       2.   President Bush's creation of Office of Homeland Security

           a)   Appointment of Governor Ridge and the blueprint for homeland security

           b)   Congressional calls for testimony about strategies

           c)   Need to coordinate personnel and budgets

       3.   Proposal of a Department of Homeland Security

           a)   Consolidation, reorganization and transformation

           b)   Need for Congress to reorganize itself to make the bureaucracy work

               (1)   Immediate protests about committee and subcommittee jurisdiction

               (2)   Congress' historical tendency to resist streamlining

    C.   The Appropriations Committee and legislative committees

       1.   Appropriations Committee most powerful

           a)   Most expenditure recommendations are approved by House

           b)   Has power to lower agency's expenditure request

           c)   Has power to influence an agency's policies by marking up an agency's budget

           d)   But becoming less powerful because of

               (1)   Trust funds: Social Security

               (2)   Annual authorizations

               (3)   Meeting target spending limits

       2.   Legislative committees are important when

           a)   A law is first passed

           b)   An agency is first created

           c)   An agency is subject to annual authorization

       3.   Informal congressional controls over agencies

           a)   Individual members of Congress can seek privileges for constituents

           b)   Congressional committees may seek *committee clearance:* right to pass on certain agency decisions

           c)   Committee heads may ask to be consulted

    D.   The legislative veto

       1.   Declared unconstitutional by Supreme Court in *Chadha* (1983)

       2.   Weakens traditional legislative oversight but Congress continues creating such vetoes

    E.   Congressional investigations

       1.   Power inferred from power to legislate

       2.   Means for checking agency discretion

3.   Means for limiting presidential control
V.   Bureaucratic "pathologies"
   A.   Red tape—complex and sometimes conflicting rules among agencies
   B.   Conflict—agencies work at cross-purposes
   C.   Duplication—two or more agencies seem to do the same thing
   D.   Imperialism—tendency of agencies to grow, irrespective of benefits and costs of programs
   E.   Waste—spending more than is necessary to buy some product or service
VI.   Reforming the bureaucracy
   A.   Numerous attempts to make bureaucracy work better for less money
     1.   Eleven attempts to reform in this century alone
     2.   National Performance Review (NPR) in 1993 designed to reinvent government
      a)   Differs from previous reforms that sought to increase presidential control
      b)   Emphasizes customer satisfaction by bringing citizens in contact with agencies
     3.   NPR calls for innovation and quality consciousness by
      a)   Less-centralized management
      b)   More employee initiatives
      c)   Customer satisfaction
   B.   Bureaucratic reform always difficult to accomplish
     1.   Most rules and red tape result from the struggle between the president and Congress.
     2.   This struggle makes bureaucrats nervous about irritating either
     3.   Periods of divided government exacerbate matters, especially in implementing policy.
      a)   Republican presidents seek to increase political control (executive micromanagement)
      b)   Democratic Congresses respond by increasing investigations and rules (legislative micromanagement)

KEY TERMS MATCH

Match the following terms and descriptions:

1.   A freely competitive economy

2.   Appointment of officials not based on the criteria specified by OPM

3.   A requirement that an executive decision lie before Congress for a specified period before it takes effect

4.   A 1993 effort, led by Vice President Al Gore, to make the bureaucracy work better and cost less

5.   Top-ranking civil servants who can be hired, fired, and rewarded in a more flexible manner than can ordinary bureaucrats

6.   A large, complex organization composed of appointed officials

7.   Appointment of officials based on selection criteria devised by the employing agency and OPM

8.   Refers to the tendency of agencies to grow without regard to the benefits their programs

a.   annual authorizations
b.   appropriation
c.   authorization legislation
d.   bureaucratic imperialism
e.   bureaucracy
f.   committee clearance
g.   competitive service
h.   Department of Homeland Security
i.   discretionary authority
j.   excepted service
k.   iron triangle
l.   issue networks
m.   laissez-faire
n.   legislative veto
o.   name-request job

without regard to the benefits their programs confer or the costs they entail.

9. Legislation that began the federal merit system

10. Governmental appointments made on the basis of political considerations

11. The right of committees to disapprove of certain agency actions

12. The ability of officials to make policies that are not spelled out in advance by laws

13. Groups that regularly debate governmental policy on subjects such as health care or auto safety

14. Government jobs having a confidential or policy-making character

15. Funds such as that of Social Security that operate outside the government budget

16. A proposal by President Bush in 2002 which would consolidate 22 federal agencies and nearly 170,000 federal employees

17. The mutually advantageous relationship among an agency, a committee, and an interest group

18. Monies that are budgeted on a yearly basis; for example Congress may set yearly limits on what agencies can spend

19. A legislative grant of money to finance a government program

20. Legislative permission to begin or continue a government program or agency

21. A job to be filled by a person whom a government agency has identified by name

22. Complex bureaucratic rules and procedures that must be followed to get something done

23. The practice of giving the fruits of a party's victory, such as jobs and contracts, to the loyal members of that party

p. National Performance Review

q. patronage

r. Pendleton Act

s. red tape

t. schedule C

u. Senior Executive Service

v. spoils system

w. trust funds

DID YOU THINK THAT . . . ?

Below are listed a number of misconceptions. You should be able to refute each statement in the space provided, referring to information or argumentation contained in this chapter. Sample answers appear at the end of this chapter.

1.   "The number of federal employees in a bureaucracy is a fairly accurate reflection of their power."

_____
_____
_____

2.   "Most bureaucrats are appointed by the president in power."

_____
_____
_____

3.   "The federal bureaucracy operates essentially like a very large corporation."

_____
_____
_____

4.   "Once an agency has accomplished its original tasks, it begins to decline in size and influence."

_____
_____
_____

DATA CHECK

Figure 13.3: Characteristics of Federal Civilian Employees, 1960 and 1999

1.   In 1960 what percentage of federal civilian employees were female?

_____

2.   In 1999 what percentage of federal civilian employees were female?

_____

3.   In 1999 what percentage of federal civilian employees were racial minorities?

_____

4.   How has the distribution of federal civilian employees–in and outside Washington–changed over the years?

_____

Table 13.2: Minority Employment in the Federal Bureaucracy, by Rank, 2000

5. On the basis of the Table what obvious conclusion can be drawn regarding the employment of minorities in the federal bureaucracy?

_____

PRACTICING FOR EXAMS

TRUE/FALSE QUESTIONS

Read each statement carefully. Mark true statements *T*. If any part of the statement is false, mark it *F*, and write in the space provided a concise explanation of why the statement is false.

1. T   F   Government agencies in this country operate under closer public scrutiny than in almost any other nation.

_____

2. T   F   World War II was the first occasion during which the government made heavy use of federal income taxes to finance its activities.

_____

3. T   F   For every single person who earns a living from the federal government there are two who work indirectly for Washington.

_____

4. T   F   In recent years, the percentage of federal employees who belong to the competitive service has decreased.

_____

5. T   F   "Schedule C" appointments involve jobs with a confidential or policy-determining character.

_____

6. T   F   When Grover Cleveland became president in 1885 he replaced forty thousand Republican postal employees with Democrats.

_____

7. T   F   A federal employee cannot appeal the decision of the Merit Systems Protection Board if it upholds his / her firing.

_____

8. T   F   The federal civil service as a whole looks very much like a cross section of American society in the education, sex, and race of its members.

_____

9. T   F   Employees of the Environmental Protection Agency are more likely to be liberal than employees of the Department of Commerce.

_____

10. T   F   People with conservative viewpoints tend to be overrepresented in defense agencies.

_____

11. T   F   Economists with the Federal Trade Commission prefer to bring cases against business firms that have done something clearly illegal.

_____

12. T   F   Lawyers with the Federal Trade Commission favor the litigation of "big" or "blockbuster" cases.

_____

13. T   F   The "layering technique" is a method designed to retain bureaucrats who are both loyal and efficient.

_____

14. T   F   Congress rarely gives any job to a single agency.

_____

15. T   F   Iron triangles are much less common today than once was the case.

_____

16. T   F   Congressional committee chairmen in both parties and in both chambers strongly supported the idea of creating a new homeland security department.

_____

17. T   F   The congressional power to investigate is not mentioned in the Constitution.

_____

18. T   F   Congress can compel a person to attend an investigation by issuing a subpoena.

_____

19. T   F   Duplication is probably the biggest criticism that people have of the bureaucracy.

_____

20. T   F   Al Gore's National Performance Review called for more specific rules to guide the federal bureaucracy and the creation of a centralized enforcement mechanism to enhance overall efficiency.

_____

MULTIPLE CHOICE QUESTIONS

Circle the letter of the response that best answers the question or completes the statement.

1.   American bureaucracy is complex because

   a.   federalism encourages the abuse of power.
   b.   the bureaucracy is so large.
   c.   the Constitution determines its structure and function.
   d.   authority is divided among several managing institutions.
   e.   civil servants are immune from firing.

2. Public enterprises in France account for what percentage of all employment?

    a. 1 percent
    b. 3 percent
    c. 6 percent
    d. 12 percent
    e. 20 percent

3. The political ideology of a presidential appointee is important because she or he

    a. must often work with radical groups.
    b. affects how the laws are interpreted.
    c. is usually bound by specific directives.
    d. is aligned with congressional ideology.
    e. typically has strong party ties.

4. The basis of appointments to the bureaucracy during most of the nineteenth century and the early part of the twentieth century was

    a. financial.
    b. patronage.
    c. nepotism.
    d. technical expertise.
    e. support for the president's policies.

5. The dramatic increase in the number of federal employees from 1816 to 1861 was the direct result of

    a. the need for Secret Service agents in the White House.
    b. expansion in the size of congressional staff.
    c. expansion of services in the Post Office.
    d. the Hatch Act.
    e. President Grant's concern over the Whiskey Ring scandal.

6. When first established, the Departments of Agriculture, Labor, and Commerce had one thing in common:

    a. their secretaries were not appointees.
    b. they all sought to regulate their clienteles.
    c. they were primarily service-oriented.
    d. they all avoided contacts with the public.
    e. they protected states' rights.

7. Which statement best describes how the text of the Constitution addresses the issue of granting power to bureaucrats?

    a. The Constitution is silent on the matter.
    b. The Constitution prohibits transfer of congressional power.
    c. The Constitution allows transfer of congressional power with presidential approval.
    d. The Constitution allows transfer of congressional power during a declared war.
    e. The Constitution prohibits transfer of congressional power during a declared war.

8. As late as 1935 the Supreme Court held that

    a. the legislature may not delegate its authority to any administrative agency.
    b. a regulatory agency was necessary to control interstate commerce.
    c. regulatory agencies could exercise wide discretion.
    d. an agency must be staffed by individuals of different parties.

e.   the creation of new agencies must be approved by Congress.

9.   Wars have generally caused the federal bureaucracy to

a.   become more decentralized.
b.   shrink in size, but increase in efficiency.
c.   respond more quickly, but make inefficient decisions.
d.   increase in size.
e.   neutralize the power of Congress.

10.   The bureaucracy of American government today is largely a product of which two events?

a.   the Depression and World War II
b.   World War I and World War II
c.   World War II and the Korean War
d.   the Korean War and the Vietnam War
e.   the Vietnam War and Watergate.

11.   Which of the following is the *most* important consideration in evaluating the power of a bureaucracy?

a.   the number of employees in it
b.   the importance of its functions
c.   the extent to which its actions are supported by the public
d.   the social status of its leaders.
e.   the amount of discretionary authority that its officials have

12.   Congress has delegated substantial authority to administrative agencies in what three areas?

a.   grants-in-aid, law enforcement, national defense
b.   law enforcement, social services, resource management
c.   grants-in-aid, subsidy payments, enforcement of regulations
d.   grants-in-aid, subsidy payments, law enforcement
e.   social services, law enforcement, national defense

13.   Which of the following is described by the text as imposing constraint on bureaucracy?

a.   political superiors
b.   legislators
c.   interest groups
d.   journalists
e.   All of the above.

14.   What percentage of all federal employees are part of the excepted service?

a.   about 20 percent
b.   about 30 percent
c.   about 40 percent
d.   about 50 percent
e.   about 80 percent

15.   A steady transfer of federal jobs from the patronage to the merit system was initiated by the passage of the

a.   Seventeenth Amendment,
b.   Eighteenth Amendment
c.   Pendleton Act.
d.   Hatch Act.

e.   Civil Service Reform Act.

16. The emergence of the merit system was, in part, prompted by

a.   the Whiskey Ring scandal of the Grant administration.
b.   the assassination of James Garfield.
c.   persistent robbery of the federal mails.
d.   Democratic control of Congress.
e.   All of the above.

17. The Administrative Procedure Act of 1946 required that

a.   every part of agency meetings be open to the public.
b.   government files about individuals be kept confidential.
c.   environmental impact statements be issued before undertaking major actions.
d.   agencies give notice before they adopt new rules, hold hearings, and solicit comments.
e.   citizens be allowed to inspect certain government records.

18. Which of the following statements about agency allies is correct?

a.   The Small Business Administration (SBA) has been part of an iron triangle.
b.   Iron triangles are far more common today than they once were.
c.   Presidential hiring from within issue networks is prohibited by law.
d.   Issue networks are often established by Congress to study key policy issues.
e.   The Department of Agriculture does not work closely with farm organizations.

19. In 2002, President Bush argued that Tom Ridge, head of the Office of Homeland Security, did not have to testify before Congress because

a.   Ridge was confirmed by the Senate.
b.   Ridge was an Assistant to the President.
c.   Congress did not have the power to supervise the newly created Office.
d.   Democrats in Congress opposed the creation of the Office.
e.   All of the above.

20. A 1987 study found that _____ of federal employees who had completed their probationary period were fired for misconduct or poor performance

a.   less than 1 percent
b.   2 percent
c.   5 percent
d.   10 percent
e.   22 percent

21. Which of the following is *not* among the procedures for firing or demoting a member of the competitive civil service?

a.   written notice of thirty days
b.   statement of reasons for dismissal
c.   right to a hearing
d.   right to an appeal
e.   review by the OPM

22. Bureaucratic conflict and duplication occur because

a.   large organizations must ensure one part of the organization does not operate out of step.
b.   Congress often wants to achieve a number of different, partially inconsistent goals.
c.   Congress can be unclear as to exactly what it wants an agency to do.

    d.   of the need to satisfy political requirements.
    e.   of the need to satisfy legal requirements.

23. Bureaucratic imperialism occurs because

    a.   large organizations must ensure one part of the organization does not operate out of step.
    b.   Congress often wants to achieve a number of different, partially inconsistent goals.
    c.   Congress can be unclear as to exactly what it wants an agency to do.
    d.   of the need to satisfy political requirements.
    e.   of the need to satisfy legal requirements.

24. The text suggests many of the "horror stories" one hears about high priced items that are purchased at the government's expense are

    a.   concocted by critics of the Hatch Act.
    b.   more accurate than public officials would like to admit.
    c.   documented in *Congressional Quarterly*.
    d.   the by-product of bureaucratic imperialism.
    e.   either exaggerated or unusual occurrences.

25. The National Performance Review attempts to reform the bureaucracy by stressing

    a.   efficiency.
    b.   rigidity.
    c.   accountability.
    d.   customer satisfaction.
    e.   consistent policies.

ESSAY QUESTIONS

Practice writing extended answers to the following questions. These test your ability to integrate and express the ideas that you have been studying in this chapter.

1. Which criteria would you want to consider if you were trying to convince someone that the federal bureaucracy is an important policy-making institution?

2. Discuss four factors that help to explain the behavior of appointed officials. Which one do you think is the most important?

3. What does the text mean by the term *bureaucratic pathologies*? What are some examples of such "pathologies"? Why does each of them exist? Can they be corrected? Why or why not?

ANSWERS TO KEY TERMS MATCH QUESTIONS

1. m
2. j
3. n
4. p
5. u
6. e
7. g
8. d
9. r
10. q
11. f
12. i
13. l
14. t
15. w
16. h
17. k
18. a
19. b
20. c
21. o
22. s
23. v

ANSWERS TO "DID YOU THINK THAT . . . ?" QUESTIONS

1. The power of civil servants is more a function of their discretionary authority than of their numbers.

2. Most bureaucrats (approximately two-thirds) compete for jobs through the OPM. The other third, called the *excepted service,* are either appointed or hired on the basis of the merit system used by the agency that is hiring. Relatively few bureaucrats are appointed by the president.

3. The federal bureaucracy operates with far more constraints than a typical corporation. Not only are hirings and firings tightly regulated in the bureaucracy, but the procedures the bureaucracy must follow in conducting its business are controlled by numerous laws, regulations, and guidelines designed to protect employees and the public. These combine to make the bureaucracy a complicated, sluggish, and clumsy institution.

4.   The phenomenon of bureaucratic imperialism reflects the tendency of agencies to grow independently of the benefits they confer or the costs entailed.

ANSWERS TO DATA CHECK QUESTIONS

1.   25 percent.

2.   43 percent.

3.   28 percent.

4.   There has been no change in this distribution.

5.   Minorities tend to be clustered in the lower levels of the federal bureaucracy.

ANSWERS TO TRUE/FALSE QUESTIONS

1.   T

2.   T

3.   F. Actually there are nearly three who work indirectly for the government.

4.   T

5.   T

6.   T

7.   F. They can appeal, to the U.S. Court of Appeals.

8.   T

9.   T

10.   T

11.   F. This would be true of the lawyers in the Commission.

12.   F. They are actually leery of such cases because the facts can be hard to prove and such cases take a long time to decide.

13.   F. This is a technique for bringing disloyal subordinates under control or simply moving them out of the way.

14.   T

15.   T

16.   T

17.   T

18.   T

19.   F. According to the text, waste is probably the biggest criticism people have of the bureaucracy.

20.   F

ANSWERS TO MULTIPLE CHOICE QUESTIONS

1.   d

2.   d

3. b
4. b
5. c
6. c
7. a
8. a
9. d
10. a
11. e
12. c
13. e
14. d
15. c
16. b
17. d
18. a
19. b
20. a
21. e
22. b
23. c
24. e
25. d

CHAPTER 14

The Judiciary

REVIEWING THE CHAPTER

CHAPTER FOCUS

This chapter introduces you to the final and perhaps most unusual branch of American government: the courts. The chapter explains how courts, particularly the Supreme Court, came to play a uniquely powerful role in forming public policy in this country and how that role has been played to very different effects at different stages of history. Other important considerations include how justices are selected, the jurisdictions of the various courts, and the steps that a case must go through on its way to Supreme Court review. The chapter concludes with an assessment of the power courts have in politics today, the limitations on that power, and why judicial activism seems to be on the increase. After reading and reviewing the material in this chapter, you should be able to do each of the following:

1. Explain what judicial review is, and trace its origin in this country to *Marbury v. Madison.*

2. List and comment on the three eras of varying Supreme Court influences on national policy from the days of slavery to the present.

3. Explain what is meant by a dual court system, and describe the effects it has on how cases are handled and appealed.

4. List the various steps that cases go through to be appealed to the Supreme Court, and explain the considerations involved at each level.

5. Discuss the dimensions of power exercised today by the Supreme Court and the opposing viewpoints on the desirability of activism by that court.

6. Develop arguments for and against an activist Supreme Court.

STUDY OUTLINE

I. Introduction
    A. Only in the United States do judges play so large a role in policy-making.
        1. Judicial review: right to rule on laws and executive acts on basis of constitutionality; chief judicial weapon in system of checks and balances
        2. In Great Britain, Parliament is supreme
        3. In other countries, judicial review means little
            Exceptions: Australia, Canada, West Germany, India, and a few others

    B. Debate is over how the Constitution should be interpreted
        1. Strict constructionist (interpretivist) approach: judges are bound by the wording of the Constitution
        2. Activist (legislative) approach: judges should look to the underlying principles of the Constitution
        3. Not a matter of liberal versus conservative

        a)   A judge can be both conservative and activist, or vice versa

        b)   Today most activists tend to be liberal, most strict constructionists conservative

II.   The development of the federal courts

    A.   Founders' view

       1.   Most Founders probably expected judicial review but not its large role in policy making

       2.   Traditional view: judges find and apply existing law

       3.   Activist judges would later respond that judges make law

       4.   Traditional view made it easy for Founders to justify judicial review

       5.   Hamilton: courts least dangerous branch

       6.   But federal judiciary evolved toward judicial activism

    B.   National supremacy and slavery: 1789–1861

       1.   *McCulloch v. Maryland:* federal law declared supreme over state law

       2.   Interstate commerce clause is placed under the authority of federal law; conflicting state law void

       3.   *Dred Scott v. Sandford:* Negroes were not and could not become free citizens of the United States; a direct cause of the Civil War

    C.   Government and the economy: Civil War to 1936

       1.   Dominant issue of the period: whether the economy could be regulated by state and federal governments

       2.   Private property held to be protected by the Fourteenth Amendment

       3.   States seek to protect local businesses and employees from the predatory activities of national monopolies; judicial activism

       4.   The Supreme Court determines what is "reasonable" regulation

       5.   The Court interprets the Fourteenth and Fifteenth Amendments narrowly as applied to blacks

    D.   Government and political liberty: 1936 to the present

       1.   Court establishes tradition of deferring to the legislature in economic cases

       2.   Court shifts attention to personal liberties and becomes active in defining rights

    E.   The revival of state sovereignty

       1.   Supreme Court rules that states have right to resist some forms of federal action

       2.   Hint at some real limits to the supremacy of the federal government

III. The structure of the federal courts

    A.   Two kinds of federal courts

       1.   Constitutional courts

          a)   Created under Article III

          b)   Judges serve during good behavior

          c)   Salaries not reduced while in office

          d)   Examples: District Courts (ninety-four), Courts of Appeals (twelve)

       2.   Legislative courts

          a)   Created by Congress for specialized purposes

          b)   Judges have fixed terms

          c)   No salary protection

    B.   Selecting judges

       1.   Party background some effect on judicial behavior but ideology does not determine behavior

       2.   Senatorial courtesy: judges for U.S. district courts must be approved by that state's senators

       3.   The litmus test

          a)   Presidential successes in selecting compatible judges

          b)   Concern this may downplay professional qualifications *c)*   Greatest effect on Supreme Court

IV. The jurisdiction of the federal courts

    A.   Dual court system

        1.   One state, one federal

        2.   Federal cases listed in Article III and the Eleventh Amendment of the Constitution

            a)   Federal question cases: involving U.S. matters

            b)   Diversity cases: involving citizens of different states

            c)   All others are left to state courts

        3.   Some cases can be tried in either court

            a)   Example: if both federal and state laws have been broken (dual sovereignty)

            b)   Justified: each government has right to enact laws, and neither can block prosecution out of sympathy for the accused

        4.   State cases sometimes can be appealed to Supreme Court

        5.   Exclusive federal jurisdiction over federal criminal laws, appeals from federal regulatory agencies, bankruptcy, and controversies between two states

    B.   Route to the Supreme Court

        1.   Most federal cases begin in U.S. district courts, are straightforward, and do not lead to new public policy.

        2.   The Supreme Court picks the cases it wants to hear on appeal

            a)   Uses writ of certiorari ("cert")

            b)   Requires agreement of four justices to hear case

            c)   Usually deals with significant federal or constitutional question

                (1)   Conflicting decisions by circuit courts

                (2)   State court decisions involving the Constitution

            d)   Only 3 to 4 percent of appeals are granted certiorari

            e)   Others are left to lower courts; this results in a diversity of constitutional interpretation

V. Getting to court

    A.   Deterrents

        1.   The Court rejects 95 percent of applications for certiorari

        2.   Costs of appeal are high

            a)   But these can be lowered by

                (1)   In forma pauperis: plaintiff heard as pauper, with costs paid by the government

                (2)   Payment by interest groups who have something to gain (American Civil Liberties Union)

            b)   Each party must pay its own way except for cases in which it is decided

                (1)   That losing defendant will pay (fee shifting)

                (2)   Section 1983 suits

        3.   Standing: guidelines

            a)   Must be controversy between adversaries

            b)   Personal harm must be demonstrated

            c)   Being taxpayer not entitlement for suit

            d)   Sovereign immunity

    B.   Class action suits

        1.   Brought on behalf of all similarly situated

        2.   Financial incentives to bring suit

        3.   Need to notify all members of the class since 1974 to limit such suits

VI. The Supreme Court in action

    A.   Oral arguments by lawyers after briefs submitted

        1.   Questions by justices cut down to thirty minutes

  2. Role of solicitor general
  3. Amicus curiae briefs
  4. Many sources of influence on justices, such as law journals
 B. Conference procedures
  1. Role of chief justice: speaking first, voting last
  2. Selection of opinion writer: concurring and dissenting opinions
 C. Strategic retirements from the U.S. Supreme Court
  1. There has been a sharp increase in the rate of retirements (contra deaths)
  2. Early duties were physically onerous, adverse to one's health
  3. More recently, retirements occur when justices and presidents share party identification
VII. The power of the federal courts
 A. The power to make policy
  1. By interpretation
  2. By extending reach of existing law
  3. By designing remedies
 B. Measures of power
  1. Number of laws declared unconstitutional (more than 120)
  2. Number of prior cases overturned; not following stare decisis
  3. Deference to the legislative branch (political questions)
  4. Kinds of remedies imposed; judges go beyond what justice requires
  5. Basis for sweeping orders from either the Constitution or the interpretation of federal laws
 C. Views of judicial activism
  1. Supporters
   a) Courts should correct injustices
   b) Courts are last resort
  2. Critics
   a) Judges lack expertise
   b) Courts not accountable; judges not elected
  3. Various reasons for activism
   a) Too many lawyers; but real cause adversary culture
   b) Easier to get standing in courts
 D. Legislation and courts
  1. Laws and the Constitution are filled with vague language
   a) Ambiguity gives courts opportunities to design remedies
   b) Courts can interpret language in different ways
  2. Federal government is increasingly on the defensive in court cases; laws induce litigation
  3. The attitudes of federal judges affect their decisions
VIII. Checks on judicial power
 A. Judges are not immune to politics or public opinion
  1. Effects will vary from case to case
  2. Decisions can be ignored
   a) Examples: school prayer, segregated schools
   b) Usually if register is not highly visible
 B. Congress and the courts
  1. Confirmation and impeachment proceedings alter the composition of the courts
  2. Changing the number of judges
  3. Revising legislation declared unconstitutional
  4. Altering jurisdiction of the courts and restricting remedies
  5. Constitutional amendment

    C.   Public opinion and the courts
          1.   Defying public opinion, especially elite opinion, frontally is dangerous
          2.   Opinion in realigning eras may energize court
          3.   Public confidence in court since 1966 has varied
          4.   Change caused by changes of personnel and what government is doing
    D.   Reasons for increased activism
          1.   Growth of government
          2.   Activist ethos of judges

KEY TERMS MATCH

Set 1

Match the following terms and descriptions:

1.   A pattern of voting behavior of two or more justices

2.   Rules defining relationships among private citizens

3.   A ruling that declared that Negroes could not be federal citizens

4.   An individual who represents the federal government before the Supreme Court

5.   The practice, authorized by statutes, under which the plaintiff is enabled to collect costs from the defendant if the latter loses

6.   The meeting at which the justices vote on cases that they have recently heard

7.   A means by which one who has an interest in a case but is not directly involved can present arguments in favor of one side

8.   A means by which one who has been injured can bring action on behalf of all similarly situated

9.   The power of the courts to determine the constitutionality of legislative and executive acts

10.   The scope of authority by which a higher court reviews a case from a lower court

11.   An issue the Court refuses to consider, believing the Constitution intends another branch to make the decision

12.   A requirement that must be satisfied before a plaintiff can have a case heard on its merits

13.   A tradition under which the Senate will defer to the judgment of a senator of the

a.   activist approach

b.   amicus curiae

c.   appellate jurisdiction

d.   bloc voting

e.   civil law

f.   class action suit

g.   constitutional court

h.   criminal law

i.   diversity case

j.   Dred Scott v. Sandford

k.   fee shifting

l.   Friday conference

m.   judicial review

n.   political question

o.   senatorial courtesy

p.   solicitor general

q.   standing

r.   stare decisis

s.   strict-constructionist approach

t.   writ of certiorari

president's party when determining the suitability of candidates for federal judgeships from the senator's state

14. The body of rules defining offenses that are considered to be offenses against society as a whole

15. Litigation in which a citizen of one state sues a citizen of another state and the amount of money in dispute is more than $50,000

16. A court established under Article III of the Constitution

17. A decision that permits a case to be heard by the Supreme Court when four justices approve

18. The rule of precedent

19. The idea that judges should amplify the vague language of the Constitution on the basis of their moral or economic philosophy and apply it to the case before them

20. The idea that judges should confine themselves to applying those rules stated in or clearly implied by the language of the Constitution

Set 2

Match the following terms and descriptions:

1. The federal courts with authority to review decisions .by federal district courts, regulatory commissions, and certain other federal courts

2. A brief, unsigned opinion issued by the Supreme Court to explain its ruling

3. The party that initiates a lawsuit to obtain a remedy for an injury to her or his rights

4. A court that is created by Congress for some specialized purpose

5. The doctrine that a citizen cannot sue the government without its consent

6. The view that judges should discern the general principles underlying the Constitution and assess how best to apply

a. activist approach (judicial)
b. brief
c. concurrent opinion
d. courts of appeal
e. dissenting opinion
f. district court
g. federal question cases
h. in forma pauperis
i. legislative court
j. litmus test
k. opinion of the court

them in contemporary circumstances

7. A Supreme Court opinion by one or more justices who agree with the majority's conclusion but for different reasons

8. A Supreme Court opinion written by one or more justices in the majority to explain the decision in a case

9. A procedure whereby a poor person can file and be heard in court as a pauper, free of charge

10. The lowest federal courts, where federal cases begin and the only federal courts in which trials are held

11. A Supreme Court opinion by one or more justices in the minority to explain the minority's disagreement with the Court's ruling

12. The view that judges should decide cases on the basis of the specific language of the Constitution

13. A legal document prepared by an attorney representing a party before a court

14. A judicial order preventing or redressing a wrong or enforcing a right

15. Cases concerning the Constitution, federal law, or treaties over which the federal courts have jurisdiction as described in the Constitution

16. A way of finding out what a person's views are on a controversial question

l. per curiam opinion

m. plaintiff

n. remedy

o. sovereign immunity

p. strict-constructionist approach

DID YOU THINK THAT . . . ?

Below are listed a number of misconceptions. You should be able to refute each statement in the space provided, referring to information or argumentation contained in this chapter. Sample answers appear at the end of this chapter.

1. "The Framers expected the Supreme Court to play the large role that it subsequently has played."

_____

_____

_____

2. "When the Supreme Court makes a decision it resolves that issue as far as national politics is concerned."

   _____

   _____

   _____

3. "Judges merely apply the law. Therefore, it does not matter what individuals are appointed to the courts so long as they are skilled lawyers."

   _____

   _____

   _____

4. "One good thing about the judiciary is that no interest groups are involved."

   _____

   _____

   _____

DATA CHECK

Table 14.2: How Partisanship Affects Judicial Attitudes

1. Is a Republican or a Democratic judge more likely to take a strict-constructionist approach to the Constitution?

   _____

2. Is a Republican or a Democratic judge more likely to agree with affirmative action considerations in hiring decisions?

   _____

3. Is a Republican or a Democratic judge more likely to favor less government regulation of business?

   _____

Figure 14.1: Female and Minority Judicial Appointments, 1963–2000

4. Did the highest total percentage of female and black judicial appointments take place during a Democratic or Republican presidency, and who was that president?

   _____

5. Did the highest total percentage of Hispanic judicial appointments take place during a Democratic or Republican presidency, and who was that president?

   _____

6.   Did the lowest total percentage of female and Hispanic judicial appointments take place during a Democratic or Republican presidency, and who was that president?

_____

7.   Did the lowest total percentage of black judicial appointments take place during a Democratic or Republican presidency, and who was that president?

_____

Tables 14.3: Supreme Court Justices in Order of Seniority, 1999

8.   What is the most commonly represented prior experience of the nine justices of the Court?

_____

9.   How many justices were appointed by Republican presidents?

_____

10.   Who is the only current justice to come to the Court without previous judicial experience?

_____

11.   If age is a reasonable predictor of who will retire / resign from the Court next, who should we expect to retire / resign next?

_____

12.   Who is the youngest member of the Court?

_____

PRACTICING FOR EXAMS

TRUE/FALSE QUESTIONS

Read each statement carefully. Mark true statements *T*. If any part of the statement is false, mark it *F*, and write in the space provided a concise explanation of why the statement is false.

1.   T   F   The only court the Constitution requires is the Supreme Court.

_____

2.   T   F   The tradition of senatorial courtesy give great weight to the preferences to the senators from the states where judges on the U.S. Courts of Appeals are to serve.

_____

3.   T   F   Democratic judges tend to be more conservative than Republican ones.

_____

4.   T   F   In two judicial circuits it is illegal for state universities to have affirmative action plans.

_____

5.   T   F   In recent years Supreme Court nominations have usually been confirmed by the Senate.

_____

6.   T   F   Under some circumstances a criminal case involving only a violation of state law can be appealed to the United Sates Supreme Court.

_____

7.   T   F   In a typical year the Supreme Court may consider over seven thousand petitions.

_____

8.   T   F   The influence of law clerks on the selection of the Supreme Court's cases and the rendering of its decisions is considerable.

_____

9.   T   F   A taxpayer brought a lawsuit in order to require the CIA to make its budget public and won.

_____

10.   T   F   The Supreme Court has made the rules governing class actions suits more lenient in recent years.

_____

11.   T   F   The Supreme Court begins each term in the month of August.

_____

12.   T   F   Interest groups lobby the Supreme Court through the use of so-called amicus briefs.

_____

13.   T   F   In conference the Chief Justice speaks first, followed by the other justices in order of seniority.

_____

14.   T   F   The vague language in congressional statutes provide additional opportunities for courts to exercise power.

_____

15.   T   F   Schools all over the country were allowing prayers long after the Supreme Court ruled such activities were not allowed in public schools.

_____

16.   T   F   No federal judge has ever been impeached.

_____

17.   T   F   Congress can change the number of members who are allowed to sit on the Supreme Court.

_____

18.   T   F   One president has gone on to become a Supreme Court justice.

_____

19.   T   F   Judicial review can be exercised in France, but only upon the request of a government official.

_____

20.   T   F   The conservative Court of Chief Justice Rehnquist has overturned most of the critical decisions that came out of the more liberal Court, headed by Chief Justice Warren.

MULTIPLE CHOICE QUESTIONS

Circle the letter of the response that best answers the question or completes the statement.

1.   The dramatic and sometimes bitter conflict surrounding some Supreme Court nominations can only be explained by the fact that

   a.   there are only nine people on the Court.
   b.   the Court plays such a large role in making public policy.
   c.   the partisan balance of the Court is quite skewed.
   d.   Presidents rarely seek the "advice" of the Senate.
   e.   nominees are rarely qualified for the job.

2.   Strict-constructionist judges differ from activist judges in that they are more likely to

   a.   adopt a liberal viewpoint on such issues as states' rights and birth control.
   b.   apply rules that are clearly stated in the Constitution.
   c.   see, and take advantage of, opportunities in the law for the exercise of discretion.
   d.   believe in the application of judicial review to criminal matters.
   e.   look for and apply the general principles underlying the Constitution.

3.   Fifty years ago judicial activists tended to be

   a.   strict constructionists.
   b.   liberals.
   c.   conservatives.
   d.   moderates.
   e.   radicals.

4.   In *Federalist* 78, Alexander Hamilton described the judicial branch as the _____ branch.

   a.   most corrupt
   b.   least political
   c.   reliable
   d.   existential
   e.   least dangerous

5.   During the period from the end of the Civil War to the beginning of the New Deal, the dominant issue that the Supreme Court faced was that of

   a.   government regulation of the economy.
   b.   rights of privacy.
   c.   states' rights versus federal supremacy.
   d.   slavery.
   e.   government regulation of interstate commerce.

6.   Which of the following statements about *McCulloch v. Maryland* is correct?

   a.   It established judicial review.
   b.   It ruled a national bank unconstitutional.
   c.   It restricted the scope of congressional power.
   d.   It allowed states to tax federal agencies.

e.   It established the supremacy of national laws over state laws.

7.   Who was defiant of Supreme Court rulings and supposedly taunted the Chief Justice to go and "enforce" one of its decisions?

a.   the Mayor of New York City
b.   the Governor of New York
c.   the Cherokee Indians of Georgia
d.   Robert Fulton
e.   President Andrew Jackson

8.   Roger B. Taney was deliberately chosen for the Supreme Court because he

a.   opposed the invention of the steamboat.
b.   opposed the creation of a national bank.
c.   favored a strong national government.
d.   was an advocate of state's rights.
e.   opposed slavery.

9.   The court-packing bill is an example of a presidential action designed to

a.   help the Court reduce its backlog.
b.   influence the way in which the Court decides its cases.
c.   make the Court more impartial.
d.   make the Court stop deciding economic questions.
e.   allow the Court to grow with society.

10. Franklin Roosevelt's plan to reorganize the Supreme Court called for

a.   the Court to meet once every other year.
b.   the total number of justices to be increased according to the age of sitting justices.
c.   the president to select justices without senatorial confirmation.
d.   the Senate to have the power to remove justices from the Court at will.
e.   all New Deal legislation to be removed from the Court's jurisdiction.

11. The two kinds of lower federal courts created to handle cases that need not be decided by the Supreme Court are

a.   constitutional and district.
b.   appeals and limited jurisdiction.
c.   district and appeals.
d.   appeals and legislative.
e.   constitutional and legislative.

12. Carp and Roland's study of twenty thousand district court cases between 1933 and 1977 discovered the decisions of judges were significantly influenced by

a.   fact patterns in cases.
b.   precedent.
c.   their party background.
d.   lower court decision-making.
e.   statutory construction.

13. When politicians complain about the use of "litmus tests" in judicial nominations, they are probably

a.   Democrats.
b.   Republicans.

    c.   Liberals.

    d.   Conservatives.

    e.   not part of the group that is currently in power.

14.   Which of the following statements about the selection of federal judges is correct?

    a.   The principle of senatorial courtesy applies to the selection of Supreme Court justices.

    b.   Presidents generally appoint judges whose political views reflect their own.

    c.   Since personal attitudes and opinions have little impact in judicial decision making, presidents are usually not too concerned about who they nominate.

    d.   Nominees for district judgeships often face tough confirmation battles in the Senate.

    e.   The application of political litmus tests to Supreme Court nominees is no longer legal.

15.   If citizens of different states wish to sue one another in a matter involving more than $75,000, they can do so in

    a.   either a federal or a state court.

    b.   a court in the plaintiff's state only.

    c.   an intermediate court of appeals.

    d.   a court in the defendant's state only.

    e.   a federal court only.

16.   If you wish to declare bankruptcy, you must do so in

    a.   a court in the state in which you reside.

    b.   a state appellate court.

    c.   a federal appellate court.

    d.   the U.S. Supreme Court.

    e.   a federal district court.

17.   *Certiorari* is a Latin word meaning, roughly,

    a.   "certified."

    b.   "made more certain"

    c.   "without certainty"

    d.   "appealed"

    e.   "judicial"

18.   What percentage of appeals court cases is rejected by the Supreme Court?

    a.   1 percent

    b.   20 percent

    c.   30 percent

    d.   50 percent

    e.   99 percent

19.   Fee shifting enables the plaintiff to

    a.   get paid by the Department of Justice.

    b.   split costs with the court.

    c.   have taxpayers pay his or her costs.

    d.   split the costs with the defendant.

    e.   collect costs from the defendant if the defendant loses.

20.   To bring suit in a court, a plaintiff must first show that

    a.   there is a defendant.

    b.   the defendant is a real person.

c. there is no true case and controversy.
d. the defendant is a citizen of the United States.
e. the plaintiff has standing.

21. The solicitor general has the job of

    a. serving as liaison between the Department of Justice and the president.
    b. deciding whether to sue large corporations.
    c. deciding who is eligible for the Supreme Court.
    d. deciding which cases the government will take to the Supreme Court.
    e. deciding which cases the Supreme Court will hear.

22. A political question is a matter

    a. involving voters.
    b. that the Constitution has left to another branch of government.
    c. that an elected state judge has dealt with.
    d. that causes conflict among average voters.
    e. that must first be acted on by Congress.

23. According to the text, the most powerful indicator of judicial power can be found in

    a. the use of judicial review.
    b. the extent to which precedent is followed.
    c. the types of political questions courts are willing to handle.
    d. the kinds of remedies that courts will impose.
    e. the use of per curiam opinions.

24. Common criticisms of judicial activism include all of the following *except*

    a. judicial activism only works when laws are devoid of ambiguous language.
    b. judges usually have no expertise in designing complex institutions.
    c. judges are not elected and are therefore immune to popular control.
    d. judicial activism often fails to account for the costs of implementing activist rulngs.
    e. judges usually have no expertise in managing complex institutions.

25. Which of the following is a major restraint on the influence of federal judges?

    a. politics, especially the results of recent elections
    b. Rule 17
    c. the lack of effective enforcement power
    d. the veto power of the president
    e. international law

26. A major reason that the courts play a greater role in American society today than they did earlier in the century is that

    a. government plays a greater role generally.
    b. lawyers are more influential than ever.
    c. public opinion is less focused.
    d. judges are better trained.
    e. the courts are more representative of American society.

ESSAY QUESTIONS

Practice writing extended answers to the following questions. These test your ability to integrate and express the ideas that you have been studying in this chapter.

1. Write an essay in which you compare and contrast the way in which the Supreme Court makes policy with the way in which the legislature makes policy.

2. Do you think that the Founders expected the Supreme Court to play the role that it has played in recent years? Why or why not?

3. What were the important constitutional and judicial issues raised in *Marbury v. Madison*? What two roles did John Marshall play in the case? What was his ruling? What were the results of the ruling?

ANSWERS TO KEY TERMS MATCH QUESTIONS

Set 1

1. d
2. e
3. j
4. p
5. k
6. l
7. b
8. f
9. m
10. c
11. n
12. q
13. o
14. h
15. i
16. g
17. t
18. r
19. a
20. s

Set 2

1. d
2. l
3. m
4. i
5. o
6. a
7. c
8. k
9. h
10. f

11. e

12. p

13. b

14. n

15. g

16. j

ANSWERS TO "DID YOU THINK THAT . . . ?" QUESTIONS

1. Sometimes the Court's decision catalyzes opposition and causes further controversy. See, for example, the aftermath of *Dred Scott v. Sandford* and New Deal legislation.

2. Vagueness in laws and in the Constitution leaves important discretion to judges. Many tend to display liberal or conservative patterns of decisions.

3. Interest groups get involved through class action suits, amicus curiae briefs, and bringing lawsuits themselves.

4. The frequency with which the Court grants review helps determine whether federal law differs in different parts of the country; it also determines the size of the Court's backlog of cases.

ANSWERS TO DATA CHECK QUESTIONS

1. Republican.

2. Democrat.

3. Democrat.

4. Democrat, Clinton.

5. Democrat, Carter.

6. Republican, Nixon.

7. Republican, Reagan.

8. Judicial experience, especially federal.

9. Seven.

10. Chief Justice Rehnquist.

11. John Paul Stevens.

12. Clarence Thomas.

ANSWERS TO TRUE/FALSE QUESTIONS

1. T

2. F. Senatorial courtesy is more of a factor in appointments to U.S. District Courts than it is appointments to U.S. Court's of Appeal.

3. F. Democratic judges tend to be more liberal.

4. T

5. T

6. T
7. T
8. T
9. F. The Court decided the taxpayer did not have standing.
10. F. The Court has drastically tightened the rules governing these cases in response to its workload.
11. F. The Court's term begins in October.
12. T
13. T
14. T
15. T
16. F. Fifteen have been impeached in our history.
17. T
18. T
19. T
20. F. As of yet, there has been no wholesale retreat from the positions of the Warren Court.

ANSWERS TO MULTIPLE CHOICE QUESTIONS

1. b
2. b
3. c
4. e
5. a
6. e
7. e
8. d
9. b
10. b
11. e
12. c
13. e
14. b
15. a
16. e
17. b
18. e

19. e

20. e

21. b

22. b

23. d

24. a

25. c

26. a

PART 3

Classic Statement: "Bureaucracy," from Max Weber: *Essays in Sociology*[1]

INTRODUCTION

Although Weber's essay on bureaucracy certainly does not focus specifically on American government, it does deal with the way in which both governments and all large private enterprises in the modern world organize themselves and operate. It is thus relevant to our study not only of the power of the executive branch of government but also of the powers of the other branches, the political parties, and privately incorporated businesses.

Weber compares the organization of the major activities of human life in traditional society and in our own times—gemeinshaft and gesellshaft, in his terminology. Face-to-face interactions based on personal loyalties give way to large, impersonal organizations run by abstract rules and loyalty to the organization itself, whether private or public.

CHARACTERISTICS OF BUREAUCRACY

Modern officialdom functions in the following specific manner:

I.   There is the principle of fixed and official jurisdictional areas, which are generally ordered by rules, that is, by laws or administrative regulations.

1.   The regular activities required for the purposes of the bureaucratically governed structure are distributed in a fixed way as official duties.

2.   The authority to give commands required for the discharge of these duties is distributed in a stable way and is strictly delimited by rules concerning the coercive means, physical, sacerdotal, or otherwise, which may be placed at the disposal of officials.

3.   Methodological provision is made for the regular and continuous fulfillment of these duties and for the execution of the corresponding rights; only persons who have the generally regulated qualifications to serve are employed.

II.   The principles of office hierarchy and of levels of graded authority mean a firmly ordered system of super- and subordination in which there is a supervision of the lower offices by the higher ones. Such a system offers the governed the possibility of appealing the decision of a lower office to its higher authority, in a definitely regulated manner. With the full development of the bureaucratic type, the office hierarchy is monocratically organized. The principle of hierarchical office

---

[1] Max Weber, a German scholar, is widely referred to as the father of sociology, yet his writings cover a variety of different fields and have been influential in many of them—political science being no exception. His essay on bureaucracy, from which this selection is taken, comes from *From Max Weber: Essays in Sociology*, edited and translated by H. H. Gerth and C. Wright Mills (New York: Oxford University Press, 1946).

authority is found in all bureaucratic structures: in state and ecclesiastical structures as well as in large party organizations and private enterprises. It does not matter for the character of bureaucracy whether its authority is called "private" or "public."

When the principle of jurisdictional "competency" is fully carried through, hierarchical subordination—at least in public office—does not mean that the "higher" authority is simply authorized to take over the business of the "lower." Indeed, the opposite is the rule. Once established and having fulfilled its task, an office tends to continue in existence and be held by another incumbent.

III.   The management of the modern office is based upon written documents ("the files"), which are preserved in their original or draught form. There is, therefore, a staff of subaltern officials and scribes of all sorts. The body of officials actively engaged in a "public" office, along with the respective apparatus of material implements and the files, make up a "bureau." In private enterprise, "the bureau" is often called "the office".

IV.   Office management, at least all specialized office management—and such management is distinctly modern—usually presupposes thorough and expert training. This increasingly holds for the modern executive and employee of private enterprises, in the same manner as it holds for the state official.

V.   When the office is fully developed, official activity demands the full working capacity of the official, irrespective of the fact that his obligatory time in the bureau may be firmly delimited. In the normal case, this is only the product of a long development, in the public as well as in the private office. Formerly, in all cases, the normal state of affairs was reversed: official business was discharged as a secondary activity.

VI.   The management of the office follows general rules, which are more or less stable, more or less exhaustive, and which can be learned. Knowledge of these rules represents a special technical learning, which the officials possess. It involves jurisprudence, or administrative or business management.

The reduction of modern office management to rules is deeply embedded in its very nature. The theory of modern public administration, for instance, assumes that the authority to order certain matters by decree—which has been legally granted to public authorities—does not entitle the bureau to regulate the matter by commands given for each case, but only to regulate the matter abstractly. This stands in extreme contrast to the regulation of all relationships through individual privileges and bestowals of favor, which is absolutely dominant in patrimonialism, at least in so far as such relationships are not fixed by sacred tradition.

THE LEVELING OF SOCIAL DIFFERENCES

Bureaucratic organization has usually come into power on the basis of a leveling of economic and social differences. This leveling has been at least relative, and has concerned the significance of social and economic differences for the assumption of administrative functions.

Bureaucracy inevitably accompanies modern *mass democracy* in contrast to the democratic self-government of small homogeneous units. This results from the characteristic principle of bureaucracy: the abstract regularity of the execution of authority, which is a result of the demand for "equality before the law" in the personal and functional sense—hence, of the horror of "privilege," and the principled rejection of doing business "from case to case." Such regularity also follows from the social preconditions of the origin of bureaucracies. The nonbureaucratic administration of any large social structure rests in some way upon the fact that existing social, material, or honorific preferences and ranks are connected with administrative functions and duties. This usually means that a direct or indirect economic exploitation or a "social" exploitation of position, which every sort of administrative activity gives to its bearers, is equivalent to the assumption of administrative functions.

We must expressly recall at this point that the political concept of democracy, deduced from the "equal rights" of the governed, includes these postulates: (1) prevention of the development of a closed status group of officials in the interest of a universal accessibility of office, and (2) minimization of the authority of officialdom in the interest of expanding the sphere of influence on "public opinion" as far as practicable. Hence, wherever possible, political democracy strives to shorten the term of office by election and recall and by not binding the candidate to a special expertness. Thereby democracy inevitably comes into conflict with the bureaucratic tendencies which, by its fight against notable rule, democracy has produced. The generally loose term "democratization" cannot be used here, in so far as it is understood to mean the minimization of the civil servants' ruling power in favor of the greatest possible "direct" rule of the *demos*, which in practice means the respective party leaders of the *demos*. The most decisive thing here—indeed it is rather exclusively so—is the *leveling of the governed* in opposition to the ruling and bureaucratically articulated group, which in its turn may occupy a quite autocratic position, both in fact and in form.

THE PERMANENT CHARACTER OF THE BUREAUCRATIC MACHINE

Once it is fully established, bureaucracy is among those social structures which are the hardest to destroy. Bureaucracy is *the* means of carrying "community action" over into rationally ordered "societal action." Therefore, as an instrument for societalizing" relations of power, bureaucracy has been and is a power instrument of the first order—for one who controls the bureaucratic apparatus.

The individual bureaucrat cannot squirm out of the apparatus in which he is harnessed. In contrast to the honorific or avocational "notable," the professional bureaucrat is chained to his activity by his entire material and ideal existence. In the great majority of cases, he is only a single cog in an ever-moving mechanism which prescribes to him an essentially fixed route of march. The official is entrusted with specialized tasks and normally the mechanism cannot be put into motion or arrested by him, but only from the very top. The individual bureaucrat is thus forged to the community of all the functionaries who are integrated into the mechanism. They have a common interest in seeing that the mechanism continues its functions and that the societally exercised authorities carries on.

The ruled, for their part, cannot dispense with or replace the bureaucratic apparatus of authority once it exists. For this bureaucracy rests upon expert training, a functional specialization of work, and an attitude set for habitual and virtuoso-like mastery of single yet methodically integrated functions. If the official stops working, or if his work is forcefully interrupted, chaos results, and it is difficult to improvise replacements from among the governed who are fit to master such chaos. More and more the material fate of the masses depends upon the steady and correct functioning of the increasingly bureaucratic organizations of private capitalism. The idea of eliminating these organizations becomes more and more utopian.

The discipline of officialdom refers to the attitude-set of the official for precise obedience within his *habitual* activity, in public as well as in private organizations. Such compliance has been conditioned into the officials, on the one hand, and, on the other hand, into the governed. If such an appeal is successful it brings, as it were, the disturbed mechanism into gear again.

The objective indispensability of the once-existing apparatus, with its peculiar, "impersonal" character, means that the mechanism—in contrast to feudal orders based upon personal piety—is easily made to work for anybody who knows how to gain control over it. A rationally ordered system of officials continues to function smoothly after the enemy has occupied the area; he merely needs to change the top officials. This body of officials continues to operate because it is to the vital interest of everyone concerned.

Such a machine makes "revolution," in the sense of the forceful creation of entirely new formations of authority, technically more and more impossible, especially when the apparatus controls the modern means of communication (telegraph, et cetera) and also by virtue of its internal rationalized structure. In classic fashion, France has demonstrated how this process has substituted *coups d'état* for "revolutions": all successful transformations in France have amounted to *coups d'état*.

Questions for Understanding and Discussion

1. What are the key characteristics of modern officialdom?

2. What relationship does Weber say exists between democratization and bureaucracy?

3. Why, according to Weber, does bureaucracy tend to become permanent, and what does this do to the prospects for social or political revolution?

PART FOUR: The Politics of Public Policy

CHAPTER 15

The Policy-Making Process

REVIEWING THE CHAPTER

CHAPTER FOCUS

In this chapter we move from the study of political and governmental institutions (president, Congress, courts, etc.) to the study of the policies that all those institutions have produced. The purpose of this chapter is to provide you with a set of categories (majoritarian, interest group, client, and entrepreneurial politics) to help you better understand politics in general and the remainder of the book in particular. After reading and reviewing the material in this chapter, you should be able to do each of the following:

1. Explain how certain issues at certain times get placed on the public agenda for action.

2. Identify the terms *costs, benefits,* and *perceived* as used in this chapter.

3. Use these terms to define the four types of politics presented in the text—majoritarian, interest group, client, and entrepreneurial—giving examples of each.

4. Review the history of business regulation in this country, using it to exemplify these four types of politics.

5. Discuss the roles played in the process of public policy formation by people's perceptions, beliefs, interests, and values.

STUDY OUTLINE

I.   Setting the agenda
     A.   Most important decision affecting policy-making is deciding what belongs on the political agenda
          1.   Shared beliefs determine what is legitimate
          2.   Legitimacy affected by
               a)   Shared political values
               b)   Weight of custom and tradition
               c)   Changes in way political elites think about politics
     B.   The legitimate scope of government action
          1.   Always gets larger
               a)   Changes in public's attitudes
               b)   Influence of events
          2.   May be enlarged without public demand even when conditions improving

3. Groups: a motivating force in adding new issues
   a) May be organized (corporations) or disorganized (urban minorities)
   b) May react to sense of relative deprivation—people's feeling that they are worse off than they expected to be
      Example: Riots of the 1960s

   c) May produce an expansion of government agenda
      Example: New commissions and laws

   d) May change the values and beliefs of others
      Example: White response to urban riots

4. Institutions a second force adding new issues
   a) Major institutions: courts, bureaucracy, Senate, national media
   b) Courts
      (1) Make decisions that force action by other branches: school desegregation, abortion
      (2) Change the political agenda
   c) Bureaucracy
      (1) Source of political innovation: size and expertise
      (2) Thinks up problems to solve
      (3) Forms alliances with senators and their staffs
   d) Senate
      (1) More activists than ever
      (2) Source of presidential candidates with new ideas
   e) Media
      (1) Help place issues on political agenda
      (2) Publicize those issues raised by others, such as safety standards proposed by Senate
5. Evolution of political agenda
   a) Changes in popular attitudes that result in gradual revision of the agenda
   b) Critical events, spurring rapid changes in attitudes
   c) Elite attitudes and government actions, occasioning volatile and interdependent change

II. Making a decision
   A. Nature of issue
      1. Affects politicking
      2. Affects intensity of political conflict
   B. Costs and benefits of proposed policy a way to understand how issue affects political power
      1. Cost: any burden, monetary or nonmonetary
      2. Benefit: any satisfaction, monetary or nonmonetary
      3. Two aspects of costs and benefits important:
         a) Perception affects politics
         b) People consider whether it is legitimate for a group to benefit
      4. Politics a process of settling disputes about who benefits and who ought to benefit
      5. People prefer programs that provide benefits at low cost.
      6. Perceived distribution of costs and benefits shapes the kinds of political coalitions that form but not who wins

III. Majoritarian politics: distributed benefits, distributed costs
   A. Gives benefits to large numbers
   B. Distributes costs to large numbers
   C. Initial debate in ideological or cost terms, for example, military budgets

IV.   Interest group politics: concentrated benefits, concentrated costs
    A.   Gives benefits to relatively small group
    B.   Costs imposed on another small group
    C.   Debate carried on by interest groups (labor unions versus businesses)
V.   Client politics: concentrated benefits, distributed costs
    A.   Relatively small group benefits; group has incentive to organize
    B.   Costs distributed widely
    C.   Most people unaware of costs, sometimes in form of pork barrel projects
VI. Entrepreneurial politics: distributed benefits, concentrated costs
    A.   Gives benefits to large numbers
    B.   Costs imposed on small group
    C.   Success may depend on people who work on behalf of unorganized majorities
    D.   Legitimacy of client claims is important, for example, the Superfund
VII. The case of business regulation
    A.   The question of wealth and power
        1.   One view: economic power dominates political power
        2.   Another view: political power a threat to a market economy
        3.   Text cautious; weighs variables
    B.   Majoritarian politics
        1.   Antitrust legislation in the 1890s
            a)   Public indignation strong but unfocused
            b)   Legislation vague; no specific enforcement agency
        2.   Antitrust legislation in the twentieth century strengthened
            a)   Presidents take initiative in encouraging enforcement
            b)   Politicians, business leaders committed to firm antitrust policy
            c)   Federal Trade Commission created in 1914
            d)   Enforcement determined primarily by ideology and personal convictions
    C.   Interest group politics
        1.   Labor-management conflict
            a)   1935: labor unions seek government protection for their rights: businesses oppose
                (1)   Unions win
                (2)   Wagner Act creates NLRB
            b)   1947: Taft-Hartley Act a victory for management
            c)   1959: Landrum-Griffin Act another victory for management
        2.   Politics of the conflict
            a)   Highly publicized struggle
            b)   Winners and losers determined by partisan composition of Congress
            c)   Between enactment of laws, conflict continues in NLRB
        3.   Similar pattern found in Occupational Safety and Health Act of 1970
            a)   Reflects a labor victory
            b)   Agency established
    D.   Client politics
        1.   Agency capture likely
        2.   Licensing of attorneys, barbers, and so on
            a)   Prevents fraud, malpractice, and safety hazards
            b)   Also restricts entry into occupation or profession; allows members to charge higher prices
            c)   Little opposition since:
                (1)   People believe regulations protect them
                (2)   Costs are not obvious
        3.   Regulation of milk industry

                         a)   Regulation prevents price competition, keeping price up

                         b)   Public unaware of inflated prices

                         c)   Consumers have little incentive to organize

                4.   Sugar quotas also benefit sugar producers

                5.   Attempts to change regulations and cut subsidies and quotas

                         a)   1996 bill replaced crop subsidies with direct cash payments

                         b)   Subsidies continued to increase

                         c)   2002 law replaced 1996 law, and new subsidies were authorized

                         d)   Subsidies: the result of history and politics

                6.   Client politics for "special interests" seems to be on decline

                         a)   Importance of appearing to be "deserving"

                         b)   Regulation can also serve to hurt a client (e.g., FCC and radio broadcasters/telephone companies)

       E.   Entrepreneurial politics; relies on entrepreneurs to galvanize

                1.   1906: Pure Food and Drug Act protected consumer

                2.   1960s and 1970s: large number of consumer and environmental protection statutes passed (Clear Air Act, Toxic Substance Control Act)

                3.   Policy entrepreneur usually associated with such measures (Ralph Nader, Edmund Muskie)

                         a)   Often assisted by crisis or scandal

                         b)   Debate becomes moralistic and extreme

                4.   Risk of such programs: agency may be "captured" by the regulated industry

                5.   Newer agencies less vulnerable

                         a)   Standards specific, timetables strict

                         b)   Usually regulate many different industries; thus do not face unified opposition

                         c)   Their existence has strengthened public-interest lobbies

                         d)   Allies in the media may attack agencies with probusiness bias

                         e)   Public-interest groups can use courts to bring pressure on regulatory agencies

VIII. Perceptions, beliefs, interests, and values

       A.   Problem of definition

                1.   Costs and benefits not completely defined in money terms

                2.   Cost or benefit a matter of perception

                3.   Political conflict largely a struggle to make one set of beliefs about costs and benefits prevail over another

       B.   Types of arguments used

                1.   "Here-and-now" argument

                2.   Cost argument

       C.   Role of values

                1.   Values: our conceptions of what is good for our community or our country

                2.   Emphasis on self-interest

                3.   Ideas as decisive forces

       D.   Deregulation

                1.   Example: airline fares, long-distance telephone rates, trucking

                2.   A challenge to "iron triangles" and client politics

                3.   Explanation: the power of ideas

                         a)   Idea: government regulation was bad

                         b)   Started with academic economists

                         c)   They were powerless but convinced politicians

                         d)   Politicians acted for different reasons

                               (1)   Had support of regulatory agencies and consumers

                               (2)   Industries being deregulated were unpopular

4. Reducing subsidies; for example, the tobacco industry
    a) Supported by members of Congress from tobacco-growing states
    b) Allowed growers to borrow against unsold tobacco and not pay back the loan
    c) Public went along until smoking became issue
    d) New system: growers pay subsidies
    e) Widely held beliefs (against smoking) defeated narrow interests (subsidies)
5. Presidents since Ford have sought to review government regulation
6. Many groups oppose deregulation
    a) Dispute focuses mostly on *how* deregulation occurs
    b) "Process regulation" can be good or bad
7. The limit of ideas
    a) Some clients are just too powerful, for example, dairy farmers, agricultural supports
    b) But trend is toward weaker client politics

KEY TERMS MATCH

Match the following terms and descriptions:

1. A business that will not employ nonunion workers

2. A situation in which government bureaucracy thinks up problems for government to solve

3. Political activity in which both benefits and costs are widely distributed

4. Deciding what belongs on the political agenda

5. Political activity in which one group benefits at the expense of many other people

6. Political activity in which benefits are distributed, costs are concentrated

7. Political activity in which benefits are conferred on a distinct group and costs on another distinct group

8. A sense of being worse off than one thinks one ought to be

9. A situation in which people are more sensitive to what they might lose than to what they might gain

10. People in and out of government who find ways of creating a legislative majority on behalf of interests not well-represented in government

11. A boycott by workers of a company other than the one against which the strike is directed

a. agenda setting

b. benefit

c. boycott

d. client politics

e. closed shop

f. cost

g. cost argument

h. entrepreneurial politics

i. interest-group politics

j. logrolling

k. majoritarian politics

l. policy entrepreneurs

m. political agenda

n. pork barrel projects

o. process regulation

p. professionalization of reform

q. relative deprivation

r. secondary boycott

s. Sherman Antitrust Act

12. A law passed in 1890 making monopolies illegal

13. Any satisfaction that people believe they will derive if a policy is adopted

14. A concerted effort to get people to stop buying from a company in order to punish and to coerce a policy change

15. The perceived burden to be borne if a policy is adopted

16. Mutual aid among politicians, whereby one legislator supports another's pet project in return for the latter's support

17. A set of issues thought by the public or those in power to merit action by government

18. Legislation that gives tangible benefits to constituents in the hope of winning their votes

19. Rules regulating manufacturing or industrial processes, usually aimed at improving consumer or worker safety and reducing environmental damage

DID YOU THINK THAT . . . ?

Below are listed a number of misconceptions. You should be able to refute each statement in the space provided, referring to information or argumentation contained in this chapter. Sample answers appear at the end of this chapter.

1. "Policy-making always operates the same way. If you know how institutions work, you know how policies are shaped."

    _____

    _____

    _____

2. "Government regulation is always opposed by industry."

    _____

    _____

    _____

3. "The bottom line in politics is money."

    _____

    _____

PRACTICING FOR EXAMS

TRUE/FALSE QUESTIONS

Read each statement carefully. Mark true statements *T.* If any part of the statement is false, mark it *F,* and write in the space provided a concise explanation of why the statement is false.

1. T   F   The expansion of government has been the result, fundamentally of a non-partisan process.

2. T   F   Congressional action has been the preferred vehicle for advocates of unpopular causes.

3. T   F   Somewhat contrary to the intent of the Framers, the House of Representatives has become a source of significant political change.

4. T   F   Conflicts between rival interest groups are not nearly so important in majoritarian politics.

5. T   F   Interest group politics often produce decisions about which the public is uninformed.

6. T   F   The Brady Bill requires background checks on gun buyers before they can purchase a firearm.

7. T   F   The Founders deliberately arranged things so that it would be difficult to pass a new law.

8. T   F   Policy entrepreneurs are outside of government.

9. T   F   Much of the antitrust legislation that was passed in this country was the result of entrepreneurial politics.

10. T   F   The Grange was an association of small businessmen who opposed the expansion of large corporations across state lines.

11. T   F   Theodore Roosevelt was influential in prompting more prosecutions for violations of antitrust laws.

12. T   F   Between 1996 and 2001 subsidies for farmers decreased.

_____

13. T   F   Our antitrust policy is perhaps the strongest found in any industrial nation.

_____

14. T   F   Antitrust enforcement in any particular administration is largely determined by the amount of interest group pressure that is applied.

_____

15. T   F   In the labor conflicts of the 1940s and 1950s, Republicans and southern Democrats tended to support the interests of businesses.

_____

16. T   F   Radio broadcasters strongly opposed the creation of the Federal Communications Commission (FCC).

_____

17. T   F   Upton Sinclair's book *The Jungle* dramatized the frightening conditions in steel mills.

_____

18. T   F   The ban on smoking on all domestic flights was enacted in 1987. _

_____

19. T   F   Environmental protection agencies are more prone to capture than other agencies.

_____

20. T   F   Tobacco subsidies are no longer paid for by taxpayers but dairy and sugar supports still are.

_____

MULTIPLE CHOICE QUESTIONS

Circle the letter of the response that best answers the question or completes the statement.

1. Policy-making is *most* affected by the decision to

    a.   enact the policy agenda.
    b.   get on the policy agenda.
    c.   enforce the policy agenda.
    d.   fund the policy agenda.
    e.   fund and enforce the policy agenda.

2. Who noted that the government "big enough to give you every thing you want" is also the government "big enough to take away everything you have?"

    a.   Richard Nixon
    b.   Ralph Nader
    c.   Dwight Eisenhower
    d.   Jimmy Carter
    e.   Gerald Ford

3.   Popular views on the legitimate scope of government action are changed primarily by

    a.   education.
    b.   sensible politics.
    c.   the impact of the Constitution.
    d.   elaborate theories.
    e.   the influence of current events.

4.   The Occupational Safety and Health Act of 1970 was passed at a time when

    a.   the number of industrial deaths had increased steadily for a decade.
    b.   the number of industrial deaths had been dropping steadily for twenty years.
    c.   industrial fatalities had remained the same for several years.
    d.   data on industrial fatalities were unavailable to Congress.
    e.   data on industrial fatalities were unreliable.

5.   According to the text, Senate attention to new proposals for safety standards for coal mines and automobiles was correlated with

    a.   the results of public opinion polls.
    b.   the pages of the *New York Times*.
    c.   editorial commentary on *CNN*.
    d.   speeches made in the House of Representatives.
    e.   a series of elections.

6.   The nature of the issue on the current political agenda has its greatest influence on

    a.   presidential policy.
    b.   the prevailing ideas of society at large.
    c.   congressional monitoring.
    d.   prevailing media opinion.
    e.   the kinds of groups that get politically involved.

7.   Because of the way in which people view the costs and benefits of policies, there is a bias toward

    a.   policies that benefit the majority at the expense of minorities.
    b.   policies that have excessive long-run costs.
    c.   making people who benefit pay the costs of the policy.
    d.   distributive and regulative policies.
    e.   regulative rather than distributive policies.

8.   The text's explanation for the urban riots in the 1960s centers on

    a.   white radicals who mobilized blacks.
    b.   organized special-interest groups in urban areas.
    c.   followers of Marcus Garvey.
    d.   blacks' sense of relative deprivation.
    e.   the Black Panther movement.

9.   Each of the following institutions plays a major role in setting the political agenda and effecting government action *except* the

    a.   council of state governors.
    b.   courts.
    c.   the Senate.
    d.   bureaucracy.
    e.   media.

10.   Which of the following statements *best* describes government bureaucracy today?

    a.   It is a tool of big business.
    b.   It is a major source of policy.
    c.   It is an impartial institution.
    d.   It is an appendage of the political parties.
    e.   It is without significant influence in the policy-making process.

11.   An example of a policy characterized by distributed benefits and distributed costs is

    a.   a tariff on bicycle chains.
    b.   farm subsidies
    c.   dairy subsidies.
    d.   the construction of a dam.
    e.   increased Social Security benefits.

12.   If you receive benefits from a policy achieved by a group to which you do not belong, you are

    a.   a majoritarian.
    b.   a policy entrepreneur.
    c.   a free rider.
    d.   a neo-institutionalist.
    e.   a secondary entrepreneur.

13.   An example of a widely distributed benefit is

    a.   the reduction of factory pollution.
    b.   dairy subsidies.
    c.   farm subsidies.
    d.   the protection of a business from competition.
    e.   a dissident group's freedom to speak.

14.   Majoritarian policies tend to reflect

    a.   interest group activity.
    b.   interest group conglomerations.
    c.   philosophies of governance.
    d.   the times.
    e.   political party activity.

15.   An example of client politics is

    a.   social welfare.
    b.   labor legislation.
    c.   licensing of barbers.
    d.   antitrust legislation.
    e.   All of the above.

16.   An example of entrepreneurial politics would be

    a.   agricultural price supports.
    b.   Social Security.
    c.   a tariff on imported cars.
    d.   requirements for antipollution and safety devices on cars.
    e.   None of the above.

17.   The type of politics that often takes on a moralistic tone, with opponents portrayed as devils and compromises strongly resisted, is

    a.   interest group politics.
    b.   majoritarian politics.
    c.   client politics.
    d.   entrepreneurial politics.
    e.   neo-institutional politics.

18.   The Superfund program was born in

    a.   1950.
    b.   1960.
    c.   1970.
    d.   1980.
    e.   1990.

19.   The Superfund was intended to force

    a.   the automobile industry to manufacture cars that were more safe.
    b.   industries to clean up their own toxic waste sites.
    c.   the coal mining industry to reduce hours and increase wages.
    d.   paper mills to reduce the emission of air pollutants.
    e.   Congress to protect the rights of consumers.

20.   The theory that the political system always operates to serve corporate interests is

    a.   Weberian.
    b.   pluralist.
    c.   Freudian.
    d.   Marxist.
    e.   sociological.

21.   A policy that did *not* pit a majority against a hostile business community was the

    a.   antitrust policy.
    b.   farm subsidy policy.
    c.   space policy.
    d.   labor policy.
    e.   All of the above.

22.   Over the years enforcement of antitrust policy has been

    a.   quite lax.
    b.   generally quite successful.
    c.   variable, depending on the president and the chief administrator.
    d.   consistently favorable to big business.
    e.   consistently biased against big business.

23.   The tobacco industry long resisted efforts to change the system under which it received federal subsidies for unsold tobacco. What finally brought about change?

    a.   concern about the health effects of smoking
    b.   President Carter's program of deregulation
    c.   a series of controversies involving shipment of tobacco products.
    d.   President Reagan's Task Force on Regulatory Relief
    e.   citizen anger at paying for unsold goods

24. The text speaks of the "power of ideas" as a key force in the deregulation of several industries that has occurred over the past two decades. Where did these ideas most often originate?

    a. with academic economists
    b. with the courts, especially the Supreme Court
    c. with broadcasters in local news stations
    d. with the national media
    e. with Congress, especially the Senate

25. One reason that the newer consumer protection agencies may not be so vulnerable to capture is that

    a. older interest groups support them.
    b. they do not impose very large costs on industry.
    c. they impose a very large cost on industry.
    d. their regulations are obviously beneficial.
    e. they regulate several industries and so do not face a single, unified opponent.

ESSAY QUESTIONS

Practice writing extended answers to the following questions. These test your ability to integrate and express the ideas that you have been studying in this chapter.

26. Write a pluralist rebuttal to the Marxist assertion that economics controls politics in the formation of public policy.

27. Why does your text assert that "the scope of legitimate government action is always getting larger"? What would be required to reduce the scope of government action?

28. What types of policies do you think are most likely to be beneficial for the nation? How might majoritarian policy be detrimental to the nation? (Consider, for example, the difficulty in modifying Social Security benefits in the interest of the larger economy.)

ANSWERS TO KEY TERMS MATCH QUESTIONS

1. e
2. p
3. k
4. a
5. d
6. h
7. i
8. q
9. g
10. l
11. r
12. s
13. b
14. c
15. f
16. j
17. m
18. n
19. o

ANSWERS TO "DID YOU THINK THAT . . . ?" QUESTIONS

1. The structure of political activity is substantially influenced by the way in which costs and benefits of a proposed policy are distributed in society.

2. Some types of regulation benefit existing businesses by keeping out competitors or by artificially raising prices. Thus businesses sometimes want regulation.

3. Most policies probably do not have an immediate effect on a person's pocketbook. Politics is also a matter of perceptions, beliefs, and values.

ANSWERS TO TRUE/FALSE QUESTIONS

1. T
2. F. The courts are the preferred vehicle for advocates of unpopular cases.
3. F. This commentary is more appropriate for the Senate.
4. T
5. T

6. T
7. T
8. F. They may be in or out of government.
9. F. Much of it was actually the result of majoritarian politics.
10. F. The Grange was an organization of farmers.
11. T
12. F. They increased.
13. T
14. F. It is more determined by the political ideology and personal convictions of the administration in power.
15. T
16. F. They supported it because they desired order and stability to their industry.
17. F. The book dealt with the meatpacking industry.
18. T
19. F. The text identifies several reasons why they are not as vulnerable to capture as some critics contend.
20. T

ANSWERS TO MULTIPLE CHOICE QUESTIONS

1. b
2. e
3. e
4. b
5. b
6. e
7. b
8. d
9. a
10. b
11. e
12. c
13. a
14. c
15. c
16. e
17. d

18. d
19. b
20. d
21. a
22. c
23. a
24. a
25. e

CHAPTER 16

Economic Policy

REVIEWING THE CHAPTER

CHAPTER FOCUS

The purpose of this chapter is to introduce you to an area of public policy that affects everyone in one way or another: economic policy. The chapter covers both the divided attitudes that voters have toward a "good" economy and the competing theories that economists offer on how to obtain a good economy. The various agencies that participate in formulating government economic policy are reviewed, along with the many stages of producing and implementing the annual federal budget. Finally, the controversial areas of government spending and tax reform are discussed. After reading and reviewing the material in this chapter, you should be able to do each of the following:

1. Show how voters have contradictory attitudes regarding their own and others' economic benefits.

2. List and briefly explain the four competing economic theories discussed in the chapter.

3. Assess the nature and effect of Reaganomics.

4. List the four major federal government agencies involved in setting economic policy, and explain the role of each.

5. Analyze federal fiscal policy in terms of the text's four categories of politics.

6. Trace the history of federal government budgeting practices up to the present day.

7. Comment on the prospects and the desirability of lowering federal spending and reforming the income tax.

STUDY OUTLINE

I.   Introduction
    A.   The politics of deficit spending
        1.   1999 / 2000 financial "miracle" (first surplus since 1969)
        2.   Uniform public opinion versus divided politicians
            a)   Cut spending?
            b)   Raise taxes?
        3.   Rapid growth of economy and increase in personal income and incoming taxes reduced deficit
        4.   New Debate: What to do with the extra money?
            a)   Republicans: return it to the taxpayers
            b)   Democrats: spend it on new programs
            c)   Economic Growth and Tax Relief Reconciliation Act of 2001
            d)   2010 expiration and increase in spending on federal programs
            e)   Future economic conditions are difficult to predict
II.   The politics of American economic prosperity

A.   Health of American economy creates majoritarian politics
    1.   Voters influenced by their immediate economic situation
    2.   Voters worry about the nation as a whole as well as their own situations
    3.   Voting behavior and economic conditions correlated at the national level but not at the individual level
        a)   People understand what government can and cannot be held accountable for
        b)   People see economic conditions as affecting them indirectly, even when they are doing well
B.   What politicians try to do
    1.   Elected officials tempted to take short-term view of the economy
    2.   Government uses money to influence elections, but government will not always do whatever is necessary
        a)   Government does not know how to produce desirable outcomes
        b)   Attempting to cure one economic problem often exacerbates another
    3.   Ideology plays a large role in determining policy
        a)   Democrats tend to want to reduce unemployment
        b)   Republicans tend to want to reduce inflation
III.   The politics of taxing and spending
  A.   Inconsistency in what people want out of majoritarian politics
    1.   No tax increases
    2.   No government deficit
    3.   Continued (or higher) government spending
  B.   Proposals to spend projected budget surplus in 1999
    1.   Tax cuts
    2.   New or enlarged government programs
    3.   Reduce the debt
  C.   Difficult to make meaningful tax cuts
    1.   Politicians get reelected by spending money
    2.   Increased spending more popular than cutting taxes
IV.   Economic theories and political needs
  A.   Monetarism—inflation occurs when there is too much money chasing too few goods (Milton Friedman); advocates increase in money supply about equal to economic growth
  B.   Keynesianism—government should create right level of demand
    1.   Assumes that health of economy depends on what fraction of their incomes people save or spend
    2.   When demand is too low, government should spend more than it collects in taxes by creating public works programs
    3.   When demand is too high, government should increase taxes
  C.   Planning—free market too undependable to ensure economic efficiency; therefore government should control it (John Kenneth Galbraith)
    1.   Wage-price controls
    2.   Industrial policy—government directs investments toward particular industries
  D.   Supply-side tax cuts—need for less government interference and lower taxes (Arthur Laffer)
    1.   Lower taxes would create incentives for investment
    2.   Greater productivity would produce more tax revenue
  E.   Ideology and theory: people embrace an economic theory partly because of their political beliefs
  F.   Reaganomics
    1.   Combination of monetarism, supply-side tax cuts, and domestic budget cutting
    2.   Goals not consistent
        a)   Reduction in size of federal government

            b)   Increase in military strength
       3.   Effects
            a)   Rate of growth of spending slowed (but not spending itself)
            b)   Military spending increased
            c)   Money supply controlled
            d)   Federal taxes decreased
            e)   Large deficits incurred and dramatically increase the size of the national debt
            f)   Unemployment decreased
V.   The machinery of economic policy-making
   A.   Fragmented policy-making; not under president's full control
       1.   Council of Economic Advisers
            a)   Members chosen are sympathetic to president's view of economics and are experts
            b)   Forecasts economic trends
            c)   Prepares annual economic report for president
       2.   Office of Management and Budget
            a)   Prepares estimates of federal government agencies; negotiates department budgets
            b)   Ensures that agencies' legislative proposals are compatible with president's program
       3.   Secretary of the Treasury
            a)   Reflects point of view of financial community
            b)   Provides estimates of government's revenues
            c)   Recommends tax changes; represents the nation before bankers and other nations
       4.   The Fed (Federal Reserve Board)
            a)   Independent of both president and Congress
            b)   Regulates supply and price of money
       5.   Congress most important in economic policy making
            a)   Approves taxes and expenditures
            b)   Consents to wage and price controls
            c)   Can alter Fed policy by threatening to reduce its powers
   B.   Effects of interest group claims
       1.   Usually majoritorian: economic health good for all
       2.   Sometimes interest group: free trade (e.g., NAFTA)
VI.   Spending money
   A.   Conflict between majoritarian and client or interest group politics
   B.   Sources of conflict reflected in inconsistencies in public opinion
   C.   Politicians have incentive to make two kinds of appeals
       1.   Keep spending down and cut deficit
       2.   Support favorite programs of voters
VII. The budget
   A.   Earlier practices
       1.   Merely adding expenditures before 1921
       2.   No unified presidential budget until 1930s
       3.   Separate committee reactions after that
   B.   Congressional Budget Act of 1974: procedures
       1.   President submits budget
       2.   House and Senate budget committees analyze budget
       3.   Budget resolution in May proposes budget ceilings
       4.   Members informed whether or not spending proposals conform to budget resolutions

5. Committees approve appropriations bills, Congress passes them, and sends them to the president for signature
6. Hard to make big changes in government spending because of entitlements
7. Big loophole: Congress not required to tighten government's financial belt
8. Failures of the process after 1981

VIII. Reducing Spending
    A. Gramm-Rudman Balanced Budget Act (1985) called for:
        1. A target cap on the deficit each year, leading to a balanced budget
        2. A spending plan within those targets
        3. If lack of agreement on a spending plan exists, automatic across-the-board percentage budget cuts (a sequester)
    B. "Smoke and mirrors" and failure of the Act
        1. Plan was unpopular, but "necessary"
        2. Congress and president found ways to increase spending about "target" anyway
    C. New strategies
        1. Congress votes for a tax increase
        2. Passage of Budget Enforcement Act of 1990
            a) Imposed a cap on discretionary spending (i.e., nonentitlements)
            b) No limit on mandatory spending (i.e., entitlements) but did impose a "pay-as-you-go" approach

IX. Levying taxes
    A. Tax policy reflects blend of majoritarian and client politics
        1. "What is a 'fair' tax law?" (majoritarian)
            a) Tax burden is kept low; Americans pay less than citizens in most other countries
            b) Requires everyone to pay something; Americans cheat less than others
        2. "How much is in it for me?" (client)
            a) Requires the better-off to pay more
            b) Progressiveness is a matter of dispute: hard to calculate
            c) Many loopholes: example of client politics
        3. Client politics (special interests) make tax reform difficult, but Tax Reform Act passed (1986)
    B. The rise of the income tax
        1. Most revenue derived from tariffs until 1913 and ratification of Sixteenth Amendment
        2. Taxes then varied with war (high), peace (low)
            a) High rates offset by many loopholes: compromise
            b) Constituencies organized around loopholes
         3. Tax bills before 1986 dealt more with deductions than with rates
        4. Tax Reform Act of 1986: low rates with smaller deductions
        5. Will Bush tax cuts expire in 2010 or be made permanent?

KEY TERMS MATCH

Match the following terms and descriptions:

1. A group that forecasts economic trends

2. The theory that the health of an economy depends on what fraction of their incomes people save or spend

3. Legislation that authorizes budget ceilings

4. An organization that provides estimates of

    a. budget

    b. budget resolution

    c. budget surplus

    d. Congressional Budget Act

    e. Council of Economic Advisers

tax revenues

5. The theory that voters worry about community and national interests

6. The use of the amount of money in bank deposits and the price of money to affect the economy

7. A combination of monetarism, tax cuts, and domestic budget cutting

8. The mechanism that regulates the supply and price of money

9. The theory that voters are mostly influenced by their own immediate economic situation

10. A budget in which expenditures exceed tax revenues

11. The use of taxes and expenditures to affect the economy

12. The theory that inflation occurs when there is too much money chasing too few goods

13. The theory that government should control wages and prices

14. A document that announces how much the government will collect in taxes and spend in revenues and how those expenditures will be allocated

15. Behaving in a manner that regards the condition of the national economy more so than one's own personal finances

16. A recommendation for budget ceilings to guide legislative committees in their spending decisions

17. A situation in which the government takes in more money than it spends

18. An economic philosophy that assumes that the government should plan some part of the country's economic activity

19. The period from October 1 to September 30 for which government appropriations are made and federal books are kept

20. An economic philosophy that would have the government planning or subsidizing investment in industries that need to recover or new and better industries that could replace them

f. deficit budget

g. economic planning

h. entitlements

i. Federal Reserve System

j. fiscal policy

k. fiscal year (FY)

l. industrial policy

m. Keynesianism

n. monetarism

o. monetary policy

p. other-regarding voters

q. planning

r. price and wage control

s. Reaganomics

t. self-regarding voters

u. sequester

v. sociotropic voting

w. supply-side theory

x. Tax Reform Act of 1970

y. Treasury Department

21. Represented a triumph for entrepreneurial politics

22. Government regulation of the maximum prices that can be charged and wages that can be paid

23. Automatic, across-the-board cuts in certain federal programs when Congress and the president cannot agree on a spending plan

24. An economic philosophy that holds that sharply cutting taxes would increase the incentive to invest, leading to more tax revenues

25. Mandatory government spending (e.g., Social Security, Medicare, Food Stamps)

DID YOU THINK THAT . . . ?

Below are listed a number of misconceptions. You should be able to refute each statement in the space provided, referring to information or argumentation contained in this chapter. Sample answers appear at the end of this chapter.

1. "The president should bear the blame when the nation's economy does not perform well, because he controls the government agencies that in turn control the economy."

_____

_____

_____

2. "Elected officials need to study the economy and respond with the appropriate tax increases or budget reductions."

_____

_____

_____

3. "The budget is so large that it should be relatively easy to find programs to cut."

_____

_____

_____

4. "It is possible to produce generous spending on programs with low taxes and no deficit."

_____

_____

_____

DATA CHECK

Figure 16.1: Bad Economic Guesses

1.   What is the general impression made by this chart?

_____

2.   Can you identify an instance where, for a period of time, the two lines are actually close?

_____

Figure 16.4: Tax Burdens in Nineteen Democratic Nations

3.   What country has the highest tax burden?

_____

4.   What country has the lowest tax burden?

_____

5.   How does the tax burden of the United States compare with other nations in the Figure?

_____

Figure 16.5: Federal Taxes on Income, Top Percentage Rates, 1913–2002

6.   How far back must we go in history to find top-bracket tax rates for individuals that are lower than they were during the Reagan era?

_____

7.   How far back must we go in history to find top-bracket corporate tax rates that are lower than they were during the Reagan era?

_____

PRACTICING FOR EXAMS

TRUE/FALSE QUESTIONS

Read each statement carefully. Mark true statements *T*. If any part of the statement is false, mark it *F*, and write in the space provided a concise explanation of why the statement is false.

1.   T   F   In 1999 and 2000 the government spent less money than it took in for the first time since 1969.

_____

2.   T   F   A "sociotropic" voter votes on the basis of his / her own pocketbook.

_____

3.   T   F   Economics played a role in the defeats of Ford (1976), Carter (1980) and Bush (1992).

_____

4. T F   Most tax issues are majoritarian issues.

5. T F   Keynes believed the market would not automatically operate at a full-employment, low inflation level.

6. T F   If you are a liberal, monetarism would appeal to you.

7. T F   If you are a socialist, economic planning would appeal to you.

8. T F   "Reaganomics" was not dictated by any single economic theory.

9. T F   Bill Clinton reappointed Ronald Reagan's choice for Fed Chairman, Alan Greenspan.

10. T F   There was no federal budget at all before 1921.

11. T F   The procedures adopted by Congress affect the policies adopted by Congress.

12. T F   The Balanced-Budget Act of 1985 was successful.

13. T F   Most other democratic nations have a higher tax rate than the United States.

14. T F   There is evidence to suggest Americans evade their income taxes more than citizens in France or Italy.

15. T F   The Seventeenth Amendment created the federal income tax.

16. T F   Progressive tax rates are not part of the federal income tax scheme.

17. T F   Democrats have traditionally accepted loopholes as part of a political compromise.

18. T F   The big gainers in the Tax Reform Act of 1986 were businesses.

19. T F   Presidents Bush (the elder) and Clinton both proposed tax increases.

20. T   F   Few Democrats voted for George W. Bush's tax cut plan in 2002.

_____

MULTIPLE CHOICE QUESTIONS

Circle the letter of the response that best answers the question or completes the statement.

1.   Which of the following statements about the power of American government to make economic policy is correct?

     a.   It is divided among rival agencies.
     b.   It is the central purpose of political parties.
     c.   It is based primarily on international politics.
     d.   It is a result of entrepreneurial politics.
     e.   It is rarely the product of more than a few influences.

2.   Self-regarding theory holds that

     a.   officials think mainly about increasing their power.
     b.   political parties encourage self-interest.
     c.   voters are influenced largely by their immediate economic situations.
     d.   citizens put the nation ahead of business or their personal economic situations.
     e.   self-interested voters will support public officials.

3.   Self-regarding theory would *not* have predicted that in a time of general prosperity, a majority of Americans would believe that _____ was (were) the nation's most important problem.

     a.   unemployment
     b.   inflation
     c.   price supports
     d.   militarism
     e.   imperialism.

4.   After the Social Security system was established, Congress voted to increase benefits

     a.   according to a specific formula.
     b.   only in times of high inflation.
     c.   for low-income recipients only.
     d.   in almost every election year.
     e.   when there were surpluses.

5.   Choices about economic policy are shaped most significantly by the

     a.   party affiliation of legislators.
     b.   occupational status of legislators.
     c.   seniority of legislators.
     d.   predictions of economists.
     e.   ideology of cabinet members

6.   Democrats tend to be more worried than Republicans about

     a.   inflation.
     b.   international politics.
     c.   unemployment.
     d.   business investment.
     e.   recessions.

7.   Lower taxes, less debt, and spending on new government programs produce _____ politics.

    a.   entrepreneurial
    b.   majoritarian
    c.   interest group
    d.   client
    e.   B and D.

8.   Politicians have a strong tendency to get reelected by

    a.   decreasing taxes.
    b.   lowering the deficit.
    c.   cutting expenditures.
    d.   spending money on specific programs that are popular.
    e.   raising taxes.

9.   Milton Friedman takes the position that inflation is caused when there is

    a.   too little money chasing too few goods.
    b.   too much money chasing too many goods.
    c.   too little money chasing too many goods.
    d.   too much money chasing too few goods.
    e.   when the government has a predictable increase in the money supply.

10. Keynesians believe that if people save too much

    a.   they will pay too little in taxes.
    b.   they will invest too little.
    c.   production and money supply will increase.
    d.   demand will decrease and production will decline.
    e.   demand and production will increase.

11. A follower of Keynes would probably agree with all of the following statements *except*

    a.   the government should make sure there is the right level of demand.
    b.   the government should take an activist role in the economy.
    c.   money should be taken out of the economy when demand is too great.
    d.   if demand increases too fast, prices will go up.
    e.   the government should balance the budget each and every year.

12. An economic policy of government's directing investments is called

    a.   wage-price controls.
    b.   industrial policy.
    c.   monetarism.
    d.   Keynesianism.
    e.   sociotropic policy.

13. A key element of the supply-side theory of the economy is the

    a.   importance of incentives.
    b.   need for careful control of the money supply.
    c.   need for a balanced budget.
    d.   need for close attention to trade imbalances.
    e.   importance of regulations.

14. All of the following were true under "Reaganomics" *except*

    a.   spending on some domestic programs was reduced.

b. military spending was sharply increased.

c. there were sharp across the board cuts in personal income taxes.

d. business activity decreased.

e. there was a drop in the unemployment rate.

15. The "fiscal year" begins on

a. April 1

b. October 1

c. December 1

d. January 1

e. April 15

16. Which statement about the Federal Reserve Board is *correct*?

a. It has fifteen members.

b. Each member is appointed by the president and confirmed by the Senate.

c. A member's term is fourteen years.

d. Since its founding in 1913 no member has ever been removed.

e. The Chairman serves a four-year term.

17. The "troika" that assists the president in making economic policy is composed of the Council of Economic Advisers, the Office of Management and Budget, and the

a. Federal Trade Commission.

b. Treasury Department.

c. Secretary of Labor.

d. Federal Reserve Board.

e. Department of Labor.

18. The most important part of the economic policy making machinery is the

a. Federal Reserve Board.

b. Congress.

c. Council of Economic Advisers.

d. General Services Administration.

e. Secretary of Labor.

19. The Congressional Budget Act of 1974 was intended to

a. impose some budget discipline on committees.

b. increase the power of the president.

c. allow interest groups more access to the budget process.

d. implement zero-based budgeting.

e. invite members of Congress to allocate funds in creative ways.

20. Entitlements (that is, mandatory spending) makes up about _____ of what government spends.

a. one-tenth

b. one-fourth

c. one-half

d. two-thirds

e. very little

21. The law enacted by Congress that imposed a cap on discretionary spending (that is, entitlements) was the

a. Budget Enforcement Act of 1990.

    b.   Balanced Budget Act of 1985.
    c.   Budget and Impoundment Act of 1974.
    d.   Budget and Accounting Act of 1921.
    e.   Monetary Control Act of 1973

22.   People are *most* likely to embrace a particular economic theory because of

    a.   their race.
    b.   the condition of the world economy.
    c.   their political beliefs.
    d.   their religious beliefs.
    e.   the condition of their state's economy.

23.   The text states that tax policy is a blend of majoritarian and client politics. What is an example of the latter?

    a.   progressive taxation
    b.   a low tax burden
    c.   tax loopholes
    d.   a requirement that everyone pay something
    e.   A and D.

24.   Tax loopholes mostly benefit

    a.   average citizens.
    b.   the very rich.
    c.   businesses.
    d.   self-employed persons.
    e.   farmers.

25.   The 1986 Tax Reform Act represented the triumph of _____ politics.

    a.   entrepreneurial
    b.   majoritarian
    c.   client
    d.   interest group
    e.   egalitartian

ESSAY QUESTIONS

Practice writing extended answers to the following questions. These test your ability to integrate and express the ideas that you have been studying in this chapter.

1.   Why is it usually unfair to blame or praise the president for the performance of the economy at any particular time?

2.   The text states that the condition of the economy as a whole and the policies aimed at improving it are examples of majoritarian politics but that the details of such policies are characterized by interest group and client politics. Explain how these types of politics will result in policies that are less than necessary to provide a stronger economy.

3.   To what extent is economic policy determined by ideology and to what extent by the economic interests of those who influence policy?

ANSWERS TO KEY TERMS MATCH QUESTIONS

1. e
2. m
3. d
4. y
5. p
6. o
7. s
8. i
9. t
10. f
11. j
12. n
13. q
14. a
15. v
16. b
17. c
18. g
19. k
20. l
21. x
22. r
23. u
24. w
25. h

ANSWERS TO "DID YOU THINK THAT . . . ?" QUESTIONS

1. Agencies that affect the economy are highly fragmented. In addition, the president shares economic leadership with Congress.

2. Officials want to get reelected, and so they respond to the opinions of voters. But many voters are self-regarding and do not want officials to adopt policies that might take away their benefits.

3. Most of the budget is relatively uncontrollable because of past commitments, contracts, and payments to individuals that are guaranteed by law.

4. It is impossible—indeed, economically contradictory—to expect greater spending with having to raise taxes and creating a budget deficit.

ANSWERS TO DATA CHECK QUESTIONS

1. The economic guesses of the experts are not always quite so accurate.

2. 1987-1990.

3. Sweden.

4. Japan.

5. Tax rate in the United States are relatively low.

6. 1930s, Hoover administration.

7. 1950s, Truman administration.

ANSWERS TO TRUE/FALSE QUESTIONS

1. T

2. F. The sociotropic voter is concerned about health of the national economy.

3. T

4. T

5. T

6. F. If you are liberal, Keynesian economics would appeal to you.

7. T

8. T

9. T

10. T

11. T

12. F. According to the text, the plan failed.

13. T

14. F. There is reason to believe Americans evade income taxes less than do citizens of France and Italy.

15. F. The 16th Amendment created the federal income tax.

16. F. Progressive tax rates have been a part of our tax scheme.

17. T

18. F. Individuals were the big winners.

19. T

20. F. Many Democrats voted for the tax cut.

ANSWERS TO MULTIPLE CHOICE QUESTIONS

1. a
2. c
3. a
4. d
5. a
6. c
7. b
8. d
9. d
10. d
11. e
12. b
13. a
14. d
15. b
16. a
17. b
18. b
19. a
20. d
21. a
22. c
23. c
24. a
25. a

CHAPTER 17

Social Welfare

REVIEWING THE CHAPTER

CHAPTER FOCUS

This chapter covers more than fifty years of the political history of efforts to establish, maintain, expand, or cut those major programs that give or claim to give government help to individuals in need. After reading and reviewing the material in this chapter, you should be able to do each of the following:

1. Describe the goals of the American social welfare system, and contrast its programs with those of the British in terms of centralization.

2. Describe the major elements of the American system, including Social Security, Medicare, and AFDC programs.

3. Explain why some welfare policies can be considered majoritarian politics and others client politics. Give examples and indicate the political consequences of each.

4. Discuss recommendations to deal with the rising costs of Social Security and Medicare as well as the Welfare Reform Act of 1996.

STUDY OUTLINE

I. Social welfare in the United States
    A. Who deserves to benefit?
        1. Insistence that it be only those who cannot help themselves
        2. Slow, steady change in deserving/undeserving line
        3. Alternative view: fair share of national income; government redistribute money
        4. Preference to give services, not money, to help deserving poor
    B. Late arrival of welfare policy
        1. Behind twenty-two European nations
        2. Contrast with Great Britain in 1908
    C. Influence of federalism
        1. Federal involvement "illegal" until 1930s
        2. Experiments by state governments
            a) Argued against federal involvement because state already providing welfare
            b) Lobbied for federal involvement to help states
    D. Majoritarian welfare programs
        1. Social Security Act of 1935
            a) Great Depression of 1929: local relief overwhelmed
            b) Elections of 1932: Democrats and Franklin Roosevelt swept in
                (1) Legal and political roadblocks; was direct welfare unconstitutional?
                (2) Fear of more radical movements
                    (a) Long's "Share Our Wealth"
                    (b) Sinclair's "End Poverty in California"

         (c)   Townsend's old age program
- *c)*   Cabinet Committee's two-part plan
  - (1)   "Insurance" for unemployed and elderly
  - (2)   "Assistance" for dependent children, blind, aged
  - (3)   Federally funded, state-administered program under means test
- 2.   Medicare Act of 1965
  - *a)*   Medical benefits omitted in 1935: controversial but done to ensure passage
  - *b)*   Opponents
    - (1)   AMA
    - (2)   House Ways and Means Committee under Wilbur Mills
  - *c)*   1964 elections: Democrats' big majority altered Ways and Means
  - *d)*   Objections anticipated in plan
    - (1)   Application only to aged, not everybody
    - (2)   Only hospital, not doctors,' bills covered
  - *e)*   Broadened by Ways and Means to include Medicaid for poor; pay doctors' bills for elderly
- E.   Reforming majoritarian welfare programs
  - 1.   Social Security
    - *a)*   Not enough people paying into Social Security
    - *b)*   Three solutions
      - (1)   Raise the retirement age to seventy, freeze the size of retirement benefits, raise Social Security taxes
      - (2)   Privatize Social Security
      - (3)   Combine first two methods and allow individual investment in mutual funds
  - 2.   Medicare
    - *a)*   Problems: huge costs and inefficient
    - *b)*   Possible solutions
      - (1)   Get rid of Medicare and have doctors and hospitals work for government
      - (2)   Elderly take Medicare money and buy health insurance
    - *c)*   Delaying the inevitable
      - (1)   Clinton and surplus, new benefits
      - (2)   Bush and attempts at new health care measures
- F.   A client welfare policy: AFDC
  - 1.   Scarcely noticed part of Social Security Act
  - 2.   Federal government permitted state to
    - *a)*   Define *need*
    - *b)*   Set benefit levels
    - *c)*   Administer program
  - 3.   Federal government increased rule of operation
  - 4.   New programs (e.g., Food Stamps, Earned Income Credit, free school meals)
  - 5.   Difficult to sustain political support
    - *a)*   States complained about federal regulations
    - *b)*   Public opinion turned against program
    - *c)*   Composition of program participants changed
- II.   Two kinds of welfare programs
  - A.   Majoritarian politics: almost everybody pays and benefits, for example, the Social Security Act and the Medicare Act
  - B.   Client politics: everybody pays, relatively few people benefit, for example, the AFDC program
  - C.   Majoritarian politics
    - 1.   Programs with widely distributed benefits and costs

        a)   Beneficiaries must believe they will come out ahead
        b)   Political elites must believe in legitimacy of program
   2.   Social Security and Medicare looked like "free lunch"
   3.   Debate over legitimacy: Social Security (1935)
        a)   Constitution did not authorize federal welfare (conservatives)
        b)   But benefits were not really a federal expenditure (liberals)
   4.   Good politics unless cost to voters exceeds benefits
  D. Client politics
   1.   Programs pass if cost to public not perceived as great and client considered deserving
   2.   Americans believe today that able-bodied people should work for welfare benefits.
   3.   Americans prefer service strategy to income strategy
        a)   Charles Murray: high welfare benefits made some young people go on welfare rather than seek jobs
        b)   No direct evidence supports Murray

KEY TERMS MATCH

Match the following terms and descriptions:

1. First U.S. legislation, in 1935, providing for an income transfer program
2. Federally funded program that provides health care to the poor
3. Legislation enacted in 1965 providing medical insurance for the elderly
4. Financial assistance to the poor that replaced the AFDC program
5. Pre-1935 state programs to aid widows with children
6. Pre-1935 state-run or locally run homes for the poor
7. Huey Long's proposal to redistribute income in the United States
8. Upton Sinclair's proposal to redistribute income in California
9. Pre-Social Security proposal that was popular because it aimed to provide financial support to elderly people
10. Benefits paid weekly to laid-off workers unable to find jobs
11. Former federally funded program that made payments to poor families with children
12. Cash payments to poor people who are aged, blind, or disabled
13. Vouchers given to the poor to buy food at grocery stores

a. AFDC
b. almshouses
c. assistance program
d. client politics
e. earned income tax credit
f. EPIC
g. food stamps
h. income strategy
i. indexing
j. insurance program
k. majoritarian politics
l. means test
m. Medicaid
n. Medicare
o. Medicare Catastrophic Coverage Act
p. mother's pension
q. service strategy
r. Share Our Wealth plan
s. Social Security Act
t. SSI
u. TANF
v. Townsend plan

14. The mechanism by which payments rise automatically when costs do

         w.   UI

15. A proviso that only those below a specified poverty level qualify for a program

16. Policy-making in which almost everybody benefits and almost everybody pays.

17. An approach to welfare that aims to give poor people job training or government jobs rather than money

18. Legislation adopted in 1988 to protect the elderly against the costs of long-term medical care; later repealed

19. Policy-making in which relatively few people benefit but everybody pays

20. An approach to welfare in which poor people are given money

21. A program financed by income taxes that provides benefits to poor citizens without requiring contributions from them

22. A self-financing program based on contributions that provides benefits to unemployed or retired persons

23. A provision of the 1975 tax law that entitles working families with children to receive money if their incomes fall below a certain level

DID YOU THINK THAT . . . ?

Below are listed a number of misconceptions. You should be able to refute each statement in the space provided, referring to information or argumentation contained in this chapter. Sample answers appear at the end of this chapter.

1. "Welfare policies are instituted primarily to redistribute income among classes."

   _____

   _____

   _____

2. "The United States has led the way in pioneering social programs."

   _____

   _____

   _____

3.   "The national government is responsible for social welfare administration."

_____

_____

_____

4.   "The public was always supportive of the old AFDC program."

_____

_____

_____

DATA CHECK

Table 17.1: Public Views on Reforming Social Security

1.   What age cohort is most optimistic about the solvency of Social Security?

_____

2.   Are a majority of Americans in favor of raising the retirement age to seventy or reducing benefits?

_____

3.   Are Americans more inclined to support individual or government investment of Social Security funds?

_____

4.   Which particular item prompted the highest level of agreement in these surveys?

_____

Table 17.2: Health Care Spending in the United States and Abroad, 1996

5.   What country spends the greatest share of its gross domestic product on health care?

_____

Table 17.3: Opinions on Welfare by Race

6.   What is the general impression when one glances over the percentages that appear in the columns for blacks and whites?

_____

7.   Which item features the greatest amount of disagreement between blacks and whites?

_____

Table 17.4: Key Votes on Major Welfare Proposals in the House

8.   How many Republicans voted for the Social Security Act of 1935?

_____

9.   Which vote featured the largest number of Democrats "against" the proposal?

    _____

10.   Which vote featured the largest number of Republicans "against" the proposal?

    _____

PRACTICING FOR EXAMS

TRUE/FALSE QUSTIONS

Read each statement carefully. Mark true statements *T*. If any part of the statement is false, mark it *F*, and write in the space provided a concise explanation of why the statement is false.

1.   T   F   Welfare programs that have no *means* test are available to everyone without regard to income.

    _____

2.   T   F   Client-based welfare programs are *means* tested.

    _____

3.   T   F   The standard measure for welfare payments has been that of a family's fair share of the national income.

    _____

4.   T   F   Progressives in the United States were less interested in welfare legislation in the early twentieth century than were Labourites in Great Britain.

    _____

5.   T   F   The first social welfare system was adopted in this country in 1935.

    _____

6.   T   F   The New Deal plan for Social Security was a radical departure in the context of the 1930s.

    _____

7.   T   F   One part of the Social Security Act of 1935 created what came to be called Aid to Families with Dependent Children (AFDC).

    _____

8.   T   F   As a result of losing political legitimacy the Aid to Families With Dependent Children (AFDC) was abolished.

    _____

9.   T   F   The most difficult hurdle for the Medicare Act of 1965 was the House Ways and Means Committee.

    _____

10.   T   F   AFDC began as a noncontroversial client program.

    _____

11. T F   In welfare policy, a service strategy is strongly preferred to an income strategy.

___

12. T F   In recent years, most Americans have come to believe that able-bodied people on welfare should be made to work for welfare benefits.

___

13. T F   There usually exists popular support in the United States for helping the needy but not for redistributing income.

___

14. T F   Social Security is an example of majoritarian politics, while the old AFDC program was an example of client politics.

___

15. T F   The key problem for Social Security is that there soon will not be enough people paying Social Security taxes to provide benefits for every retired person.

___

16. T F   As a means of saving Social Security, most Americans favor raising the retirement age to seventy and raising Social Security taxes.

___

17. T F   The only problem associated with Medicare is its huge costs.

___

18. T F   Welfare programs that emphasize job training are based on an income strategy.

___

19. T F   Under the Welfare Reform Act of 1996, adults receiving benefits are required to work within two years.

___

20. T F   Americans pay less for health care than do citizens in most other western democracies.

___

MULTIPLE CHOICE QUESTIONS

Circle the letter of the response that best answers the question or completes the statement.

1. Welfare programs in which nearly everyone benefits and nearly everyone pays are characterized by

   a. overlapping politics.
   b. minoritarian politics.
   c. club-based politics.
   d. congruent politics.
   e. majoritarian politics.

2. The biggest problem facing majoritarian welfare programs is

   a. their cost.

b. their legitimacy.
c. their goals.
d. who will benefit.
e. how should clients be served.

3. The biggest problem facing client-oriented welfare programs is

a. their cost.
b. their legitimacy.
c. their goals.
d. who will pay.
e. how will costs be determined.

4. A welfare program such as the old Aid to Families with Dependent Children (AFDC) is a good example of

a. client politics.
b. club-based politics.
c. majoritarian politics.
d. interest group politics.
e. entrepreneurial politics.

5. Most of the welfare policies in the United States have attempted to

a. redistribute income.
b. change the existing tax structure.
c. help people with disabilities.
d. provide everyone with a guaranteed income.
e. balance the haves and the have-nots.

6. Which of the following beliefs is *not* held by the American people?

a. Income redistribution is a good thing.
b. Helping the needy is a good thing.
c. Assisting those who cannot help themselves is a good thing.
d. Giving people money will produce a class of welfare chiselers.
e. Giving people services rather than money is a good thing.

7. In distinct contrast to many other European nations, America's national welfare system

a. has emphasized the provision of money more than services.
b. has been a top priority of lawmakers since the 1880s.
c. is more oriented toward the basic notion of each person's "fair share."
d. is far less adversarial.
e. arrived quite late in our history.

8. By 1935 most states had adopted a _____ program.

a. mother's pension.
b. food stamp.
c. unemployment insurance.
d. work training
e. medicaid

9. Which of the following is a noncontributory, or public assistance, program, as opposed to a contributory program?

a. Medicare

b.   Aid to Families with Dependent Children
c.   Old Age and Survivors Disability Insurance
d.   unemployment insurance
e.   A and C.

10.   Following the creation of federal welfare programs in the early 1930s, the chief concern of the federal government was

a.   the states' acceptance of social welfare programs.
b.   how people would be compensated.
c.   how states would administer the program without proper funding.
d.   seeking qualified individuals to run the programs.
e.   the constitutionality of the programs.

11.   Dr. Francis E. Townsend's organization led a nationwide movement that demanded

a.   food stamps for all persons over the age of seventy-five.
b.   government pensions of $200 a month.
c.   health benefits for persons who were both elderly and disabled.
d.   free health insurance for all persons over the age of seventy-five.
e.   government run hospitals in each state.

12.   Which presidents initially supported the idea of having the government pay the medical and hospital bills of the elderly and the poor?

a.   Democrats
b.   Republicans
c.   both Democrats and Republicans
d.   those who were chosen in close elections
e.   those who were former governors

13.   The American Medical Association considered the idea of medical support for the elderly and poor to be

a.   "absolutely necessary."
b.   "consistent with the principles of our government."
c.   "a sure way to bankrupt the government."
d.   "incompatible with the rights of patients."
e.   "socialized medicine."

14.   By the 1960s a majority of the House favored a health care plan, but did not expect such legislation to ever reach the floor because

a.   presidents had so roundly condemned the idea.
b.   the Social Security system was unpopular.
c.   it was expected that the Supreme Court would probably rule such a plan unconstitutional.
d.   the Ways and Means Committee adamantly opposed the idea.
e.   All of the above.

15.   The _____ government program provides health care for poor people.

a.   Medicare
b.   Poverty Fund.
c.   Medifund
d.   Medicaid
e.   Temporary Assistance to Needy Families (TANF)

16. Which of the following is *not* a problem under Medicare?

    a.   Some doctors charge the government for their services.
    b.   A lot of people use medical services when they really do not need them.
    c.   There is fraud and abuse.
    d.   Old people are not "deserving" recipients.
    e.   Doctors and hospitals are paid on the basis of a government-approved payment plan.

17. A national advisory commission examined the Social Security crisis and proposed to President Clinton that

    a.   the retirement age be raised to eighty-five.
    b.   retirement benefits be increased.
    c.   Social Security taxes be lowered.
    d.   the program be privatized by investments in the stock market.
    e.   citizens be allowed to invest some portion of Social Security taxes in mutual funds.

18. Over the years AFDC recipients were eligible for the following new program:

    a.   Medicare.
    b.   Earned Income Credit.
    c.   unemployment compensation.
    d.   Food Stamp Program.
    e.   workman's compensation.

19. By 1994, about _____ of AFDC mothers had been on it for eight years or longer.

    a.   one-eighth
    b.   one-fourth
    c.   one-third
    d.   one-half
    e.   two-thirds

20. Programs such as Social Security and Medicare are the product of

    a.   client politics.
    b.   association politics.
    c.   majoritarian politics.
    d.   interest group politics.
    e.   entrepreneurial politics.

21. The big debate in 1935 and 1965 over Social Security and Medicare was over

    a.   whether the public wanted them.
    b.   whether they were too costly.
    c.   whether they constituted unnecessary duplication.
    d.   whether they were needed.
    e.   whether it was legitimate for government to provide them.

22. Which one of the following statements about the four major welfare programs is *not* true?

    a.   Each new policy was proposed by a president.
    b.   The debate on three of the four policies was heavily ideological.
    c.   Voting on each new welfare policy tended to follow party lines.
    d.   Public opinion was against passage of all four programs.
    e.   Public opinion was favorable to each.

ESSAY QUESTIONS

Practice writing extended answers to the following questions. These test your ability to integrate and express the ideas that you have been studying in this chapter.

1. Why did Great Britain develop a much more comprehensive social welfare system than the United States and institute it long before the United States?

2. Discuss what made it impossible to sustain political support for AFDC, which had begun as a noncontroversial form of client politics.

3. Discuss several ideas to save Social Security and Medicare and why none have been adopted to date.

4. Show how majoritarian politics has often worked better than client politics with respect to social welfare, giving examples of the results of each.

ANSWERS TO KEY TERMS MATCH QUESTIONS

1. s
2. m
3. n
4. u
5. p
6. b
7. r
8. f
9. v
10. w
11. a
12. t
13. g
14. i
15. l
16. k
17. q
18. o
19. d
20. h
21. c
22. j
23. e

ANSWERS TO "DID YOU THINK THAT . . . ?" QUESTIONS

1. After-tax income of all social classes has hardly changed as a proportion of the national income. The poor receive welfare not because they are poor but rather on the basis of certain specific circumstances: blindness, disability, age, or families with dependent children.

2. The United States has lagged behind other nations in passing social laws. Even today the welfare and medical programs of the United States have fewer benefits and less coverage than those of Canada, Australia, Japan, and most nations of Western Europe.

3. The major programs are decentralized, with states paying some costs, setting some policies, and administering most programs. The major exceptions, in which the national government runs the entire program, are the Social Security program and payments to the elderly, blind, and disabled.

4.   The AFDC program has been increasingly criticized over the last several decades. First, the public hated a program they thought was weakening the family by encouraging out-of-wedlock births. Second, the public worried that AFDC recipients were working covertly on the side. Third, the public complained that healthy parents were taking AFDC instead of working. Finally, the composition of the people in the program changed (that is, from women who had experienced the death or divorce of their husband to women who had never been married, from women who had been on the program for a short period of time to women who had been on AFDC for extended periods of time).

ANSWERS TO DATA CHECK QUESTIONS

1.   Those sixty-five years and older.

2.   No.

3.   Individual.

4.   Let some workers shift some of their Social Security taxes payments into personal retirement accounts to invest on their own.

5.   United States.

6.   The attitudes of blacks and white about welfare are very similar.

7.   "System does not give one skills and help they need to get people off of welfare."

8.   1.

9.   Family Assistance Plan (1970).

10.   Economic Opportunity (1964).

ANSWERS TO TRUE/FALSE QUESTIONS

1.   T

2.   T

3.   F. Such a notion of redistributing income has never been adopted here.

4.   T

5.   F. All but two of the states already had various social welfare programs.

6.   F. The Long, Townsend, and Sinclair plans would have gone even further.

7.   T

8.   T

9.   T

10.   T

11.   T

12.   T

13.   T

14.   T

15.   T

16. F. Polls indicate that they oppose both ideas.
17. F. It is also an inefficient form of health care.
18. F. They are based on a service strategy. An income strategy involves cash benefits directly.
19. T
20. F. They pay the most for health care.

ANSWERS TO MULTIPLE CHOICE QUESTIONS

1. e
2. a
3. b
4. a
5. c
6. a
7. e
8. a
9. b
10. e
11. b
12. a
13. e
14. d
15. d
16. d
17. e
18. b
19. e
20. c
21. e
22. d

CHAPTER 18

Civil Liberties

REVIEWING THE CHAPTER

CHAPTER FOCUS

This chapter surveys quite a number of pressure points that have developed in the American political system regarding the liberties of individuals and the government's involvement in protecting or restricting those liberties. Included among these pressure points are national security, federal versus state enforcement of rights, First Amendment freedoms, and criminal law. After reading and reviewing the material in this chapter, you should be able to do each of the following:

1.   Discuss the relationship of the Bill of Rights to the concept of democratic rule of the majority, and give examples of tension between majority rule and minority rights. Explain how the politics of civil liberties may at times become a mass issue, and offer several examples.

2.   Describe the conflicts that have arisen between those who claim First Amendment rights and those who are in favor of sedition laws that might restrict freedom of speech. Explain how the Supreme Court attempts to balance competing interests. Describe the various tests that the Court has applied.

3.   Explain how the structure of the federal system affects the application of the Bill of Rights. How has the Supreme Court used the Fourteenth Amendment to expand coverage in the federal system? Discuss changing conceptions of the due process clause of the Fourteenth Amendment.

4.   List the categories under which the Supreme Court may classify "speech." Explain the distinction between protected and unprotected speech, and name the various forms of expression that are not protected under the First Amendment. Describe the test used by the Court to decide the circumstances under which freedom of expression may be qualified.

5.   State what the Supreme Court decided in *Miranda* v. *Arizona,* and explain why that case illustrates how the Court operates in most such due process cases.

6.   Analyze why the resolution of civil liberties issues involves politics as well as law. Discuss the political factors that influence the Supreme Court when it decides fundamental civil liberties issues.

STUDY OUTLINE

I.   The politics of civil liberties
  A.   The objectives of the Framers
    1.   Limited federal powers
    2.   Constitution: a list of dos, not don'ts
    3.   Bill of Rights: specific do nots
      a)   Not intended to affect states
      b)   A limitation on popular rule
II.   Politics, culture, and civil liberties

A. Liberties become a major issue for three reasons
B. Rights in conflict: Bill of Rights contains competing rights
  1. *Sheppard* case (free press versus fair trial)
  2. *New York Times* and Pentagon Papers (common defense versus free press)
  3. Kunz anti-Jewish speeches (free speech versus public order)
  4. Struggles over rights show same pattern as interest group politics
C. Policy entrepreneurs most successful during crises, especially war, by arousing people
  1. Sedition Act of 1789, during French Revolution
  2. Espionage and Sedition Acts of World War I
  3. Smith Act of World War II
  4. Internal Security Act of 1950, Korean War
  5. Communist Control Act of 1954, McCarthy era
D. Cultural conflicts
  1. Original settlement by white European Protestants produced Americanism
  2. Waves of immigration brought new cultures, conflicts
    a) Non-Christians offended by government-sponsored creches at Christmas
    b) English speakers prefer monolingual schools
    c) Boy Scouts of America exclude homosexuals from being scout leaders
  3. Differences even within cultural traditions
III. Interpreting and applying the First Amendment
A. Speech and national security
  1. Original Blackstone view: no prior press censorship
  2. Sedition Act of 1789 followed Blackstone view
  3. By 1917–1919, Congress defines limits of expression
    a) Treason, insurrection, forcible resistance
    b) Upheld in *Schenck* via test of "clear and present danger"
    c) Justice Holmes dissents, saying test not met
  4. Fourteenth Amendment "due process" not applied to states originally; *Gitlow* elicits "fundamental personal rights"
  5. Supreme Court moves toward more free expression after WWI
    a) But communists convicted under Smith Act under "gravity of evil"
    b) By 1957, test of "calculated to incite"
    c) By 1969 (*Brandenburg*), "imminent" unlawful act
    d) 1977 American Nazi march in Skokie, Illinois, held lawful
    e) "Hate" speech permissible but not "hate crime"
B. What is speech?
  1. Some forms of speech not fully protected; four kinds
  2. Libel: written statement defaming another by false statement
    a) Oral statement: slander
    b) Variable jury awards
    c) Malice needed for public figures
  3. Obscenity
    a) Twelve years of decisions; no lasting definition
    b) 1973 definition: patently offensive by community standards of average person
    c) Balancing competing claims remains a problem
    d) Localities decide whether to tolerate pornography but must comply with strict rules
    e) Protection extended: nude dancing only marginally protected
    f) Indianapolis statute: pornography degrading but court disagreed
    g) Zoning ordinances upheld
    h) Regulation of electronic Internet (computer-simulated child pornography)

        4.   Symbolic speech
             a)   Acts that convey a political message: flag burning, draft card burning
             b)   Not generally protected
             c)   Exception is flag burning: restriction of free speech

IV.   Who is a person?
    A.   Corporations, etc., usually have same rights as individuals
        1.   Boston bank, antiabortion group, California utility
        2.   More restrictions on commercial speech
             a)   Regulation must be narrowly tailored and serve public interest
             b)   Yet ads have some constitutional protection
        3.   Young people may have fewer rights; Hazelwood; school newspaper can be restricted

V.   Church and state
    A.   The free exercise clause: no state interference, similar to speech
        1.   Law may not impose special burdens on religion
        2.   But no religious exemptions from laws binding all
        3.   Some cases difficult to settle
             a)   Conscientious objection to war, military service
             b)   Refusal to work Saturdays; unemployment compensation
             c)   Refusal to send children to school beyond eighth grade
    B.   The establishment clause
        1.   Jefferson's view: "wall of separation"
        2.   Congress at the time: "no national religion"
        3.   Ambiguous phrasing of First Amendment
        4.   Supreme Court interpretation: "wall of separation"
             a)   1947 New Jersey case (reimbursements)
                 (1)   Court: First Amendment applies to the states
                 (1)   Court: State must be neutral toward religion
             b)   Later decisions struck down
                 (1)   School prayers (voluntary, nonsectarian, delivered by a rabbi or minister or student elected by others students)
                 (2)   Teaching of creationism
                 (3)   In-school released time programs
             c)   Public aid to parochial schools particularly controversial
                 (1)   Allowed: aid for construction of buildings, textbook loans, tax-exempt status, state deductions for tuition, computers, and sign language interpreters
                 (2)   Disallowed: teacher salary supplements, tuition reimbursements, various school services, money to purchase instructional materials, special districts
                 (3)   Though the Court can (and does) change its mind
             d)   Development of a three-part test for constitutional aid
                 (1)   It has a strictly secular purpose
                 (2)   It neither advances nor inhibits religion
                 (3)   It involves no excessive government entanglement
             e)   Failure of the Court's test to create certainty in our law
                 (1)   Nativity scenes, menorahs, and Christmas trees
                 (2)   Seeming anomalies: Prayer in Congress, chaplains in the armed services, "In God We Trust" on currency
                 (3)   Deep division / confusion among members of the Court

VI.   Crime and due process
    A.   The exclusionary rule
        1.   Most nations punish police misconduct apart from the criminal trial

2. United States punishes it by excluding improperly obtained evidence
3. Supreme court rulings
   a) 1949: declined to use exclusionary rule
   b) 1961: changed, adopted it in *Mapp* case
B. Search and seizure
   1. When can "reasonable" searches of individuals be made?
      a) With a properly obtained search warrant with probable cause
      b) Incident to an arrest
   2. What can police search incident to an arrest?
      a) The individual being arrested
      b) Things in plain view
      c) Things under the immediate control of the individual
   3. What of an arrest while driving?
      a) Answer changes almost yearly
      b) Court attempts to protect a "reasonable expectation of privacy"
      c) Privacy in body and home but not from government supervisor
   4. Testing for drugs and AIDS
      a) Mandatory AIDS testing called for, not yet in place
      b) Government drug testing now in courts but private testing OK
      c) Supreme Court: some testing is permissible
         (1) Law enforcement and railroad employees
         (2) Random sobriety checks on drivers
         (3) Key: concern for public safety or national security
         (4) High school athletes
C. Confessions and self-incrimination
   1. Constitutional ban originally against torture
   2. Extension of rights in the 1960s
      a) *Escobedo*
      b) *Miranda* case: "Miranda rules" to prove voluntary confession
D. Relaxing the exclusionary rule
   1. Positions taken on the rule
      a) *Any* evidence should be admissible
      b) Rule had become too technical to work
      c) Rule a vital safeguard
   2. Supreme Court moves to adopt second position
E. Terrorism and Civil Liberties
   1. USA Patriot Act
      a) Telephone and internet taps, voice mail seizure
      b) Grand jury information exchange
      c) Detainment of non-citizens and deportation of aliens
      d) Money laundering
      e) Crime and punishments
   2. Executive order for use of military courts
      a) Trial before commission of military officers, may be secret
      b) two-thirds vote for conviction, appeal to secretary of defense and the president
   3. Intensified investigations and concerns of civil liberties organizations

KEY TERMS MATCH

Match the following terms and descriptions:

1. The government suppression of American leftists after the 1917 Bolshevik Revolution in Russia

2. A Federalist bill of 1789 criminalizing criticism of government

3. A 1940 act criminalizing the advocacy of violent revolution

4. A 1950 act requiring the registration of all communists

5. A 1954 act denying legal rights to the Communist party

6. A Supreme Court formula to legitimate the abridgement of the right of free speech

7. Harming another by publishing defamatory statements

8. A government action to prevent rather than punish certain expressions

9. The supposed superiority of rights of expression over other constitutional rights

10. The use of only minimal measures to restrict potentially dangerous expression

11. The First Amendment clause guaranteeing religious freedom

12. The First Amendment clause prohibiting an official religion

13. A teaching on the origin of the world found to be religiously inspired

14. A period during the public school day when students get religious instruction

15. The prohibition against the use of illegally obtained evidence in court

16. A written authorization to police officers to conduct a search

17. The legal basis for the issuance of a search warrant

18. A Supreme Court case that led to rules that police officers must follow in warning arrested persons of their rights

a. "clear and present danger" test

b. Communist Control Act

c. conscientious objector

d. creationism

e. due process clause

f. establishment clause

g. exclusionary rule

h. free exercise clause

i. freedom of expression

j. freedom of religion

k. good-faith exception

l. Internal Security Act

m. least means

n. libel

o. McCarthyism

p. Miranda

q. preferred position

r. prior restraint

s. probable cause

t. Red scare

u. released time

v. search warrant

w. Sedition Act

x. Smith Act

y. symbolic speech

z. wall-of-separation principle

19. One who refuses military service on religious or ethical grounds

20. Protection against arbitrary deprivation of life, liberty, or property as guaranteed in the Fifth and Fourteenth Amendments

21. Part of the First Amendment protecting freedom of speech, press, assembly, and the right to petition the government

22. Part of the First Amendment protecting the free exercise of religion and prohibiting an establishment of religion

23. Admission of illegally obtained evidence if illegality results from a technical or minor error

24. Originated during communist witch-hunt in the 1950s, unfair accusations that tarnish a person's reputation

25. An act that conveys a political message, such as burning a draft card to protest the draft

26. An interpretation of part of the First Amendment that prevents government involvement with religion

DID YOU THINK THAT . . . ?

Below are listed a number of misconceptions. You should be able to refute each statement in the space provided, referring to information or argumentation contained in this chapter. Sample answers appear at the end of this chapter.

1. "Civil rights are a clear standard that can be fully enforced at all times to protect minorities."

   _____

   _____

   _____

2. "All of the Bill of Rights applies to state officials."

   _____

   _____

   _____

3. "Flag burning and draft card burning are afforded the same free speech protection under the law."

   _____

   _____

   _____

4. "The language of the First Amendment clearly requires the separation of church and state."

_____

_____

_____

DATA CHECK

FIGURE 18.1: Annual Immigration, 1840–1996

1. In approximately what years do the statistics for annual immigration reach their peak?

_____

2. Where does the number of annual immigrants appear to hit its lowest point in the Figure?

_____

FIGURE 18.2: Changing Composition of U.S. Immigration, 1901–1996.

3. From 1901 to 1960, a majority of U.S. immigrants came from where?

_____

4. From 1961 to 1996, a plurality (or most) of immigrants to the U.S. came from where?

_____

5. What source of immigrants has maintained a fairly steady percentage from 1921 to 1996?

_____

PRACTICING FOR EXAMS

TRUE/FALSE QUESTIONS

Read each statement carefully. Mark true statements _T._ If any part of the statement is false, mark it _F,_ and write in the space provided a concise explanation of why the statement is false.

1. T   F   The inevitable debates which accompany a time of war have generally been met with expansion in First Amendment liberties by Congress.

_____

2. T   F   When legislatures have chosen to restrict freedom of speech, the Supreme Court has had a general tendency to oppose such efforts and defend the First Amendment rights of citizens.

_____

3. T   F   Sedition laws are no longer used today.

_____

4. T   F   The Sedition Act of 1798 entrusted judges to convict persons charged under the Act.

_____

5.   T   F   Charles T. Schenck was convicted of planting bombs in key government buildings.

_____

6.   T   F   In the *Gitlow* case, the Supreme Court incorporated the freedom of speech and of the press to the states via the due-process clause of the Fourteenth Amendment.

_____

7.   T   F   The Court has considered nude dancing a form of "speech" or "expression."

_____

8.   T   F   The Court upheld a statute banning total nude dancing.

_____

9.   T   F   In the 1989 case that declared flag burning protected speech, the Supreme Court's decision was unanimous.

_____

10. T   F   When Congress passed a law that would make flag burning a federal crime, the Supreme Court declared it unconstitutional.

_____

11. T   F   A constitutional amendment that would have made flag burning a crime received a majority of votes in both the House and the Senate.

_____

12. T   F   The Court upheld a Florida city's ban on animal sacrifices that were being made by members of an Afro-Caribbean religion.

_____

13. T   F   Draft laws have only recently made exceptions for conscientious objectors.

_____

14. T   F   The Supreme Court's first attempt at interpreting the Establishment Clause was in 1947.

_____

15. T   F   The House and the Senate have opened with prayer every session since 1789.

_____

16. T   F   Initially, the Supreme Court refused to apply the exclusionary rule to the states.

_____

17. T   F   Private employers have little freedom to search an employee's desk and files.

_____

18. T   F   The USA Patriot Act proclaimed a national emergency and gave military courts jurisdiction over cases involving suspected terrorists.

_____

19. T   F   Military commissions can operate in secret.

_____

20.   T   F   The verdict of a military commission can be appealed to a civilian court.

___

MULTIPLE CHOICE QUESTIONS

Circle the letter of the response that best answers the question or completes the statement.

1.   Which of the following statements about the Bill of Rights is true?

    a.   It is part of the Declaration of Independence.
    b.   It was written during the Constitutional Convention.
    c.   It was part of the original draft of the Constitution.
    d.   It was added to the Constitution before ratification.
    e.   It was added to the Constitution shortly after ratification.

2.   The Framers saw no need for a bill of rights because

    a.   in their view, civil liberties were a matter for the states, not for the federal government.
    b.   they were convinced that in a democratic republic, public opinion was a sufficient protection.
    c.   no one bothered to even bring up the topic at the Convention.
    d.   they assumed that the federal government could not do things that it was not explicitly authorized to do.
    e.   their chief concern was protecting public order, not guaranteeing rights.

3.   Civil liberties issues are most likely to be issues of

    a.   majoritarian politics.
    b.   reciprocal politics.
    c.   interest group politics.
    d.   client politics.
    e.   party politics.

4.   The leading entrepreneur of the Red scare around the time of World War I was

    a.   Joseph McCarthy.
    b.   A. Mitchell Palmer.
    c.   Kate Richards O'Hare.
    d.   Theodore Roosevelt.
    e.   Woodrow Wilson.

5.   Blackstone argued that the press should be free

    a.   from any restrictions whatsoever.
    b.   only when it published the truth.
    c.   from censorship prior to publication.
    d.   from seditious libel restrictions alone.
    e.   from libel laws regarding government officers.

6.   The debate between the Federalists and the Jeffersonians over the Sedition Act was largely a debate over

    a.   the fundamentals of individual liberty.
    b.   the role of the press in a democratic republic.
    c.   states' rights.
    d.   the interpretation of elastic clauses in the Constitution.

e.   the role of government in the economy.

7.   The Jeffersonian Republicans believed that the press

    a.   should be free from governmental controls.
    b.   should be free from governmental controls except when the nation is at war.
    c.   should be punished by the federal government for slander and defamation.
    d.   could be punished by federal courts but only when malice was shown.
    e.   could be punished by the states for slander and defamation.

8.   The effect of the "clear and present danger" rule seems to have been to

    a.   clarify the law but not keep anyone from prison.
    b.   greatly clarify and expand the scope of free expression.
    c.   increase convictions for sedition and incitement in the states.
    d.   make guarantees of freedom of expression as binding on state as on federal officials.
    e.   bring the process of incorporation to its logical conclusion.

9.   The Framers intended the Bill of Rights to apply to

    a.   the states only.
    b.   the federal government only.
    c.   both the states and the federal government.
    d.   all governmental units outside of the nation's capital.
    e.   private institutions as well as governments.

10.   Which of the following would be illegal under current Supreme Court doctrines?

    a.   giving secret government documents to the press
    b.   drawing a hilarious, but quite insulting cartoon, of a Senator
    c.   showing the movie *Carnal Knowledge*
    d.   stating that the violent overthrow of the government would be a good thing
    e.   inciting someone to an illegal act

11.   The display of an odious symbol, such as a swastika or a burning cross, has been deemed by the Supreme Court to be

    a.   punishable as a hate crime.
    b.   punishable as incitement.
    c.   an unconstitutional act.
    d.   protected by the Constitution.
    e.   not a case for Supreme Court review.

12.   *Libel* is defined as

    a.   stating something untrue about another person.
    b.   writing something false about someone without their knowledge.
    c.   an oral statement defaming another person.
    d.   a written statement defaming another person.
    e.   maliciously intending to defame a public official.

13.   Justice Hugo Black and a few others took the position that obscenity is

    a.   protected by the First Amendment.
    b.   easy to define, but difficult to punish.
    c.   difficult to define, but easy to punish.
    d.   subject to federal but not state prosecution.
    e.   subject to state but not federal prosecution.

14. The definition of what is obscene and therefore not a form of protected speech

    a. is left almost entirely up to localities.
    b. can be decided by localities but only within narrow limits.
    c. is finely detailed in the Court's decision in the Roth case.
    d. has to be decided by the Supreme Court on pretty much a case-by-case basis.
    e. has to be decided by the Supreme Court on the basis of reasonably clear guidelines.

15. The Supreme Court struck down a 1996 law that addressed the issue of child pornography because it attempted to ban images that were

    a. graphic.
    b. violent.
    c. psychologically harmful.
    d. in the public domain.
    e. computer simulated.

16. The Supreme Court has ruled that which one of the following sorts of symbolic speech is protected by the Constitution?

    a. burning draft cards
    b. burning the flag
    c. making obscene gestures toward a police officer
    d. sleeping in a public park to draw attention to the plight of the homeless
    e. protesting loudly directly outside a court building

17. In general, high school students have the same rights as adults. An exception is when

    a. their actions are specifically prohibited by the Constitution.
    b. their actions offend other students.
    c. they exercise these rights as individuals rather than as part of a school-sponsored activity.
    d. some form of symbolic speech is involved.
    e. their exercise of these rights impedes the educational process.

18. The First Amendment states that Congress may not make any law prohibiting the free exercise of religion. It also specifically states that

    a. church and state must be clearly separate.
    b. there will no official church in the United States.
    c. citizens are exempt from laws binding other citizens when the law goes against their religious beliefs.
    d. Congress may not make any law respecting an establishment of religion.
    e. nonsectarian, voluntary, or limited prayer is permissible in public schools.

19. The phrase "wall of separation" between church and state comes from:

    a. the pen of Thomas Jefferson.
    b. the Bill of Rights.
    c. the debates in the First Congress that drafted the Bill of Rights.
    d. the 14th Amendment.
    e. George Washington's farewell address.

20. Interestingly, the wording of the Establishment Clause that was originally debated by Congress was _____ than what finally emerged.

    a. more abstract.
    b. longer and even more confusing.
    c. more brief

d. quite different and much plainer
e. more partial to the federal government

21. The Supreme Court's three part controversial "test" for Establishment Clause cases focuses specifically on

a. whether there is a secular purpose for an action.
b. the effect of an act advances or inhibits religion.
c. whether an action fosters excessive governmental entanglement with religon.
d. All of the above.
e. None of the above.

22. The exclusionary rule is the means by which the Supreme Court implements its decisions in matters of

a. criminal due process.
b. cruel and unusual punishment.
c. freedom of speech.
d. establishment of religion.
e. civil liberties generally.

23. Instead of using the exclusionary rule, our courts might do as European courts do and

a. refuse to include illegally obtained evidence at a trial.
b. ignore the legality or illegality of the method used to obtain the evidence.
c. levy civil or criminal penalties against law enforcement officers who obtain evidence illegally.
d. refuse to hear cases tainted with official illegality.
e. use the rule only when cases do not involve murder.

24. The exclusionary rule was not applied to the states until the

a. 1940s
b. 1950s
c. 1960s
d. 1980s
e. 1990s

25. In the *Miranda* case the Supreme Court ruled that for a confession to be considered voluntary, the suspect must

a. not be subject to coercion.
b. not be subject to undue coercion.
c. be told that he or she need not talk to the police.
d. be told to speak slowly.
e. have his or her lawyer present.

26. All of the following are true of the USA Patriot Act (passed in the aftermath of the attack of September 11) *except*

a. the penalties for terrorist crimes were increased.
b. the government can seize voice mail without a court order.
c. information in secret grand jury hearings can be shared by officials.
d. non-citizens who pose a national security risk can be detained for up to seven days.
e. the government can tap Internet communications with a court order.

ESSAY QUESTIONS

Practice writing extended answers to the following questions. These test your ability to integrate and express the ideas that you have been studying in this chapter.

27. List several eras in which U.S. governments have enacted laws aimed at taking away the civil liberties of certain Americans. Are these eras always associated with war? Discuss whether the government is usually the friend or the enemy of free expression.

28. Summarize the history of the incorporation process. Do you believe that the process is complete today, or can you imagine its going further in the future?

29. What competing claims has the Supreme Court typically weighed in dealing with obscenity cases? Why do you believe that it has had such difficulty in arriving at lasting standards?

30. What are the ambiguities in the establishment clause on religion, and what problems have these created for the courts over the years?

ANSWERS TO KEY TERMS MATCH QUESTIONS

1. t
2. w
3. x
4. l
5. b
6. a
7. n
8. r
9. q
10. m
11. h
12. f
13. d
14. u
15. g
16. v
17. s
18. p
19. c
20. e
21. i
22. j
23. k
24. o
25. y
26. z

ANSWERS TO "DID YOU THINK THAT . . . ?" QUESTIONS

1. Often rights compete, and enforcing the rights of one group may deny the rights of others. Examples include the right to privacy versus freedom of the press, freedom of speech versus preservation of public order, "right to life" versus "freedom of choice" in abortion cases, and rights of defendants in criminal trials versus rights of reporters to shield their sources in investigations.

2. The Bill of Rights originally applied only to national officials. Then several rights were "incorporated" by the Court into the Fourteenth Amendment due process clause, to protect citizens against certain acts of state officials. Activist courts have expanded the list of actions prohibited under the due process clause, whereas judges practicing judicial conservatism have consolidated or cut back on protections. Individuals are protected not only by the Bill of Rights but also by state constitutions, which contain their own bills of rights.

3. It is illegal to burn a draft card; it is not illegal to burn the American flag. The key distinction is that the government has a right to run a military draft and so can protect draft cards. But the only motive the government has in banning flag burning is to restrict this form of symbolic speech, and that makes it improper.

4. What the First Amendment says is that Congress shall pass no law prohibiting the "free exercise" of religion, nor shall it make any law "respecting the establishment of religion." The Supreme Court allows government involvement in religious activities so long as this involvement has a secular purpose, neither advances nor inhibits religion, and does not foster an excessive entanglement with religion.

ANSWERS TO DATA CHECK QUESTIONS

1. 1988–1989.

2. Mid-1940s.

3. Europe.

4. Asia.

5. Mexico.

ANSWERS TO TRUE/FALSE QUESTIONS

1. F. War has generally facilitated entrepreneurial politics aimed at restricting the liberty of some minority.

2. F. In most instances the Court tended to uphold the legislatures.

3. F. Some use is still made of such laws.

4. F. The Act entrusted juries to make the decision.

5. F. Schecnk simply mailed out circulars encouraging men to resist the draft.

6. T

7. T

8. T

9. F. The vote was 5–4.

10. T

11. T

12. F. The courts ruled against the ban.

13. F. They have always made such exemptions.

14. T

15. T

16. T
17. F. A private employer has a great deal of freedom to search your desk and files.
18. T
19. T
20. F. Appeals can be made to the secretary of defense and the president, but not to a civilian court.

ANSWERS TO MULTIPLE CHOICE QUESTIONS

1. e
2. d
3. c
4. b
5. c
6. c
7. e
8. a
9. b
10. e
11. d
12. d
13. a
14. b
15. e
16. b
17. e
18. d
19. a
20. d
21. d
22. a
23. b
24. c
25. e
26. b

CHAPTER 19

Civil Rights

REVIEWING THE CHAPTER

CHAPTER FOCUS

This chapter focuses on the two most intense and protracted struggles for civil rights in recent times: that of blacks and that of women. After reading and reviewing the material in this chapter, you should be able to do each of the following:

1. Contrast the experience of economic interest groups with that of black groups in obtaining satisfaction of their interests from the government. Indicate why in most circumstances the black movement involved interest group rather than client politics. Describe the strategies used by black leaders to overcome their political weaknesses, and explain why the civil rights movement has become more conventional in its strategy in recent years.

2. Summarize the legal struggles of blacks to secure rights under the Fourteenth Amendment, and state how the Court construed that amendment in the civil rights cases and in *Plessy* v. *Ferguson*. Discuss the NAACP strategy of litigation, and indicate why it was suited to the political circumstances. Summarize the rulings in *Brown v. Board of Education* and compare them with those in *Plessy v. Ferguson.*

3. Discuss the rationale used by the Supreme Court in ordering busing to achieve desegregation. Explain the apparent inconsistency between *Brown* and *Charlotte-Mecklenburg*. State why these decisions are not really inconsistent, and explain why the courts chose busing as an equitable remedy to deal with de jure segregation.

4. Trace the campaign launched by blacks for a set of civil rights laws. Explain why they used nonviolent techniques. Discuss the conflict between the agenda-setting and the coalition-building aspects of the movement. Demonstrate how civil rights advocates could overcome sources of resistance in Congress.

5. Describe the differences between the black civil rights movement and the women's movement. List the various standards used by the courts in interpreting the Fourteenth Amendment, and explain how these standards differ depending on whether blacks or women are involved.

6. Summarize the debate over "compensatory action" versus "preferential treatment" and targets versus quotas in affirmative action.

STUDY OUTLINE

I. Introduction
    A. Civil rights issue
        1. Group is denied access to facilities, opportunities, or services available to other groups, usually along ethnic or racial lines
        2. Issue is whether differences in treatment are "reasonable"
            a) Some differences are: progressive taxes

                    b)   Some are not: classification by race subject to "strict scrutiny"

II.   The black predicament
- A.   Perceived costs of granting black rights not widely shared
  1. Concentrated in small, easily organized populations
  2. Interest-group politics versus lower-income whites
  3. Blacks at a disadvantage in interest group politics because they were not able to vote in many areas
- B.   Majoritarian politics worked against blacks
  1. Lynchings shocked whites, but little was done
  2. General public opinion was opposed to black rights
  3. Those sympathetic to granting black rights opposed the means
- C.   Progress depended on
  1. Finding more white allies or
  2. Shifting policy-making arenas
- D.   Civil rights movement both
  1. Broadened base by publicizing grievances
  2. Moved legal struggle from Congress to the courts

III.   The campaign in the courts
- A.   Ambiguities in the Fourteenth Amendment
  1. Broad interpretation: Constitution color-blind
  2. Narrow interpretation: equal legal rights
  3. Supreme court adopted narrow view in *Plessy* case
- B.   "Separate but equal"
  1. NAACP campaign objectives in education through courts
     - *a)* Obviously unequal schools
     - *b)* Not so obviously unequal schools
     - *c)* Separate schools inherently unequal
- C.   Can separate schools be equal?
  1. Step 1: obvious inequalities
     - *a)* Lloyd Gaines
     - *b)* Ada Lois Sipuel
  2. Step 2: deciding that a separation creates inequality in less obvious cases
     - *a)* Heman Sweatt
     - *b)* George McLaurin
  3. Step 3: making separation inherently unequal; 1950 strategy to go for integration
  4. *Brown v. Board of Education* (1954)
     - *a)* Implementation
       - (1) Class action suit
       - (2) All deliberate speed
     - *b)* Collapse of resistance in the 1970s
  5. The rationale
     - *a)* Detriment to pupils by creating sense of inferiority
     - *b)* Social science used because intent of Fourteenth Amendment unclear; needed unanimous decision
  6. Desegregation versus integration
     - *a)* Ambiguities of *Brown*
       - (1) Unrestricted choice or integrated schools?
       - (2) De jure or de facto segregation?
     - *b)* 1968 rejection of "freedom of choice" plan settles matter; mixing
     - *c)* *Charlotte-Mecklenburg,* 1971
       - (1) Proof of intent to discriminate

(2)   One-race school creates presumption of intent
(3)   Remedies can include quotas, busing, redrawn lines
(4)   Every school not required to reflect racial composition of school system
   d)   Some extensions to intercity busing
   e)   Busing remains controversial
(1)   Some presidents oppose but still implement it
(2)   Congress torn in two directions
   f)   1992 decision allows busing to end if segregation caused by shifting housing patterns
IV.   The campaign in Congress
  A.   Mobilization of opinion by dramatic event to get on agenda
    1.   Sit-ins and freedom rides
    2.   Martin Luther King, Jr.
    3.   From nonviolence to long, hot summers
  B.   Mixed results
    1.   Agenda-setting success
    2.   Coalition-building setbacks: methods seen as law breaking
  C.   Legislative politics
    1.   Opponents' defensive positions
     a)   Senate Judiciary Committee controlled by southern Democrats
     b)   House Rules Committee controlled by Howard Smith
     c)   Senate filibuster threat
     d)   President Kennedy reluctant
    2.   Four developments broke deadlock
     a)   Change of public opinion
     b)   Violent white reactions of segregationists became media focus
     c)   Kennedy assassination
     d)   1964 Democratic landslide
    3.   Five bills pass, 1957–1968
     a)   1957, 1960, 1965: voting rights laws
     b)   1968: housing discrimination law
    4.   1964 civil rights bill: the high point—employment, public accommodations
     a)   Broad in scope, strong enforcement mechanisms
     b)   Johnson moves after Kennedy assassinated
     c)   Discharge petition, cloture invoked
    5.   Effects since 1964
     a)   Dramatic rise in black voting
     b)   Mood of Congress shifted to pro-civil rights; 1988 overturn of Reagan veto of bill that extended federal ban on discrimination in education
  D.   Racial Profiling
    1.   Stopping drivers for "driving while black"
    2.   Condemned by Clinton, Bush, and Congress
    3.   A complex issue, worthy of debate
     a)   Inherently discriminatory and always wrong?
     b)   Trends can exist and possibly provide useful clues
    4.   Weighing costs and benefits
     a)   Does profiling increase the ability of police to catch criminals?
     b)   If so, by how much?
     c)   When is profiling justified (young, male, Middle Easterners involved in September 11 attacks)?
     d)   What impact does profiling have on innocent people?

       5.   A major political issue, but few firm facts

V.   Women and equal rights

    A.   Supreme Court's position altered after the 1970s

       1.   Somewhere between reasonableness and strict-scrutiny standard

       2.   Gender-based differences prohibited by courts

          a)   Age of adulthood

          b)   Drinking age

          c)   Arbitrary employee height-weight requirements

          d)   Mandatory pregnancy leaves

          e)   Little League exclusion

          f)   Jaycees exclusion

          g)   Unequal retirement benefits

       3.   Gender-based differences allowed by courts

          a)   All-boy/all-girl schools

          b)   Widows' property tax exemption

          c)   Delayed promotions in Navy

          d)   Statutory rape

       4.   Women must be admitted to all-male, state-supported military colleges

    B.   The military

       1.   *Rostker v. Goldberg* (1981): Congress may draft men only

       2.   Secretary of Defense in 1993 allows women in air and sea combat

    C.   Sexual harassment

       1.   Requesting sexual favors as condition for employment

          a)   "quid pro quo" rule

          b)   Employer "strictly liable"

       2.   Hostile or intimidating work environment

          a)   Employer not strictly liable

          b)   Employer can be at fault if "negligent"

       3.   Almost no federal laws governing it

       4.   Vague and inconsistent court and bureaucratic rules tell us what it is

    D.   Abortion

       1.   Until 1973 regulated by states

       2.   1973: *Roe v. Wade*

          a)   Struck down Texas ban on abortion

          b)   Woman's freedom to choose protected by Fourteenth Amendment ("right to privacy")

             (1)   First trimester: no regulations

             (2)   Second trimester: no ban but regulations to protect health

             (3)   Third trimester: abortion ban

          c)   Critics claim life begins at conception

              (1)   Fetus entitled to equal protection

             (2)   Supporters say no one can say when life begins

             (3)   Pro-life versus pro-choice

          d)   Hyde Amendment (1976): no federal funds for abortion

          e)   Gag order on abortion referrals imposed under Bush, removed under Clinton

       3.   1973–1989: Supreme Court withstood attacks on *Roe v. Wade*

       4.   1989: Court upheld Missouri law restricting abortion

       5.   *Casey* decision lets *Roe* stand but permits more restrictions: twenty-four-hour wait, parental consent, pamphlets

       6.   Supreme Court and anti-abortion activists

VI. Affirmative action

    A.   Equality of results
        1.   Racism and sexism overcome only by taking them into account in designing remedies
        2.   Equal rights not enough; people need benefits
        3.   Affirmative action should be used in hiring
    B.   Equality of opportunities
        1.   Reverse discrimination to use race or sex as preferential treatment
        2.   Laws should be color-blind and sex neutral
        3.   Government should only eliminate barriers
    C.   Targets or quotas?
        1.   Issue fought out in courts
            a)   No clear direction in Supreme Court decisions
            b)   Court is deeply divided; affected by conservative Reagan appointees
            c)   Law is complex and confusing
                (1)   *Bakke:* numerical minority quotas not permissible
                (2)   But Court ruled otherwise in later cases
        2.   Emerging standards for quotas and preference systems
            a)   Must be "compelling" justification
            b)   Must correct pattern of discrimination
            c)   Must involve practices that discriminate
            d)   Federal quotas are to be given deference
            e)   Voluntary preference systems are easier to justify
            f)   Not likely to apply to who gets laid off
        3.   Congressional efforts to defend affirmative action not yet successful
        4.   "Compensatory action" (helping minorities catch up) versus "preferential treatment" (giving minorities preference, applying quotas)
            a)   Public supports former but not latter
            b)   In line with American political culture
                (1)   Support for individualism
                (2)   Support for needy
        5.   Courts divided
            a)   Court of Appeals for Fifth Circuit ruled race to be used in admissions decisions for law school
            b)   Supreme Court ruled that racial classifications subject to strict scrutiny
VII. Gays and the Supreme Court
    A.   State laws could ban homosexual activities
    B.   Court struck down amendment to state constitution prohibiting cities from adopting an ordinance banning discrimination against gays

KEY TERMS MATCH

Match the following terms and descriptions:

1.   A legal distinction that the Supreme Court scrutinizes especially closely

2.   Post-Civil War era when southern laws protected blacks' freedoms

3.   A Supreme Court decision upholding state-enforced racial segregation

4.   The standard under which the Court once upheld racial segregation

    a.   affirmative action

    b.   aliens

    c.   Bakke

    d.   Brown v. Board of Education

    e.   civil rights

    f.   compensatory action

5. The term for laws forcing second-class status on blacks

6. A black interest group active primarily in the courts

7. A Supreme Court decision declaring segregated schools inherently unequal

8. Segregation created by law

9. Segregation that exists but that was not created by law

10. A school integration plan mandating no particular racial balance

11. An early nonviolent leader in black civil rights

12. Offering the races an equal chance at desired things

13. Distributing desired things equally to the races

14. The standard by which the Court judges gender-based classifications

15. A ruling that held that Congress may draft men but not women

16. A ruling that declared all state laws prohibiting abortion unconstitutional

17. Legislation that barred the use of federal funds for nearly any abortion

18. A leading feminist organization

19. A philosophy of peaceful violation of laws considered unjust and accepting punishment for the violation

20. The standard by which the Supreme Court judges classifications based on race: they must have a compelling public purpose

21. The use of race or sex to give preferential treatment to blacks or women

22. Helping disadvantaged people catch up, usually by giving them extra education, training, or services

23. Giving minorities preference in hiring, promotions, college admissions, and contracts

24. Designing remedies for overcoming racism and sexism by taking race and sex into

g. de facto segregation

h. de jure segregation

i. equality of opportunity

j. equality of results

k. freedom of choice

l. Hyde Amendment

m. Jim Crow

n. Martin Luther King, Jr.

o. NAACP

p. nonviolent civil disobedience

q. NOW

r. Plessy v. Ferguson

s. preferential treatment

t. reasonableness

u. Reconstruction

v. reverse discrimination

w. Roe v. Wade

x. Rostker v. Goldberg

y. separate-but-equal doctrine

z. strict scrutiny

aa. suspect classification

account

25. A Supreme Court ruling stating that a college may not use an explicit numerical quota in admitting minorities but could "take race into account:"

26. Any persons who are not U.S. citizens

27. The rights of citizens to vote, receive equal treatment before the law, and share benefits of public facilities

DID YOU THINK THAT . . . ?

Below are listed a number of misconceptions. You should be able to refute each statement in the space provided, referring to information or argumentation contained in this chapter. Sample answers appear at the end of this chapter.

1. "The Supreme Court has had the full cooperation of Congress in implementing its decisions."

_____

_____

_____

2. "Violent tactics have irreparably harmed and retarded the black struggle for civil rights."

_____

_____

_____

3. "Most presidents have been staunch supporters of the goals of the civil rights movement."

_____

_____

_____

4. "There are numerous federal laws dealing with the issue of sexual harassment."

_____

_____

_____

DATA CHECK

Figure 19.2: Growing Support Among Southern Democrats in Congress for Civil Rights Bills

1. In which years did less than 25 percent of the Southern Democrats in the House and the Senate support Civil Rights legislation?

2. In which years did more than 50 percent of the Southern Democrats in the House and the Senate support Civil Rights legislation?

_____

Table 19.1: Increase in Number of Black Elected Officials

3. Which category of elected officials has seen the sharpest increase in the number of black officeholders during the period covered by the table? The next sharpest increase?

_____

4. The next sharpest increase?

_____

5. In which category of elected officials has the number of black officeholders increased the *least*?

_____

PRACTICING FOR EXAMS

TRUE/FALSE QUESTIONS

Read each statement carefully. Mark true statements *T*. If any part of the statement is false, mark it *F*, and write in the space provided a concise explanation of why the statement is false.

1. T F   In the 1940s President Roosevelt approved of the army's removal of Japanese Americans from their homes and their placement in "relocation centers."

_____

2. T F   Civil Rights violations occur when laws and policies make distinctions among people and treat them differently.

_____

3. T F   The series of test cases that led up to the Court's decision in *Brown* began in the 1950s.

_____

4. T F   Over one hundred members of Congress signed a declaration that the Court's decision in *Brown* constituted an abuse of judicial power.

_____

5. T F   In 1964 and 1968, over two-thirds of whites told pollsters that they thought the civil rights movement was too violent.

_____

6. T F   When an increase in arrests of crack cocaine dealers led to an increase in the arrests of African Americans dealers, the Supreme Court found violations of civil rights.

_____

7. T F   The Court applies the strict scrutiny standard to gender discrimination cases.

_____

8.   T   F   The Court tends to give little deference to congressional policy related to national defense.

9.   T   F   There are almost no federal laws governing sexual harassment.

10.   T   F   The Court's decision in *Roe v. Wade* was unanimous.

11.   T   F   Constitutional amendments have been introduced to overturn *Roe*.

12.   T   F   The Supreme Court began to uphold state restrictions on abortion in part because of the influence of justices appointed by President Bush.

13.   T   F   In 1997 the Court upheld the notion of "buffer zones" around clinics in which antiabortion demonstrations could not be held.

14.   T   F   Affirmative action programs are just about always upheld by the Supreme Court.

15.   T   F   Aliens cannot vote or run for office, but they must pay taxes.

16.   T   F   Legally admitted aliens are entitled to welfare benefits.

17.   T   F   States cannot bar aliens from serving on juries.

18.   T   F   The Republicans in Congress introduced a bill to ban affirmative action, but withdrew it.

19.   T   F   Colorado's state constitutional amendment disallowing legal protections based on sexual orientation was upheld by the United States Supreme Court.

20.   T   F   The Court is deeply divided over the issue of gay rights.

MULTIPLE CHOICE QUESTIONS

Circle the letter of the response that best answers the question or completes the statement.

1.   Blacks are an example of a group that we would expect to benefit from

    a.   majoritarian politics.
    b.   client politics.

    c.   entrepreneurial politics.

    d.   interest group politics.

    e.   club-based politics.

2.   Which of the following was *not* one of the reasons that blacks for many years failed to gain redress of their grievances?

    a.   They were excluded from normal political activity such as voting.

    b.   They lacked material and institutional support for effective political organization.

    c.   Public opinion opposed black equality.

    d.   Blacks could not agree among themselves on the proper policies to combat discrimination.

    e.   White allies were few.

3.   When Congress, in 1883, passed a law that outlawed racial discrimination in public accommodations such as hotels

    a.   the president exercised the veto power.

    b.   the Supreme Court declared the law unconstitutional.

    c.   the state legislatures immediately passed similar laws.

    d.   governors applauded the legislation as "progressive."

    e.   None of the above.

4.   The Supreme Court's decision in *Plessy v. Ferguson* (whatever its wider implications) directly concerned

    a.   segregation on railroad cars.

    b.   voting rights for blacks.

    c.   interracial marriage.

    d.   lynching.

    e.   the ability of Congress to regulate race relations in the states.

5.   "Jim Crow" is a slang expression referring to

    a.   laws and policies that segregated blacks.

    b.   discrimination against blacks in the military.

    c.   the early civil rights movement.

    d.   discrimination against blacks in other countries.

    e.   the difficulty that blacks had in getting a fair trial.

6.   The National Association for the Advancement of Colored People (NAACP) was founded

    a.   immediately after the Civil War.

    b.   in 1909, in the aftermath of an anti-black riot.

    c.   during the presidential election of 1968.

    d.   during the Great Depression.

    e.   in 1955, following the Montgomery bus boycott.

7.   Which of the following statements about *Brown v. Board of Education* is true?

    a.   It was handed down by a divided Court.

    b.   It was ultimately rather narrow in its implications.

    c.   It explicitly banned *de facto* segregation.

    d.   It was almost unnoticed when it was decided.

    e.   It was the logical extension of a line of related cases.

8.   *Brown* called for the desegregation of public schools

    a.   "with all deliberate speed."

   b.   as soon as the state legislatures could fund the enterprise.
   c.   "in an acceptable amount of time."
   d.   "immediately"
   e.   immediately following the next school year.

9.   In 1954 the Supreme Court ruled that segregation is "inherently unequal" on the basis of

   a.   the fact that black children were not achieving success academically.
   b.   the Equal Protection Clause of the Fourteenth Amendment.
   c.   apparent psychological harm done to black children in separate schools.
   d.   inadequate expenditures on black education.
   e.   a philosophical understanding of the essentials of equality.

10.   According to the text, the authors of the Fourteenth Amendment

   a.   intended to outlaw segregated schools in the Washington area.
   b.   intended to outlaw segregated schools throughout the United States.
   c.   may not have intended to outlaw segregated schools.
   d.   were pleased four years later when a civil rights act proposed an end to segregated schools.
   e.   thought desegregated schools would cure certain social ills.

11.   Segregation maintained by law is labeled

   a.   prima facie.
   b.   de facto
   c.   statist.
   d.   de jure.
   e.   post facto suspect.

12.   In the late 1960s the Supreme Court rejected a so-called "freedom of choice" plan because

   a.   *Brown* had explicitly ruled against such plans.
   b.   too many children chose different schools under the plan.
   c.   most students chose to stay in the same schools under the plan.
   d.   school administrators were not actually allowing students to make a choice.
   e.   few people could make up their minds easily about such decisions.

13.   Which of the following was *not* among the key factors that put civil rights on the national agenda in the early 1960s?

   a.   lynchings of blacks in the South
   b.   demonstrations in southern cities
   c.   freedom rides
   d.   long, hot summers of rioting in the North
   e.   sit-ins

14.   Three young civil rights workers were killed in June 1964 in

   a.   Montgomery, Alabama.
   b.   Selma, Alabama.
   c.   Memphis, Tennessee.
   d.   DeKalb County, Georgia.
   e.   Neshoba County, Mississippi.

15.   According to the Supreme Court differences based on sex are permitted for:

   a.   the ages at which men and women are allowed to buy beer.
   b.   the age at which men and women legally become adults.

c.   allowing women to remain officers longer than men without being promoted in the Navy.
d.   excluding girls from playing on Little League baseball teams.
e.   insisting women pay more insurance benefits because, on average, they live longer.

16.   The Court uses the _____ standard in cases involving gender discrimination.

a.   "strict rationality"
b.   "strict scrutiny"
c.   "substantial relationship"
d.   "suspect"
e.   "reasonableness"

17.   Which of the following gender discriminations has been permitted by the Supreme Court?

a.   a property tax exemption for widows that is not given to widowers
b.   barring girls from little league baseball teams
c.   preference given to men in the appointment of administrators of estates
d.   different legal drinking ages for males and females
e.   mandatory pregnancy leaves for women

18.   The Court's 1996 ruling on gender discrimination at the Virginia Military Institution was especially important because the Court

a.   upheld VMI's right to engage in such discrimination.
b.   came close to using the strict scrutiny standard.
c.   upheld VMI's so-called "adversarial method" of training.
d.   the Court ignored the VMI's sources of financial support.
e.   VMI refused to even offer a course at another college.

19.   Under the "quid pro quo" rule pertaining to sexual harassment

a.   the employer is "strictly liable" even if he/she did not know that sexual harassment was occurring.
b.   the employer cannot be held liable if he/she did not know that sexual harassment was occurring.
c.   an employee is never liable for the sexual harassment of an employee.
d.   a pattern of sexual harassment must be proven before the employer is liable.
e.   the employer is liable but not the employee in sexual harassment cases.

20.   The Supreme Court's decision in *Roe v. Wade* had as its constitutional basis the

a.   due process clause of the Fourteenth Amendment, implying a right to privacy.
b.   Eighth Amendment, implying that denying women the right to abortion constitutes cruel and unusual punishment.
c.   First Amendment, implying that abortion is covered under the free exercise of speech.
d.   Equal Rights Amendment, passed in 1982, granting women the right to control their own bodies.
e.   All of the above.

21.   The so-called Hyde Amendment

a.   restricts the use of federal funds for abortions.
b.   was upheld by the United States Supreme Court.
c.   has resulted in the denial of Medicaid funds for abortions for low-income women.
d.   All of the above.
e.   was declared unconstitutional by the United States Supreme Court

22. The position that the Constitution neither is nor should be color-blind is taken by those who advocate

    a. equality of results.
    b. the incorporation of the Bill of Rights.
    c. the abolition of affirmative action.
    d. freedom-of-education plans.
    e. equal opportunity.

23. In the *Bakke* case the Supreme Court held that a university medical school, in admitting students, may

    a. use quotas for blacks and whites.
    b. use quotas for men, but not women.
    c. use quotas for men and women.
    d. take gender into account.
    e. take race into account.

24. Among the standards that appear to be emerging in the Supreme Court's rulings on quota systems and preference systems are all of the following *except*

    a. such systems must correct a present or past pattern of discrimination.
    b. those systems involving hiring practices are more defensible than those involving layoffs.
    c. those systems created by state law will be given deference to those created by federal law.
    d. there must be compelling justification for such systems.
    e. such systems should be flexible and limited in scope.

25. In a 2000 case, the Supreme Court ruled by a vote of 5–4 that the _____ could prevent gay boys and men from being members.

    a. American Civil Liberties Union
    b. Boy Scouts of America
    c. American Bar Association
    d. Lion's Club
    e. International Brotherhood of Electrical Workers

ESSAY QUESTIONS

Practice writing extended answers to the following questions. These test your ability to integrate and express the ideas that you have been studying in this chapter.

1. List the political weaknesses of the black civil rights movement earlier in this century, and discuss the strategies followed to overcome those weaknesses.

2. Explain the effect of *Brown* in the line of Supreme Court decisions on civil rights and the kinds of political change *Brown* in turn produced.

3. Review the debate between those who favor equality of results and those who favor equality of opportunity. State and defend your own position on the issue.

4. Compare and contrast the movement for black civil rights with that for women's rights.

ANSWERS TO KEY TERMS MATCH QUESTIONS

1. aa
2. u
3. y
4. r
5. m
6. o
7. d
8. h
9. g
10. k
11. n
12. i
13. j
14. t
15. x
16. w
17. l
18. q
19. p
20. z
21. v
22. f
23. s
24. a
25. c
26. b
27. e

ANSWERS TO "DID YOU THINK THAT . . . ?" QUESTIONS

1. Congress has limited or prohibited the use of federal funds to implement court-ordered busing decisions and has defined *desegregation* in a way that has attempted (thus far unsuccessfully) to limit the reach of court decisions.

2. It was never a strategy of the movement to use violence. It was the use of nonviolent demonstrations, designed to provoke violence from white-supremacist law enforcement officials that catalyzed public opinion and convinced many Americans that the time to put an end to

segregation was at hand. In the last forty years support for integration in schools, housing, and transportation has increased dramatically among whites.

3.   Hayes was a supporter of southern whites who were attempting to remove black officials from state government in the aftermath of Reconstruction. Wilson introduced segregation in federal employment to Washington, D.C. Franklin Roosevelt took no action during the Depression to desegregate public facilities or to provide New Deal programs on an integrated basis. Eisenhower seemed to oppose the decision to integrate public schools, although he did enforce the Court order at Little Rock, Arkansas, in 1957 in a major test of national authority versus states' rights. Kennedy took several actions to reduce segregation in federally assisted public housing, but it took public pressure to induce him to introduce his civil rights bill. Lyndon Johnson, a southerner, was the first president to identify with the black movement, and during his administration two civil rights bills and a voting rights bill were passed. Nixon claimed to favor desegregation but opposed court-ordered busing of children to overcome racial imbalance. Reagan tried, rather successfully, to eviscerate the Civil Rights Commission.

4.   Since there has been almost no federal laws passed governing sexual harassment, we are left with somewhat vague and often inconsistent court and bureaucratic rules as the only basis for knowing what to do about it. In fact, the Supreme Court has drawn very heavily on rulings issued by the Equal Employment Opportunities Commission to determine what sexual harassment is.

ANSWERS TO DATA CHECK QUESTIONS

1.   1957, 1960, 1964, 1968.

2.   1965, 1970, 1988, 1991.

3.   City and county officials.

4.   Boards of education.

5.   Congress and state legislatures.

ANSWERS TO TRUE/FALSE QUESTIONS

1.   T

2.   F. Laws make distinctions and treat people differently all of the time. Civil Rights involve distinctions that are considered unacceptable.

3.   F. The cases that led up to Brown actually began in the 1930s.

4.   T

5.   T

6.   F. The Court disagreed noting there was no evidence to show drug dealers of other races had not been prosecuted.

7.   F. In gender discrimination cases the Court applies the reasonableness standard, or the rational basis test.

8.   F. The Court gives great deference to Congress in the area of national defense.

9.   T.

10.   F. The vote was 7–2.

11.   T

12.   F. The restrictions were largely upheld by Reagan appointees.

13. T

14. F. Such programs appear to have a fifty-fifty chance before the Court.

15. T

16. T

17. F. States can bar aliens from serving on juries.

18. T

19. F. The Court ruled that the Amendment violated the Equal Protection Clause of the Fourteenth Amendment.

20. T

ANSWERS TO MULTIPLE CHOICE QUESTIONS

1. b
2. d
3. b
4. a
5. a
6. b
7. e
8. a
9. c
10. c
11. d
12. c
13. a
14. e
15. c
16. e
17. a
18. b
19. a
20. a
21. a
22. a
23. e
24. c
25. b

CHAPTER 20

Foreign and Military Policy

REVIEWING THE CHAPTER

CHAPTER FOCUS

This chapter presents a survey of selected topics in United States foreign policy (or rather policies), focusing on the political processes involved in arriving at those policies. After reading and reviewing the material in this chapter, you should be able to do each of the following:

1. List the constitutional powers of the president and compare them with the authority of Congress in foreign affairs. Indicate why it is naive to read the Constitution literally in order to determine which institution has the major responsibility to conduct foreign policy. Explain why the president has a larger role than the Framers intended.

2. Compare the president's powers with those of a prime minister in a parliamentary system.

3. Explain why checks on the powers of the national government in foreign affairs are primarily political rather than constitutional.

4. Give reasons for the volatility of public opinion on foreign affairs. Explain the advantages that the president obtains when he acts resolutely in crises. Describe the problems that the president may face, using public opinion on the Vietnam War as an example.

5. Explain the worldview concept, and describe the containment strategy of Mr. X. Summarize essential elements of the Munich–Pearl Harbor and post-Vietnam worldviews. Discuss the revisionist argument that it is the material interests of elites, rather than their principles, that explain American foreign policy. Indicate the potential objections to this view.

6. Analyze the key allocative decisions about the defense budget. List factors that make the decisions on the budget incremental. Explain how the congressional role in deciding on weapons systems has changed in recent years.

7. Explain how the condition of the defense industry makes necessary a follow-up system in the distribution of contracts. Indicate the extent to which client defense politics affects U.S. industry, and compare the performance of defense contractors with that of similar nondefense companies.

8. Explain why the cost-overrun problem is primarily the result of bureaucratic rather than political factors, and describe proposed reforms of the system.

9. Explain why the 1947 and 1949 Defense Reorganization Acts prevented the merger of services in the Defense Department. Review the current structure of the department, and explain how it contributes to interservice rivalries. Explain why presidents find it difficult to use the Joint Chiefs of Staff to control defense policy making. Discuss the reforms adopted in 1986.

STUDY OUTLINE

I.   Introduction
    A.   Effects of the September 11 attacks
        1.   Public consciousness about international terrorism
        2.   Outbursts of patriotism
        3.   Confidence in government
        4.   Emergence of important fundamental questions
            a)   How to wage a "war" against terrorism?
            b)   How to hold other nations accountable?
            c)   How to act when other nations fight terrorism?
            d)   Does such a war require military to be redesigned?
        5.   Reemergence of classic questions
            a)   Do we only support nations that are reasonably free and democratic?
            b)   Are we the world's policemen?
    B.   Democratic politics and foreign and military policy
        1.   Tocqueville and weakness of democracy
        2.   Others blame reckless policies of presidents

II.   Kinds of foreign policy
    A.   Majoritarian politics
        1.   Perceived to confer widespread benefits, impose widespread costs
        2.   Examples
            a)   War
            b)   Military alliances
            c)   Nuclear test ban or strategic arms limitation treaties
            d)   Response to Berlin blockade by Soviets
            e)   Cuban missile crisis
            f)   Covert CIA operations
            g)   Diplomatic recognition of People's Republic of China
    B.   Interest group politics
        1.   Identifiable groups pitted against one another for costs, benefits
        2.   Examples
            a)   Cyprus policy: Greeks versus Turks
            b)   Tariffs: Japanese versus steel
    C.   Client politics
        1.   Benefits to identifiable group, without apparent costs to any distinct group
        2.   Example: Israel policy (transformation to interest group politics?)
    D.   Who has power?
        1.   Majoritarian politics: president dominates; public opinion supports but does not guide
        2.   Interest group or client politics: larger congressional role
        3.   Entrepreneurial politics: Congress the central political arena

III.   The constitutional and legal context
    A.   The Constitution creates an "invitation to struggle"
        1.   President commander in chief but Congress appropriates money
        2.   President appoints ambassadors, but Senate confirms
        3.   President negotiates treaties, but Senate ratifies
        4.   But Americans think president in charge, which history confirms
    B.   Presidential box score
        1.   Presidents relatively strong in foreign affairs
            a)   More successes in Congress on foreign than on domestic affairs
            b)   Unilateral commitments of troops upheld but stronger than Framers intended

            (1)   1801: Jefferson sends navy to Barbary

            (2)   1845: Polk sends troops to Mexico

            (3)   1861: Lincoln blockades Southern ports

            (4)   1940: FDR sends destroyers to Britain

            (5)   1950: Truman sends troops to Korea

            (6)   1960s: Kennedy and Johnson send forces to Vietnam

            (7)   1983: Reagan sends troops to Grenada

            (8)   1989: Bush orders invasion of Panama

            (9)   1990: Bush sends forces into Kuwait

            (10) 1999: Clinton orders bombing of Serbian forces

            (11) 2000: Bush sends troops to Afghanistan

   2.   Presidents comparatively weak in foreign affairs; other heads of state find U.S. presidents unable to act

       a)   Wilson and Franklin Roosevelt unable to ally with Great Britain before World War I and World War II

       b)   Wilson unable to lead U.S. into the League of Nations

       c)   Reagan criticized on commitments to El Salvador and Lebanon

       d)   Bush debated Congress on declaration of Gulf War

C.   Evaluating the power of the president

   1.   Depends on one's agreement/disagreement with policies

   2.   Supreme Court gives federal government wide powers; reluctant to intervene in Congress-president disputes

       a)   Nixon's enlarging of Vietnam war

       b)   Lincoln's illegal measures during Civil War

       c)   Carter's handling of Iranian assets

       d)   Franklin Roosevelt's "relocation" of 100,000 Japanese-Americans

D.   Checks on presidential power: political rather than constitutional

   1.   Congress: control of purse strings

   2.   Limitations on the president's ability to give military or economic aid to other countries

       a)   Arms sales to Turkey

       b)   Blockage of intervention in Angola

       c)   Legislative veto (previously) on large sale of arms

   3.   War Powers Act of 1973

       a)   Provisions

            (1)   Only sixty-day commitment of troops without declaration of war

            (2)   All commitments reported within forty-eight hours

            (3)   Legislative veto (previously) to bring troops home

       b)   Observance

            (1)   no president has acknowledged constitutionality

            (2)   Ford, Carter, Reagan, Bush, and Clinton sent troops without explicit congressional authorization

       c)   Supreme Court action (*Chadha* case)

            (1)   Struck down the legislative veto

            (2)   Other provisos to be tested

       d)   Effect of act doubtful even if upheld

            (1)   Brief conflicts not likely to be affected; Congress has not challenged a successful operation

            (2)   Even extended hostilities continue: Vietnam and Lebanon

   4.   Intelligence oversight

       a)   Only two committees today, not the previous eight

   b) No authority to disapprove covert action
   c) But "covert" actions less secret after congressional debate
   d) Congress sometimes blocks covert action: Boland Amendment
   e) Congressional concern about CIA after attacks of September 11

IV. The machinery of foreign policy
 A. Consequences of major power status
  1. President more involved in foreign affairs
  2. More agencies shape foreign policy
 B. Numerous agencies not really coordinated by anyone
 C. Secretary of State unable to coordinate
  1. Job too big for one person
  2. Most agencies owe no political or bureaucratic loyalty
 D. National Security Council created to coordinate
  1. Chaired by president and includes vice president, secretaries of State and Defense, director of CIA, chair of joint chiefs
  2. National security adviser heads staff
  3. Goal of staff is balanced view
  4. Grown in influence since Kennedy but downgraded by Reagan
  5. NSC rivals secretary of state
 E. Consequences of multicentered decision-making machinery
  1. "It's never over" because of rivalries within and between branches
  2. Agency positions influenced by agency interests

V. Foreign policy and public opinion
 A. Outlines of foreign policy shaped by public and elite opinion
  1. Before World War II, public opposed U.S. involvement
  2. World War II shifted popular opinion because
   a) Universally popular war
   b) War successful
   c) United States emerged as world's dominant power
  3. Support for active involvement persisted until Vietnam
   a) Yet support for internationalism highly general
   b) Public opinion now mushy and volatile
 B. Backing the president
  1. Public's tendency to support president in crises
   a) Foreign crises increases presidential level of public approval
   b) Strong support to rally 'round the flag for some but not all foreign military crises
  2. Presidential support does not decrease with casualties
  3. Americans support escalation rather than withdrawal in a conflict
 C. Mass versus elite opinion
  1. Mass opinion
   a) Generally poorly informed
   b) Generally supportive of president
   c) Conservative, less internationalist
  2. Elite opinion
   a) Better informed
   b) Opinions change more rapidly (Vietnam)
   c) Protest on moral or philosophical grounds
   d) More liberal and internationalist

VI. Cleavages among foreign policy elites
 A. Foreign policy elite divided
 B. How a worldview shapes foreign policy

    1.   Definition of *worldview:* comprehensive mental picture of world issues facing the United States and ways of responding

    2.   Example: Mr. X article on containment of USSR

    3.   Not unanimously accepted but consistent with public's mood, events, and experience

  C.   Four worldviews

    1.   Isolation paradigm

        a)   Opposes involvement in European wars

        b)   Adopted after World War I because war accomplished little

    2.   Appeasement (containment) paradigm

        a)   Reaction to appeasement of Hitler in Munich

        b)   Pearl Harbor ended isolationism in United States

        c)   Postwar policy to resist Soviet expansionism

    3.   Disengagement ("Vietnam") paradigm

        a)   Reaction to military defeat and political disaster of Vietnam

        b)   Crisis interpreted in three ways

            (1)   Correct worldview but failed to try hard enough

            (2)   Correct worldview but applied in wrong place

            (3)   Worldview itself wrong

        c)   Critics believed worldview wrong and new one based on new isolationism needed

        d)   Elites with disengagement view in Carter administration but were replaced during Reagan and Bush administrations

    4.   Human rights

        a)   Clinton had a disinterest in foreign policy and his advisors believed in disengagement.

        b)   Clinton's strongest congressional supporters argued against the Gulf War but advocated military intervention in Kosovo.

        c)   Change in view explained by concern for human rights and belief that situation in Kosovo amounted to genocide

        d)   Conservatives who supported containment in Gulf War urged disengagement in Kosovo

    5.   The politics of coalition building

        a)   Should the United States act "alone?"

        b)   If so, in what circumstances?

VII. The Use of Military Force

  A.   Military power more important after collapse of Soviet Union and end of Cold War

    1.   Military force used to attack Iraq, defend Kosovo, maintain order in Bosnia, and occupy Haiti and Somalia

    2.   Several nations have long-range rockets and weapons of destruction

    3.   Many nations feel threatened by neighbors

    4.   Russia still has nuclear weapons

  B.   Majoritarian view of military

    1.   Almost all Americans benefit, almost all pay

    2.   President is the commander-in-chief

    3.   Congress plays largely a supportive role

  C.   Client view of military

    1.   Real beneficiaries of military spending—general, admirals, big corporations, members of Congress whose districts get fat defense contracts—but everyone pays

    2.   Military-industrial complex shapes what is spent

VIII. The defense budget

  A.   Total spending

    1. Small peacetime military until 1950
       a) No disarmament after Korea because of Soviet threat
       b) Military system designed to repel Soviet invasion of Europe and small-scale invasions
    2. Public opinion supports a large military
    3. Demise of USSR produced debate
       a) Liberals: sharp defense cuts; United States should not serve as world's police officer
       b) Conservatives: some cuts but retain well-funded military because world still dangerous
    4. Desert Storm and Kosovo campaigns made clear no escaping U.S. need to use military force
    5. Kosovo campaign indicated that military had been reduced too much
    6. Clinton and Republican Congress called for more military spending

IX. What do we buy with our money?
  A. Changing circumstances make justification of expenditures complex
    1. World War II and Cold War: big armies, artillery, tanks, ships, etc.
    2. War on Terrorism: small groups, special forces, high-tech communications, precision guided bombs, and rockets
    3. Joint operations now also seem more necessary
  B. Secretary of defense
    1. Must transform conventional military for wars on terrorism
    2. Must budget in an atmosphere of debate and pressure from members of both the military and Congress
  C. Debating big new weapons
    1. Washington folks are used to it (B-1, B-2 bombers, MX missiles, M1 tank, etc.)
    2. Strategic Defense Initiative (SDI, or "Star Wars") debate particularly protracted
       a) Major scientific and philosophical quarrels
       b) Reluctance among the military
          (1) Mutually Assured Destruction (MAD) requires more missiles and bombers
          (2) SDI may reduce spending on missiles and bombers
       c) Concern MAD only works against rational leaders

X. What do we get for our money?
  A. Personnel
    1. From draft to all-volunteer force in 1973
    2. Volunteer force improved as result of:
       a) Increases in military pay
       b) Rising civilian unemployment
    3. Changes in military
       a) More women in military
       b) Ban of women on combat ships lifted in 1993 but Congress to be consulted if ground combat involved
       c) "Don't ask, don't tell" compromise adopted by Clinton on homosexuals in military
  B. Big-ticket hardware
    1. Main reasons for cost overruns
       a) Unpredictability of cost of new items
       b) Contractor incentives to underestimate at first
       c) Military chiefs want best weapons money can buy
       d) "Sole sourcing" of weapons without competitive bids
       e) Holding down budget by "stretching out" production

    2.   Latter four factors can be controlled; first cannot
  C. Small-ticket items
    1.   Seemingly outrageous prices come from allocation of overhead, small run of items produced
    2.   Others result from "gold-plating" phenomenon
  D. Readiness, favorite area for short-term budget cutting
    1.   Other cuts would hurt constituents
    2.   Cuts here show up quickly in money saved
  E. Bases
    1.   At one time, a lot of bases opened and few closed
    2.   Commission on Base Realignment and Closure created to take client politics out of base closings
XI. Structure of defense decision-making
  A. National Security Act of 1947
    1.   Department of Defense
      a) Secretary of Defense (civilian, as are secretaries of the army, navy, and air force)
      b) Joint Chiefs of Staff (military)
    2.   Reasons for separate uniformed services
      a) Fear that unified military will become too powerful
      b) Desire of services to preserve their autonomy
      c) Interservice rivalries intended by Congress to receive maximum information
  B. 1986 defense reorganization plan
    1.   Joint Chiefs of Staff
      a) Composed of uniformed head of each service with a chair and vice chair appointed by the president and confirmed by the Senate
      b) Chair since 1986 principal military adviser to president
    2.   Joint Staff
      a) Officers from each service assisting JCS
      b) Since 1986 serves chair; promoted at same rate
    3.   The services
      a) Each service headed by a civilian secretary responsible for purchasing and public affairs
      b) Senior military officer oversees discipline and training
    4.   The chain of command
      a) Chair of JCS does not have combat command
      b) Uncertainty whether 1986 changes will work

KEY TERMS MATCH

Set 1

Match the following terms and descriptions:

1. A policy perceived to confer wide benefits, and impose wide costs

2. A policy perceived to confer benefits on one group and costs on another

3. A policy perceived to benefit distinct groups but not to cost others

4. A stoppage by the USSR of Allied access to

a. antiappeasement

b. Berlin blockade

c. Chadha

d. CIA

e. client foreign policy

Germany's capital

5. The situation that followed the USSR's installation of hostile missiles in the Caribbean

6. A cabinet-level body charged with the execution of foreign policy

7. The agency charged with collecting sensitive foreign information

8. The committee appointed by statute that advises the president on foreign policy

9. International agreements submitted to the Senate for approval

10. International agreements not submitted to the Senate for approval

11. Schlesinger's depiction of presidential power under Nixon

12. A proviso allowing Congress to overrule the president's actions

13. Legislation passed in 1973 that attempted to limit the president's power to make war

14. The group of developing nations in Africa, Asia, Latin America, and the Middle East

15. A Supreme Court case voiding the legislative veto in the War Powers Act

16. The constitutional role played by the president in time of war

17. A private but powerful foreign policy think tank funded by the Rockefellers

18. A relatively consistent picture of the world problems facing the United States

19. The U.S. strategy that has dominated its post-World War II policy on the USSR

20. Where Neville Chamberlain sought peace through appeasement

21. The site of the Japanese attack on U.S. naval forces in 1941

22. Churchill's view of the barrier separating the Western powers from the USSR-dominated countries after World War II

23. A business operating in more than one country

f. cold war

g. commander in chief

h. containment

i. Council on Foreign Relations

j. Cuban missile crisis

k. disengagement view

l. domino theory

m. executive agreements

n. imperial presidency

o. interest group foreign policy

p. iron curtain

q. isolationism

r. legislative veto

s. majoritarian foreign policy

t. multinational corporation

u. Munich

v. NSC

w. Pearl Harbor

x. State Department

y. Third World

z. treaties

aa. War Powers Act

bb. worldview

24. The worldview that emerged as a result of World War II and in particular as a reaction to the Munich conference

25. The worldview that emerged in the aftermath of the Vietnam War suggesting that the United States ought to limit foreign intervention

26. The nonmilitary struggle between the United States (and its allies) and the former Soviet Union (and its allies) following World War II

27. The theory that if one nation fell into communist hands, neighboring nations would follow

28. The view that the United States should withdraw from world affairs, limit foreign aid, and avoid involvement in foreign wars

Set 2

Match the following terms and descriptions.

1. Participants in client politics in U.S. defense spending

2. Legislation enacted in 1947 that created the current Department of Defense

3. Competition among the army, navy, air force, and marines

4. In military terms, the tendency to ask for everything at once

5. Congressional bodies charged with oversight of the military

6. The decision hierarchy, starting with the president at the top and including the secretary of Defense and various unified and specified commands

7. Money presumably made available for "butter" as a consequence of cuts in military spending

8. A group of several hundred officers from the four services who assist the Joint Chiefs of Staff

9. A committee consisting of the heads of the

a. chain of command

b. cost overruns

c. defense reorganization plan

d. Desert Storm

e. "gold plating"

f. House Armed Services Committee

g. interservice rivalry

h. Joint Chiefs of Staff

i. Joint Staff

j. military-industrial complex

k. National Security Act

l. peace dividend

m. readiness

n. "sole sourcing"

o. Strategic Defense Initiative (SDI)

four military services plus an appointed chair
and vice chair

10. The procedure by which new weapons are
purchased from a single contractor

11. The amounts by which the prices of systems
exceed initial estimates

12. Controversial defense weapons system

13. The 1991 war in the Persian Gulf involving
U.S. troops

14. Training, supplies, munitions, fuel, and food

15. A plan signed in 1986 that increased the
power of officers who coordinate the
activities of different services

DID YOU THINK THAT . . . ?

Below are listed a number of misconceptions. You should be able to refute each statement in the space
provided, referring to information or argumentation contained in this chapter. Sample answers appear at
the end of this chapter.

1. "The Constitution gives the president the major role in foreign affairs."

   _____
   _____
   _____

2. "Because the public always rallies 'round the flag in crises, the president has great freedom of
action to do whatever he wants in international affairs."

   _____
   _____
   _____

3. "The amount of money spent on defense has been increasing steadily since the 1950s."

   _____
   _____
   _____

4. "With the collapse of the Soviet Union and the end of the Cold War, military power has become
less important."

   _____
   _____
   _____

DATA CHECK

Table 20.1: Popular Reactions to Foreign Policy Crises

1. What conclusion can be drawn regarding the effect of a foreign policy crisis on the president's approval rating?

2. Which crisis features the least amount of positive change in the "before" and "after" columns?

3. Which two crises are associated with downward trends in the level of public approval?

Table 20.2: How the Public and the Elite See Foreign Policy, 1999

Indicate whether the following views would most likely be expressed by the average member of the public or by a foreign policy leader.

4. Russia should solve its problems alone.

5. It is acceptable to assassinate a terrorist leader in order to combat terrorism.

6. Reducing illegal immigration is very important.

Figure 20.1: Trends in Military Spending

7. Which presidents noticeably increased military spending after taking office?

8. Which presidents noticeably decreased military spending after taking office?

Figure 20.2: Public Sentiment on Defense Spending, 1969–2002

9. Which sentiments most often have been expressed by Americans since 1973?

PRACTICING FOR EXAMS

TRUE/FALSE QUESTIONS

Read each statement carefully. Mark true statements *T*. If any part of the statement is false, mark it *F*, and write in the space provided a concise explanation of why the statement is false.

1.   T   F   Tocqueville argued that democratic nations were the best adapted to handle foreign affairs.

   _____

2.   T   F   The U.S. policy toward Israel is regarded as an example of majoritarian politics.

   _____

3.   T   F   U.S. presidents have less freedom in foreign affairs than do most other Western heads of state.

   _____

4.   T   F   The Supreme Court has consistently held that the federal government has foreign policy powers beyond those enumerated in the Constitution.

   _____

5.   T   F   Congress has yet to use its power to restrict the president's granting military or economic aid to foreign countries.

   _____

6.   T   F   In *Chadha*, the Supreme Court upheld the constitutionality of the War Powers Act.

   _____

7.   T   F   Before Pearl Harbor most Americans seemed to oppose U.S. entry into World War II.

   _____

8.   T   F   As wars continue, Americans usually become more determined to win them.

   _____

9.   T   F   Elites tend to give more support to the president's foreign policy than does public opinion in general.

   _____

10. T   F   Young people opposed U.S. involvement in Vietnam more than other age groups.

   _____

11. T   F   The disengagement worldview held that the Munich worldview had not merely been misapplied but was fundamentally wrong.

   _____

12. T   F   The antiappeasement approach to foreign policy emerged at the end of the Vietnam War.

   _____

13.　T　F　The four branches of the military are four separate entities and cannot by law be commanded by a single military officer.

14.　T　F　The Joint Chiefs of Staff are charged with the execution of national defense policy.

15.　T　F　In the 1960s Congress became more willing to question proposed military outlays.

16.　T　F　In 1940 President Roosevelt sent fifty destroyers to England to help fight Germany even though we were technically at peace.

17.　T　F　The size of the military budget, says the text, is best explained by majoritarian politics.

18.　T　F　Keeping a defense plant open is a matter of interest group and client politics as well as defense policy.

19.　T　F　The opening and closing of military bases is a good example of client politics.

20.　T　F　The military-industrial complex theory of defense procurement portrays military spending as an example of majoritarian politics.

MULTIPLE CHOICE QUESTIONS

Circle the letter of the response that best answers the question or completes the statement.

1.　The division of constitutional authority between the president and Congress is *best* characterized as

　　a.　congressional dominance.
　　b.　presidential dominance.
　　c.　an "invitation to struggle."
　　d.　"provocative silence."
　　e.　a true case and controversy.

2.　Decisions as to the total level of defense spending and the size of the armed forces as a whole are made by

　　a.　the secretary of Defense and the Pentagon.
　　b.　the Joint Chiefs of Staff.
　　c.　the Speaker of the House.
　　d.　Congress.
　　e.　the president.

3. Of the thirteen major wars fought by this country, _____ have followed a formal declaration of war by Congress.

    a. three
    b. five
    c. ten
    d. twelve
    e. thirteen

4. The Supreme Court has generally held the view that the conduct of foreign affairs

    a. is chiefly a congressional responsibility.
    b. is chiefly a presidential responsibility.
    c. involves important constitutional rights.
    d. is a political question for Congress and the president to work out.
    e. is best handled by the lower federal courts.

5. The most important congressional check on the president in the area of foreign affairs is the power to

    a. impeach.
    b. control the purse strings.
    c. approve ambassadors.
    d. reorganize those federal agencies that make foreign policy—the State Department, the CIA, and so forth.
    e. restrict access to the White House.

6. The War Powers Act of 1973 was designed as a check on the

    a. president.
    b. the Courts.
    c. CIA.
    d. Pentagon.
    e. congressional hawks.

7. The War Powers Act calls for Congress to provide a formal declaration or statutory authorization within _____ after troops are sent into a hostile situation.

    a. forty-eight hours
    b. one week
    c. two weeks
    d. sixty days
    e. six monts

8. According to the text

    a. the Director of the CIA authored the War Powers Act.
    b. the Pentagon whole-heartedly supported the War Powers Act.
    c. every president has obeyed the War Powers Act.
    d. every president but Clinton has obeyed the War Powers Act.
    e. no president has acknowledged the War Powers Act is constitutional.

9. The only war in which public support remained high was

    a. the Korean War.
    b. the Vietnam War.
    c. A and B.
    d. World War II.

    e.   World War I.

10.   Support for an internationalist American foreign policy is

    a.   heavily dependent on the phrasing of poll questions.
    b.   narrowly tailored and specific.
    c.   rarely affected by the opinions of popular leaders.
    d.   immune to world events.
    e.   All of the above.

11.   The "rally round the flag" effect and boost in presidential approval ratings which accompany many foreign crises were not evident when

    a.   John F. Kennedy accepted responsibility for the failed invasion of Cuba.
    b.   George W. Bush responded to the attack of September 11.
    c.   Ronald Reagan invaded Grenada.
    d.   George Bush sent troops to fight Iraq.
    e.   Bill Clinton launched bombing attacks on Iraq.

12.   A careful study of public opinion has concluded that, as American lives are lost during a time of war, the public tends to

    a.   desire escalation and swift victory.
    b.   seriously rethink the general premises behind our involvement.
    c.   withdraw support from its political leaders.
    d.   lose faith in our ability to "win."
    e.   None of the above.

13.   Where foreign policy—particularly declaring and conducting war—is concerned, _____ have the most volatile opinions.

    a.   the college-educated elite
    b.   the working class
    c.   women
    d.   blacks and other minorities
    e.   the elderly

14.   American elites adopted the isolationist worldview as a result of our experience with

    a.   the War Between the States.
    b.   World War I.
    c.   World War II.
    d.   the Korean War.
    e.   Vietnam.

15.   Containment was the policy of

    a.   the British and French during the rise of Hitler in Germany.
    b.   General Patton.
    c.   the United States toward Japan before Pearl Harbor.
    d.   Admiral Alfred T. Mahan.
    e.   the United States toward Russia after World War II.

16.   The "lessons of Munich," which shaped American foreign policy for a generation, were that

    a.   the United States cannot police the world.
    b.   nationalism is the predominant force in Third World politics.
    c.   aggression could best be met by negotiation and compromise.

d. aggression should be forcefully opposed.

e. economic development and foreign aid serve U.S. interests better than military aid.

17. The disengagement worldview was adopted by younger elites as a result of experience with

a. the War Between the States.
b. World War I.
c. World War II.
d. the Korean War.
e. Vietnam.

18. Opponents of the Gulf War were supportive of American intervention in Kosovo, suggesting a shift to the _____ paradigm of foreign policy.

a. isolationist
b. containment
c. disengagement
d. human rights
e. antiappeasement

19. The size and the division of the defense budget represent, respectively

a. entrepreneurial and majoritarian politics.
b. client and entrepreneurial politics.
c. majoritarian and interest group politics.
d. interest group and client politics.
e. reciprocal and club-based politics.

20. The reason for the great increase in the defense budget in 1950 was the

a. Korean War.
b. Cuban missile crisis.
c. escalation of the U.S.-Soviet arms race.
d. U2 spy plane incident.
e. oil embargo in the Middle East.

21. All of the following statements correctly describe the situation before the "War on Terrorism" *except*

a. Each of the four services developed its own tactics and weapons.
b. Each service was independent of every other one.
c. The Joint Chiefs of Staff took the idea of "joint operations" quite seriously.
d. In conflicts, each service typically performed a different task in different places.
e. Each of the four services developed its own communication services.

22. The strategic Defense Initiative (SDI) is an effort to

a. build coalitions of interests in the international community.
b. strengthen the efficiency of the M-12 tank.
c. employ B-1 bombers to provide a moving shield from attack.
d. require membership in NATO.
e. destroy incoming enemy missiles.

23. Among the causes of defense overruns noted in the text are all of the following *except*

a. the key players' incentive to underestimate costs going in.
b. the difficulty of estimating the costs of new programs in advance.
c. the cumbersome process of competitive bidding even for minor items.

d. the speed with which bids and contracts are obtained.
e. "stretch-outs" used to keep annual budgets low.

24. The Department of Defense was created by the

   a. Marshall Plan.
   b. Twenty-second Amendment.
   c. Twenty-third Amendment.
   d. Truman Doctrine.
   e. National Security Act.

25. The creation of separate uniformed services within a single department reflects the concern that

   a. the military budget would not be kept accountable.
   b. the military budget would not be kept below acceptable levels.
   c. interservice rivalry would escalate.
   d. intelligence sources should not communicate.
   e. a unified military might become too powerful politically.

26. The 1986 defense reorganization plan did all of the following *except*

   a. designate the chair of the Joint Chiefs of Staff as the president's principal military adviser.
   b. give control to the Joint Chiefs of Staff.
   c. give more power to the commander in chief of each unified command.
   d. A and C.
   e. create a civilian head for each service.

ESSAY QUESTIONS

Practice writing extended answers to the following questions. These test your ability to integrate and express the ideas that you have been studying in this chapter.

27. Compare the powers of U.S. presidents with those of heads of state in other Western governments with respect to the making of foreign policy.

28. Discuss the provisions of the War Powers Act and the effects that those provisions seem likely to have on presidential war-making abilities.

29. Since the 1920s American elite opinion has moved through four dominant worldwide views: isolation, containment (or antiappeasement), disengagement ("Vietnam"), and human rights. Compare and contrast each of these views.

30. Discuss the drawbacks and the advantages of interservice rivalries.

31. Outline and discuss the bureaucratic factors that tend to create the cost-overrun problem, and describe any solution that you believe might work.

ANSWERS TO KEY TERMS MATCH QUESTIONS

Set 1

1. s
2. o
3. e
4. b
5. j
6. x
7. d
8. v
9. z
10. m
11. n
12. r
13. aa
14. y
15. c
16. g
17. i
18. bb
19. h
20. u
21. w
22. p
23. t
24. a
25. k
26. f
27. l
28. q

Set 2

1. j
2. k

3. g
4. e
5. f
6. a
7. l
8. i
9. h
10. n
11. b
12. o
13. d
14. m
15. c

ANSWERS TO "DID YOU THINK THAT . . . ?" QUESTIONS

1. The president is given the title of commander in chief, receives ambassadors, and shares power with the Senate to nominate ambassadors to foreign countries and negotiate treaties. But Congress has the power to regulate foreign commerce and declare war and has powers of appropriation and legislation in foreign affairs. In fact, the Constitution gives more specific powers in foreign affairs to Congress than to the president.

2. Such an effect occurs immediately after an international crisis. Support tends to erode if the crisis is not resolved quickly (Iran), if there is a stalemate (Korea), or if people believe the president deceived them (Vietnam, Mexican-American War).

3. There was a dramatic increase in spending in 1950, but less was spent after the Korean War ended. There were ups and downs in spending for the next forty years and then a dramatic cut when the Soviet Union ceased to exist.

4. The fact is that the military remains as important as it once was. Since the USSR was abolished and the Berlin Wall came down in 1989, the United States has used military force to attack Iraq, defend Kosovo, maintain order in Bosnia, and occupy Haiti and Somalia. Various rogue nation, such as Iraq, Libya, and North Korea, have acquired or are about to acquire long-range rockets and weapons of mass destruction. Many nations that feel threatened by their neighbors, such as China, India, Pakistan, and Israel, have nuclear bombs. And Russia still has many of the nuclear weapons that the old Soviet Union built.

ANSWERS TO DATA CHECK QUESTIONS

1. Foreign policy crises are associated with an increase in positive approval ratings for the president.
2. The U2 spy plane incident (1960) and the failed attempt to rescue hostages from Iran (1980).
3. Troops sent to Bosnia (1995) and Kosovo (1998).
4. Public.

5.   Public.

6.   Public

7.   Nixon and Reagan.

8.   Carter and Clinton.

9.   "Too little / about right."

ANSWERS TO TRUE/FALSE QUESTIONS

1.   F. Perseverance and secrecy were among the qualities he said they lacked.

2.   F. It is an example of client politics.

3.   T

4.   T

5.   F. It cutoff of military sales to Turkey was an example.

6.   F. It struck the legislative veto portion of the act.

7.   T

8.   F. Usually only short wars remain popular.

9.   F. The masses are usually more supportive.

10.   F. Older people opposed it the most.

11.   T

12.   F. It emerged at the end of World War II.

13.   T

14.   F. They act only in an advisory capacity.

15.   T

16.   T

17.   T

18.   T

19.   F. No longer. The creation of the Commission on Base Realignment and Closure in 1988 changed the decision-making process.

20.   F. Client politics.

ANSWERS TO MULTIPLE CHOICE QUESTIONS

1.   c

2.   e

3.   b

4.   d

5.   b

6.   a

7. d
8. e
9. d
10. a
11. e
12. a
13. a
14. b
15. e
16. d
17. e
18. d
19. c
20. a
21. c
22. e
23. c
24. e
25. e
26. e

CHAPTER 21

Environmental Policy

REVIEWING THE CHAPTER

CHAPTER FOCUS

Environmental policy, like economic or welfare policy, reflects the unique nature of the American political system. Unlike economic or welfare issues, however, environmental issues lend themselves to entrepreneurial politics, which requires mobilizing the media, dramatizing the issue, and convincing members of Congress that their political reputations will suffer if they do not cast the right vote. It is politics in which an unorganized public benefits at the expense of a well-organized group, such as a manufacturer. After reading and reviewing the material in this chapter, you should be able to do each of the following:

1. List three reasons environmental policy tends to be so controversial, providing examples of each reason.

2. Describe the role of the American political system and local politics in shaping environmental policy. Contrast these with environmental policy making in England.

3. Distinguish among the following styles of politics in terms of who benefits and who pays: entrepreneurial, majoritarian, interest group, and client.

4. Describe the role of entrepreneurial politics in government's efforts to deal with the issues of global warming and endangered species.

5. Outline the major provisions of the Clean Air Act (1970), the Water Quality Improvement Act (1970), the revised Clean Air Act (1990), and the National Environmental Policy Act (1969).

6. Describe the role of majoritarian politics in government's efforts to reduce automobile emissions. Explain why majoritarian politics worked in some cases and not in others.

7. Describe the role of interest group politics in government's efforts to resolve the acid rain controversy. List proposed alternative solutions, and outline the terms of the compromise that was reached by Congress and the Bush administration.

8. Describe the role of client politics in government's efforts to regulate the use of agricultural pesticides and timber cutting in U.S. forests.

9. Give three reasons why it is so difficult to develop a sane environmental policy in this country. Provide examples of how the EPA is dealing with these problems.

10. Discuss the results of environmental protection measures that have been taken since 1970.

STUDY OUTLINE

I. Introduction
   A. Why is environmental policy so controversial?
      1. Creates both winners and losers

         a)   Losers may be interest groups or average citizens
         b)   Losers may not want to pay costs
              Example: auto exhaust control
    2.   Shrouded in scientific uncertainty
           Example: greenhouse effect

    3.   Takes the form of entrepreneurial politics
         a)   Encourages emotional appeals: "good guys" versus "bad guys"
         b)   May lead to distorted priorities
              Example: cancer versus water pollution
II.   The American context
   A.   Environmental policy is shaped by unique features of American politics
      1.   More adversarial than in Europe
         a)   Rules are often uniform nationally (auto emissions)
         b)   But require many regulators and rules, strict deadlines, and expensive technologies
         c)   Often government (pro-) versus business (anti-)
         d)   Example: Clean Air Act, which took thirteen years to revise in Congress
         e)   In England, rules are flexible and regional
             (1). Compliance is voluntary
             (2). Government and business cooperate
             (3). Policies are effective
      2.   Depends heavily on states
         a)   Standards are left to states, subject to federal control
         b)   Local politics decides allocations
         c)   Federalism reinforces adversarial politics; separation of powers provides multiple points of access
   B.   Types of politics
      1.   Entrepreneurial politics
         a)   Most people benefit, few companies pay costs
         b)   Example: factories and other stationary sources
      2.   Majoritarian
         a)   Most people benefit, most people pay
         b)   Example: air pollution from automobiles
      3.   Interest group
         a)   Some groups benefit, other groups pay
         b)   Example: acid rain controversy
      4.   Client
         a)   Most people pay, some groups benefit
         b)   Example: pesticide control
III. Entrepreneurial politics: global warming
   A.   Entrepreneurial politics gave rise to environmental movement
      1.   Santa Barbara oil spill, Earth Day
      2.   Led to the formation of EPA and passage of the Water Quality Improvement Act and tougher Clean Air Act in 1970
      3.   Two years later Congress passed laws designed to clean up water
      4.   Three years later Congress adopted the Endangered Species Act
      5.   New laws passed into the 1990s
      6.   Existing environmental organizations grew in size and new ones formed
      7.   Public opinion rallied behind environmental slogans
   B.   Global warming

          1.   Earth's temperature rises from trapped gases in the atmosphere
          2.   Predicted result: floods on coastal areas as the polar ice caps melt; wilder weather as more storms are created; and tropical diseases spread to North America
          3.   Activist scientists versus skeptics scientists
               a)   Activists agree with predicted results and say we should act now, despite scientific doubts
               b)   Skeptics say we should learn more before doing anything
               c)   Survey indicates skeptics outnumber activists
          4.   Activists have greatest influence
          5.   U.S. signed Kyoto Protocol in 1997
    C.   Endangered species
          1.   Endangered Species Act of 1973 prohibits buying or selling plants or animals on "endangered" species list
          2.   Over six hundred species on list with about half plants
          3.   Firms and government agencies seeking to build in areas with endangered species must comply with federal regulations
          4.   Complaints outweigh public support for law
IV. Majoritarian politics: pollution from automobiles
    A.   Clean Air Act imposed tough restrictions
          1.   Public demanded improvements
          2.   1975: 90 percent reduction of hydrocarbons and carbon monoxide
          3.   1976: 90 percent reduction in nitrous oxides
          4.   Required catalytic converters
    B.   Emergence of majoritarian politics in auto pollution
          1.   States were required to restrict public use of cars
               a)   If auto emissions controls were insufficient—Los Angeles, Denver, New York—parking bans required, implementation of car pools, gas rationing
               b)   Efforts failed: opposition too great
               c)   Congress and the EPA backed down, postponed deadlines
          2.   Consumers, auto industry, and unions objected
               a)   Loss of horsepower
               b)   Loss of competitiveness
               c)   Loss of jobs
          3.   The Clean Air Act was weakened in 1977 but revived in 1990 with tougher standards
    C.   Public will support tough laws
          1.   If costs are hidden (catalytic converters)
          2.   But not if they have to change habits (car pools)
    D.   Majoritarian politics when people believe the costs are low: National Environmental Policy Act of 1969 (NEPA)
          1.   Requires environmental impact statement (EIS)
          2.   Does not require specific action
          3.   Passed Congress with overwhelming support
          4.   But encouraged numerous lawsuits that block or delay projects
          5.   Popular support remains strong: costs appear low, benefits high
    E.   Majoritarian politics when people believe the costs are high
          1.   Increased gasoline taxes
               a)   Would discourage driving, save fuel, and reduce smog
               b)   Most would pay, most would benefit
               c)   But costs come long before benefits
               d)   And benefits may not be obvious

2.   Easier to raise gas tax if benefits are concrete, for example, highways, bridges, and so forth

V.   Interest group politics: acid rain
   A.   Source of acid rain
      1.   Burning of high-sulfur coal in midwestern factories
      2.   Winds carry sulfuric acid eastward
      3.   Rains bring acid to earth
   B.   Effects of acid rain
      1.   Acidification of lakes
      2.   Destruction of forests
      3.   Long-term and some short-term effects are unclear
   C.   Regional battle
      1.   East versus Midwest, Canada versus United States
      2.   Midwestern businesses deny blame and costs
   D.   Solutions and compromise
      1.   Burn low-sulfur coal one alternative
         a)   Effective but expensive
         b)   Low-sulfur coal comes from West, high-sulfur coal is local
      2.   Install smokestack scrubbers a second alternative
         a)   Costly, not always effective, and leave sludge
         b)   But allow use of inexpensive high-sulfur coal
      3.   Congress voted for scrubbers for all new plants
         a)   Including those that burned low-sulfur coal
         b)   Even if plant was next to low-sulfur coal mine
      4.   Political advantages
         a)   Protected jobs of high-sulfur coal miners; powerful allies in Congress
         b)   Environmentalists preferred scrubbers; "definitive" solution to problem
         c)   Scrubber manufacturers preferred scrubbers
         d)   Eastern governors preferred scrubbers; made their plants more competitive
      5.   Practical disadvantages
         a)   Failed to allow for plants that burn low-sulfur coal; why spend money on scrubbers?
         b)   Scrubbers didn't work well
         c)   Failed to address problem of existing plants
      6.   Stalemate for thirteen years
      7.   Two-step regulation proposed by Bush
         a)   Before 1995: some plants could choose their approach; fixed reduction but plants decide how to do
         b)   After 1995: sharper reductions for many more plants, requiring some use of scrubbers
         c)   Sulfur dioxide allowances could be bought and sold
         d)   Financial compensation for coal miners who lose jobs
      8.   Became part of Clean Air Act of 1990
   E.   Another example of interest group politics: zoning regulations, residents versus developers
   F.   New interest groups
      1.   More fervent and committed than before
      2.   Able to block change in policies
      3.   Examples
         a)   Environmental protection industry
         b)   Environmental Defense Fund
         c)   Labor unions

        4.   Momentum remains with policy makers

VI. Client politics: agricultural pesticides

    A.   Issue: control of use and runoff of pesticides; farmers have mostly resisted policy entrepreneurs, with DDT an exception

    B.   EPA efforts to evaluate safety of all pesticides

        1.   Given mandate by Congress in 1972

        2.   Program has not succeeded

           a)   Too many pesticides to evaluate

              (1). Many have only long-term effects needing extended study

              (2). Expensive and time-consuming to evaluate

           b)   Benefits of pesticide may outweigh harm

        3.   Political complications

           a)   Farmers are well-represented in Congress

           b)   Subsidies encourage overproduction, which encourages overuse of pesticides

           c)   Damage is hard to see and dramatize

        4.   The EPA budget is small

        5.   Few pesticides have been removed from the market; only those receiving heavy media coverage such as DDT in 1972

        6.   Client politics has won out

    C.   Environmentalists versus loggers

        1.   Issue: clear-cutting of forests

        2.   Congress has supported loggers

           a)   Forest Service forced to sell lumber at below-market prices

           b)   Subsidizes industry

        3.   Spotted owl: getting the media involved—entrepreneurial politics

VII. The environmental uncertainties

    A.   Why is it so difficult to have a sane environmental policy?

        1.   Many environmental problems are not clear cut

        2.   Goals are often unclear; public opinion can shift

        3.   Means of achieving goals (command-and-control strategy) are complicated by

           a)   Local circumstances

           b)   Technological problems

           c)   Economic costs

    B.   Examples of EPA and politics

        1.   What is the problem?

           a)   The EPA not left alone to define problem

           b)   Scandals and congressional demands can shift priorities

        2.   What are our goals?

           a)   Many are completely unrealistic

           b)   The EPA forced to ask for extensions and revisions

        3.   How do we achieve our goals?

           a)   Rules have been replaced by incentives

              (1). Offsets

              (2). Bubble standards

              (3). Pollution allowances

           b)   Complaints about command-and-control strategy are now coming from environmental groups and government

              (1). Clinton administration is reexamining old approaches

              (2). People are learning from experience

VIII. The results: the environment has improved since 1970 in some aspects

    A.   Less air pollution

B.   Maybe less water pollution but harder to judge
C.   Hazardous wastes remain a problem

KEY TERMS MATCH

Match the following terms and descriptions:

1.   The type of politics best illustrated by the acid rain controversy

2.   An EPA incentive that allows a company to decide how best to reduce air pollution from a given factory

3.   A national event held on April 22, 1970, celebrating the new environmental movement

4.   A device designed to remove sulfurous pollutants from smoke as it comes out of coal-burning plants

5.   The type of politics best illustrated by auto emission control rules

6.   The setting of pollution standards and rules in order to improve air and water quality

7.   The EPA incentive that allows a company higher pollution at one plant in exchange for lower pollution at another

8.   A law that includes the compromise reached by Congress on acid rain

9.   A pesticide banned by the EPA in 1972

10. Precipitation that may be caused by the burning of high-sulfur coal

11. The type of politics best illustrated by the continued use of agricultural pesticides

12. A law enacted in 1970 that made oil companies responsible for cleanup costs of oil spills

13. A document required before any federal agency undertakes an activity that "significantly" affects the environment

14. A major cause of acid rain

15. An EPA incentive that allows a company to apply credits for low-polluting emissions to future plant expansions, or to sell the credits.

16. A law passed in 1969 that included a provision requiring environmental impact

a.   acid rain
b.   bank (or pollution allowance)
c.   bubble standard
d.   catalytic converter
e.   Clean Air Act of 1970
f.   Clean Air Act of 1990
g.   clear-cutting
h.   client politics
i.   command-and-control strategy
j.   DDT
k.   Earth Day
l.   entrepreneurial politics
m.   environmental impact statement (EIS)
n.   Environmental Protection Agency (EPA)
o.   interest group politics
p.   majoritarian politics
q.   National Environmen-tal Policy Act (NEPA)
r.   offset
s.   scrubber
t.   sulfur dioxide
u.   Water Quality Im-provement Act of 1970

statements

17. The type of politics best illustrated by controversies over factory pollution

18. A logging method in which all trees in an area are removed

19. The device used in automobile engines to remove emission pollutants

20. The government agency established in 1970 to implement environmental legislation

21. Landmark environmental legislation that established national air-quality standards with specified deadlines.

DID YOU THINK THAT . . . ?

Below are listed a number of misconceptions. You should be able to refute each statement in the space provided, referring to information or argumentation contained in this chapter. Sample answers appear at the end of this chapter.

1. "Environmental policy in Europe, as in the United States, generally pits government interests against business interests."

    _____

    _____

    _____

2. "The costs of cleaning up the environment are generally paid for by the companies that do the polluting."

    _____

    _____

    _____

3. "The public will generally oppose environmental protection legislation that requires the average citizen to shoulder the costs."

    _____

    _____

    _____

4. "The environment has been steadily deteriorating over the past century."

    _____

    _____

    _____

DATA CHECK

Figure 21.1: Government Regulation

1. Summarize the opinions of Americans on government regulation and involvement in the area of environmental protection throughout the 1980s.

    _____

2. Summarize the opinions of Americans on government regulations and involvement in the area of environmental protection throughout the 1990s

    _____

PRACTICING FOR EXAMS

TRUE/FALSE QUESTIONS

Read each statement carefully. Mark true statements *T*. If any part of the statement is false, mark it *F*, and write in the space provided a concise explanation of why the statement is false.

1. T F Environmental policy making in the United States tends to be more adversarial than in European countries.

    _____

2. T F Allocation decisions regarding environmental policy are typically made on the basis of scientific evidence gathered by the federal government.

    _____

3. T F Majoritarian politics best explains the nation's policy approach to global warming.

    _____

4. T F With entrepreneurial politics, most people benefit at the expense of a well-organized group.

    _____

5. T F The Environmental Protection Agency was formed during the Great Depression as a means of lowering unemployment.

    _____

6. T F Interest group politics crated the environmental movement.

    _____

7. T F Citizens have a right to sue the EPA.

    _____

8. T F The Clean Air Act of 1970 required states to restrict the public's use of cars.

    _____

9. T F Popular support for the National Environmental Policy Act of 1969, including its call for environmental impact statements, remains strong.

    _____

10. T F   The average citizen will support increased gasoline taxes if the benefits include cleaner air and a reduction of oil consumption.

_____

11. T F   The controversy over the problem of acid rain illustrates the importance of client politics in environmental policy making.

_____

12. T F   The major source of sulfur dioxide in the atmosphere is the burning of low-sulfur coal.

_____

13. T F   The two major opposing groups in the acid rain controversy are midwestern power and coal companies and eastern environmentalists.

_____

14. T F   Environmentalists generally prefer the burning of low-sulfur coal to the use of scrubbers to reduce acid rain.

_____

15. T F   Under the compromise acid rain plan adopted by Congress, a power plant situated next to a low-sulfur coal mine must nevertheless install smokestack scrubbers.

_____

16. T F   A battle between residents and developers over the use of farmland is most likely to involve client politics.

_____

17. T F   Farmers have effectively resisted the efforts of policy entrepreneurs to restrict the use of agricultural pesticides.

_____

18. T F   Agricultural subsidies tend to discourage the use of pesticides.

_____

19. T F   Command-and-control strategies are typically used to achieve environmental policy goals.

_____

20. T F   Offsets, bubble standards, and banks (pollution allowances) are incentives used by the EPA to achieve its environmental protection goals.

_____

MULTIPLE CHOICE QUESTIONS

Circle the letter of the response that best answers the question or completes the statement.

1. One reason environmental policy tends to be so controversial is that

    a.   so many environmental policy decisions are based on scientific evidence, which tends to be highly political.

b. environmental policy often takes the form of majoritarian politics, which requires strong emotional appeals to overcome the political advantage of client groups.
c. environmental policy creates losers, who must pay the costs without getting enough of the benefits.
d. most people feel that government is already doing enough to control pollution; new programs are therefore likely to face stiff opposition.
e. All of the above.

2. The text speaks of the importance of *entrepreneurial politics* in many areas of environmental policy making. This term refers to a style of policy making in which

a. an unorganized public benefits at the expense of a well-organized group.
b. an unorganized public benefits at its own expense.
c. two organized groups with a material stake in the outcome fight over who will pay and who will benefit.
d. an organized group benefits at the expense of an unorganized public.
e. an organized group benefits at the expense of a well-organized public.

3. An example cited in the text of the adversarial nature of environmental policy making in the United States is the fact that

a. rules designed to reduce air pollution were written by government and business acting cooperatively.
b. most environmental issues are settled through majoritarian politics.
c. the public is prohibited by law from suing the Environmental Protection Agency.
d. it took Congress thirteen years to revise the Clean Air Act.
e. Congress has not passed a substantive environmental law in over twenty-seven years.

4. Compared with U.S. regulations, rules controlling air pollution in Great Britain involve

a. strict deadlines.
b. voluntary compliance.
c. expensive technology.
d. a uniform national policy.
e. rigorous assessments.

5. According to the text, federalism and the separation of powers

a. have reduced the scope of conflicts in environmental policy making.
b. ensure efficiency in environmental policy making.
c. are responsible for the broad-based public support for anti-pollution laws.
d. reinforce adversarial politics in environmental policy making.
e. None of the above.

6. All of the following are correct pairings of different styles of politics and examples of these styles in environmental policy making *except*

a. entrepreneurial politics and global warming.
b. majoritarian politics and pollution from automobiles.
c. client politics and land-use controls.
d. interest group politics and acid rain.
e. A and D.

7. The Environmental Protection Agency (EPA) was created by

a. Franklin D. Roosevelt.
b. Theodore Roosevelt

c.   Richard Nixon.
d.   Gerald Ford.
e.   Jimmy Carter.

8.   Which of the following statements is *incorrect*?

a.   Most scientists agree the earth has gotten warmer over the last century.
b.   Global warming is caused when gases are trapped in the earth's atmosphere.
c.   Global warming "activists" have had significant impact on policy-making.
d.   Almost all scientists agree that global warming will occur in ways that hurt humankind.
e.   The United States signed the Kyoto Protocol pledging to reduce greenhouse gas emission.

9.   Currently, there are over ____ species on the "protected" species list.

a.   six hundred
b.   one hundred
c.   fifty
d.   thirty
e.   fifteen

10.   One provision of the Clean Air Act of 1970 required cities in which smog was still a problem, despite emissions controls placed on new cars, to impose rules restricting the public's use of cars. Why did this provision fail?

a.   The EPA adopted an overly zealous command-and-control strategy.
b.   The provision was ruled unconstitutional.
c.   Powerful client groups worked to defeat the provision.
d.   Public opposition was too great.
e.   Legislators vowed to strengthen the measure if there were not immediate results.

11.   Why is environmental policy making on auto emissions control standards cited by the text as an example of majoritarian politics?

a.   because almost everyone benefits and almost everyone pays
b.   because the issue involves two powerful and competing interests
c.   because such politics involves mobilizing the media and dramatizing the issues
d.   because costs can be minimized, deferred, or phased on to small groups
e.   because few people were aware of the standards and the media ignored the issue

12.   When is the average citizen most likely to support tough environmental protection measures?

a.   when people believe the benefits are great enough
b.   when almost everyone benefits from the measures
c.   when costs of the measures are hidden or deferred
d.   when benefits are deferred to some later date
e.   when benefits are perceived as legitimate

13.   Which of the following statements about environmental impact statements (EISs) is correct?

a.   They were first mandated by a provision of the Clean Air Act of 1970.
b.   They have most frequently been used by businesses to block or change projects.
c.   They require specific action in response to a proposed project.
d.   They apply only to federal agencies.
e.   They apply only to state agencies.

14. Your state proposes an increase in gasoline taxes. The citizens of the state are most likely to support such an increase if the tax revenues will be used to

    a.   build a new highway.
    b.   reduce air pollution.
    c.   pay for measures to reduce traffic congestion.
    d.   finance a new crime prevention program.
    e.   finance a new weapons-exchange program.

15. If burning low-sulfur coal significantly reduces the emission of sulfurous fumes and therefore reduces acid rain, why don't plants in the Midwest and Great Lakes region burn only low-sulfur coal?

    a.   because it can be burned only if plants are equipped with scrubbers
    b.   because it is expensive
    c.   because it produces far less energy than does high-sulfur coal
    d.   because the major source of low-sulfur coal is Canada
    e.   because the major source of low-sulfur coal is Mexico

16. Why should many residents of Canada be concerned about the type of coal burned in midwestern U.S. power plants?

    a.   because acid rain caused by these plants affects lakes and forests in eastern Canada
    b.   because the Canadian economy is heavily dependent on the sale of high-sulfur coal
    c.   because the Canadian economy benefits directly from the sale of smokestack scrubbers
    d.   because Canada is a major producer of sulfur dioxide and a source of acid rain
    e.   because the extraction of low-sulfur coal in Canada is quite damaging to farm land

17. The compromise worked out by Congress to deal with acid rain calls for

    a.   scrubbers in all new plants.
    b.   the burning of only low-sulfur coal in all new plants.
    c.   both scrubbers and the burning of only low-sulfur coal in all new plants.
    d.   both scrubbers and the burning of only low-sulfur coal in all plants, both new and existing.
    e.   scrubbers in old plants and the burning of low-sulfur coal in half of all new plants.

18. In cases in which pesticides, such as DDT, have been taken off the market, public debate of their effects tends to lend itself to

    a.   majoritarian politics.
    b.   entrepreneurial politics.
    c.   interest group politics.
    d.   client politics.
    e.   club-based politics.

19. Many policy entrepreneurs favor measures to control the use of agricultural pesticides. One reason they have not been successful in enacting legislation to do this is that

    a.   the EPA is opposed to such legislation.
    b.   extensive media coverage has lent support to farmers.
    c.   the benefits to the public of pesticide use are high.
    d.   farmers are well-represented in Congress.
    e.   Congress and the EPA cannot agree on relevant standards.

20. Under this program chemical and petroleum industries would be taxed and the proceeds, along with general tax revenues, were to be used to pay for cleaning up abandoned hazardous waste sites.

    a. Off-set
    b. Superfund
    c. Command-and-Control
    d. Koyoto Protocol
    e. A and D.

21. Congress orders the U.S. Forest Service to sell timber to the timber industry at below-market prices and thereby subsidizes the timber industry. Such a program best illustrates

    a. entrepreneurial politics.
    b. majoritarian politics.
    c. interest group politics.
    d. client politics.
    e. club-based politics.

22. Offsets, bubble standards, and banks (pollution allowances) are all

    a. pollution control devices that effectively reduce air contamination.
    b. tests conducted by the EPA on agricultural pesticides.
    c. EPA incentives for companies to reduce pollution.
    d. rules devised by the EPA under its command-and-control strategy to improve air and water quality.
    e. standards which are employed in order to control the amount of hazardous nuclear waste that is discarded in waterbeds.

23. When a company reduces its polluting emissions by more than the law requires and uses the excess amount to cover a future plant expansion, it is taking advantage of

    a. an air proxy card.
    b. an offset.
    c. the command-and-control strategy.
    d. the bubble standard.
    e. a pollution allowance.

24. The EPA was given responsibility to administer certain laws governing

    a. air.
    b. water.
    c. pesticides.
    d. All of the above.
    e. None of the above.

25. The inability of Superfund to treat more than 2,000 waste sites by the year 2000 was, in part, attributable to the fact that

    a. Superfund money went straight to the waste removers.
    b. finding and suing responsible parties were difficult.
    c. the government provided little in the way of funding.
    d. President Reagan signed a bill which weakened the EPA.
    e. environmental lobbyists were no longer able to exert pressure on the EPA.

ESSAY QUESTIONS

Practice writing extended answers to the following questions. These test your ability to integrate and express the ideas that you have been studying in this chapter.

26. In this chapter much is made of the role of entrepreneurial politics in environmental policy making. Why should this form of politics lend itself to environmental issues? What other types of policy issues would involve entrepreneurial politics?

27. Most environmental policy decisions do not have an immediate or a visible effect on the environment; in fact, it may take years before reduced levels of water or air pollution become apparent to the public. Why then should the public be willing to support such decisions, especially when it must bear the costs? What issues are likely to be most popular with average citizens? Least popular?

28. Environmental policy making is described in the chapter as "adversarial." What does this mean? Who are some of the usual adversaries? What factors contribute to the adversarial nature of environmental policy making?

ANSWERS TO KEY TERMS MATCH QUESTIONS

1. o
2. c
3. k
4. s
5. p
6. i
7. r
8. f
9. j
10. a
11. h
12. u
13. m
14. t
15. b
16. q
17. l
18. g
19. d
20. n
21. e

ANSWERS TO "DID YOU THINK THAT . . . ?" QUESTIONS

1. Whereas environmental policy making in the United States is adversarial—often pitting government against business—in England, for example, rules designed to reduce pollution are written by government and business leaders cooperatively.

2. Majoritarian politics, of the sort that produced current auto emission standards, means that almost everyone benefits but almost everyone pays. The public also pays when client politics rewards certain organized groups, as in the use of agricultural pesticides and in timber cutting. The public may also pay, indirectly, when polluting companies pass along their cleanup costs to consumers.

3. The public will pay if the benefits to them are obvious and the costs are low or hidden. An example is public willingness to support auto emission control standards when the costs are hidden in the price of a car or to support higher gas taxes if the money is going directly into new highways or bridges.

4. Air quality has improved since passage of the Clean Air Act in 1970. Water quality may also be improving, but it is more difficult to gauge water contamination when pollutants do not come from some fixed source (such as a sewer).

ANSWERS TO DATA CHECK QUESTIONS

1. Worse.

2. Specific environmental catastrophes (e.g., Chernobyl, the *Exxon Valdez* spill); concern over global warming; increased media coverage, especially at the local level; and the general political and economic climate.

ANSWERS TO TRUE/FALSE QUESTIONS

1. T
2. F. They are controlled mainly by local politics.
3. F. Entrepreneurial politics.
4. T
5. F. It was formed in 1970 as an outgrowth of the environmental movement.
6. F. It was entrepreneurial politics.
7. T
8. T
9. T
10. F. They are more likely to support increased gasoline taxes if the benefits are concrete—new highways, bridges, and so on.
11. F. Interest group politics.
12. F. High-sulfur coal.
13. T
14. F. They prefer scrubbers.
15. T
16. F. Interest group politics.
17. T
18. F. They encourage overproduction and therefore the use of pesticides.
19. T
20. T

ANSWERS TO MULTIPLE CHOICE QUESTIONS

1. c
2. a
3. d
4. b

5. d
6. c
7. c
8. d
9. a
10. d
11. a
12. c
13. d
14. a
15. b
16. a
17. a
18. b
19. d
20. b
21. d
22. c
23. e
24. d
25. b

PART 4

Classic Statement: *West Virginia Board of Education v. Barnette* (1943)

INTRODUCTION

Occurring during World War II, the Barnette case presented an explosive issue to the Supreme Court. Under state law, children attending public schools in West Virginia were required to salute the American flag before class. Failure to comply was considered insubordination and resulted in expulsion from school.

Children who were Jehovah's Witnesses refused to participate in the patriotic exercise for religious reasons. They believed that saluting the flag violated the biblical commandment against worshiping graven images. According to their parents, obedience to the law risked the children's eternal salvation. Consequently, the children were expelled from school.

In 1940, the Supreme Court had ruled in a similar case that compulsory flag saluting in public schools was a permissible means of fostering "national unity" and vital to the national security. Much controversy followed this decision. In Barnette, Justice Robert Jackson reversed the earlier ruling and wrote a classic statement about the position of the Bill of Rights in American society.

The very purpose of a Bill of Rights was to withdraw certain subjects from the vicissitudes of political controversy, to place them beyond the reach of majorities and officials and to establish them as legal principles to be applied by the courts. One's right to life, liberty, and property, to free speech, a free press, freedom of worship and assembly and other fundamental rights may not be submitted to vote; they depend on the outcome of no elections.

Struggles to coerce uniformity of sentiment in support of some end thought essential to their time and country have been waged by many good as well as by evil men. Nationalism is a relatively recent phenomenon but at other times and places the ends have been racial or territorial security, support of a dynasty or regime, and particular plans for saving souls. As first and moderate methods to attain unity have failed, those bent on its accomplishment must resort to an ever-increasing severity. As governmental pressure toward unity becomes greater, so strife becomes more bitter as to whose unity it shall be. Probably no deeper division of our people could proceed from any provocation than from finding it necessary to choose what doctrine and whose program public educational officials shall compel youth to unite in embracing. Ultimate futility of such attempts to compel coherence is the lesson of every such effort from the Roman drive to stamp out Christianity as a disturber of its pagan unity, the Inquisition, as a means to religious and dynastic unity, the Siberian exiles as a means to Russian unity, down to the fast failing efforts of our present totalitarian enemies. Those who begin coercive elimination of dissent soon find themselves exterminating dissenters. Compulsory unification of opinion achieves only the unanimity of the graveyard.

It seems trite but necessary to say that the First Amendment to our Constitution was designed to avoid these ends by avoiding these beginnings. There is no mysticism in the American concept of the State or of the nature or origin of its authority. We set up government by consent of the governed, and the Bill of Rights denies those in power any legal opportunity to coerce that consent. Authority here is to be controlled by public opinion, not public opinion by authority.

The case is made difficult not because the principles of its decision are obscure but because the flag involved is our own. Nevertheless, we apply the limitations of the Constitution with no fear that freedom to be intellectually and spiritually diverse or even contrary will disintegrate the social organization. To believe that patriotism will not flourish if patriotic ceremonies are voluntary and spontaneous instead of a compulsory routine is to make an unflattering estimate of the appeal of our institutions to free minds. We can have intellectual individualism and the rich cultural diversities that we owe to exceptional minds only at the price of occasional eccentricity and abnormal attitudes. When they are so harmless to others or to the State as those we deal with here, the price is not too great. But freedom to differ is not limited to things that do not matter much. That would be a mere shadow of freedom. The test of its substance is the right to differ as to things that touch the heart of the existing order.

If there is any fixed star in our constitutional constellation, it is that no official high or petty, can prescribe what shall be orthodox in politics, nationalism, religion, or other matters of opinion or force citizens to confess by word or act their faith therein. If there are any circumstances which permit an exception, they do not now occur to us.

We think the action of the local authorities in compelling the flag salute and pledge transcends constitutional limitations on their power and invades the sphere of intellect and spirit which it is the purpose of the First Amendment to our Constitution to reserve from all official control.

Questions for Understanding and Discussion

1. According to Justice Jackson, what is the purpose of the Bill of Rights?

2. Does Justice Jackson's position contradict the democratic ideal of majoritarian rule? Explain.

3. According to Jackson, what evils are associated with the government's attempting to compel unanimity at a time of national crisis? Is the justice making patriotism an object of ridicule?

4. Does Justice Jackson imply that the Bill of Rights is superior to the other provisions of the Constitution? Defend your position.

PART FIVE:
The Nature of American Democracy
CHAPTER 22

Who Governs? To What Ends?

REVIEWING THE CHAPTER

CHAPTER FOCUS

This chapter provides an overview of American politics and central themes of the text, namely, "Who Governs? To What Ends?" A broad perspective of the history of American politics is utilized in order to provide a basis for understanding the politics of the past and present, and also to allow you to consider what the future may hold. After reading and reviewing the material in this chapter, you should be able to do each of the following:

1. Explain why the size of the federal government and the scope of its power did not increase in many significant ways for almost 150 years.

2. Identify and explain specific historical events and developments that triggered the transformation of the federal government into a common candidate for solving an amazing variety of social and economic problems.

3. Explain the general consequences of the enlarged scope of government activity.

4. Understand how our political culture played a critical role in the foundation of our government and continues to shape political processes and our nation's development.

STUDY OUTLINE

I.   Introduction
    A.   Assumption the president and Congress are to address social and economic problems
        1.   Limited concern of government as recently as the Eisenhower administration
        2.   The Founders and the role of the federal government
    B.   Constitutional hurdles to effective federal action
        1.   Separation of powers and checks and balances
        2.   Federalism
        3.   Bicameralism
II. Restraints on the growth of government
    A.   For first 150 years government grew slowly
        1.   Supreme Court defined government authority narrowly
        2.   Popular opinion supported a limited governmental role
        3.   The political system was designed to limit government
    B.   System limiting government makes it difficult to abolish programs

1. Under Reagan spending increased for many programs
2. Bush has also proposed programs that would increase spending

III. Relaxing the Restraints
   A. Changes in Constitutional interpretation
      1. Bill of Rights incorporated to the states
      2. Special protection of property rights reduced, business regulation increased
      3. Congress allowed to give broad discretionary powers to administrative agencies
   B. Changes in public opinion
      1. Public demand for government action during Great Depression
      2. Opinions of political elites changed even faster
      3. Some programs have been popular with the masses
   C. Changes in the distribution of political resources
      1. Number and variety of interest groups have increased
      2. Funds from organization pursuing causes have grown
      3. Greater access to the federal courts
      4. Technological advances have enhanced the power to communicate ideas
   D. The Old System v. the New System

IV. Consequences of activist government
   A. Need to assess costs and benefits of programs
   B. General political consequences of the enlarged scope of activity
      1. Bureaucratization of all organizations
      2. Rise of competing policies
      3. Less control by the electorate through the decline of parties and turnout and of public confidence
      4. Greater risk of government failure

V. The influence of structure
   A. Parliamentary model; if adopted here, would do the following:
      1. Fewer legislative restraints on the executive
      2. More bureaucratic centralization
      3. Less citizen participation to challenge or block policies
      4. Higher taxes and more secrecy
   B. U.S. model
      1. More local authority
      2. Greater citizen participation

VI. The influence of ideas
   A. Preoccupation with rights
      1. Assumption that affected groups have a right to participate in policy formation
      2. Willingness to resort to courts
   B. Effects of rights on government functions
      1. Harder to make government decisions
      2. More red tape
   C. Elite opinion influences which rights have priority
      1. Favors freedom of expression over management of property
      2. Mass opinion less committed to freedom of expression
   D. Freedom versus equality an enduring tension
      1. Advantages of freedom are remote
      2. Advantages of equality are obvious
   E. Fragmentation of political system increases role of ideas
      1. Widespread enthusiasm for an idea can lead to rapid adoption of new programs
      2. Competing ideas make change difficult; change today may require the persuading of thousands of special interests

F.   Fundamental challenge: to restore confidence in the legitimacy of government itself

PRACTICING FOR EXAMS

TRUE/FALSE QUESTIONS

Read each statement carefully. Mark true statements *T*. If any part of the statement is false, mark it *F*, and write in the space provided a concise explanation of why the statement is false.

1.   T   F   The Founders generally expected the scope of the power of the federal government to be quite limited.

2.   T   F   Previous to the 1930's, the Supreme Court prevented the government from regulating business and levying an income tax.

3.   T   F   Racial segregation was practiced only in the South.

4.   T   F   The Great Depression made people even more hesitant to give power to the federal government.

5.   T   F   The Court has incorporated key provisions of the Bill of Rights through the Equal Protection Clause of the Fourteenth Amendment.

6.   T   F   Political resources have become more widely distributed.

7.   T   F   It is now easier to get access to the federal courts.

8.   T   F   Campaign finance laws and court rulings have eliminated the influence that interest groups can wield by spending money.

9.   T   F   Under the Old System, the presidency was small and somewhat personal.

10.   T   F   Lyndon Johnson became president with a small share of the popular vote.

11.   T   F   Medicare and Medicaid were part of Johnson's "Great Society" legislation.

12.   T   F   Members of the House began to enjoy security in the retention of their seats in the 1960s.

13.   T   F   Television began to play a major role in shaping the political agenda in the 1960s.

14. T F   Party conventions came to supplant primary elections in the 1960s.

15. T F   When the people in Washington did little, elections made less difference in policy.

16. T F   Individual members of Congress are far more important than congressional leaders.

17. T F   We expect more from government but are less and less certain that we are going to get it.

MULTIPLE CHOICE QUESTIONS

Circle the letter of the response that best answers the question or completes the statement.

1. As recently as the Eisenhower administration

    a. domestic political issues and foreign affairs were given an equal amount of attention in Washington.
    b. major domestic political issues dominated the attention of Washington.
    c. the national political agenda was short on major domestic political issues.
    d. civil rights were not thought to be a matter of federal policy.
    e. Congress was preoccupied with solving social and economic problems nationwide.

2. Which of the following is *not* an explanation for why there was no rapid growth in the power and scope of the federal government for the better part of a century and a half?

    a. prevailing interpretations of the Constitution
    b. constitutional amendments
    c. separation of powers
    d. popular opinion
    e. checks and balances

3. Who took office after promising to reduce the size of government, but learned that existing programs have entrenched defenders.

    a. John F. Kennedy
    b. Harry Truman
    c. Franklin D. Roosevelt
    d. Dwight Eisenhower
    e. Ronald Reagan

4. In recent decades,

    a. the Supreme Court has permitted Congress to give broad discretionary power to administrative agencies.
    b. important provisions of the Bill of Rights have been incorporated to the states.
    c. citizens have been able to alter state policy to a greater degree than before.
    d. court rulings have allowed a greater degree of business regulation.
    e. All of above.

5. Once enough proposals for new government programs were passed, former debates about legitimacy shifted to arguments about

    a.   reciprocity.
    b.   costs.
    c.   effectiveness.
    d.   popularity.
    e.   creativity.

6. Under the Old System of policy-making,

    a.   the government's agenda was large.
    b.   the legitimacy of federal action was rarely questioned.
    c.   state's rights were almost irrelevant.
    d.   the president was frequently quoted directly by the press.
    e.   the people voted at a high rate.

7. The "New System" of policy making began in the

    a.   1860s
    b.   1890s
    c.   1920s
    d.   1930s
    e.   1990s

8. What made it difficult to start a new program under the Old System and makes it difficult to change a new program in the New System?

    a.   checks and balances
    b.   federalism
    c.   state's rights
    d.   the electoral college
    e.   None of the above.

9. Under the New System, it is much more difficult to resolve conflicts because

    a.   individual members of Congress are less influential.
    b.   the Supreme Court has limited the impact of interest groups.
    c.   the distribution of political resources is shrinking.
    d.   power is centralized.
    e.   power is decentralized.

10. The shift from the Old System to the New System was, in part, accelerated by

    a.   the election of Republican presidents in the 1950s and 1970s.
    b.   the election of Democrat majorities in the House and Senate in the 1930s and 1960s.
    c.   the selection of Republican Supreme Court justices in the 1930s.
    d.   economic instability in the 1960s.
    e.   constant turnover in the membership of Congress.

11. The text suggests the consequences of an increasingly activist government include all of the following *except*

    a.   Members of government spend more time managing.
    b.   The government appears to act in inconsistent, uncoordinated and cumbersome ways.
    c.   The government is less susceptible to control by electoral activity.
    d.   Interest groups have lost their influence.
    e.   The government is held responsible for more things.

12. More than the citizens of perhaps any other nation, Americans define their relationships with one another and political authority in terms of

    a.   rights
    b.   liberties
    c.   duties
    d.   economics
    e.   social class

13. The authors suggest that, had the Founders adopted a centralized parliamentary regime similar to that of Great Britain, the least amount of historical variation would have probably concerned

    a.   social welfare
    b.   national planning
    c.   war
    d.   congressional investigations
    e.   taxes

14. If the United States had adopted a parliamentary structure of government, it probably would

    a.   be more sensitive to local concerns.
    b.   have stronger parties.
    c.   be less sensitive to local concerns.
    d.   have weaker parties.
    e.   experience a decrease in voter turnout.

15. According to the text, elite opinion tends to favor freedom of _____ over freedom to manage or dispose of property.

    a.   choice
    b.   travel
    c.   conscience
    d.   religion
    e.   expression

16. Tocqueville felt that Americans, as a part of a democratic community, were primarily attached to

    a.   feeedom.
    b.   equality.
    c.   fraternity.
    d.   community.
    e.   reciprocity.

17. Perhaps the greatest challenge to statesmanship in the years ahead is to find a way to serve the true interests of the people and, at the same time,

    a.   reduce partisan conflicts in Washington.
    b.   restore their confidence in government.
    c.   increase voter participation.
    d.   satisfy the demands of a multiplicity of interest groups.
    e.   satisfy the demand of the military-industrial complex.

ESSAY QUESTIONS

Practice writing extended answers to the following questions. These test your ability to integrate and express the ideas that you have been studying in this chapter.

1. Describe the Constitutional arrangements that make it hard for the federal government to act.

2. Explain the role that the United States Supreme Court played in the expansion of federal power.

3. Identify the two major differences between the Old and New Systems of politics in the United States.

4. Explain why increases in government activism are likely to be associated with a public that is increasingly dissatisfied.

ANSWERS TO TRUE/FALSE QUESTIONS

1. T
2. T
3. F.
4. F. The Great Depression helped swing public opinion toward the idea of big government.
5. T
6. T
7. T
8. F. Law and rulings have given legal status and constitutional protection to thousands of such groups.
9. T
10. F. Johnson came to power with a larger share of the popular vote than any other president in modern times.
11. T
12. T
13. T
14. F. Primary elections came to supplant the party conventions.
15. F. When the people in Washington did little, elections made a larger difference in policy.
16. T
17. T

ANSWERS TO MULTIPLE CHOICE QUESTIONS

1. b
2. c
3. b
4. a
5. c
6. b
7. c
8. b
9. d
10. a
11. d
12. d
13. d

14. c
15. a
16. d
17. b

PART 5

Classic Statement: "Why Democratic Nations Show a More Ardent and Enduring Love of Equality Than of Liberty, and How That Leads Them to Concentrate Political Power," from *Democracy in America,* by Alexis de Tocqueville[1]

INTRODUCTION

Earlier (in the Classic Statement section for Part II), we read of Tocqueville's concern about the power of the majority. Here he examines another problem that democracies face—how to preserve freedom when it is more natural, he argues, for people to love equality more than freedom. He makes a subtle argument about why equality should be more attractive than freedom; read it closely and see whether you agree. Then he turns to one consequence of a love of equality—its tendency to promote the concentration, or centralization, of political power. Tocqueville was writing in 1840; see whether you can think of present-day examples that support or contradict his argument.

WHY DEMOCRATIC NATIONS SHOW A MORE ARDENT AND ENDURING LOVE OF EQUALITY THAN OF LIBERTY

The first and most intense passion that is produced by equality of condition is, I need hardly say, the love of that equality.

It is possible to imagine an extreme point at which freedom and equality would meet and blend. Let us suppose that all the people take a part in the government, and that each one of them has an equal right to take a part in it. As no one is different from his fellows, none can exercise a tyrannical power; men will be perfectly free because they are all entirely equal; and they will all be perfectly equal because they are entirely free. To this ideal state democratic nations tend. This is the only complete form that equality can assume upon earth; but there are a thousand others which, without being equally perfect, are not less cherished by those nations.

Although men cannot become absolutely equal unless they are entirely free, and consequently equality, pushed to its furthest extent, may be confounded with freedom, yet there is good reason for distinguishing the one from the other. The taste which men have for liberty and that which they feel for equality are, in fact, two different things; and I am not afraid to add that among democratic nations they are two unequal things.

---

[1] Alexis de Tocqueville, *Democracy in America* (New York: Knopf, 1944, first published in 1840), Book 2, Chapter 1, and Book 4, Chapter 3.

Freedom has appeared in the world at different times and under various forms; it has not been exclusively bound to any social condition, and it is not confined to democracies. Freedom cannot, therefore, form the distinguishing characteristic of democratic ages. The peculiar and preponderant fact that marks those ages as its own is the equality of condition; the ruling passion of men in those periods is the love of this equality. Do not ask what singular charm the men of democratic ages find in being equal, or what special reasons they may have for clinging so tenaciously to equality rather than to the other advantages that society holds out to them: equality is the distinguishing characteristic of the age they live in; that of itself is enough to explain that they prefer it to all the rest.

That political freedom in its excesses may compromise the tranquility, the property, the lives of individuals is obvious even to narrow and unthinking minds. On the contrary, none but attentive and clear-sighted men perceive the perils with which equality threatens us, and they commonly avoid pointing them out. They know that the calamities they apprehend are remote and flatter themselves that they will only fall upon future generations, for which the present generation takes but little thought. The evils that freedom sometimes bring with it are immediate; they are apparent to all, and all are more or less affected by them. The evils that extreme equality may produce are slowly disclosed; they creep gradually into the social frame; they are seen only at intervals; and at the moment at which they become most violent, habit already causes them to be no longer felt.

The advantages that freedom brings are shown only by the lapse of time, and it is always easy to mistake the cause in which they originate. The advantages of equality are immediate, and they may always be traced from their source.

Political liberty bestows exalted pleasures from time to time upon a certain number of citizens. Equality every day confers a number of small enjoyments on every man. The charms of equality are every instant felt and are within the reach of all; the noblest hearts are not insensible to them, and the most vulgar souls exult in them. The passion that equality creates must therefore be at once strong and general. Men cannot enjoy political liberty unpurchased by some sacrifices, and they never obtain it without great exertions. But the pleasures of equality are self-proffered; each of the petty incidents of life seems to occasion them, and in order to taste them, nothing is required but to live.

Democratic nations are at all times fond of equality, but there are certain epochs at which the passion they entertain for it swells to the height of fury. This occurs at the moment when the old social system, long menaced, is overthrown after a severe internal struggle, and the barriers of rank are at length thrown down. At such times men pounce upon equality as their booty, and they cling to it as to some precious treasure which they fear to lose. The passion for equality penetrates on every side into men's hearts, expands there and fills them entirely. Tell them not that by this blind surrender of themselves to an exclusive passion they risk their dearest interests; they are deaf. Show them not freedom escaping from their grasp while they are looking another way; they are blind, or rather they can discern but one object to be desired in the universe.

I think that democratic communities have a natural taste for freedom; left to themselves, they will seek it, cherish it, and view any privation of it with regret. But for equality their passion is ardent, insatiable, incessant, invincible; they call for equality in freedom; and if they cannot obtain that, they still call for equality in slavery. They will endure poverty, servitude, barbarism, but they will not endure aristocracy.

This is true at all times, and especially in our own day. All men and all powers seeking to cope with this irresistible passion will be overthrown and destroyed by it. In our age freedom cannot be established without it and despotism itself cannot reign without its support.

THAT THE SENTIMENTS OF DEMOCRATIC NATIONS ACCORD WITH THEIR OPINIONS IN LEADING THEM TO CONCENTRATE POLITICAL POWER

If it is true that in ages of equality men readily adopt the notion of a great central power, it cannot be doubted, on the other hand, that their habits and sentiments predispose them to recognize such a power and to give it their support.

As the men who inhabit democratic countries have no superiors, no inferiors, and no habitual or necessary partners in their undertakings, they readily fall back upon themselves and consider themselves as beings apart. Hence such men can never, without an effort, tear themselves from their private affairs to engage in public business; their natural bias leads them to abandon the latter to the sole visible and permanent representative of the interests of the community; that is to say, to the state. Not only are they naturally wanting in a taste for public business, but they have frequently no time to attend it. Private life in democratic times is so busy, so excited, so full of wishes and of work, that hardly any energy or leisure remains to each individual for public life.

As in periods of equality no man is compelled to lend his assistance to his fellow men, and none has any right to expect much support from them, everyone is at once independent and powerless. These two conditions, which must never be either separately considered or confounded together, inspire the citizen of a democratic country with very contrary propensities. His independence fills him with self-reliance and pride among his equals; his debility makes him feel from time to time the want of some outward assistance, which he cannot expect from any of them, because they are all impotent and unsympathizing. In this predicament he naturally turns his eyes to that imposing power which alone rises above the level of universal depression. Of that power his wants and especially his desires continually remind him, until he ultimately views it as the sole and necessary support of his own weakness.[2]

. . . The hatred that men bear to privilege increases in proportion as privileges become fewer and less considerable, so that democratic passions would seem to burn most fiercely just when they have least fuel. I have already given the reason for this phenomenon. When all conditions are unequal, no

---

[2] In democratic communities nothing but the central power has any stability in its position or any permanence in its undertakings. All the citizens are in ceaseless stir and transformation. Now, it is in the nature of all governments to seek constantly to enlarge their sphere of action; hence it is almost impossible that such a government should not ultimately succeed, because it acts with a fixed principle and a constant will upon men whose position, ideas, and desires are constantly changing.

   It frequently happens that the members of the community promote the influence of the central power without intending to. Democratic eras are periods of experiment, innovation, and adventure. There is always a multitude of men engaged in difficult or novel undertakings, which they follow by themselves without shackling themselves to their fellows. Such persons will admit, as a general principle, that the public authority ought not to interfere in private concerns; but, by an exception to that rule, each of them craves its assistance in the particular concern on which he is engaged and seeks to draw upon the influence of the government for his own benefit, although he would restrict it on all other occasions. If a large number of men applies this particular exception to a great variety of different purposes, the sphere of the central power extends itself imperceptibly in all directions, although everyone wishes it to be circumscribed.

   Thus a democratic government increases its power simply by the fact of its permanence. Time is on its side; every incident befriends it; the passions of individuals unconsciously promote it; and it may be asserted that the older a democratic community is, the more centralized will its government become.

inequality is so great as to offend the eye, whereas the slightest dissimilarity is odious in the midst of general uniformity; the more complete this uniformity is, the more insupportable the sight of such a difference becomes. Hence it is natural that the love of equality should constantly increase together with equality itself, and that it should grow by what it feeds on.

This never dying, ever kindling hatred which sets a democratic people against the smallest privileges is peculiarly favorable to the gradual concentration of all political rights in the hands of the representative of the state alone. The sovereign, being necessarily and incontestably above all the citizens, does not excite their envy, and each of them thinks that he strips his equals of the prerogative that he concedes to the crown. The man of a democratic age is extremely reluctant to obey his neighbor, who is his equal; he refuses to acknowledge superior ability in such a person; he mistrusts his justice and is jealous of his power; he fears and he despises him; and he loves continually to remind him of the common dependence in which both of them stand to the same master.

Every central power, which follows its natural tendencies, courts and encourages the principle of equality; for equality singularly facilitates, extends, and secures the influence of a central power.

In like manner it may be said that every central government worships uniformity; uniformity relieves it from inquiry into an infinity of details, which must be attended to if rules have to be adapted to different men, instead of indiscriminately subjecting all men to the same rule. Thus the government likes what the citizens like and naturally hates what they hate. These common sentiments, which in democratic nations constantly unite the sovereign and every member of the community in one and the same conviction, establish a secret and lasting sympathy between them.

Thus by two separate paths I have reached the same conclusion. I have shown that the principle of equality suggests to men the notion of a sole, uniform, and strong government; I have now shown that the principal of equality imparts to them a taste for it. To governments of this kind of nations of our age are therefore tending. They are drawn thither by the natural inclination of mind and heart; and in order to reach that result, it is enough that they do not check themselves in their course.

I am of the opinion that, in the democratic ages which are opening upon us, individual independence and local liberties will ever be the products of art; that centralization will be the natural government.

Questions for Understanding and Discussion

1. In Tocqueville's opinion, in what ways do the pleasures of freedom differ from the pleasures of equality?

2. Why does democracy tend to make its citizens nonparticipants in the affairs of their state?

3. Why does a centralized government prefer that all citizens have the same rights and duties?

4. Tocqueville states that "the government likes what the citizens like and naturally hates what they hate." Do you think this observation is still valid in light of all the controversial issues, protests, and debates of today?

5. Has the course of government in the past century and a half tended mostly to confirm or to refute Tocqueville's ideas in these segments? Give examples to support your answer.

Practice Examination, Chapters 1 to 14

True/False Questions

Read each statement carefully. Mark true statements *T*. If any part of the statement is false, mark it *F,* and write in the space provided a concise explanation of why the statement is false.

1. Some writers of the Constitution opposed democracy on the grounds that the people would be unable to make wise decisions.

   _____

2. *Democracy* as used in this book refers to the rule of the many.

   _____

3. The Declaration of Independence contained more paragraphs naming specific complaints against the king than paragraphs announcing the goals of the Revolution.

   _____

4. James Madison, like Aristotle, thought that government had an obligation to cultivate virtue among those who were governed.

   _____

5. Federalism was intended by the Founders to operate as a protection for personal liberty.

   _____

6. The most important attraction of federal grants-in-aid has been federal budget surpluses.

   _____

7. A thoroughly shared civic culture renders such phenomena as civil war impossible.

   _____

8. Because of the separation of church and state, religious dogmas and practices have been irrelevant in the formation of American civic culture.

   _____

9. In recent years, women have "deserted" Democratic candidates for Republican ones.

   _____

10. Elite opinion does not address economic issues in U.S. politics.

    _____

11. The percentage of Americans voting in elections is lower than the percentage of voters who go to the polls in most European countries.

    _____

12. Schooling appears to correlate strongly with high levels of political participation.

    _____

13. The Founders recognized the inevitability of political parties.

_____

14. Since 1984, most independents have voted for the Republican presidential candidates..

_____

15. The federal campaign reform law of 1974 has largely succeeded in its goal of eliminating fat cats from the election process.

_____

16. A realigning election marks a shift in the coalitions that make up the major parties.

_____

17. Interest groups tend to proliferate more in such cities as Chicago, where the political party is strong, than in Los Angeles, where political parties are weaker.

_____

18. The American Association of Retired Persons is an example of an interest group that offers material incentives to prospective members.

_____

19. Public interest lobbies often do best when faced with a hostile administration in Washington.

_____

20. Because of its visual nature, television is able to cover more politicians than newspapers can.

_____

21. Newspapers can be sued simply for printing false and damaging information about government officials.

_____

22. The principal work of a congress is representation.

_____

23. Until the twentieth century the struggles for national political power that occurred periodically in American history were between Congress and the president.

_____

24. Ideological differences between party members in the House are more important than regional differences.

_____

25. The greatest source of presidential power is the authority of the president to introduce legislation.

_____

26. The most frequent concern expressed at the Constitutional Convention in regard to the presidency was the possibility of perpetual reelection.

_____

27. The number of employees is a good indicator of the power of the bureaucracy.

_____

28. Most top federal bureaucrats have worked in several agencies and thus bring a wealth of experience to their jobs.

   _____

29. Unlike the legislative process, the judicial process is not affected by interest groups.

   _____

30. *McCulloch v. Maryland* established the supremacy of federal laws over state laws.

   _____

Multiple Choice Questions

Circle the letter of the response that best answers the question or completes the statement.

1. Which of the following statements about authority is correct?

   a. It is defined as the right to use power.
   b. It resides in government, not in the private sector.
   c. It typically results from the naked use of force.
   d. It is the opposite of *legitimacy*.
   e. It is rarely the product of brute force.

2. In the Marxist view government is a reflection of underlying _____ forces.

   a. social
   b. political
   c. ideological
   d. economic
   e. teleological

3. Max Weber felt that the dominant social and political fact of modern times was

   a. that "the Establishment" was dominated by Wall Street lawyers.
   b. that all institutions have fallen under the control of large bureaucracies.
   c. that capitalism is essential to modern-day forms of government.
   d. the conflict between the government and the press.
   e. communism is the inevitable result of a dialectical process.

4. The kinds of answers that political scientists usually give to the fundamental political questions tend to be

   a. highly abstract and speculative.
   b. clear, concrete, and consistent.
   c. partial, contingent, and controversial.
   d. qualified to the point of unintelligibility.
   e. empirical and void of theory.

5. The logical place to begin the study of how power is distributed in our national politics is

   a. the broadcast of yesterday's news
   b. your local town hall or courthouse.
   c. the day-to-day lives of Americans.
   d. the pages of this morning's newspaper.
   e. the Constitutional Convention.

6. The original purpose of the Constitutional Convention was to

   a. draw up a bill of rights.
   b. discuss trade regulation.
   c. levy taxes.
   d. revise the Articles of Confederation.
   e. establish an army.

7. The philosophy of John Locke strongly supported the idea that

   a. government ought to be limited.
   b. property rights should be subordinated to human rights.
   c. reason is an inadequate guide in establishing a political order.
   d. equality of goods and income is necessary for the political order.
   e. the state of nature provided a perfect protection for natural rights.

8. The American version of representative democracy was based on two major principles:

   a. self-interest and institutionalism.
   b. separation of powers and federalism.
   c. liberty and equality.
   d. unification and centralism.
   e. idealism and fraternity.

9. The Framers believed that equality was

   a. protected by limited government.
   b. inconsistent with liberty.
   c. guaranteed by political privilege.
   d. a meaningless abstraction.
   e. beyond the comprehension of the average citizen.

10. Which of the following statements most accurately characterizes the support given to the Constitution by different Framers?

   a. Most Framers acted out of a mixture of motives, with economic interests' playing only a modest role.
   b. Those Framers who held government debt and who did not own slaves tended to oppose the Constitution.
   c. Most Framers were more concerned about establishing a central government that was too weak than one that was too strong.
   d. The Framers tended to divide along class lines in the support they gave to the Constitution.
   e. Most supported the Constitution to the extent that they believed it would increase the value of their own personal property.

11. Which of the following statements about the size of the average monthly welfare payments received by an AFDC family is correct?

   a. The amount is determined by Congress.
   b. It varies greatly from state to state.
   c. It is about the same in every state.
   d. It is based on a legislative formula.
   e. It is rarely determined in the same manner twice.

12. Tensions in the federal system most commonly arise from

   a. the failures of local and state government.
   b. the arrogance of federal officials.

    c.   competing demands on federal versus local officials.

    d.   the increasingly local orientation of Congress.

    e.   the advantage incumbents enjoy in congressional elections.

13.   Reagan's proposal in 1981 for more clearly sorting out national from state and local responsibilities was unsuccessful largely because it would have

    a.   turned responsibility for education over to the national government.

    b.   made welfare a purely local matter.

    c.   ended the kinds of ambiguity on which courts thrive.

    d.   created huge federal budget deficits.

    e.   caused an exceptional decline in business activity.

14.   The U.S. government primarily regulates

    a.   individual citizens.

    b.   states.

    c.   regions of the country.

    d.   areas of the world.

    e.   community organizations.

15.   The standard used to determine when the national government may exercise powers not specifically mentioned in the Constitution is

    a.   "necessary and proper."

    b.   "preferred freedoms."

    c.   "clear and present."

    d.   "mutual noninterference."

    e.   "full faith and credit"

16.   Which of the following statements about a political culture is correct?

    a.   It implies the existence of an ideology.

    b.   It is the result of an ideology.

    c.   It is the same as an ideology.

    d.   It does not vary across regions within a nation.

    e.   It does not reflect long-term sentiment or opinions.

17.   The text uses the phrase "equality of results" in discussing economic equality in America and Sweden. This phrase refers to equality in

    a.   access to government funds.

    b.   people's opportunity to get ahead.

    c.   what people earn.

    d.   political participation.

    e.   bureaucratic access.

18.   Which of the following statements about class-consciousness in America is true?

    a.   It is the primary determinant of the vote in a presidential election.

    b.   It powerfully affects attitudes.

    c.   It is particularly salient among the unemployed.

    d.   It implies an ideology of class struggle.

    e.   It has been relatively unimportant.

19. When people feel that they have a say in what the government does, that public officials will pay attention to them, and that politics is understandable, they have a sense of

   a. political trust.
   b. political tolerance.
   c. political efficacy.
   d. political legitimacy.
   e. political reciprocity.

20. Americans think it important everyone be

   a. economically equal.
   b. politically equal.
   c. both politically and economically equal.
   d. neither politically nor economically equal.
   e. politically equal when economically successful.

21. The Framers of the Constitution understood that _____ would be the chief source of opinion on most matters.

   a. the general public
   b. elected representatives
   c. factions and interest groups
   d. intellectuals
   e. educators and theorists

22. Which of the following goals is *not* listed in the Preamble to the Constitution?

   a. justice
   b. domestic tranquility
   c. equality
   d. the general welfare
   e. the common defense

23. In recent years the influence of the family on party identification has

   a. decreased.
   b. increased slightly.
   c. remained the same.
   d. disappeared.
   e. increased significantly.

24. Changes in the occupational structure during the past few decades have

   a. caused liberals to forsake the Democratic party.
   b. produced the Moral Majority.
   c. increased differences between manual and nonmanual workers.
   d. increased cohesion within the Democratic party.
   e. produced the new class.

25. If you favor universal medical insurance and a woman's right to choose abortion, according to the text you would be labeled a

   a. pure liberal.
   b. pure conservative.
   c. libertarian.
   d. populist.
   e. neo-populist.

26. Adoption of the Australian ballot enabled United States citizens to vote

    a.   early and often.
    b.   more easily.
    c.   by absentee ballot.
    d.   in secret.
    e.   without state supervision.

27. In which of the following forms of political participation does the smallest portion of Americans engage?

    a.   voting in presidential elections
    b.   voting in local elections
    c.   working for a candidate or party during an election
    d.   belonging to a political club
    e.   belonging to an organization

28. In states that have instituted same-day voter registration, the effect on voter turnout has been

    a.   a decline.
    b.   a slight increase.
    c.   a major increase.
    d.   no impact at all.
    e.   too complex to analyze.

29. The number of elective offices in the United States, compared with European nations, is

    a.   much lower.
    b.   about the same.
    c.   slightly higher.
    d.   much higher.
    e.   slightly lower.

30. Why should George Washington, among other founders of our nation, have been so opposed to political parties?

    a.   because the Constitution made clear the dangers of partisanship in government
    b.   because political parties during the early years of the Republic were both strong and centralized
    c.   because disputes over policies and elections were not easily separated from disputes over governmental legitimacy
    d.   because political parties during the early years of the Republic represented clear, homogeneous economic interests
    e.   because Washington feared Hamilton would organize a party to win the presidency.

31. A Northerner who opposed the Civil War was most likely to belong to which party?

    a.   Democratic
    b.   Republican
    c.   Whig
    d.   Federalist
    e.   Know-Nothing

32. Almost all elections in the United States are based on

    a.   the retention system.
    b.   the majority system.
    c.   proportional representation.

d.   a combination of systems.
e.   the plurality system.

33. The disadvantage to parties of the current system of presidential nomination is that it

a.   increases the chances of nominating a candidate unappealing to the rank and file.
b.   decreases the chances of a faction bolting the party.
c.   increases the chances of a faction bolting the party.
d.   affords little opportunity to minorities to voice their concerns.
e.   gives an unfair advantage to non-ideological candidates.

34. To obtain power within a political party, an individual must usually

a.   avoid anything that remotely resembles ideology.
b.   move away from the center.
c.   avoid publicity.
d.   reflect the views of the average voter.
e.   move toward the center.

35. The campaign activity most on the increase now is

a.   large parades.
b.   radio and television appearances.
c.   whistle-stop train tours.
d.   appearances at malls and factories.
e.   rallies.

36. A major difference between presidential and congressional campaigns is that

a.   more people vote in congressional elections.
b.   presidential races are generally less competitive.
c.   presidential incumbents can better provide services for their constituents.
d.   congressional incumbents can more easily duck responsibility.
e.   the president can more plausibly take credit for improvements in a district.

37. Unlike funding for presidential campaigns, the money for congressional campaigns comes from

a.   both private and public sources.
b.   public sources only.
c.   private sources only.
d.   federal matching grants only.
e.   state taxes.

38. Campaign contributions by political action committees generally favor

a.   incumbents.
b.   conservatives.
c.   Republicans.
d.   supporters of organized labor.
e.   liberal challengers.

39. If presidential campaigns were decided simply by party identification, the

a.   Democrats would always win.
b.   Republicans would always win.
c.   Democrats would win most of the time.
d.   Republicans would win most of the time.
e.   impact could not be intelligently guessed.

40. Where political parties are strong, interest groups are likely to be

    a. equally strong.
    b. independent.
    c. weak.
    d. more numerous.
    e. more representative.

41. Interest groups with large staffs are likely to take political positions in accordance with

    a. rank-and-file opinion.
    b. the view of the general public.
    c. staff beliefs.
    d. government policy.
    e. members of key committees in Congress.

42. Although farmers today have difficulty getting Congress to enact bills in their favor, they are still able to

    a. block bills that they don't like.
    b. appeal to public sentiment.
    c. win court cases.
    d. manipulate prices by withholding their produce.
    e. stall collective bargaining agreements.

43. Probably the best measure of an interest group's ability to influence legislators and bureaucrats is

    a. the size of its membership.
    b. the dollar amount of its contributions.
    c. its organizational skill.
    d. its contacts.
    e. the socio-economic status of its leadership.

44. The revolving door between government and business raises the possibility of

    a. poor communications.
    b. revenue sharing.
    c. conflicts of interest.
    d. ticket splitting.
    e. interest group proliferation.

45. The most significant legal constraints on interest groups currently come from

    a. the 1946 Federal Regulation of Lobbying Act.
    b. the tax code.
    c. antitrust legislation.
    d. the Supreme Court.
    e. the Senate Judiciary Committee.

46. Compared with other Western democracies, the United States has

    a. a more nationally-oriented media.
    b. a greater variety of extreme left- and right-wing views.
    c. more private ownership of broadcast media.
    d. greater concentration of control over the media in a few hands.
    e. more rigorous government supervision of the content of news.

47. The invention of radio was a politically important media development because it

    a.   more than doubled the number of voters in the following election.
    b.   gave rise to the era of mass politics and a large electorate.
    c.   rendered image more important than substance in seeking political office.
    d.   reinforced the influence of political parties when it was first introduced.
    e.   allowed public officials to reach the public in a less-filtered manner.

48. One of Jimmy Carter's signal achievements in dealing with the media in the 1976 primary campaign was

    a.   keeping a low profile.
    b.   taking newsworthy positions on important issues.
    c.   defusing an initial bias against him among reporters.
    d.   getting himself mentioned with great frequency.
    e.   refusing to buckle under the pressure of special interest groups.

49. If we compare the issues that citizens feel are important with the issues that newspapers and television newscasts feature, we find that

    a.   the media are far too "mainstream" to handle the major issues of concern.
    b.   they are vastly different.
    c.   the media are more likely to feature the concerns of political liberals.
    d.   the media ignore the economic concerns of many citizens.
    e.   they are very much the same.

50. In deciding which stories to include in the daily newspaper, editors

    a.   are rigidly constrained by the volume of hard news that must be included.
    b.   are rigidly constrained by the limited amount of material available to them.
    c.   are rigidly constrained by the need to include popular or catchy feature stories.
    d.   have considerable latitude to express their ideological biases in the selection of background or feature stories.
    e.   are rigidly constrained by the willingness of federal courts to prosecute cases under the *Chaplinsky* ruling.

51. Whereas the principal work of a parliament is debate, that of a congress is

    a.   representation.
    b.   oversight.
    c.   administration.
    d.   discussion.
    e.   investigation.

52. In the twentieth century the trend in congressional decision-making has been toward

    a.   centralization.
    b.   increasing the power of the Speaker.
    c.   increasing the power of the president.
    d.   decentralization.
    e.   logrolling.

53. Today House membership is still characterized by a(n)

    a.   high turnover of members.
    b.   increase in marginal districts.
    c.   decrease in safe districts.
    d.   low turnover of members.

e.   centralization.

54. The real leadership in the Senate rests with the

a.   majority leader.
b.   president pro tempore.
c.   vice president.
d.   Senate whip.
e.   floor managers.

55. Which of the following statements is true of U.S. presidents but not of British prime ministers?

a.   Presidents and the legislature often work at cross-purposes.
b.   Presidents are selected by the legislature.
c.   Presidents are most often government insiders.
d.   Presidents generally choose their cabinets from among members of Congress.
e.   Presidents are more distant from the media.

56. Of the three audiences that the president confronts, the one most important for maintaining and exercising power is

a.   other politicians and leaders in Washington.
b.   the mass public throughout the nation.
c.   party activists and officeholders outside Washington.
d.   foreign leaders.
e.   fundraisers.

57. Which of the following statements is true of a bill that is not signed or vetoed within ten days while Congress is still in session?

a.   It is considered to have received a pocket veto.
b.   It is returned to Congress.
c.   It must be given a veto message.
d.   It becomes law until the following Congress.
e.   It becomes law automatically.

58. The doctrine of executive privilege is based on separation of powers and on the

a.   constitutional requirements for secrecy.
b.   War Powers Act.
c.   president's need for confidential advice.
d.   integrity of each branch of government.
e.   the Eleventh Amendment.

59. If a president is deeply interested in attaining a particular goal, he will be most likely to

a.   seek Congress's assistance.
b.   assign it high priority.
c.   create a new agency.
d.   appeal to the media.
e.   A and C.

60. The basis of appointments to the bureaucracy during most of the nineteenth century and the early part of the twentieth century was

a.   financial.
b.   patronage.
c.   technical expertise.

    d.   support for the president's policies.

    e.   nepotism.

61. Congress has delegated substantial authority to administrative agencies in which three areas?

    a.   grants-in-aid, law enforcement, and national defense

    b.   law enforcement, social services, and resource management

    c.   grants-in-aid, subsidy payments, and enforcement of regulations

    d.   grants-in-aid, subsidy payments, and law enforcement

    e.   social services, law enforcement and national defense

62. Which of the following is the *most* important consideration in evaluating the power of a bureaucracy?

    a.   the number of employees in it

    b.   the importance of its functions

    c.   the extent to which its actions are supported by the public

    d.   the amount of discretionary authority that its officials have

    e.   the socio-economic status of its leaders.

63. One major constraint under which the bureaucracy operates is the

    a.   communication of goals by the president to the media.

    b.   power of issue networks to determine agency policy.

    c.   absence of competing forces in the public sector.

    d.   presence of many highly structured roles.

    e.   assignment of single jobs to several agencies.

64. All of the following have weakened the power of appropriations committees over government agencies *except*

    a.   the establishment of trust funds that operate outside the regular government budget.

    b.   the change in authorization of many programs from permanent or multiyear to annual authorizations.

    c.   the need for these committees to focus on huge budget deficits and target spending limits.

    d.   the requirement that these committees mark up an agency's budget request.

    e.   B, C, and D.

65. Which of the following statements is true of the written opinion in a Supreme Court case?

    a.   It is always written by the Chief Justice.

    b.   It is a statement of the legal reasoning behind the decision.

    c.   It is jointly written by all nine justices.

    d.   It is nearly always unanimous.

    e.   It is never influenced by a justice's personal opinions or views of public policy.

66. A political question is a matter

    a.   involving voters.

    b.   that the Constitution has left to another branch of government.

    c.   that an elected state judge has dealt with.

    d.   that must first be acted on by Congress.

    e.   that affects the decisions of voters in an election.

67. A major reason that the courts play a greater role in American society today than they did earlier in the century is that

    a.   government plays a greater role generally.

b.   public opinion is less focused today.

c.   judges are better trained today than in the past.

d.   the courts are more representative of American society.

e.   the appellate jurisdiction of courts has been contracted.

68.   During the period from the end of the Civil War to the beginning of the New Deal, the dominant issue that the Supreme Court faced was that of

a.   government regulation of the economy.

b.   states' rights versus federal supremacy.

c.   slavery.

d.   government regulation of interstate commerce.

e.   state compliance with the "Full Faith and Credit" Clause.

69.   Which of the following statements about the selection of federal judges is correct?

a.   The principle of senatorial courtesy applies to the selection of Supreme Court justices.

b.   Presidents generally appoint judges whose political views reflect their own.

c.   Nominees for district court judge often face tough confirmation battles in the Senate.

d.   The application of political litmus tests to Supreme Court nominees is no longer legal.

e.   Appointments rarely have an impact because the personal opinions and views of judges do not have an impact in their decision-making.

70.   What is the relationship between an appeal and a writ of certiorari?

a.   Judges must hear all appeals but only some writs.

b.   A case granted certiorari may be heard in either state or federal court.

c.   Appeals are paid for by plaintiffs, writs by defendants.

d.   Only some appeals are granted certiorari.

e.   A writ of certiorari requires at least seven votes from the Court.

ANSWERS TO TRUE/FALSE QUESTIONS

1. T

2. F. It is used in the sense of representative democracy.

3. T

4. F. He feared a government so strong.

5. T

6. F. The attractiveness to state officials of money they did not have to raise has been the most important.

7. F. As the U.S. Civil War demonstrates, some issues can arise that are not handled by even a well-accepted civic culture.

8. F. Puritanism, Congregationalism, and religious diversity are three examples to the contrary.

9. F. In recent years, men rather than women have "deserted" Democratic candidates for Republican ones, while the voting behavior of women has remained unchanged.

10. T

11. T

12. T

13. F. They opposed them.

14. F. While most independents voted for the winning Republican in 1984 and 1988, pluralities of independents voted for the winning Democrat in 1992 and 1996.

15. T

16. T

17. F. The party is stronger in Chicago, where interest groups must work with the party.

18. T

19. T

20. F. It covers far fewer.

21. F. Malice or "reckless disregard" must also be shown.

22. T

23. F. Struggles took place within Congress.

24. T

25. F. It is found in politics and public opinion.

26. T

27. F. The power depends on the discretionary authority of the officials.

28. F. Most have spent their entire careers in one agency.

29. F. Interest groups sometimes promote litigation.

30. T

ANSWERS TO MULTIPLE CHOICE QUESTIONS

1. a	2. d	3. b	4. c	5. e	6. d	7. a
8. b	9. a	10. a	11. b	12. c	13. b	14. b
15. a	16. c	17. c	18. e	19. c	20. b	21. c
22. c	23. a	24. e	25. a	26. d	27. d	28. b
29. d	30. c	31. a	32. e	33. a	34. e	35. b
36. d	37. c	38. a	39. b	40. c	41. c	42. a
43. c	44. c	45. b	46. c	47. e	48. d	49. e
50. d	51. a	52. d	53. d	54. a	55. a	56. a
57. e	58. c	59. c	60. b	61. c	62. d	63. e
64. d	65. b	66. b	67. a	68. a	69. b	70. d

Practice Examination, Chapters 15 to 22

True/False Questions

Read each statement carefully. Mark true statements *T*. If any part of the statement is false, mark it *F*, and write in the space provided a concise explanation of why the statement is false.

1. The bureaucracy has acquired a new significance in American politics simply because of its power.

    _____

2. Congress, especially the Senate, has often initiated consumer and environmental protection laws.

    _____

3. The main reason the deficit went away in 1999 is that the American economy grew so rapidly that Washington was flooded with more tax money.

    _____

4. A Keynesian believes that inflation occurs when there is too much money chasing too few goods.

    _____

5. Client-based welfare programs are means tested.

    _____

6. As a result of losing political legitimacy, the Aid to Families With Dependent Children (AFDC) was abolished.

    _____

7. School authorities in the United States can legally search students' lockers without asking permission.

    _____

8. The congress that adopted the Bill of Rights never considered applying it to state governments.

    _____

9. During World War II Americans of Japanese origin were forced by the federal government to relocate in camps.

    _____

10. Presidents of the United States have less freedom in foreign affairs than do most other Western heads of state.

    _____

11. Elites tend to give more support to the president's foreign policy than public opinion in general does.

    _____

12. Keeping a defense plant open is a matter of interest group and client politics as well as defense policy.

_____

13. Majoritarian politics best explains the nation's policy approach to global warming.

_____

14. Citizens have a right to sue the EPA.

_____

15. Elitist theory argues that the same social grouping decides or influences public policy across a wide spectrum of issues.

_____

16. Growth in the size of the bureaucracy is associated with growth in the scope of government activity.

_____

17. The more rights are asserted by individuals, the harder it is for government to make decisions.

_____

18. Since congressional enactment of the Welfare Reform Act in 1996, state spending for social service programs has declined.

_____

19. Majoritarian politics influences relatively few issues in this country.

_____

20. In the 1920s it was widely assumed that the federal government would play a small role in citizens' lives.

_____

21. Shays's Rebellion seemed to indicate the inability of state governments alone to cope with serious popular uprisings.

_____

22. The U.S. Constitution is the world's oldest written national constitution still in operation.

_____

23. The fact that one party can control Congress and the other the presidency is related to the decentralization of American parties.

_____

24. Party delegates to national conventions tend to be less ideological than average voters.

_____

25. The Ford Foundation has contributed millions of dollars to predominantly conservative interest groups.

_____

26. Politicians generally like to avoid situations in which disruptive tactics are pursued by interest groups.

_____

27. A filibuster is the means by which cloture is invoked.

_____

28. Just because one party has a majority in the House or Senate does not mean that it controls that chamber.

_____

29. White House staff appointments must be confirmed by the Senate.

_____

30. Andrew Johnson is the only president to be impeached.

_____

Multiple Choice Questions

Circle the letter of the response that best answers the question or completes the statement.

1. Popular views on the legitimate scope of government action are changed primarily by

    a.   education.
    b.   sensible politics.
    c.   the influence of the Constitution.
    d.   the influence of current events.
    e.   exposure to the media.

2. Which of the following statements *best* describes government bureaucracy today?

    a.   It is a tool of big business.
    b.   It is a major source of policy.
    c.   It is an impartial institution.
    d.   It is an appendage of the political parties.
    e.   It rarely plays a significant role in the implementation of policy.

3. An example of a widely-distributed benefit is

    a.   dairy subsidies.
    b.   farm subsidies.
    c.   the protection of a business from competition.
    d.   a dissident group's freedom to speak.
    e.   the reduction of factory pollution.

4. Majoritarian policies tend to reflect

    a.   interest group activity.
    b.   philosophies of governance.
    c.   the times.
    d.   political party activity.
    e.   interest group formation.

5. Self-regarding theory holds that

   a. officials think mainly about increasing their power.
   b. political parties encourage self-interest.
   c. voters are influenced largely by their immediate economic situation.
   d. citizens put the nation ahead of business or their personal economic situations.
   e. sociotropic voters will focus on the state of the nation's economic health..

6. After the Social Security system was established, Congress voted to increase benefits

   a. according to a specific formula.
   b. only in times of high inflation.
   c. for low-income recipients only.
   d. in almost every election year.
   e. when surpluses were available.

7. Tax loopholes mostly benefit

   a. average citizens.
   b. the very rich.
   c. businesses.
   d. self-employed persons.
   e. farmers.

8. Lower taxes, less debt, and spending on new government programs produce _____ politics.

   a. entrepreneurial
   b. majoritarian
   c. interest group
   d. client
   e. reciprocal.

9. The most important part of the economic policy-making machinery is the

   a. Federal Reserve Board.
   b. Congress.
   c. Council of Economic Advisors.
   d. General Services Administration.
   e. Secretary of Labor.

10. Which of the following is a noncontributory, or public assistance, program, as opposed to a contributory program?

   a. Medicare
   b. Aid to Families with Dependent Children
   c. Old Age and Survivors Disability Insurance
   d. unemployment insurance
   e. Food Stamp Program

11. The Welfare Reform Act of 1996

   a. made illegal aliens eligible for TANF.
   b. increased federal regulations over the states.
   c. relaxed work requirements for TANF recipients.
   d. placed a two-year limit on how long a TANF recipient could receive benefits.
   e. increased benefits and relaxed requirements for TANF.

12. The public's distrust of welfare programs is the result of

a. a preference for relief over insurance-type programs.
b. the fear that welfare discourages work.
c. a preference for a negative income tax rather than a guaranteed annual income.
d. the public's desire to have local authorities retain greater control over the distribution of welfare funds
e. a fear of bureaucrats who have too much discretion.

13. By 1994 about _____ of AFDC mothers had been on it for eight years or longer.

a. one-fourth
b. one-third
c. one-half
d. two-thirds
e. 99 percent.

14. Regarding the relationship between church and state, the First Amendment states that Congress may not make any law prohibiting the free exercise of religion. It also specifically states that

a. church and state must be clearly separate.
b. citizens are exempt from laws binding other citizens when the law goes against their religious beliefs.
c. government must be neutral toward religion.
d. nonsectarian, voluntary, or limited prayer is permissible in public schools.
e. Congress may not make any laws respecting an establishment of religion.

15. The Supreme Court has ruled that which one of the following sorts of symbolic speech is protected by the Constitution?

a. burning draft cards
b. burning the flag
c. making obscene gestures toward a police officer
d. sitting in to disrupt traffic at a draft board
e. sleeping in a public park overnight.

16. The definition of what is obscene and therefore not a form of protected speech

a. is left almost entirely to localities.
b. can be decided by localities but only within narrow limits.
c. has to be decided by the Supreme Court on pretty much a case-by-case basis.
d. has to be decided by the Supreme Court on the basis of reasonably clear guidelines.
e. is meticulously detailed in the Court's decision in *Roth*.

17. The text cites a number of cases involving religious issues that the Supreme Court refused to hear. The lower court decisions

a. at least for now are the law.
b. are automatically reversed.
c. await further appeal.
d. remain subject to reversal at the discretion of the Court of Appeals.
e. is certified and declared void.

18. *Libel* is defined as

a. stating something untrue about another person.
b. an oral statement defaming another person.
c. a written statement defaming another person.

    d.   maliciously intending to defame a public official.

    e.   writing something false about someone without their knowledge.

19. "Jim Crow" is a slang expression referring to

    a.   laws and policies that segregated blacks.

    b.   discrimination against blacks in the military.

    c.   the early civil rights movement.

    d.   the difficulty that blacks had in getting a fair trial.

    e.   discrimination faced by blacks in other countries.

20. Which of the following statements about *Brown v. Board of Education* is true?

    a.   It was handed down by a divided Court.

    b.   It was ultimately rather narrow in its implications.

    c.   It was almost unnoticed when it was decided.

    d.   It was the logical extension of a line of related cases.

    e.   It announced a specific deadline for compliance.

21. Segregation maintained by law is labeled

    a.   prima facie.

    b.   statist.

    c.   de jure

    d.   post facto suspect.

    e.   de facto

22. Under the "quid pro quo" rule pertaining to sexual harassment

    a.   the employer is "strictly liable" even if he/she did not know that sexual harassment was occurring

    b.   the employer cannot be held liable if he/she did not know that sexual harassment was occurring.

    c.   an employee is never liable for the sexual harassment of an employee.

    d.   a pattern of sexual harassment must be proven before the employer is liable.

    e.   the employer is liable but not the employee in sexual harassment cases.

23. The position that the Constitution neither is nor should be color-blind is taken by those who advocate

    a.   equality of results.

    b.   the incorporation of the Bill of Rights.

    c.   freedom-of-education plans.

    d.   equal opportunity.

    e.   abolition of affirmative action.

24. The Supreme Court has generally held the view that the conduct of foreign affairs

    a.   is chiefly a congressional responsibility.

    b.   is chiefly a presidential responsibility.

    c.   involves important constitutional rights.

    d.   is a political question for Congress and the president to work out.

    e.   is an executive prerogative until war is declared.

25. Containment was the policy of

    a.   the British and French during the rise of Hitler in Germany.

    b.   the United States toward Japan before Pearl Harbor.

    c.   Admiral Alfred T. Mahan.
    d.   the United States toward Russia after World War II.
    e.   General Patton.

26. Among the causes of defense overruns noted in the text are all of the following *except*

    a.   the key players' incentive to underestimate costs going in.
    b.   the difficulty of estimating the costs of new programs in advance.
    c.   the cumbersome process of competitive bidding even for minor items.
    d.   "stretch-outs" used to keep annual budgets low.
    e.   the blinding speed with which bids and contracts are obtained.

27. The most important congressional check on the president in the area of foreign affairs is the power to

    a.   impeach.
    b.   control the purse strings.
    c.   approve ambassadors.
    d.   reorganize those federal agencies that make foreign policy—the State Department, the CIA, and so forth.
    e.   investigate.

28. The creation of separate uniformed services within a single department reflects the concern that

    a.   the military budget would not be kept accountable.
    b.   the military budget would not be kept below acceptable levels.
    c.   interservice rivalry would escalate.
    d.   a unified military might become too powerful politically.
    e.   intelligence data should not be communicated widely.

29. How members of Congress vote on defense matters can best be explained by

    a.   the economic interests of their states or districts.
    b.   their party.
    c.   their ideology.
    d.   the public relations skills of military leaders.
    e.   experience (or lack of experience) in the military.

30. Cost overruns in the military are *most* likely to be the result of

    a.   excessive profits of defense contractors.
    b.   the desire of military officers to have quantity, rather than quality, in their weapons.
    c.   the blinding speed with which bids and contracts are obtained.
    d.   an unwillingness on the part of defense contractors to submit low bids.
    e.   the fact that most weapons must be invented rather than bought off the shelf.

31. The size and the division of the defense budget represent, respectively,

    a.   entrepreneurial and majoritarian politics.
    b.   majoritarian and interest group politics.
    c.   interest group and client politics.
    d.   client and entrepreneurial politics.
    e.   club-based and neo-institutional politics.

32. One way that government can correct cost overruns is to

    a.   limit contracts to just a few bidders.
    b.   refuse to pay for cost overruns.

    c.   avoid "gold plating."

    d.   incorporate the latest technology from the initial planning stage.

    e.   streamline the intelligence community.

33.   One reason environmental policy tends to be so controversial is that

    a.   so many environmental policy decisions are based on scientific evidence, which tends to be highly political.

    b.   environmental policy often takes the form of majoritarian politics, which requires strong emotional appeals to overcome the political advantage of client groups.

    c.   environmental policy creates losers, who must pay the costs without getting enough of the benefits.

    d.   most people feel that government is already doing enough to control pollution; new programs are therefore likely to face stiff opposition.

    e.   A and D.

34.   The text speaks of the importance of *entrepreneurial politics* in many areas of environmental policy making. This term refers to a style of policy making in which

    a.   an unorganized public benefits at the expense of a well-organized group.

    b.   an unorganized public benefits at its own expense.

    c.   two organized groups with a material stake in the outcome fight over who will pay and who will benefit.

    d.   an organized group benefits at the expense of an unorganized public.

    e.   two unorganized groups benefit at the expense of an organized group.

35.   When is the average citizen most likely to support tough environmental protection measures?

    a.   when people believe the benefits are great enough

    b.   when almost everyone benefits from the measures

    c.   when costs of the measures are hidden or deferred

    d.   when benefits are deferred to some later date

    e.   when the costs are great and the benefits are deferred

36.   Many policy entrepreneurs favor measures to control the use of agricultural pesticides. One reason they have not been successful at enacting legislation to do this is that

    a.   the EPA is opposed to such legislation.

    b.   extensive media coverage has lent support to farmers.

    c.   the benefits to the public of pesticide use are high.

    d.   farmers are well-represented in Congress.

    e.   Congress and the EPA cannot agree on objective standards of assessment.

37.   Offsets, bubble standards, and banks or pollution allowances are all

    a.   pollution-control devices that effectively reduce air contamination.

    b.   tests conducted by the EPA on agricultural pesticides.

    c.   EPA incentives for companies to reduce pollution.

    d.   rules devised by the EPA under its command-and-control strategy to improve air and water quality.

    e.   devices employed to restrict the disposal of nuclear wastes in river beds.

38.   When the benefits are concentrated on a relatively small group and the costs are widely distributed over the public as a whole, the situation involves

    a.   entrepreneurial politics.

    b.   majoritarian politics.

   c.   teleological politics
   d.   interest group politics.
   e.   client politics.

39. Which of the following policy areas *best* demonstrates the elitist theory of American politics?

   a.   a tax revolt
   b.   the Occupational Safety and Health Act
   c.   Social Security
   d.   foreign policy
   e.   Medicare

40. The role of the judiciary is *best* explained in terms of

   a.   Marxist theory: courts serve capitalist interests.
   b.   elitist theory: judges have a common profession and need pay little attention to public opinion.
   c.   bureaucratic theory: we should look at the formal organization of the court system.
   d.   pluralist theory: judges are a group with interests like any other group.
   e.   mechanistic theory: judges merely apply the law.

41. The theory of American politics that emphasizes conflict and bargaining among various interests is the

   a.   Marxist theory.
   b.   bureaucratic theory.
   c.   pluralist theory.
   d.   entrepreneurial theory.
   e.   cluster-response theory.

42. The value of any government program can be assessed only by considering

   a.   public opinion.
   b.   economics.
   c.   supply and demand.
   d.   costs and benefits.
   e.   theoretical ramifications.

43. Which of the following statements is true of every country in which public opinion plays a major role in politics?

   a.   Citizens have a high degree of confidence in government.
   b.   The country has as many emigrants as immigrants.
   c.   The government is basically authoritarian.
   d.   Citizens are cynical about government performance.
   e.   The bureaucracy is distant, but efficient.

44. The text argues that public opinion has been changed by such factors as

   a.   crises and the spread of higher education.
   b.   political campaigns and crises.
   c.   interest groups and political campaigns.
   d.   the spread of higher education and interest groups.
   e.   demagogues and interest groups.

45. The decline since the 1960s of public confidence in government seems to reflect

   a.   a loss of faith in the American form of government.

    b.   discontent with the design of various institutions.
    c.   a cynicism about government's performance.
    d.   loss of admiration for the Founding Fathers.
    e.   all of the above.

46. Procedural rules on governmental behavior, included in the Freedom of Information Act, are

    a.   more complex and demanding than the rules binding any other democratic government.
    b.   honored more in the breach than in the observance.
    c.   less stringent than were the restrictions on the behavior of the U.S. government in earlier generations.
    d.   impossible to enforce.
    e.   an important buffer between bureaucrats and investigating committees.

47. Entitlements (that is, mandatory spending) makes up about ____ of what government spends.

    a.   one-tenth
    b.   one-fourth
    c.   one-half
    d.   two-thirds
    e.   an unknown amount

48. The most popular idea to save Social Security is to

    a.   allow citizens to invest some of their Social Security taxes.
    b.   raise the retirement age to seventy.
    c.   freeze retirement benefits.
    d.   raise Social Security taxes.
    e.   decrease benefits.

49. Civil liberties issues are most likely to be issues of

    a.   majoritarian politics.
    b.   interest group politics.
    c.   client politics.
    d.   party politics.
    e.   theological politics

50. In the *Bakke* case the Supreme Court held that a university medical school, in admitting students, may

    a.   use quotas for blacks and whites.
    b.   use quotas for men and women.
    c.   take gender into account.
    d.   take race into account.
    e.   take gender, but not race into account.

51. Which of the following has (have) grown fastest in recent years?

    a.   categorical grants
    b.   block grants
    c.   revenue sharing
    d.   All have grown at about the same rate.
    e.   None have grown in recent years.

52. Which of the following institutions suffered the *least* from a great loss of confidence on the part of the American people between 1966 and 1992?

    a.   the media
    b.   Congress
    c.   major companies
    d.   the U.S. Supreme Court
    e.   public schools

53. There is a popular commitment in America to government programs to aid

    a.   all those in need.
    b.   those who are truly in need.
    c.   those who are without work.
    d.   no one.
    e.   those who are loyal to the nation.

54. In recent years the influence of the family on party identification has

    a.   decreased.
    b.   increased.
    c.   remained the same.
    d.   disappeared.
    e.   increased dramatically.

55. If you favor reducing federal taxes and quarantining AIDS sufferers, you would be classified as a

    a.   pure liberal.
    b.   pure conservative.
    c.   libertarian.
    d.   populist.
    e.   neo-populist.

56. Popular election to the House of Representatives is required by

    a.   the Voting Rights Act of 1832.
    b.   the Constitution.
    c.   the Declaration of Independence.
    d.   state laws.
    e.   Rule 17 of the U.S. Code.

57. Those who prefer to participate in politics by joining nonpartisan groups and dealing with various issues in them are referred to as

    a.   voting specialists.
    b.   campaigners.
    c.   communalists.
    d.   parochial participants.
    e.   neo-institutionalists.

58. To win the party nomination, candidates need to appear particularly

    a.   liberal.
    b.   conservative.
    c.   liberal if Democrats, conservative if Republicans.
    d.   conservative if Democrats, liberal if Republicans.
    e.   void of anything that remotely resembles ideology.

59. Which of the following was *not* associated with the rise of national magazines around the turn of the century?

    a.   the middle class
    b.   muckraking
    c.   high-impact photojournalism
    d.   nationally-known writers
    e.   scandal mongering.

60. An irony concerning government regulation of the news media is that

    a.   American media are less regulated than the media in foreign countries despite the greater need for regulation here.
    b.   legislation designed to intimidate the media has in fact made them more hostile toward officials.
    c.   the media are highly restricted by a government that does not even obey its own laws.
    d.   the most influential media, the broadcast media, show highly-concentrated patterns of ownership by a few large corporations.
    e.   the least competitive part of the media is almost entirely unregulated, whereas the most competitive part is substantially regulated.

61. The first president to engage in the systematic cultivation of news reporters was

    a.   Theodore Roosevelt.
    b.   Franklin Roosevelt.
    c.   Harry Truman.
    d.   Richard Nixon.
    e.   John F. Kennedy.

62. A person ordinarily becomes a candidate for representative or senator by

    a.   appealing to party leaders.
    b.   serving first in the state legislature.
    c.   serving in the state judiciary.
    d.   serving first in a government agency.
    e.   running in a primary election.

63. In the House a stalled bill can be extracted from a committee and brought to the floor by means of

    a.   a discharge petition.
    b.   a committee rule.
    c.   cloture.
    d.   a unanimous consent vote.
    e.   a pop-start amendment.

64. Recent ethics rules in Congress appear to favor

    a.   liberals over conservatives.
    b.   members supported by wealthy interest groups.
    c.   persons who were wealthy before entering Congress.
    d.   members of Congress who earn large fees on the lecture circuit.
    e.   members of Congress who are young.

65. Contemporary critics of Congress disagree with the Framers' vision of Congress in that the critics

    a.   believe that Congress should normally proceed slowly in its deliberations.
    b.   view Congress as designed to check and balance strong leaders in the executive branch.
    c.   wish to see the House and the Senate based on population.

d.   wish to make changes to prevent the American political system from resembling a parliamentary system.

f.   wish to end policy gridlock by making Congress capable of speedily adopting sweeping changes in national policies.

66. In a parliamentary system the prime minister is chosen by the

a.   people.
b.   electors.
c.   legislature.
d.   monarch.
e.   nocturnal councils.

67. The text suggests that policy gridlock is a necessary consequence of

a.   representative democracy.
b.   direct democracy.
c.   divided government.
d.   unified government.
e.   big government.

68. Which of the following statements about efforts to reorganize the federal bureaucracy is true?

a.   It may trigger bitter political battles.
b.   It typically takes place at the time of the election of a new president.
c.   It has seldom been tried.
d.   It requires the support of the voters.
e.   It usually works, but has little impact.

69. Which of the following government agencies duplicate each other's functions in important ways?

a.   Federal Communications Commission and Federal Aviation Agency
b.   Office of Management and Budget and Central Intelligence Agency
c.   Customs Service and Drug Enforcement Administration
d.   Agricultural Research Service and Agricultural Stabilization and Conservation Service
e.   B and D

70. The National Performance Review attempts to reform the bureaucracy by stressing

a.   efficiency.
b.   accountability.
c.   customer satisfaction.
d.   consistent policies.
e.   reconciliation.

ANSWERS TO TRUE/FALSE QUESTIONS

1. F. Its significance is that it is now a source of political innovation.

2. T

3. T

4. F. A Keynesian believes that the health of the economy depends on what fraction of their incomes people save or spend.

5. T

6. T

7. T

8. T

9. T

10. F

11. F. The masses are usually more supportive.

12. T

13. T

14. T

15. T

16. T

17. T

18. F. To the contrary, state spending for social services has increased. In fact, many states are spending at least part of their so-called welfare surpluses on other social service programs.

19. T

20. T

21. T

22. T

23. T

24. T

25. F. Rather, to liberal public interest groups.

26. T

27. F. A filibuster is extended debate in the Senate.

28. T

29. F. They do not have to be confirmed.

30. F. Bill Clinton was impeached in 1998.

ANSWERS TO MULTIPLE CHOICE QUESTIONS

1. d	2. b	3. e	4. b	5. c	6. d	7. a
8. b	9. b	10. b	11. d	12. b	13. d	14. e
15. b	16. b	17. a	18. c	19. a	20. d	21. c
22. a	23. a	24. d	25. d	26. c	27. b	28. d
29. c	30. e	31. b	32. c	33. c	34. a	35. c
36. d	37. c	38. e	39. d	40. b	41. c	42. d
43. d	44. a	45. c	46. a	47. d	48. a	49. c
50. d	51. a	52. a	53. b	54. c	55. b	56. b
57. c	58. c	59. c	60. e	61. a	62. e	63. d
64. d	65. e	66. c	67. a	68. a	69. c	70. c